New Perspectives on Virtual and Augmented Reality

New Perspectives on Virtual and Augmented Reality discusses the possibilities of using virtual and augmented reality in the role of innovative pedagogy, where there is an urgent need to find ways to teach and support learning in a transformed learning environment. Technology creates opportunities to learn differently and presents challenges for education. Virtual reality solutions can be exciting, create interest in learning, make learning more accessible and make learning faster.

This book analyses the capabilities of virtual, augmented and mixed reality by providing ideas on how to make learning more effective, how existing VR/AR solutions can be used as learning tools and how a learning process can be structured. The virtual reality (VR) solutions can be used successfully for educational purposes as their use can contribute to the construction of knowledge and the development of metacognitive processes. They also contribute to inclusive education by providing access to knowledge that would not otherwise be available.

This book will be of great interest to academics, researchers and postgraduate students in the field of educational technology.

Linda Daniela is Professor, Chair of the Council for PhD Defense in Education, Dean of the Faculty of Education, Psychology and Art at the University of Latvia in Riga, Latvia.

Perspectives on Education in the Digital Age
Series Editors: David Kergel and Birte Heidkamp

The process of digitalization is leading to a fundamental social change affecting all spheres of social life. In the pedagogical field, there is a need for re-structuring key concepts such as learning, teaching and education that consider socio-economic and cultural changes.

Perspectives on Education in the Digital Age explores the process of coming to terms with socio-economic and socio-cultural shifts arising from digitalization and discusses this process with reference to its effects on education. The series provides a forum for discussion of critical, integrative analyses of social transformations in the digital age, drawn from different fields such as the humanities, social sciences and economics. The aim of the series is to analyse the implications of cultural change on education in the digital age by bringing together interdisciplinary dialogue and different theoretical approaches.

New Perspectives on Virtual and Augmented Reality

Finding New Ways to Teach in a Transformed Learning Environment

Edited by Linda Daniela

Routledge
Taylor & Francis Group

LONDON AND NEW YORK

First published 2020
by Routledge
2 Park Square, Milton Park, Abingdon, Oxon OX14 4RN

and by Routledge
52 Vanderbilt Avenue, New York, NY 10017

Routledge is an imprint of the Taylor & Francis Group, an informa business

British Library Cataloguing-in-Publication Data
A catalogue record for this book is available from the British Library

Library of Congress Cataloging-in-Publication Data
A catalog record has been requested for this book

ISBN: 978-0-367-43211-9 (hbk)
ISBN: 978-1-003-00187-4 (ebk)

Typeset in Bembo
by Integra Software Services Pvt. Ltd.

Contents

Figures

Tables

Preface

Why do we need new ways to teach?
Virtual reality perspective

Technological advances and the opportunities created by digitalization are transforming the educational environment by creating different types of transformations. Technology creates opportunities to learn differently and presents challenges for education, as it is necessary to ensure the acquisition of competencies that are essential in today's world and to ensure that the fascination with technology does not take precedence over learning goals. Virtual reality solutions can be exciting, create interest in learning, make learning more accessible and make learning faster.

In this volume, researchers have sought to analyse the capabilities of virtual, augmented and mixed reality by providing ideas on how to make learning more effective, how existing VR/AR solutions can be used as learning tools, and how a learning process can be structured. VR/AR and haptic solutions can provide opportunities to acquire knowledge and competencies that would otherwise be impossible or difficult to acquire. There are a number of reasons VR solutions can be used successfully for educational purposes: i) their use can contribute to the construction of knowledge and the development of metacognitive processes; ii) they may help to reduce barriers to otherwise inaccessible places, either because of changes in the historical period or because it is necessary to preserve historical and natural values from human influence; iii) they can help to ensure that abstract learning becomes concrete by helping to master complex concepts; iv) they can contribute to inclusive education by providing access to knowledge that would not otherwise be available; v) they can serve as facilitators of sustainable development by addressing virtual reality and vi) they can help to visualize things that are impossible in reality. These opportunities can and should be used to make learning more effective. The next steps educational researchers need to take are to analyse learning outcomes and offer specific learning strategies, as VR/AR solutions also have educational shortages that can result from under-achievement, neglected skills and an inability to distinguish the real world from virtual reality.

Researchers are currently looking at various ways to use VR/AR solutions in education to make the education process more efficient, modern and diverse. They are also looking for technical solutions that can make VR more accessible and technically and aesthetically pleasing.

Organization of the book

The present book consists of 18 chapters, in which the authors try to explain different approaches using VR and AR possibilities. Some of the authors analyse these possibilities from the perspective of knowledge gain; some take the perspective of the effectiveness of the learning process and others point out the need for changes to traditional learning and the necessity to change attitudes to VR. One chapter proposes ideas on how the learning process should be organized and its outcomes evaluated; another introduces a tool for how VR/AR solutions can be evaluated from the educational perspective. There are also ideas on how to organize a safer learning process and how to analyse historical events and historical achievements. A brief description of each of the chapters follows.

Lana Frančeska Dreimane, in her chapter **Virtual reality learning experience evaluation tool for instructional designers and educators**, presents a VR learning experience evaluation tool that highlights the pivotal aspects that should be considered by instructors and educators who wish to successfully design and/or apply VR learning experiences.

Gregory Quinn and *Fabian Schneider*, in their chapter **A+Ha!: combining tactile interaction with augmented reality to transform secondary and tertiary STEM education**, claim that the effectiveness of, accessibility to and engagement in teaching and learning STEM subjects can be significantly improved by 1) making use of novel technologies that combine haptic interaction with pedagogically strategic digital augmentation; 2) exploiting the benefits of the 'haptic bond' between visual and auditory stimuli; 3) the application of gamification techniques and 4) facilitating active learning and explorative design.

Neus Lorenzo Galés and *Ray Gallon*, in **Transcendent Learning Spaces**, claim that the emerging technologies of augmented and virtual reality can be used to model daily life situations that learners have to face in the digital world. Transcendent learning spaces can be extremely powerful for a variety of learner populations, including, as the case studies show, populations at risk of exclusion or in educational crisis.

Linda Daniela and *Yipaer Aierken*, in the chapter **The educational perspective on virtual reality experiences of cultural heritage**, discuss the possibilities of VR experiences for educational purposes and propose an evaluation tool that was developed to evaluate VR applications from the educational perspective.

The chapter **How to enhance the trustworthiness of virtual reality systems**, by *Davide Salanitri, Glyn Lawson* and *Brian Waterfield*, describes a study to validate trust in a VR model, where usability, technology acceptance and presence are theorized to be the factors influencing trust. The results are a starting point for validating the model, which, when fully demonstrated, could shape the design of VR technologies to enhance users' trust in the system and, consequently, improve the human–system interaction and the effectiveness of the technology.

Joshua A. Fisher, in his chapter **Applied theatre with mixed reality on university campuses**, puts forward instructional concepts for the use of mixed reality (MR) as part of an applied theatre class on a university campus. Participatory performance tactics from Augusto Boal's Theatre of the Oppressed, an applied theatre practice, are connected to MR's interaction design patterns to develop a lesson plan.

In the chapter **Development of professional skills in higher education: Problem-based learning supported by immersive worlds**, *Elvira Femández-Ahumada and her co-authors* provide results from developing professional competencies in the areas of engineering and mathematics teaching, using environments recreated in immersive worlds.

Charles Hand, Raphael Olaiya and *Mohamed Elmasry*, in their chapter **Virtual reality for teaching clinical skills in medical education**, explore the application of VR in healthcare education and whether it is more effective than traditional methods of teaching clinical skills to medical students.

Michael Spitzer, Manfred Rosenberger and *Martin Ebner*, in the chapter **Simulation data visualization using mixed reality with Microsoft HoloLens**[TM], introduce the HoloLens app and a CAD/simulation workflow to visualize CAD models, sensors and the simulation data of a test run on an air conditioning system test bed. They implemented examples coloured the temperature or pressure changes of the test bed parts as MR overlays. The main purpose of the HoloLens app is to reduce the learning effort and time required to understand such simulations and test bed settings.

In the chapter **Towards a virtual photoreality for construction safety education**, *Hai Chien Pham, Anh-Tuan Pham-Hang* and *Thi-Thanh-Mai Pham* propose an innovative Virtual Photoreality (VP)-based learning approach for improving construction safety education. A VP prototype is developed and validated, derived from case studies of accidents that often happen on real construction sites.

Encarnación V. Taguas and her co-authors, in their chapter **Encouraging immersion in the soil sciences through virtual conferences where ideas are shared among avatars to improve the educational background of young scientists**, present a teaching experience where an immersive virtual conference was set up to hold participative meetings on the soil sciences between senior researchers and young scientists.

Giuseppe Abrami, Alexander Mehler, Christian Spiekermann, Attila Kett, Simon Lööck and *Lukas Schwarz*, in **Educational technologies in the area of ubiquitous historical computing in virtual reality**, explain the use of VAnnotatoR, which is a versatile framework for the creation and use of virtual environments that serve to model historical processes in historical education. The chapter describes the building blocks of VAnnotatoR and describes its applications in historical education.

Jin Rong Yang, Fabian Hadipriono Tan and *Adrian Hadipriono Tan*, in the chapter **he use of fuzzy angular models and 3D models on a construction method assessment on the Great Wall of China in Jinshanling as a case study of the history and heritage of civil engineering in education**, introduce three possible construction methods that were likely to have been implemented during the building of the walls and towers of the Jinshanling section of the Great Wall of China during the Ming Dynasty. Fuzzy angular models were selected and employed to determine the most likely and feasible construction methods and sequences. The results can be displayed in VR with or without the fuzzy logic methodology, which is suitable for teaching in primary, secondary and/or university classroom settings.

The chapter **Virtual and augmented reality applications for environmental science education and training** by *Ibrahim Demir* and *Yusuf Sermet* presents seven case studies to demonstrate the potential benefits of XR as an educational tool in the environmental sciences for K-12 and college-level students, as an exhibit for community outreach to increase awareness about environment and to present data resources in an engaging way, as a decision support system for environmental planning and disaster management and as a training platform for technical staff and first responders.

Marko Orel, in **The potentials of virtual reality in entrepreneurship education**, explores the various possibilities of VR for entrepreneurship education that could provide future entrepreneurs with necessary skills and functional knowledge.

In the chapter **ViMeLa: Interactive educational environment for mechatronics lab in virtual reality**, a blended-learning method using theory classes and VR as an experimentation tool is presented by *Toomas Tikk and his co-authors* The main objective is to create a virtual mechatronic laboratory for learning and teaching students in mechatronics.

Tomas Blazauskas and *Daina Gudoniene* in **Virtual reality and augmented reality in educational programs** present the educational fields of VR and AR and discuss their implementation in educational programs by using different technologies and practices related to medicine, sport, military science and history.

Finally, *Oli Howson*, in his chapter **An exploration of the impact of augmented and virtual reality within compulsory education**, explores the uses of AR and VR in the education of those within the age range of 5 to 18.

I am very grateful to all the authors for their efforts in the preparation of their chapters and for sharing their ideas.

I hope that the book will contribute to the field and open up new lines of research, new ideas and new concepts.

Professor Linda Daniela
University of Latvia, Latvia

Contributors

Giuseppe Abrami is a scientific assistant in the Text Technology Lab (TTLab) at Goethe-University in Frankfurt. He is responsible for the various technological developments of the working group, and his research interests include the opportunities of collaborative virtual and augmented realities for the use of multicodal information and the creation of virtual annotation environments.

Yipaer Aierken is a Design, Environment and the Arts (History, Theory and Criticism) Ph.D. student and teaching assistant at Arizona State University supervised by professor Claudia Brown. Currently, she works on ethnicity and identity in Chinese art and artificial intelligence storytelling in virtual worlds. Her master's thesis is titled *Ethnicity and Identity in the Art of Giuseppe Castiglione.* Yipaer Aierken's previous research of includes visual reality in art history and museums applications, ancestor portraits in Chinese art, Japanese emaki, the art and culture of Sogdian and the Silk Road map.

Purificación Alarcón Ramírez studied Architecture at the University of Seville and in the University of Rome La Sapienza, and earned the master's degree *Representation and Design in Engineering and Architecture* in the University of Córdoba. She has worked as an architect in Spain and Germany and has collaborated in research works at the universities of Cordoba and Seville. Currently she works as a mathematics teacher.

Gholamreza Anbarjafari is a team member of the ViMeLa project, which has been co-funded by the Erasmus+ Programme of the European Union (Strategic Partnership, ViMeLa, 2017-1-PL01-KA203-038675).

Paolo Di Barba is a team member of the ViMeLa project, which has been co-funded by the Erasmus+ Programme of the European Union (Strategic Partnership, ViMeLa, 2017-1-PL01-KA203-038675).

Maria Benlloch-González is an agricultural engineer at the Agronomy Department of the Higher School of Agricultural and Forestry Engineering

(University of Cordoba). She belongs to a teaching group related to crop production and currently is immersed in the research of topics related to future scenarios associated to climate change.

Tomas Blazauskas holds a doctoral degree in the Technological sciences, Informatics Engineering field. He is the head of Software Engineering Department at Kaunas University of Technology. His areas of interest include software engineering solutions, virtual reality technologies and applications.

M.C. del Campillo - Agriculture engineer expert on bioavailability of critical nutrients such as phosphorus, iron and zinc, in soils of the Mediterranean area and in the synthesis of new sustainable and economic fertilizers. M.C. is motivated by new technologies in teaching, especially those that promote creativity, imagination, curiosity, research and knowledge.

María del Carmen Beato is forest engineer at the University of Cordoba. She earned a master's degree in *Representation and design in engineering and architecture* at the University of Cordoba. She specialized in 3D design and is currently Councillor Delegate of Lucena City Council, Cordoba.

Sebastián Castillo-Carrión has finished his studies in computer engineering developing a virtual reality platform. Since then, he is involved in diverse research projects, but most of all virtual worlds, specifically Opensim, designing and implementing scenarios for conferences, learning and teaching environments, among other areas.

Maja Celeska is a team member of the ViMeLa project, which has been co-funded by the Erasmus+ Programme of the European Union (Strategic Partnership, ViMeLa, 2017-1-PL01-KA203-038675).

Goga Cvetkovski is a team member of the ViMeLa project, which has been co-funded by the Erasmus+ Programme of the European Union (Strategic Partnership, ViMeLa, 2017-1-PL01-KA203-038675).

Linda Daniela is professor, Chair of the Council for PhD Defence in Education and Dean of the Faculty of Education, Psychology and Art at the University of Latvia. Her expertise spans Technology-enhanced learning, Smart Pedagogy, Smart Education, Educational technologies for learning, Educational robotics, etc. Professor Daniela is an author and co-author of more than 80 publications about processes in all dimensions of education. She has been involved in more than 30 research projects, editing books and journals on technological aspects in education.

Ibrahim Demir is an assistant professor in the Civil and Environmental and Electrical and Computer Engineering departments at the University of Iowa. Dr. Demir's research focuses on hydroinformatics, environmental information systems, scientific visualization, big data analytics, intelligent systems and information communication.

Mihail Digalovski is a team member of the ViMeLa project, which has been co-funded by the Erasmus+ Programme of the European Union (Strategic Partnership, ViMeLa, 2017-1-PL01-KA203-038675).

Lana Frančeska Dreimane is a PhD candidate and a lecturer at the University of Latvia. Her research expertise is educational applications of immersive technology for learning, spanning from immersive technologies for learning, to cognitive pedagogy, instructional design strategies, transversal competences and technology enhanced learning. She has authored several publications on the topic of immersive learning, and transversal competences and developed a Master's course on educational applications of immersive technology for learning. Lana is also a member of the Immersive Learning Research Network (iLRN)'s State of XR and Immersive Learning Expert Panel.

Martin Ebner is currently the head of the Department of Educational Technology at Graz University of Technology and is therefore responsible for all university wide e-learning activities. He is an Adjunct Professor on media informatics (research area: educational technology) and works also at the Institute for Interactive Systems and Data Science as senior researcher. His research focuses strongly on seamless learning, learning analytics, open educational resources, maker education and computer science for children.

Mohamed Elmasry is a general surgery registrar at Oxford University Hospitals, and a PhD student at the University of Liverpool. He has obtained his bachelor's degree in medicine and surgery from Ain Shams University, Cairo, Egypt in 2008, and has started his surgical training in the UK in 2011. Mohamed's area of interest is Hepato-Pancreato-Biliary (HPB) surgery, alongside general surgery and medical education.

Mohamed's research work focuses on liver regeneration after surgical resection, and he has been the author and co-author of several published articles in peer-reviewed journals.

Elvira Fernández-Ahumada is assistant professor in the Department of Mathematics of the University of Cordoba. Her main research deals with mathematical competence of pre-service teachers, problem solving and modelling in mathematics teaching, use of immersive virtual worlds for educational purposes and multivariate analyses of different types of data.

Anna Firych-Nowacka is a team member of the ViMeLa project, which has been co-funded by the Erasmus+ Programme of the European Union (Strategic Partnership, ViMeLa, 2017-1-PL01-KA203-038675).

Joshua A. Fisher, Ph.D. is an expert in participatory, community-focused platforms for XR storytelling and experiences. Fisher has published through a variety of conferences including ACM Multimedia, International Conference on Interactive Digital Storytelling, Virtual Reality 4 Good, CHI-Play and IEEE VR. Currently, he is an Assistant Professor of Immersive Media at Columbia College Chicago.

Ray Gallon is president and co-founder of the Transformation Society, which promotes digital transformation and organizational learning, and currently teaches at the universities of Barcelona and Strasbourg. He is cochair of the Transformation and Information 4.0 Research and Development group of the World Federation of Associations for Teacher Education (WFATE). Earlier, Ray was an award-winning radio producer and was programme manager of New York's public radio station, WNYC-FM. Since 1992 Ray has focused on the convergence of communication, culture, and technology, He is a speaker at conferences and events throughout the world, and has contributed to many books, journals and magazines. He currently serves as president of the Information 4.0 Consortium.

Daina Gudoniene has a doctoral degree in the Technological sciences, Informatics Engineering field. Since 2010, she works on the Informatics faculty at the Kaunas University of Technology as a lecturer in the distance study program. Areas of interest include learning object design and models for technologies enhanced learning, virtual reality and applications for education.

José Emilio Guerrero-Ginel has Ph.D. in Agricultural Engineering and is a Full Professor at the University of Córdoba, Coordinator and teacher of several courses of initial and continuing training in Spain, Europe and Latin America on animal production, environment and rural development. He is also the author of more than 150 publications on topics related to animal production, environment and regional development, is responsible for R & D projects and supervises numerous masters and doctoral theses.

Rain Eric Haamer is a team member of the ViMeLa project, which has been co-funded by the Erasmus+ Programme of the European Union (Strategic Partnership, ViMeLa, 2017-1-PL01-KA203-038675).

Charles Hand is a neurosurgical trainee at Southmead Hospital in Bristol, UK. He has a background in academia and his interests include virtual reality for use in medical education and clinical neurosurgical research. He believes that virtual reality will have a large part to play in the future of medical education and will be especially relevant to surgical trainees.

Oli Howson is an experienced teacher of Computer Science at Secondary, Post-16 and Higher Education levels. As a teacher, he believes that virtual reality has as much potential to improve educational provision as the BBC Micro did in the 1980s.

Dorota Kamińska is a team member of the ViMeLa project, which has been co-funded by the Erasmus+ Programme of the European Union (Strategic Partnership, ViMeLa, 2017-1-PL01-KA203-038675).

Attila Kett chose Computer Science as his second study at the Goethe-University Frankfurt after his music studies and will soon start his Computer Science Master. He is especially interested in virtual reality and the visualization of data.

Glyn Lawson is a Chartered Ergonomist and Human Factors Specialist and has spent his career researching the human factors of virtual reality technologies for applications such as health and safety training and vehicle design.

Marcin Lefik is a team member of the ViMeLa project, which has been co-funded by the Erasmus+ Programme of the European Union (Strategic Partnership, ViMeLa, 2017-1-PL01-KA203-038675).

Simon Lööck studied Computer Science at the Goethe University in Frankfurt am Main, Germany, from 2016 to 2019 where he wrote his bachelor's thesis at the Text Technology Lab. For this thesis, he developed the network capability and usability of the virtual reality application 'StolperwegeVR'.

Neus Lorenzo Galés is an Inspector of Education and cofounder of the Transformation Society, which promotes digital organizational learning. She is the former Subdirector General of Educational Transformation in Catalonia (Spain), and Co-Chair of the 'Transformation Society and Information 4.0' Research and Development Group of the World Federation of Associations for Teacher Education (WFATE). She teaches at the Universitat Autònoma de Barcelona (UAB), is a member of the Information 4.0 Consortium and has been researcher and assessor for the Education Commission of the European Parliament, the Council of Europe, Pestalozzi Programmes, Erasmus +, etc. She is an international speaker and also presents webinars and online seminars.

Juan José Martínez Molina is a Forest engineer at the University of Cordoba; he earned a master's degree in *Representation and design in engineering and architecture* in the University of Cordoba. He specialized in 3D design and calculation of structures and currently works calculating and designing metal structures in a company in Alicante, Spain.

Alexander Mehler is a Professor of Computational Humanities/Text-technology at Goethe University Frankfurt where he heads the Text Technology Lab (TTLab). Alexander Mehler is a member of the executive committee of the Center for Digital Research in the Humanities, Social Sciences and Education Sciences (CEDIFOR). He is a founding member of the German Society for Network Research (DGNet). His research interests include quantitative analysis, simulative synthesis and formal modelling of textual units in spoken and written communication. To this end, he investigates linguistic networks based on contemporary and historical languages (using models of language evolution). A current research interest concerns 4D text technologies based on VR, AR and Augmented Virtuality.

Maria Evelina Mognaschi is a team member of the ViMeLa project, which has been co-funded by the Erasmus+ Programme of the European Union (Strategic Partnership, ViMeLa, 2017-1-PL01-KA203-038675).

Jesús Montejo-Gámez is an Assistant Professor at the department of Mathematical Education of the University of Granada, researcher of the Spanish Society of Research on Mathematics Education and a member of the Education Committee of the Spanish Royal Mathematical Society. He is focused on collaborative learning supported by ICT, mathematics teacher formation and mathematical modelling in problem solving.

Raphael Olaiya is currently an acute and emergency medicine resident doctor at the Central London Deanery Hospitals and the director of the Lewisham and Greenwich Hospital's Health Data Science Group, a team that focuses on the research and application of machine learning to clinical medicine. He achieved his medical degree at University of Liverpool and his Masters of Data Science post-graduate degree at University College London. He has lead several UK based commercial and academic oriented health innovation implementation projects utilising virtual reality and machine learning. Raphael's research and work focuses on translating state of the art emerging technologies towards improving healthcare.

Marko Orel is an assistant professor at the University of Economics, Prague qualitative researcher specializing in the exploration of the changing nature of the global workplace and research of digital age that presents major new challenges to entrepreneurs. He is exploring projects and operational networks of influences, community engagement moderation and its inter-relational participation within flexible workspaces.

Leovigilda Ortiz-Medina is an agronomist attached to the Unit of Production Systems Engineering, in the Higher School of Agricultural and Forestry Engineering (University of Cordoba). Since 2002, she has mainly worked in the management of post-graduate programs and in projects for the improvement of teaching quality, especially in the field of employment and business creation. She is also involved in projects related to innovation in the agroforestry sector.

Cristina Pérez Martínez is an architect and currently works as a secondary school teacher. She was born on 20 February 1988 in Jaén (Spain). In 2016 Cristina obtained two Masters: in *Representation and Design in Engineering and Architecture* and another in *Teaching*. After her degree in 2012, she worked as an architect in numerous places (such as Antwerp in Belgium and in Valencia, Córdoba, Jaén and Madrid in Spain) until the year 2019, when she started working as a secondary teacher in the specialty of Mathematics.

Lidija Petkovska is a team member of the ViMeLa project, which has been co-funded by the Erasmus+ Programme of the European Union (Strategic Partnership, ViMeLa, 2017-1-PL01-KA203-038675).

Anh-Tuan Pham-Hang is currently a student of the School of Computer Science and Engineering at the International University, Vietnam. His research interests consist of virtual reality, augmented reality and photoreality, focusing on computer-assisted pedagogical tools.

Hai Chien Pham received his Ph.D. in Construction Engineering and Management from Chung-Ang University, Seoul, South Korea. His research interests consist of Building Information Modeling (BIM), Virtual Reality, Augmented Reality, Photoreality and mobile computing, focusing on technology-enhanced application for construction education, training and management. He is currently the Head of the Department of Construction Engineering and Management (DCEM) of Faculty of Civil Engineering at Ton Duc Thang University, Vietnam. He has taught many construction management courses for undergraduate and graduate students and guided a large number of Ph.D. and master's students. Furthermore, he has coordinated and participated in several research projects.

Thi-Thanh-Mai Pham is currently a lecturer of Faculty of International Trade, College of Foreign Economic Relation, Vietnam. She has taught many international trade and business management courses for undergraduate and graduate students, as well as participated in several research projects. Her research interests focus on assessing the innovative pedagogy methods for improving learning outcome.

Gregory Quinn: As course leader for Architectural Engineering at the Swinburne University of Technology, Gregory Quinn pursues innovation by navigating between the arts and sciences in all of his professional pursuits. His research strengths lie in research through design, lightweight architecture, education and computation.

Najmeh Rezaei is a team member of the ViMeLa project, which has been co-funded by the Erasmus+ Programme of the European Union (Strategic Partnership, ViMeLa, 2017-1-PL01-KA203-038675).

Manfred Rosenberger holds a Bachelor of Education from Pädagogische Hochschule Steiermark and received his MSc in Software Engineering Leadership from campus02 in Graz in 2016. His work is focused on Requirements Engineering in research und software projects.

Davide Salanitri achieved his Ph.D. in Human Factors at The University of Nottingham in 2018. Davide is a Human Factors researcher, a specialist in the study of Human Factors in Virtual Reality.

Pedro Sánchez-Zamora (Córdoba, 1984) is Lecturer at the Department of Agricultural Economics, Sociology and Policy at ETSIAM-University of Cordoba (Spain). He was trained as agricultural engineer (2009) and has a Ph.D. in Rural Development (2014) from the University of Cordoba. His areas of expertise are focused on the study of territorial dynamics and territorial resilience in rural areas and the analysis and evaluation of Public Policies for rural areas.

Tomasz Sapiński is a team member of the ViMeLa project, which has been co-funded by the Erasmus+ Programme of the European Union (Strategic Partnership, ViMeLa, 2017-1-PL01-KA203-038675).

Fabian Schneider is a researcher and computational architect exploring the boundaries between practice, design and human interface. His research focus lies with multi-platform interfacing, computational design and visualisations.

Lukas Schwarz has been studying Computer Science at the Goethe University Frankfurt since 2014. His work as a student assistant at the Text Technology Lab mainly consists of creating virtual 3D models of real-world buildings and assisting other students in creating these models.

Yusuf Sermet is a Ph.D. candidate in the Department of Electrical and Computer Engineering at the University of Iowa, while working as a Graduate Research Assistant at the IIHR—Hydroscience & Engineering. His research focuses on next-generation environmental knowledge generation and communication.

Christian Spiekermann has been studying Computer Science at the Goethe University Frankfurt since 2014. There he has focused on computer graphics and mixed reality, especially in his position as student assistant at the TTLab.

Michael Spitzer received his MSc in Information and Computer Engineering from Graz University of Technology in 2015. As his master's thesis, he implemented a collaborative sketch tool (Teamsketch) for iPads to train in collaborative work with primary school pupils. Since then he has focused his work on technology-enhanced learning (TEL). In 2016 he started the Ph.D. program at Graz University of Technology as a researcher in the field of technology-enhanced learning with augmented reality.

Encarnación V. Taguas works as an Assistant Professor in the Department of Rural Engineering of the University of Cordoba. She is a Ph.D. Forest Engineer, and her specific fields are 'Innovative teaching techniques in

Geosciences and Engineering Projects' and 'Soil and Water Measurements, Modelling and Conservation in olive groves'.

Adrian Hadipriono Tan is a Ph.D. alumnus of the Ohio State University. He has a B.S. in Computer Science and Engineering and an M.S. and Ph.D. in Civil Engineering. Adrian's Ph.D. work was in civil engineering with a focus on computer graphics and virtual simulation in the construction industry.

Fabian Hadipriono Tan has an M.S. in structural engineering, an M.E. in construction engineering and management and a Dr. Eng. in construction engineering and management from the University of California in Berkeley. He has worked in the areas of construction of infrastructures and buildings, failure assessment of buildings and bridges, construction accident investigations, forensic engineering, ancient buildings, ancient bridges and the ancient history of science and engineering for over 50 years. The tools Professor Tan uses for his research include fault tree analysis, fuzzy logic, artificial intelligence and virtual reality.

Ana M. Tarquis has been teaching Mathematics at UPM under different graduate programs since 1991. In addition to classroom instruction, she is mentoring students on appropriate research topics at Master and PhD programs.

Toomas Tikk is a team member of the ViMeLa project, which has been co-funded by the Erasmus+ Programme of the European Union (Strategic Partnership, ViMeLa, 2017-1-PL01-KA203-038675).

Brian Waterfield is a Specialist in Virtual Reality & High-end Visualisation Technical Lead, who has driven jaguar LandRover's immersive development over the last 12 years.

Slawomir Wiak is a team member of the ViMeLa project, which has been co-funded by the Erasmus+ Programme of the European Union (Strategic Partnership, ViMeLa, 2017-1-PL01-KA203-038675).

Jin Rong Yang holds a B.S., M.S. and Ph.D. in Civil Engineering from The Ohio State University. He has worked as a graduate teaching associate for the Department of Engineering Education at the university, as well as a construction inspector for the City of Columbus. Dr. Yang is currently a civil engineer in the U.S. Army Aviation and Missile Command.

Grzegorz Zwoliński is a team member of the ViMeLa project, which has been co-funded by the Erasmus+ Programme of the European Union (Strategic Partnership, ViMeLa, 2017-1-PL01-KA203-038675).

Part I

Virtual reality in humanities and social sciences

Virtual reality learning experience evaluation tool for instructional designers and educators

Lana Frančeska Dreimane

Introduction

Virtual reality (VR) has been used for learning since the 1970s for flight simulation and military training. VR has been applied to create learning experiences in various fields that require complex conceptualisation, drill-training (repetition, automation) and complex contextual problem-solving (individuals and teams). The emerging availability of low-cost, high fidelity VR environments opened new possibilities for direct learning that is both cost effective and scalable.

For the past decade, VR has transformed human-computer interface and in fact humanised it much further than ever before. Immersive experiences – either reality or fantasy based, allow us to interact with content and other people in a way that previously could only have been possible in science fiction. New outlooks on the prevailing importance of learning environments and technology enhanced learning strategies led by the educational and immersive technology research community offered new terminology to advance the discussion on immersive learning. Thus, the new terms – three-dimensional (3-D) virtual learning environments (VLEs) (Dalgarno & Lee, 2010) and virtual immersive experiences (VIEs) (Kapp & O'Driscoll, 2010) allowed for new opportunities to further and more effectively structure the academic discourse on the educational potential and applications of VR technology.

The field of VR research can be viewed in two main categories – technical solutions and applications. This study discusses technical solutions in context, but the focus of the research will be on applications, specifically VR applications for learning purposes. There is a significant body of research available on technical solutions and limitations of VR technology; however, in 2020 it is still very challenging for educators and instructional designers to find and navigate the guidelines on how VR learning experiences should be designed in order to ensure that learning objectives will be achieved. Thus, a major problem of VR learning research today seems to be the lack of understanding of the general principles that govern the process and how they are interconnected with the existing knowledge about learning, instructional strategies and curricula. With the explosive development in the field of VR learning, there is a need for systematisation of pedagogical principles that govern and facilitate learning in VR. This chapter presents a VR learning experience evaluation tool consisting of 3 macro-level criteria, 21 mezzo-level criteria and 90 sub-criteria that will highlight pivotal aspects that should be considered by instructors and educators who wish to successfully design and/ or apply VR learning experiences.

As Ron Burns concluded in the Foreword for *Learning in 3-D: Adding a New Dimension to Enterprise Learning and Collaboration* (Burns in Kapp & O'Driscoll, 2010): 'Now learning in context will become the most empowering component for learning and collaboration or humans and the human computer interface will be more naturalistic' (p. xi). Today, with emergence of virtual learning environments, we have the opportunity to go beyond content, beyond hierarchies and set environments – classrooms or desktops – and focus on the context of learning. Contrary to the general belief that VR has changed or will completely change the way we interact, entertain and learn, the author of this article argues that VR in fact offers a possibility to create more natural extensions to existing modes of interaction, entertainment and learning. This conviction also relates to the application and effectiveness of the existing approved instructional models (Bloom's, SOLO, ADDIE, Gagne's, 4C ID model) in the VR environment. Furthermore, this view is shared by Oral Roberts University's (a world pioneer in the use of VR in university programmes) vice president of technology and innovation, Michael Mathews (2017). The main benefit of introducing VR into the learning process is that there is no need to change the learning objectives and strategies; VR rather aids in achieving these objectives and amplifies (deepens) the residue and speeds up the learning process.

VR has already shown great potential; nevertheless, it is very new technology and there is much more to be understood and studied on how to use it effectively and further incorporate VR technology into our daily lives in order to harness the unique opportunities. Several authors argue that the success of VR learning relies on the quality of the chosen visualisation and interaction mode (Bryson, 1995; Erickson, 1993). The VR technology industry is exceedingly competitive and has developed with remarkable speed; nevertheless, today's VR technologies bear several significant technical limitations, including, for some users, cybersickness or simulation sickness. Also called VR sickness, it occurs when exposure to a virtual environment causes symptoms that are similar to those of motion sickness (Kolasinski, 1995; LaViola, 2000). Other issues include the quality of lenses (including the lack of comfortable and affordable optometric solutions for VR headsets, eliminating the need to wear glasses/ lenses beneath the headset), as well as increasing need to improve the resolution and display quality and improvements in terms of latency (response) including spatial queues and haptic responses.

Why do we need an evaluation tool for VR learning experiences?

Since the advent of computer technologies, various research has raised the question of whether and how technology can potentially enhance the learning process and outcomes and what value can be added to learners' experiences. Unlike other terms, technology enhanced learning (TEL) implies a value judgement, as 'enhanced' suggests that something is improved or superior in some way. The proposed description itself suggests that enhancement should be understood as a value judgement meaning improved quality or added value. Thus, several academics (Chatti, Schroeder, & Jarke, 2012; Kapp & O'Driscoll, 2010; Kirkwood & Price, 2013) have raised questions such as what exactly can and should be, or in particular instances is, enhanced when technology is used for teaching and learning. How will the enhancement be achieved, and how can enhancement be determined, evaluated and monitored? Is enhancement concerned with increasing technology use or improving the circumstances/environment in which educational activities take place?

Instructional strategies for learning approaches in VR

Learning taxonomies and instructional design models present a most suitable platform for further discussion about the approaches learning in VR. A variety of field-specific (case-study) based inquiries draw on several field-specific principles (e.g. medical training, first-response teams, military, pilot, as well as navy training and engineering, manufacturing and sales); however, it is important to note that very little research is available on the general principles governing learning in VR.

Chwen Jen Chen (2006) asserts that

> Although VR is recognized as an impressive learning tool, there are still many issues that need further investigation including, identifying the appropriate theories and models to guide its design and development, investigating how its attributes are able to support learning (…).
>
> (2006, p. 39)

Her research resulted in insights to a feasible instructional design theoretical framework, as well as an instructional development framework for VR-based learning environments.

Kapp & O'Driscoll (2010) combine technological knowledge with instruction and learning approaches and present a model to approach learning in VR through a variety of components and levels. The model defines 7 Sensibilities; 9 Principles; 4 Macrostructures and 11 Learning Archetypes (Figure 1.1.).

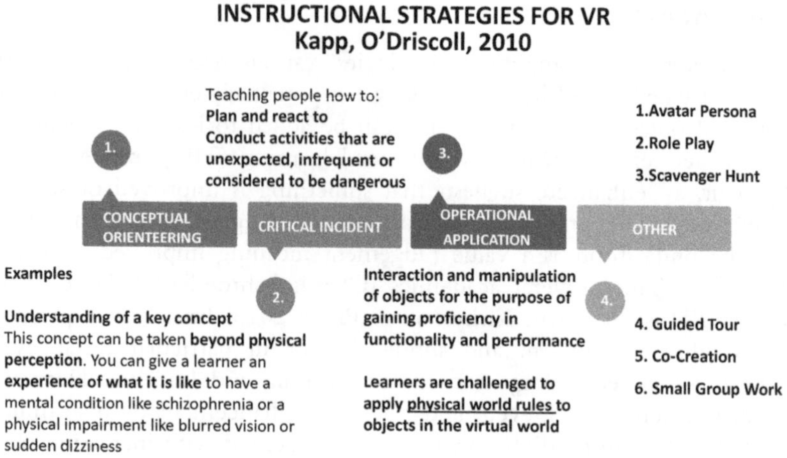

INSTRUCTIONAL STRATEGIES FOR VR
Kapp, O'Driscoll, 2010

Teaching people how to:
Plan and react to
1. **Conduct activities that are**
unexpected, infrequent or
considered to be dangerous

3.

1.Avatar Persona

2.Role Play

3.Scavenger Hunt

CONCEPTUAL ORIENTEERING   CRITICAL INCIDENT   OPERATIONAL APPLICATION   OTHER

Examples

2.

Understanding of a key concept
This concept can be taken **beyond physical**
perception. You can give a learner an
experience of what it is like to have a
mental condition like schizophrenia or a
physical impairment like blurred vision or
sudden dizziness

Interaction and manipulation
of objects for the purpose of
gaining proficiency in
functionality and performance

Learners are challenged to
apply <u>physical world rules</u> to
objects in the virtual world

4.

4. Guided Tour

5. Co-Creation

6. Small Group Work

Figure 1.1 Instructional strategies for VR adopted from Kapp and O'Driscoll (2010) Author's concept.

Method

The first step involved constructing VR learning ecosystem and typologies, which necessitated extensive literature analysis and practical case analysis. For the purposes of this research, VR learning archetypes and typologies defined by Kapp and O'Driscoll (2010) as well as the unique characteristics and affordances of VR learning environment proposed by Dalgarno and Lee (2010) were adopted.

The second step consisted of drawing comparisons through cross-analysis of the established learning theories and approaches of the 20th and 21st century in order to establish aspects and attributes that are fully or partially applicable to the process of learning in VR (see Table 1.1). The following educational theories and approaches were analysed: Behaviourism, Cognitivism, Constructivism, Generative learning, Problem-based learning, Activity theory, Significant learning, Constructionism, Connectivism, Situated learning, Experiential learning and Learning as a Network (LaaN) theory.

Step 3 involved highlighting aspects of the VR learning ecosystem that fit with the key aspects of each of the pedagogic and instructional design theory frameworks Table 1.2 maps out some of the aspects of the VR learning ecosystem that fit with the key facets of each of the learning frameworks set out in Table 1.1.

Based on the literature analysis and extensive VR learning content testing, a qualitative data analysis tool for evaluating VR learning experiences was developed. The evaluation tool included 3 macro-criteria, 21 criteria and 90 sub-criteria. The full evaluation tool template can be found in Annex 1.

Table 1.1 Cross-analysis of the learning theories and approaches of the 20th and 21st centuries.

	20th century learning theories			21st century learning theories
Theory/ approach	Behaviourism	Cognitivism	Constructivism	Connectivism
	TEACHING $\longrightarrow$		LEARNING	
Theorists	I. Pavlov, E. Thorndike, B.F. Skinner	D. Merril, R. Gagne, J. Bruner	L. Vygotsky, A. Bandura, J. Piaget, J. Dewey, S. Papert, M.C. Wittrock, L.D. Fink (significant learning), D.H. Jonassen	Y. Engestrom, G. Siemens, S. Downes, J. Lave, D.A. Kolb, M.A. Chatti
Related approaches/ theories	Cognitive behaviourism	Instructional theory	Constructionism Generative learning approach; Problem-based learning (reflection, scaffolding); Significant learning – authentic experiential activity theory experiences + reflection, self-assessment	Situated learning/ Experiential learning, Active learning and learning-by-doing (such as role-play), scaffolded, collaborative learning, Learning as a Network (LaaN) theory, actor-network theory, gamification
Learner's role	Passive – reactive	Reactive	Active	Proactive
Main assumption	correct instructional stimuli will elicit the desired learning outcomes, with an emphasis on practice and performance	Focus on understanding of mental processes; mind as an information processor	Student-centered view of the learner as an active participant in the learning process and the teacher as a facilitator; learning occurs as a result of active engagement or experience in a social context; importance of social context in which the learning occurs importance of interaction,	knowledge and learning are today defined by connections; learning as a connection/ network-forming process; the half-life of knowledge is shrinking; learning consists of the ability to construct and traverse networks; understands learning as a socially

(Continued)

Table 1.1 (Cont.)

	20th century learning theories			21st century learning theories
Theory/ approach	Behaviourism	Cognitivism	Constructivism	Connectivism
	TEACHING ⟶		LEARNING	
			communication and experience; assistance of a more capable peer, scaffolding	constructed process where learners interact in pursuit of a shared goal; the connections that enable us to learn are more important than our current state of knowing. Knowledge networks, fluidity, some learning environments with no spatial and time restrictions, collective value creation, exchange of knowledge and virtual co-construction
Types of learning facilitated	Task-based	Reasoning, problem-solving	Social, hands-on, contextual	Creation of knowledge through connection creating, creating collective knowledge, leveraging internal and external knowledge networks
How the learning environment is viewed	Design of learning environment as potential facilitator of learning	Learning environment is constructed as a projection of internal mental processes (schema)	Authenticity of learning environment Contextual learning Technology enhanced	Learning environment is fundamental and can be also viewed in multiple ways – internal, external, artefacts, groups of people, information, technology, activities, etc.

Table 1.2 Relation to learning in VR.

Aspects of VR learning ecosystem that fit with the key facets of each learning framework

BEHAVIOURISM	COGNITIVISM	CONSTRUCTIVISM	CONNECTIVISM
1. Stimuli are effective in controlling learning outcomes and learner behaviour – VR environment stimuli guide learner through experience and potentially impact one's behaviour and values.	1. Internalising knowledge construction – shift from teaching to learning.	1. Authentic experiential experiences – learning environment becomes paramount	1. Collective intelligence
2. Focus on stimulation of learner's attention through reinforcement – stimulation of learner's attention is quintessential to VR learning.	2. Emphasis on knowledge deconstruction/architecture – cognitive processes, knowledge dimensions	2. Personal interpretation and knowledge representation	2. Enabling internal and external knowledge networks of a learner in order to facilitate new knowledge building or constructing new meaning to existing knowledge.
3. Achieving learning outcomes by stimulating learner engagement through presenting the correct stimuli.	3. Learning is a change in cognitive processes and knowledge dimensions	3. Learning in and from context	3. Shift of emphasis from knowing to the ability to navigate through knowledge networks
4. E. Thorndike, B.F. Skinner – (the law of effect, Operant conditioning) Selective reinforcement – positive/negative response in VR learning environment (or avatars)	4. Importance of differentiating short-term and long-term memory	4. Reflection, self-assessment	4. Ability to incorporate and interpret new knowledge
	5. By applying the correct stimulus, the learner can be engaged in cognitive processes of different complexity in order to facilitate learning	5. Learning process is self-directed, experiment and discovery driven	5. Fluidity of self across the different networks
	6. Replicating mental models when constructing a learning experience	6. Learning is facilitated and enabled by VR space	6. Personal knowledge network
		7. Online collaboration – VR artefacts (Vygotsky tools)	7. Internal and external knowledge nodes
		8. Prior knowledge	8. Networks of knowledge and applications
		9. Sense of self (Bandura) – avatar persona	
		10. sense of self-efficacy – engagement in VR learning through experimentation, engagement with other avatars, co-creation	
		11. Guidance (Vygotsky ZPD)	

(Continued)

Table 1.2 (Cont.)

Aspects of VR learning ecosystem that fit with the key facets of each learning framework

BEHAVIOURISM	COGNITIVISM	CONSTRUCTIVISM	CONNECTIVISM
5. E. Thorndike, B.F. Skinner – learner must play an active role in order to acquire knowledge 6. E. Thorndike, B.F. Skinner – learners learn by doing – trial and error – VR presents a safe and engaging space for practical training. 7. Evaluation of behaviour to measure learning progress and objectives – VR learning provides an opportunity to evaluate natural human interaction with artefacts and other humans; thus, it is possible to evaluate not only separate forms of behaviour (e.g. writing, talking, movement), but also enable to evaluate whole-some behaviour aspects – decisions, reaction time, collaboration, etc.	7. Organising new knowledge as 'related' to already existing knowledge	12. VR learning space and arte-facts within shape cultural conditions of learning 13. Play as a significant element of learning, which also ensures learner engagement 14. Importance of transfer and prior knowledge	

Three macro-criteria, 21-mezzo criteria and 90 sub-criteria

The proposed VR experience evaluation tool was essentially developed to serve as a purposeful quality control or design development instrument that would inform instructional designers, educators, learners and VR content and technology professionals by providing a clear and multi-purpose framework that allows one to outline the alignment of the instructional, pedagogical and VR learning environment to ensure and strengthen the efficiency of the VR learning design and instructional strategies.

These typologies were developed through analysis of 130 VR learning experience designs and then drawing similar characteristics of learning environments and strategies applied in VR, thus establishing broader types of VR learning experiences. The tool has been further developed through rigorous approbation and modifications for variant use. These types are based on the current technology and learning needs; nevertheless, this only means that these types will be evolving hand in hand with the development of VR technologies and the ever-evolving job-market appetite for knowledgeable and skilled professionals.

A compact schema for the framework of the evaluation tool is provided in Figure 1.2.

The first macro criterion is labelled 'Purpose', which includes 5 mezzo-level criteria (see Table 1.3.).

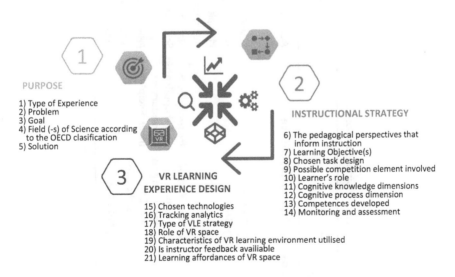

Figure 1.2 Framework of the evaluation tool.

Table 1.3 First macro criterion 'purpose'.

Macro-criterion	Criterion	Sub-criteria						
1. Purpose	1) Type of Experience	Activity	Lesson	Experience	Interactive simulation	Experience + activity	Experience + lesson	Immersive Virtual World
	2) Problem	Learning problem that has to be addressed						
	3) Goal	Single / Multiple/interdisciplinary / Adjustable						
	4) Field (-s) of Science according to the OECD classification	Primary FOS and if applicable secondary or interdisciplinary						
		Natural Sciences	Engineering and Technology	Medical and Health Sciences	Agricultural Sciences	Social Sciences	Humanities	
		Primary FOS / Secondary FOS						
	5) Solution	Presented learning solution						

The second macro criterion proposes 9 mezzo-level 'Instructional Strategy' criteria (see Table 1.4.).

The third macro criterion proposes 6 mezzo-level criteria for evaluating VR learning experience designs (see Table 1.5.).

Table 1.4 Second macro criterion 'instructional strategy'.

Macro-criterion	Criterion	Sub-criteria	
2. Instructional Strategy	6) The pedagogical perspectives that inform instruction	Single	
		Multiple	
		Mixed	
		Behaviourism	
		Cognitivism	
		Constructivism	
		Connectivism	
	7) Learning objective(s)	Single	
		Multiple	
	8) Chosen task design	Sequential	Interrelated
	9) Possible competition element	Individual	Ranking
		Team	Time-count score
		Adjustable	Other
	10) Learner's role	Passive explorer – learner absorbs the experience yet has no additional control over the environment in the speed or mode of interaction	
		Re-active – learner is actively responding to and interacting with the learning environment	
		Proactive – learner drives and controls the learning environment	
	11) Cognitive knowledge dimensions	Factual	
		Conceptual	
		Procedural	
		Meta-cognitive	
	12) Cognitive process dimension	Remember	
		Understand	
		Apply	
		Analyse	
		Evaluate	
		Create	
	Knowledge	Disciplinary knowledge	

(Continued)

Table 1.4 (Cont.)

Macro-criterion	Criterion		Sub-criteria
	13) Competences developed		Interdisciplinary knowledge
			Practical knowledge
		Skills developed	Cognitive and meta-cognitive skills
			Social and emotional
			Physical and practical skills
		Attitudes and values	Attitudes and values
	14) Monitoring and assessment		Learner is assessed in real-time (wright or wrong signals, score, points, levels, number of errors, completion time, other real-time metrics)
			Learner is assessed after completing several sessions
			Self-assessment
			No assessment is incorporated into the experience

Table 1.5 Third macro criterion 'VR learning experience design'.

Macro-criterion	Criterion	Sub-criteria
3. VR learning experience design	15) Chosen technologies	High compatibility (numerous headsets devices/platforms)
		Low compatibility
		Web VR friendly
		VR/AR/MR mode
	16) Tracking analytics (e.g. attention, eye movement, facial expressions, EEG, ECG, EMG, EDA)	Engagement, interaction
		Eye tracking, viewpoint monitoring
		Sensory tracking (facial expressions, EEG, ECG, EMG, EDA)
		Haptic interaction
	17) Type of VLE strategy	Individual
		Group
		Adjustable (real-time; multi-user; synchronous)
		Avatar persona
		Role play

(Continued)

Table 1.5 (Cont.)

Macro-criterion	Criterion	Sub-criteria
		Scavenger hunt
		Guided tour
		Operational application
		Conceptual orienteering
		Critical incident
		Co-creation
		Small group work
		Group forums
		Social networking
	18) Role of VR space (including artefacts within the space) in achieving learning objectives	Primary significance – learning occurs from interaction with the space
		Important – not a primary driver of learning experience, yet important in conveying contextual knowledge and cues
		Supportive/entertaining
	19) Characteristics of VR learning environment utilised	Representational fidelity
		Learner interaction
		Social fidelity (including social familiarity and social reality)
		Social presence
		Immediacy of discourse
	20) Availability of instructor or feedback	Yes
		No
		Statistical data (success rate, progress)
		Test
	21) Learning affordances of VR space	Spatial knowledge representation
		Experiential learning
		Engagement
		Contextual learning
		Collaborative learning

Conclusions and recommendations

This chapter highlights a framework for ensuring an alignment between learning goals (pedagogy), instructional strategy and affordances of VR technology. The VR learning experience evaluation tool aims to serve a ready-to-use and adaptable instrument for instructional designers, educators, VR technology developers and potentially learners. Perhaps the most notable contribution of this study is in systematising already existent yet fragmented knowledge and developing practical recommendations, as well as defining the area for further considerations and research.

First conclusion and recommendation

VR learning experiences can be used for all cognitive processes and knowledge dimensions; however, if we aim to utilise the specific and unique affordances of the virtual learning environment, the most beneficial choice of learning objectives for such experiences would be, in fact, a higher cognitive dimensions starting with remembering factual knowledge and moving all the way to creation of metacognitive knowledge.

It is especially beneficial to utilise VR learning technology in order to develop students' ability to create and engage in critical thinking and innovation, as VR learning experiences allow students to express and create complex metacognitive concepts, as well as perfect complex procedural knowledge including where procedural and cognitive processes fuse together.

Second conclusion and recommendation

It is important to note that the majority of the current research on learning in VR draws a connection with learning principles of constructivism, constructionism and connectivism; however, it often disregards other learning frameworks such as behaviourism and cognitivism.

For this reason, the author argues that all of the relevant learning facets highlighted in Table 1.1 should be taken into account when approaching learning in VR from the pedagogic perspective (Table 1.2), as the teachings of each of the learning frameworks discussed in Table 1.1 should be fully leveraged in order to better understand how learning takes place in relation to affordances of VR technology and user experience. However, the author stresses that numerous aspects are unique to the VR learning ecosystem and are not covered by the existing learning frameworks, such as those included in the third macro criterion 'VR learning experience design' (see Table 1.5). Thus, when attempting to define the most appropriate pedagogic theory outlook, the author argues, a mixed or fused outlook should be adapted.

Third conclusion and recommendation

In order to avoid creating ineffective VR learning content and wasting hours and resources, it is immensely important to ensure the effective use of VR technology. Thus, it is crucial to analyse and map out the characteristics of the strategically set learning objectives and the role of the VR learning environment before undertaking the creation of VR learning content (including instructional design and 3D visual and multi-media content creation).

Table 1.6 Preliminary cross-analysis.

	Criterion	Sub-criteria
Preliminary cross-analysis	How the affordances of the VR environment contribute to qualities of active, collaborative learning	*(Free form)*
	Is (was) the learning strategy successful *because* of the affordances of 3D VLE?	*(Free form)*
	VR user experience (What is the role of learner using the VLE?)	*(Free form)*
	Does the learning experience clearly manifest the benefits of using VR as the learning mode	Yes, the reasons for choosing VR as the learning mode are clear
		Reasons for choosing VR as the learning mode can be identified
		Reasons for choosing VR as the learning mode cannot be identified

The author proposes preliminary cross-analysis (see Table 1.6.) in order to ensure further effectiveness and successful alignment of all of the affordances involved in VR learning experience.

Annex 1 'Evaluation tool'

Macro-criterion	Criterion	Sub-criteria	Title of the learning experience
1. Purpose Type of Experience	1) Type of Experience	Activity Lesson Experience Interactive simulation Experience + activity Experience + lesson Immersive Virtual World	
	2) Problem	Learning problem that has to be addressed	
	3) Goal	Single Multiple/interdisciplinary Adjustable	

(Continued)

Macro-criterion	Criterion	Sub-criteria		Title of the learning experience
	4) Field(-s) of Science according to the OECD classification	1. Natural Sciences 2. Engineering and Technology 3. Medical and Health Sciences 4. Agricultural Sciences 5. Social Sciences 6. Humanities Primary FOS Secondary FOS (interdisciplinary)		
	5) Solution			
2. Instructional strategy	6) The pedagogical perspectives that inform instruction	Single Multiple Mixed Behaviourism Cognitivism Constructivism Connectivism		
	7) Learning objective(s)	Single Multiple		
	8) Chosen task design	Sequential Interrelated		
	9) Possible competition element involved	Individual RankingScore Adjustable	Team Time count Other	
	10) Learner's role	Passive explorer – learner absorbs the experience yet has no additional control over the environment in the speed or mode of interaction Re-active – learner is actively responding and interacting with the learning environment Proactive – learner drives and controls the learning environment		

Macro-criterion	Criterion		Sub-criteria	Title of the learning experience
	11) Cognitive knowledge dimensions		Factual	
			Conceptual	
			Procedural	
			Meta-cognitive	
	12) Cognitive process dimension		Remember	
			Understand	
			Apply	
			Analyse	
			Evaluate	
			Create	
	13) Competences developed	Knowledge	Disciplinary knowledge	
			Interdisciplinary knowledge	
			Practical knowledge	
		Skills developed	Cognitive and meta-cognitive	
			Social and emotional	
			Physical and practical	
		Attitudes and values	Attitudes and values	
	14) Monitoring and assessment		Learner is assessed in real time (right or wrong signals, score, points, levels, number of errors, completion time, other real-time metrics)	
			Learner is assessed after completing several sessions	
			Self-assessment	
3. VR learning experience design	15) Chosen technologies		High compatibility (numerous headsets devices/platforms)	
			Low compatibility	
			Web VR friendly	
			VR/AR/MR mode	
	16) Tracking analytics (e.g. attention, eye movement, facial expressions, EEG, ECG, EMG, EDA)		Engagement, interaction	
			Eye tracking, viewpoint monitoring	
			Sensory tracking (facial expressions, EEG, ECG, EMG, EDA)	
			Haptic interaction	
	17) Type of VLE strategy		Individual	
			Group	

(Continued)

Macro-criterion	Criterion	Sub-criteria	Title of the learning experience
		Adjustable	
		Real time	
		Multi user	
		Synchronous	
		Avatar persona	
		Role play	
		Scavenger hunt	
		Guided tour	
		Operational application	
		Conceptual orienteering	
		Critical incident	
		Co-creation	
		Small group work	
		Group forums	
		Social networking	
	18) Role of VR space (including artefacts within the space) in achieving learning objectives	Primary significance – learning occurs from interaction with the space	
		Important – not a primary driver of learning experience, yet important in conveying contextual knowledge and cues	
		Supportive/entertaining	
	19) Characteristics of VR learning environment utilised	Representational fidelity	
		Learner interaction	
		Social fidelity (including social familiarity and social reality)	
		Social presence	
		Immediacy of discourse	
	20) Availability of instructor or feedback	Yes	
		No	
		Statistical data (success rate, progress)	
		Test	
	21) Learning affordances of VR space	Spatial knowledge representation	
		Experiential learning	
		Engagement	
		Contextual learning	
		Collaborative learning	

References

Bryson, S. (1995). Approaches to the successful design and implementation of VR applications. in R. A. Earnshaw, J. A. Vince, H. Jones, eds. *Virtual Reality Applications*. London: Academic Press Limited. p. 328.

Chatti, M. A., Schroeder, U., & Jarke, M. (2012). LaaN: Convergence of knowledge management and technology-enhanced learning. *IEEE Transactions on Learning Technologies, 5*, 177–189.

Chen, C. J. (2006). The design, development and evaluation of a virtual reality based learning environment. *Australasian Journal of Educational Technology, 22*(1), 39–63. Retrieved from https://ajet.org.au/index.php/AJET/article/download/1306/678

Dalgarno, B., & Lee, M. (2010). What are the learning affordances of 3-D virtual environments? *British Journal of Educational Technology, 41*, 10–32. doi:10.1111/j.1467-8535.2009.01038.x

Erickson, T. (1993). Artificial realities as data visualization environments: Problems and prospects. In A. Wexelblat (Ed.), *Virtual reality – Applications and explorations*. London: Academic Press. p. 3–22.

Kapp, K. M., & O'Driscoll, T. (2010). *Learning in 3-D: Adding a new dimension to enterprise learning and collaboration*. San Francisco, CA: Pfeiffer.

Kirkwood, A., & Price, L. (2013). Technology-enhanced learning and teaching in higher education: What is 'enhanced' and how do we know? A critical literature review. *Learning, Media and Technology, 39*(1), 6–36. doi:10.1080/17439884.2013.770404 Retrieved from www.tandfonline.com/doi/full/10.1080/17439884.2013.770404?scroll=top&needAccess=true

Kolasinski, E. M. (1995). Simulator sickness in virtual environments (ARI 1027). *U.S. Army Research Institute for the Behavioral and Social Sciences*, Retrieved from www.dtic.mil/dtic/tr/fulltext/u2/a295861.pdf

LaViola, J. J., Jr. (2000). A discussion of cybersickness in virtual environments. *ACM SIGCHI*.

Mathews, M. (2017). "Full Bloom with Mixed Reality". Published in Talentquest. Retrieved August 2018: http://www.talentquest.com/full-bloom-with-mixed-reality/ .Bulletin, 32, 47–56. doi:10.1145/333329.333344

Chapter 2

The educational perspective on virtual reality experiences of cultural heritage

Linda Daniela and Yipaer Aierken

Introduction

Learning from personal experience is widely accepted as a powerful tool to construct knowledge, to develop a deeper understanding of different concepts, and to develop new competencies, and Virtual Reality (VR) and Augmented Reality (AR) can support such learning by providing tools to widen possibilities (hereafter, the authors will use the generic term VR for AR as well, as it is a sub-branch of VR). The use of VR, including in the educational environment, has been growing rapidly in recent years, but as Fowler (2015) has pointed out, in most cases, the technological perspective is at the forefront. Currently, VR solutions are offered in a wide variety of applications where VR simulations can be used to master skills and develop competencies needed for specific purposes, the development of which can be dangerous in real situations if dealing with hazardous substances or located in war zones. VR simulations can reduce financial expenditure to ensure the possibility for each student to practice (as it can be resource-intensive in real-life situations), and it can make the impossible possible from a technological point of view; VR simulations of the human body allow one to enter various human organs or reproduce historical situations that are impossible to experience because of the time-lapse. VR can support sustainability from different perspectives – for instance, as a tool for preserving cultural, historical and natural heritage by preventing the damage that can be inflicted by big masses of touristic flows. VR can also serve as a tool for sustainability from the perspective of inclusive education by reducing some of the barriers to education. It can also serve as a tool for knowledge transfer. In this chapter, the authors will focus on the use of VR learning in cultural heritage and offer an evaluation tool (rubric) for analyzing VR experiences from an educational perspective. The objective of this research is to develop and test the evaluation tool, not to evaluate all possible VR experiences, and the decision to evaluate four experiences was based on Virzi (1992), who says that four experiences are enough to test usability problems and that more subjects are less likely to reveal new information. Such an evaluation tool can be used by educators to enable them to select and use the most appropriate VR learning experiences and be able to plan their pedagogical activities to enhance the learning experiences of students and cover the learning gaps that can exist in VR experiences. The proposed tool can also be useful for the developers of VR experiences who are eager to make them engaging and useful for learning purposes, since the fascination effect is usually short-term and students may switch their attention to other activities that bring new fascination. The tool can also help museums ensure that the VR experiences they provide serve as ladders for learning support. The proposed tool will make it possible to structure the VR experiences offered for teaching cultural heritage, but it should be borne in mind that with the rapid development of technology, which also affects the field of VR, this tool can be refined, adapted and supplemented by other criteria. More about the developed tool will be described in the methodology section, and the tool itself can be found in Appendix 2.1.

VR cultural heritage experiences and possibilities

VR techniques are prevalent in diverse scientific fields, businesses, museums, educational settings, art, medicine, military fields, etc. Many companies, like Samsung and Sony, are putting VR onto their smartphones, making it available for the general public. VR techniques require an interface between hardware and software, goggles and gloves, and all of this works together to create a new world to feel, touch, smell and see (Gerard, 2005). VR techniques include headsets, multi-projected environments and physical environments to produce real-life images, sounds and other sensations (Zyda, 2005). VR extends the possibilities of discovery and exploration (Regian, Shebilske, & Monk, 1992) and supports the sense of self; the death of distance; the power of presence; the sense of space; the capability to co-create; the pervasiveness of practice; and the enrichment of experience (Kapp & O'Driscoll, 2010).

Craig and colleagues define it as a medium composed of interactive computer simulations that sense the participant's position and actions, providing synthetic feedback to one or more senses, giving the feeling of being immersed or present in the simulation (Craig, Sherman, & Will, 2009). Slater (2017) says that there are at least five reasons VR may contribute to education: transforming the abstract into the concrete; doing rather than only observing; the infeasible or impossible becoming practical; exploring the manipulation of reality; and going beyond reality with a positive advantage. VR experiences can serve as learning agents (Bickmore, Pfeifer, & Schulman, 2011; Daniela & Strods, 2018) helping students find deeper meaning in content while developing critical observation skills; they can be transferred when students visit or otherwise study historically significant locations in the physical world (Sweeney, Newbill, Ogle, & Terry, 2018).

Museums and VR exhibitions as learning spaces

The use of museums for learning is no longer a novelty. Semper (1990) previously called museums '*an educational country fair*'. By now, we have reached the stage where museums are no longer seen as a place to gather knowledge, but rather as a place to learn (Andre, Durksen, & Volman, 2017). This type of learning ensures that students are actively involved in their knowledge-building (Daniela, 2019; Gutiérrez-Braojos Montejo-Gámez, J., Ma, L., Chen, B., de Escalona-Fernández, M.M., Scardamalia, M., and Bereiter C., 2019; Scardamalia & Bereiter, 2010) and also sets certain requirements for the museum environment, which must become open and accessible for learning. However, some constraints exist, such as the space constraint that prevents all artefacts held by the museum from being displayed at the same time, and the contradiction between active learning, where students are perceived as active participants in the learning process, and the need to preserve historical cultural values for future generations; as a result, students' direct interaction with the museum's artefacts cannot be permitted. Another limitation is connected with access to museums located in particular premises or in particular countries. Although there are museums that provide free access to their exhibitions or offer flexible discount systems for students to reduce the financial barriers to accessing the knowledge concentrated in museums, these solutions only reduce access barriers for the people of a particular country. For people from other countries, it can be quite an expensive experience to reach such a museum, and it means that the knowledge preserved there is a luxury in a way. To reduce these barriers, many museums around the world have begun using VR solutions, offering their exhibits in a VR experience that allows people to connect to them from anywhere with an Internet connection. One of the first museums to display VR was the Ars Electronica Center for electronic art in Linz, Austria, which contains a CAVE-projection VR display in which the user stands between six walls in a room-sized cube (Craig et al., 2009). Thus, VR in museums already has some history. It is believed that using various technological tools and projecting objects will become mainstream in museum development. A great example is Situating Hybrid Assemblies in Public Environments (SHAPE), a project that extends public space areas with mixed reality installations. In this case, VR is used as a new medium (Hindmarsh et al., 2001). For example, an archaeological site can be simulated by a computer with VR tools, helping museum visitors to explore each object. VR possibilities provide an opportunity to learn from historical and cultural experiences and to visit certain objects that cannot be visited in reality. The use of VR not only solves problems of accessibility, but some researchers believe that VR experiences scaffold learning because there is a synergy between visual and textual information, as a narration or spoken text is longer and easier to remember than individual media elements (Moro, Stromberga, & Stirling, 2017). VR is an opportunity for constructivist learning, with important emphasis laid on knowledge experimentation and interactivity, allowing students to acquire knowledge based on meaningful experience by exploring the content to be learned in a real-world, face-to-face context (Fowler, 2015; Yoon, 2010). For example, Fowler emphasizes three stages of learning through VR: conceptualization (the learner learns and interprets facts, concepts and theories and receives information), construction (the learner evaluates facts and concepts, applies knowledge in an interactive way, solves or analyzes problems, tests the use of concepts in new situations and observes real-life experiences by building on his/her own knowledge of the experience) and discussion (the student engages in discussions about what he/she has learned and his/her own learning) (Fowler, 2015). Since the VR environment itself does not offer discussion, it is up to educators to bridge this gap to scaffold learning. Falk and Dierking believe that sociocultural theory is a more appropriate theory of education for learning in the museum environment and that what is important is not only what happens in the museum, but also how learning happens in it and what the learning context is for students (Falk & Dierking, 2000; Falk & Storksdieck, 2005). To encourage learning in the museum or during learning with VR experiences, the interaction with knowledgeable adults (teachers, curators, parents) is essential (Andre, Durksen, & Volman, 2017) to scaffold knowledge-building and the development of metacognitive processes. Prior learning, spoken text while using VR and discussions, feedback or questions at the end of the activity are crucial (Foote, 2017; Ott & Pozzi, 2011). This is also one of the reasons it is necessary to analyze VR experiences from a learning perspective to make sure that the experience offered provides this aspect of learning and to allow educators to anticipate their own pedagogical action scenarios, in order to fill the gap if specific information is not provided by the VR experience. As VR can provide the possibility to visit any place at any time with a virtual tour (Hu-Au & Lee, 2017), teachers can support students' learning by using the fascination effect of VR as a powerful tool to ensure the acquisition of certain knowledge and to develop the abilities to analyze facts, compare information, respect cultural heritage and support the development of 'historical empathy' (Brooks, 2009). Gehlbach (2004) has demonstrated in his research that perspective-taking, one aspect of historical empathy, positively correlates to conflict resolution skills.

Duncan, Miller and Jiang (2012) have defined the educational activities that can be used to support learning: problem-based learning; enquiry-based learning; game-based learning; role-playing; virtual quests; collaborative simulations (learn by simulation); collaborative construction (building activities); design courses (game, fashion, architectural); language teaching and learning; virtual laboratories; virtual fieldwork and attending lectures or classes.

Methodology

To evaluate the VR cultural heritage experiences provided by museums and companies that develop such experiences from an educational perspective, the authors developed an evaluation tool (rubric) according to the principles of an analytical rubric (Quinlan, 2012) in which 21 criteria were included, all of which were evaluated on three levels; each level has its own description. During the quantitative analyses of the results, the levels were indicated by numbers where 1 indicated the lowest level, 2 the medium level and 3 the highest level of the criterion. The structure of the evaluation tool was adapted from Stevens and Levi (2013).

Four VR experiences were evaluated, based on the idea that four are enough to test usability problems and more subjects are less likely to reveal new information (Virzi, 1992). The evaluation tool included such criteria as are important for ensuring that learning can happen: how information is structured, the ease of information flow, whether elements of gamification and knowledge tests are included, the level of interactivity, etc. A few technical criteria are also included (e.g. whether it is possible to download the experience, the quality of the material's graphics, whether there is a possibility of cybersickness). These criteria are supposed to be evaluated by ticking the appropriate level, and only one of the levels can be chosen for each criterion. A possibility to add comments to let the evaluator explain why a particular level was chosen is provided. The last criterion in the rubric provides a possibility to evaluate the age group for which the material can be used, for which there were also three levels: appropriate for minors (up seven years old), for school-age children (7–18) and for adults (18 and above). This is the only criterion in the tool where all levels can be chosen if the VR experience is suitable for all ages. This criterion is very important for adults who wish to choose an appropriate VR experience for their children or students. Such evaluation of age level should be done from the perspective of the regularities of cognitive, psychomotor and emotional development to ensure that younger students are not faced with information that is too hard to understand.

The complete evaluation tool (rubric) can be found in Appendix 2.1.

Once the evaluation tool was developed, we started to evaluate VR experiences, in July 2019.

Results

One of the most important parts of VR techniques is interaction, and there are three ways of interacting: first, physical interaction, with which the audience can actually go into the virtual world through devices; second, interaction via an agent, which means users communicate with computers and the computers help them and third, virtual interaction, where users' 'devices' are inside the virtual world itself (Craig et al., 2009).

Quantified results of the evaluated experiences were entered into Excel; the resulting graph (Figure 2.1) indicates that the evaluated VR experiences differ; the best scores are in the technical criteria, where for all analyzed VR/AR experiences the total score is 12 (number of scores are given in brackets), which is the maximum score possible. The technical criteria are the use of the material; perception of the material; connectivity with other information and the graphics

Results of the evaluation

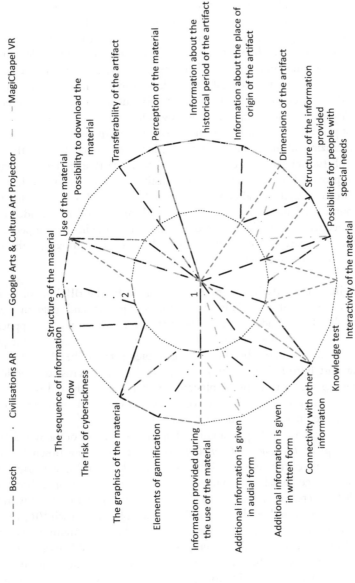

Figure 2.1 Results of the evaluation.

of the material, which indicates that the materials are well-designed and well-resourced. Conversely, lower scores are found in the transferability of the artefact (6); the interactivity of the material (8); knowledge test (8); additional information given as audial text (7) and additional information given as written text (7). Bearing in mind that people learn better if information is given in different ways (i.e. when visual information is combined with audial and written), some problems of interpreting the information can arise; this means that knowledgeable adults (parents, teachers, museum educators) should follow the learning and fill the gap in understanding if such is apparent. There is one low evaluation point in the criterion – possibilities to download the material (6) – but we assume this is a criterion that is mainly important for situations in which the availability of Internet connections is low. Otherwise, this technical criterion does not play an important role in the accessibility of the material.

Summarizing all the quantitative results, it can be concluded that the evaluation tool (rubric) can be used to evaluate the VR/AR experiences of cultural heritage provided by museums or other institutions who work on developing such materials, but it should be kept in mind that this tool is intended for educational purposes. Sub-criteria can be developed for each of the included criteria to get a deeper view on the knowledge gained or on the inclusive aspects.

In the next part of the results section, the authors will explain the results of evaluation of VR experiences.

1. **Civilisations AR** is the first AR application by the BBC in collaboration with Nexus Studio. This application brings art and cultural heritage together for its audience throughout the world. By using this application, the audience can experience the secret mummies of ancient Egypt and the hidden material behind the masterpieces from the Renaissance and learn art historical information of cultural heritage across the world. AR provides a tool to bring all objects together realistically and without limitations of space. The X-Ray technique allows the audience to discover the hidden material behind each artwork.

2. **Bosch VR** is a VR application with a VR experience of the world-famous masterpiece *The Garden of Earthly Delights* by Hieronymus Bosch. Flying and riding on a catfish into the Garden of Eden, the virtual noises inadvertently send strange signals. Surrounded by giant fruits and strange half-human, half-beast creatures, *The Garden of Earthly Delights* becomes a real world. On the left is hell, and on the right is the Garden of Eden. Bosch VR, according to its official website, is available on iPhone, iPad and Android smartphones so that everyone can deeply engage with this new VR world of a 14th-century painting. Most surprisingly, the background music includes one of the sacred bells in the Hertogenbosch Cathedral, which is a great feature. Sounds influence what we think and how we react to what we see; real sounds make an audience feel what is real. Sounds, like storytelling, play an extra role in the VR experience.

3. **The Magi Chapel VR** has frescoes painted by Benozzo Gozzoli (Luchinat, 1994). These frescoes show the journey of the Magi and are richly painted. Hence, it offers an opportunity to see the beautiful cultural environment and political life of the high Renaissance period; initially, these frescoes were made for the Medici family around 1459 (Oxley, 1994). However, very few people have the chance to travel to the Magi Chapel in Italy and experience it directly. Thus, a world-famous, leading VR production company called EON Reality created an application offering a VR tour of the Magi Chapel for the user in 360 degrees and in every detail with an explanation of the historical background. This application belongs to the World Heritage Initiative made by EON Reality, which is trying to save and protect valuable cultural treasures. The Magi Chapel is a real place with real objects, and using VR as a tool helps more people to experience and know about it. One outstanding aspect of the Magi Chapel is that there is storytelling behind it, which gives its audience a sense of getting into the Renaissance period, especially for those who have no knowledge of Renaissance art and its historical background.

4. **Google Arts & Culture Art Projector** uses the camera on a smartphone or tablet to transfer a life-size work of art into any real space. Using the Google Arts & Culture Art Projector, the experiencer is presented with a life-size painting in real space; each line of text allows him or her to learn about the color, material and information of the artwork. There are 50 paintings available in the Art Projector, and the experiencers can adjust the size of the paintings to capture every detail in super high resolution. There are Vincent Van Gogh's *Irises*, Frida Kahlo's portraits and Japanese Ukiyo-e for the audiences to learn about, study and engage with.

Conclusions

The objective of this research was to develop an evaluation tool (rubric) that can be used to evaluate VR cultural heritage experiences from an educational perspective to let teachers and other knowledgeable adults select VR experiences and develop pedagogical strategies to support learning. The authors evaluated four experiences, which is assumed to be enough (Virzi, 1992) to test usability problems. In this research, the usability of the developed tool (rubric) was tested, and it can be concluded that such an evaluation tool gives the possibility to evaluate VR experiences and structure them according to educational needs.

The main objective is the development of the tool, but some results from the evaluation of four VR cultural heritage experiences showed some educational shortages, and they were found in the following criteria:

Transferability of the artefact. In the evaluation of this criterion, the highest number was given if *it is easy to transverse the artefact in smaller details.* The highest level of this criterion was given for only one of the evaluated experiences (Google Arts & Culture Art Projector). Such a possibility is important to let students understand details and develop their computational thinking.

Interactivity of the material. The highest number was given if *there are different forms of interactivity.* Again, only one of the evaluated experiences (Bosch VR) was given the highest possible level. Engaging interactivity is important if educators wish to ensure that technology-enhanced learning allows the achievement of the learning objectives and not only fascination with technological possibilities.

Knowledge test. The highest level was given if *the possibility to test knowledge is included in different parts of the material and from different aspects of the information provided.* None of the evaluated experiences was given the highest level. If the provided experiences are used for purposes of entertainment, there is no need to include knowledge tests, but if educators wish to use them for learning purposes then the possibility to test the knowledge acquired should be added, as it gives students the feeling that they are learning, and it can support motivation to learn something new. Teachers can add knowledge evaluations outside of VR experiences, but the developers of VR experiences should incorporate such a possibility in the experiences for educational purposes.

Additional information is given as audial text. The highest level was *a lot of additional information in audial form is given.* Only the MagiChapel VR experience got the highest amount of points.

Additional information is given as written text. The highest level was expressed as *a lot of additional information in written form is given,* and the highest evaluation was given to the Civilisations AR experience. The students perceive information with different sensors, and there is no need to always include all the sensors when providing information, but an evaluation of the methods of information flow in VR experiences is important in order to know which of them are present and to ensure that other ways are provided in different activities. It is also important from the perspective of inclusive education, because not all students can perceive audial texts, not all of them can understand visual symbols, etc.

The current products on the market already play a role in the cultural heritage field. At present, the development of VR experiences is quite an expensive activity and is not affordable for all museums, but the tendency for technologies to become more affordable and new VR solutions to be provided in which no specific coding skills are needed let us make the prediction that more experiences will be developed in the near future. These VR solutions can be used for educational purposes to experience historical sites and historical moments and to support the development of historical empathy, but an understanding of the strengths and weaknesses of all the technological possibilities should also be developed, and the tool developed during this research can help to structure VR experiences for educational purposes.

More research should be done in this field to develop the grounds for the use of VR in educational purposes and to support students in the learning process.

References

Andre, L., Durksen, T., & Volman, M. L. (2017). Museums as avenues of learning for children: A decade of research. *Learning Environment Research, 20*(1), 47–76.

Bickmore, T., Pfeifer, L., & Schulman, D. (2011). Relational agents improve engagement and learning in science museum visitors. In H. H. Vilhjálmsson, S. Kopp, S. Marsella, & K. R. Thórisson (Eds.), *Intelligent virtual agents. IVA 2011. Lecture notes in computer science, Vol. 6895*. Berlin and Heidelberg: Springer. 55–67.

Brooks, S. (2009). Historical empathy in the social studies classroom: A review of the literature. *The Journal of Social Studies Research, 33*(2), 213–234.

Craig, A. B., Sherman, W. R., & Will, J. D. (2009). *Developing virtual reality applications: Foundations of effective design*. Burlington, MA: Morgan Kaufmann.

Daniela, L. (2019). Smart pedagogy for technology enhanced learning. In L. Daniela (Ed.), *Didactics of smart pedagogy: Smart pedagogy for technology enhanced learning* (pp. 3–22). Cham: Springer.

Daniela, L., & Strods, R. (2018). Robot as agent in reducing risks of early school leaving. In L. Daniela (Ed.), *Innovations, technologies and research in education* (pp. 140–158). Newcastle upon Tyne: Cambridge Scholars Publishing.

Duncan, I., Miller, A., & Jiang, S. (2012). A taxonomy of virtual worlds usage in education. *British Journal of Educational Technology, 43*, 949–964.

Falk, J. H., & Dierking, L. D. (2000). *Learning from museums: Visitor experiences and the making of meaning*. Walnut Creek, CA: AltaMira Press.

Falk, J. H., & Storksdieck, M. (2005). Using the contextual model of learning to understand visitor learning from a science center exhibition. *Science Education, 89*, 744–778.

Foote, C. (2017). Mobile technology goes virtual: Using virtual reality in education. *Internet@Schools, 24*(3), 12–13.

Fowler, C. (2015). Virtual reality and learning: Where is the pedagogy? *British Journal of Educational Technology, 46*(2), 412–422.

Gehlbach, H. (2004). Social perspective taking: A facilitating aptitude for conflict resolution, historical empathy, and social studies achievement. *Theory and Research in Social Education, 32*(1), 39–55.

Gerard, K. (2005). *Designing virtual reality systems: The structured approach*. London: Springer-Verlag.

Gutiérrez-Braojos, C., Montejo-Gámez, J., Ma, L., Chen, B., de Escalona-Fernández, M.M., Scardamalia, M., and Bereiter C. (2019). Exploring collective cognitive responsibility through the emergence and flow of forms of engagement in a knowledge building community. In L. Daniela (Ed.), *Didactics of smart pedagogy* (pp. 213–232). Cham: Springer.

Hindmarsh, J., Heath, C., Vom Lehn, D., Ciolfi, L., Hall, T., Bannon, L., ... Hall, J. (2001). Interaction as a public phenomenon. *SHAPE Deliverable, 2*(1). 9–23

Hu-Au, E., & Lee, J. J. (2017). Virtual reality in education: A tool for learning in the experience age. *International Journal of Innovation in Education, 4*(4), 215–226.

Kapp, K. M., & O'Driscoll, T. (2010). *Learning in 3-D: Adding a new dimension to enterprise learning and collaboration.* San Francisco, CA: Pfeiffer.

Luchinat, A. C. (1994). *The Chapel of the Magi: Benozzo Gozzoli's Frescoes in the Palazzo Medici-Riccardi Florence.* (E. Daunt, Trans.). London and New York, NY: Thames & Hudson.

Moro, C., Stromberga, Z., & Stirling, A. (2017). Virtualisation devices for student learning: Comparison between desktop-based (oculus rift) and mobile-based (gear VR) virtual reality in medical and health science education. *Australasian Journal of Educational Technology, 33*(6), 1–10.

Ott, M., & Pozzi, F. (2011). Towards a new era for cultural heritage education: Discussing the role of ICT. *Computers in Human Behavior, 27*(4), 1365–1371.

Oxley, M. (1994). The Medici and Gozzoli's Magi. *History Today, 44*(12), 16.

Quinlan, A. M. (2012). *A complete guide to Rubrics: Assessment made easy for teachers of K-College* (2nd ed.). Lanham, MD: Rowman & Littlefield Education.

Regian, J. W., Shebilske, W. L., & Monk, J. M. (1992). Virtual reality: An instructional medium for visual-spatial tasks. *Journal of Communication, 42*(4), 136–149.

Scardamalia, M., & Bereiter, C. (2010). A brief history of knowledge building. *Canadian Journal of Learning and Technology, 36*(1). Retrieved from www.cjlt.ca/index.php/cjlt/article/view/26367/19549

Semper, R. J. (1990). Science museums as environments for learning. *Physics Today, 43*(11), 50–56.

Slater, M. (2017). Implicit learning through embodiment in immersive virtual reality. In D. Liu, C. Dede, R. Huang, & J. Richards (Eds.), *Virtual, augmented, and mixed realities in education. Smart computing and intelligence.* Singapore: Springer. 19–33.

Stevens, D. D., & Levi, A. J. (2013). *Introduction to Rubrics: An assessment tool to save grading time, convey effective feedback, and promote student learning* (2nd ed.). Sterling, VA: Stylus Publishing.

Sweeney, S. K., Newbill, P., Ogle, T., & Terry, K. (2018). Using augmented reality and virtual environments in historic places to scaffold historical empathy. *TechTrends, 62*(1), 114–118.

Virzi, R. A. (1992). Refining the test phase of usability evaluation: How many subjects is enough? *Human Factors, 34*(4), 457–468.

Yoon, S. (2010). *Virtual reality in art education* (Master's thesis). Virginia Commonwealth University, USA.

Zyda, M. (2005). From visual simulation to virtual reality to games. *Computer, 38*, 25–32.

VR experiences analyzed

BBC Media Applications Technologies Limited. Civilisations AR [Computer software]. Retrieved August 8, 2019 from www.bbc.co.uk/taster/pilots/civilisations-ar

BDH. Bosch VR – Immersive – BDH [Computer software]. Retrieved July 23, 2019 from www.bdh.net/immersive/bosch-vr

EON Reality. Magi Chapel VR [Computer software]. Retrieved February 23, 2020 from https://eonreality.com/eon-reality-and-virtualiter-bring-the-medici-familys-magi-chapel-to-virtual-reality/

Google LLC. The google art & culture art projector [Computer software]. Retrieved August 8, 2019 from https://artsandculture.google.com/theme/6AISWNxkfTniIA.

Appendix 2.1 Criteria for the evaluation of VR/AR experiences in museums from an educational perspective.

All criteria should be evaluated by ticking the correct answer according to the evaluator's opinion. Only in the last row, where the evaluator's opinion on the age group should be given, can more than one answer be chosen.

	The content is well structured.	The content is structured but the structure is not logical.	The content is fragmented and not structured according to some kind of logic.
Structure of the material			
Comments can be added here:			
	It is easy to understand how to use the material.	It is not very understandable how to use the material.	It is hard to understand how the material should be used.
Use of the material			
Comments can be added here:			
	It can be downloaded to all possible devices.	It can be downloaded to some particular devices.	It can be downloaded to devices that have a specific program.
Possibility to download the material			
Comments can be added here:			
	It is easy to transverse the artefact in smaller details.	It is possible to transverse the artefact in a few details.	It is not possible to transverse the artefact in detail.
Transferability of the artefact			
Comments can be added here:			
	It is easy to perceive the material.	The material is well prepared, but sometimes it is hard to perceive due to the	It is hard to perceive the material.

		complexity of the information.	
Perception of the material			

Comments can be added here:

	Information about the historical period is given and it is clear.	Information about the historical period is given, but it is hard to understand.	Information about the historical period is not given.
Information about the historical period of the artefact			

Comments can be added here:

	Information about the place of origin of the artefact is given, and it is clear to understand,	Information about the place of origin of the artefact is given, but it is hard to understand.	Information about the place of origin of the artefact is not given.
Information about the place of origin of the artefact			

Comments can be added here:

	It is easy to move the artefact and see it from different dimensions (outside and inside).	It is possible to move the artefact and see it from different outside dimensions.	It is possible to see the artefact only from a few outside dimensions.
Dimensions of the artefact			

Comments can be added here:

	The information provided is well structured and easy to understand.	Some parts of the information are well structured, but some information lacks structure and it is not easy to understand.	There is no structured information provided.
Structure of the information provided			

Comments can be added here:

	The material is prepared in a way that people with diverse special needs can use it, and it is clearly indicated how to use it.	The material is prepared in a way that people with some specific special needs can use it, but it is not available for all groups of special needs, and it is indicated which groups can use it.	The material is prepared for the general public, and there is no way to switch the way in which the information is provided.
Possibilities for people with special needs			

Comments can be added here:

	There are different forms of interactivity.	There is some interactivity.	People cannot interact with the material.
Interactivity of the material			

Comments can be added here:

	The possibility to test knowledge is included in different parts of the material and on different aspects of the information provided.	There is a possibility to test knowledge, but it is only on a few aspects of the material.	There is no possibility to test the knowledge included.
Knowledge test			

Comments can be added here:

	There is smooth connectivity with other parts of the information, other artefacts, other historical facts, etc.	There is fragmented connectivity with other parts of the information, other artefacts, other historical facts, etc.	There is no connectivity with other information.
Connectivity with other information			

Comments can be added here:

	A lot of additional information in written form is given.	Some additional information in written form is given.	No additional information in written form is given.
Additional information in written form			
Comments can be added here:			
	A lot of additional information in audial form is given.	Some additional information in audial form is given.	No additional information in audial form is given.
Additional information in audial form			
Comments can be added here:			
	All the information is given in an easy-to-understand way even without previous knowledge on the topic.	Some parts of the information are given in an easy-to-understand way, but some parts are hard to understand without previous knowledge on the topic.	The information is hard to understand (due to complexity, fragmentation or other problems).
Information provided during the use of the material			
Comments can be added here:			
	Elements of gamification are used to attract people and to keep them focused.	Some elements of gamification are used but on a fragmented basis.	Elements of gamification are not used.
Elements of gamification			
Comments can be added here:			
	The graphical elements are well structured, and visualizations are in high quality.	The graphical elements are randomly structured, and visualizations could be of a better quality.	The graphical elements are poorly structured, and visualizations are in low quality.

The graphics of the material			

Comments can be added here:

	The risk of cyber-sickness is completely reduced.	The risk of cybersickness can be a problem for some groups of people.	There is a high risk of cybersickness.
The risk of cybersickness			

Comments can be added here:

	The sequence of the information flow can be changed according to the decision of the person who explores the material.	Some parts of the information can be skipped or changed.	The sequence of the information flow cannot be changed according to the decision of the person who explores the material.
The sequence of information flow			

Comments can be added here:

	Adults (18+)	School-age children (7–18)	Minors (up to 7)
The age group for which the material can be used			

Comments can be added here:

Chapter 3

The potentials of virtual reality in entrepreneurship education

Marko Orel

Introduction

In December 2018, a handful of pixelated avatars met near a virtual campfire site within the digital world of AltspaceVR, one of the leading social platforms for virtual reality (Altspacevr, 2019). Individuals, immersed in their floating-yet-digitalised counterparts that automatically mimicked their body language, and after some informal chatter, exchanged their entrepreneurial stories and discussed their start-up ideas. This entrepreneurial meetup was not a single entrepreneurial event. The next edition of the same meetup, entitled 'Fail Fast, Fail Forward' has been organised within the same setting of AltspaceVR in the first quarter of 2019 with entrepreneurs discussing their ideas and sharing their fails – something that could be emotionally challenging in our competitive reality.

Virtual reality is progressively transforming digital social worlds and making them vibrant places for gatherings (Maffei, Masullo, Pascale, Ruggiero, & Romero, 2016), where individuals can meet up in custom-built environments, use creative tools and showcase their ideas, discuss their work and seek supportive communities (Rubin, 2019). In two entrepreneurial meetups held in the virtual setting of AltspaceVR, individuals from around the globe potentially faced less anxiety over rejection when sharing their entrepreneurial fails (Singh, Corner, & Pavlovich, 2007; Zhao, Seibert, & Hills, 2005), gaining temporal focus (Rusko, Härkönen, & Liukkonen, 2016; Sheail, 2018; Tata, Laureiro-Martínez, & Brusoni, 2016) and discussing their past, business-related actions with the digital community. Simultaneously, they could present their work in an immersive environment that resembles reality (Bertram, Moskaliuk, & Cress, 2015), enabling them to develop necessary entrepreneurial skills through peer-assessed presentation (Faherty, 2015). The sharing of tacit knowledge is best achieved through face-to-face interaction and the reciprocal relationship between actors involved in the process of knowledge transfer (Macpherson, Jones, & Zhang, 2005).

Contemporary entrepreneurship draws individuals to engage their capacity, efforts and abilities in the creation of new services and products that compete for market demand and attention (Bellotti et al., 2012). Klein and

Bullock (2006) found that there is little connection between the leading approaches to entrepreneurship education and economists' understanding of the entrepreneurial function. As starting a new business is commonly an uncertain undertaking and precarious process, the entrepreneur must develop a mental model (through the sense-making procedure) of how the environment of the newly developed business will operate. Moreover, preparing entrepreneurs to be able to communicate their entrepreneurial undertakings to others and gain support through sense giving process is both demanding and challenging (Hill & Levenhagen, 1995). Entrepreneurship education is the process of providing individuals with not only the required skills and knowledge, but also the ability to recognise commercial opportunities (Jones & English, 2004).

Virtual reality shows much promise in educational contexts (Kizilkaya, Vince, & Holmes, 2019) as it enables users to provoke individual reflection while interacting with the materiality and concreteness of the intangible aspects of oneself (Schneider, 2019). Shen and Eder (2009) explored the immersive potential of virtual worlds and found that social engagement and interactions among learners in a virtual setting can maximise learning outcomes.

By conducting a narrative review, this chapter explores the different streams and possibilities of virtual reality in entrepreneurship education. Not only do individuals traverse into immersive digital reality, where they can enhance necessary cognitive capabilities, but they can also undergo captivating learning courses that provide skills and functional knowledge related to their entrepreneurial careers.

The perspectives of entrepreneurship education

Contemporary entrepreneurship is defined by generating new opportunities in uncertain and unknowable environments (Neck & Greene, 2011) and can be perceived as a vital source of competitiveness and the engine for economic growth and future development (Nabi & Holden, 2008). From this standpoint, modern entrepreneurs are not inclined to maximise personal interest; for them, the pursuit of collective interest is important (Van de Ven, Sapienza, & Villanueva, 2007). The optimisation of these interests is thus important for the general society, and entrepreneurship education appears to play a crucial role in mobilising available resources through entrepreneurial opportunity realisation. Moreover, effective entrepreneurship education contributes to obtaining better results (Cruz, Rodriguez Escudero, Hernangomez Barahona, & Saboia Leitao, 2009) and positively affects the general business skills needed by individuals in creating and managing their ventures (Premand, Brodmann, Almeida, Grun, & Barouni, 2016).

According to Raposo and Do Paço (2011), entrepreneurship education seeks to link knowledge with the ability to recognise and pursue opportunities, by generating new ideas and allocating needed resources, and the ability to create and operate a business venture in a creative and critical manner. The ultimate goal of processing entrepreneurial knowledge is for individuals to master communication skills derived from open and constant communication with the environment; share and evaluate challenging goals and finally form the ability to adapt to unforeseen conditions (Neck & Greene, 2011).

Karlsson and Moberg (2013) relate that a trait-based view of entrepreneurship, where only some individuals are born with the necessary competencies to become entrepreneurs, is still prevalent in modern society. Thus, it is not a surprise that the debate of whether entrepreneurship can be taught with supportive and stimulating learning processes is ongoing for several decades (Henry, Hill, & Leitch, 2005; Hynes, 1996; Jack & Anderson, 1999; Kantor, 1988; Kirby, 2004; Ronstadt, 1985; Taatila, 2010). At both theoretical and ontological levels, there is a lack of firm consensus regarding entrepreneurship education due to the ever-changing landscape of contemporary entrepreneurship as a concept (Huq & Gilbert, 2017).

Nabi and Holden (2008) conclude that no universal approach to entrepreneurship works for all contexts – the individual needs of different contexts require tailored and customised approaches, and there is substantial diversity of target groups in the educational process. Mwasalwiba (2010) emphasises that there is still non-alignment between what educators and other stakeholders wish to achieve in training and transferring relevant entrepreneurial knowledge through applied pedagogical approaches and relevant success indicators.

Learning entrepreneurial methods and approaches facilitates the formation of a way of thinking and acting, built on assumptions using a portfolio of techniques to motivate individuals towards creating (Neck & Greene, 2011). While these methods and approaches can be taught within entrepreneurial teaching courses at primary, secondary, graduate and postgraduate levels, individuals can gain relevant knowledge by involving themselves in self-taught processes (Katz, 2014). The shaping of individuals' entrepreneurial intentions does not solely depend on their personalities, personal aims, goals and tendencies; rather, they are directly linked to the level of engagement and priority entrepreneurial objectives they hold (Top, Çolakoğlu, & Dilek, 2012).

A critical factor in determining one's level of interest in pursuing an entrepreneurial career is self-confidence with entrepreneurial self-efficiency in gaining access to skills needed to succeed in creating a business (Wilson, Kickul, & Marlino, 2007). Entrepreneurial self-efficiency is one's discernment about their skills and abilities to cope with a newly established business venture and a personal motivation for facing the associated challenges and difficulties. Individuals with high entrepreneurial self-efficiency are more likely to investigate and explore entrepreneurial opportunities and persist to achieve their entrepreneurial vision (Pihie & Bagheri, 2011). What is more, not all aspects and angles of entrepreneurship can be taught, with characteristics such as ambition, persistence, self-confidence and risk-taking being the domain of extensive training (Matlay, Rae, Henry, & Treanor, 2012).

The emergence of new technologies has eased access to relevant knowledge and enabled individuals to receive effective teaching and training. Furthermore, the reduction of hierarchical barriers potentially common in traditional educational environments empowers individuals to become more congenial in realising their learning journeys and creating accountability in acting on that learning (Huq & Gilbert, 2017). Entrepreneurship education is therefore slowly moving from teacher-led to more student-centred and focused on existential and experimental learning practices (Robinson, Neergaard, Tanggaard, & Krueger, 2016).

For more than two decades now, with a computer and the access to the Internet, for instance, individuals can independently create and carry through their business plans, learn about product development and marketing and master the theoretical concepts of business operationalisation (Al-Atabi & DeBoer, 2014; Daly, 2001). Distance training and education can be managed by using e-mentoring (Homitz & Berge, 2008; Perren, 2003) that enables individuals to obtain remote feedback on the development of their conceptual capability, interpersonal capability, leading capability and entrepreneurial capability (Jiao, Ogilvie, & Cui, 2010). In addition, online learning not only lowers the importance of the geographic distance component, but the strict adhesion to adjusted timetables can be hypothetically utilised at any time (Bourne, Harris, & Mayadas, 2005).

Nevertheless, widely accessible entrepreneurial knowledge and the student-centred approach still have several limitations with a questionable self-efficacy and realised entrepreneurial intentions. There are implications that the relationships between individuals' self-efficacy beliefs and entrepreneurial intentions lean negatively in theoretically orientated courses and positively in practically orientated courses (Piperopoulos & Dimov, 2015). Huq and Gilbert (2017) demonstrate that learning outcomes can be improved with the integration of a design-driven pedagogy delivered in an open and constructivist environment; thus, it is expected that obtaining practical knowledge first-hand is preferred by individuals.

Consequently, formal and informal learning processes can be effectively based not solely on access to relevant online databases (Sampson, Ifenthaler, Isaias, & Spector, 2014), but also through simulations and games as digital tools for supporting entrepreneurship education (Bellotti et al., 2012; Panoutsopoulos, Lykourentzou, & Sampson, 2011). The impact of these tools can vary due to their effectiveness on learning outcome based on factors such as attitude, intrinsic and extrinsic motivation and perception that is dependent on immersive multi-user environments (Kira & Saade, 2006; Lorenzo, Sicilia, & Sánchez, 2012). On that account, virtual reality as a computer-generated and immersive simulation of the selected learning environment could be recognised as a potentially useful learning tool for entrepreneurship education as it can help individuals to understand events, situations and other people (Rogers, 2019).

Challenges and possibilities of Virtual Reality for entrepreneurship education

The potential uses of virtual reality as an educational tool have been the subject of several discussions and studies in the past (e.g. Hedberg & Alexander, 1994; Kaufmann, Schmalstieg, & Wagner, 2000; Martín-Gutiérrez, Mora, Añorbe-Díaz, & González-Marrero, 2017; Merchant, Goetz, Cifuentes, Keeney-Kennicutt, & Davis, 2014; Psotka, 1995; Virvou & Katsionis, 2008; Wickens, 1992; Winn & Jackson, 1999). Yet, the potential of virtual reality that would allow future entrepreneurs to gain necessary skills, helping them tackle everyday obstacles on their entrepreneurial pathways, is a virtually unresearched subject. Recent research suggests that individuals can retain more information and can effectively use learned skills and obtained knowledge after participating in virtual reality simulations (Krokos, Plaisant, & Varshney, 2019), making virtual reality a vital learning tool.

A handful of existing and freely accessible virtual reality environments deal with the STEM domain, and generic courses on entrepreneurship are also available. These environments are designed to boost individuals' active learning as well as teachers' lecture conduct by interacting with various virtual objects and peers. Perikos, Grivokostopoulou, Paraske, Kovas, and Hatzilygeroudis (2018) explored a particular virtual reality world, the 3D Virtual World, and investigated the potential for entrepreneurship education. The 3D Virtual World is a cloud-based software component that is implemented in OpenSim, an open-source multi-user virtual environment where individuals can interact with various objects, devices and other users, represented by avatars that are delegated into the roles of students or tutors. Students take an active role in virtual classes that involve interactive quizzes and exercises, while tutors provide simultaneous feedback on their performance. Additionally, individuals can actively participate in different activities in order to visualise procedures that are relevant for obtaining entrepreneurial knowledge of specific work field.

While utilising this virtual reality environment has not yet been widely adopted, it appears that The Sloan School of Management at Massachusetts Institute for Technology (MIT) is one of the first educational institutions engaging their business students in a sophisticated virtual reality exercise by using World Climate, a simulated role-playing game. In this game, students are challenged to negotiate a climate agreement to reduce greenhouse gas emissions. The students have several options for approaching the decision-making process with negotiation tactics and advancing their improvisation and public speaking techniques (Childers, 2019). Relatedly, Niebuhr and Tegtmeier (2019) have investigated how the virtual reality environment helps entrepreneurs give more charismatic investor pitches and thus raise their effectiveness and chances to obtain desired funding. Through their empirical study, they found that rehearsing business pitches in a virtual reality setting gradually improves the speaker's charismatic tone of voice and enhances the presentation when the student returns to the traditional rehearsal setting. The latter would also explain why discussing and pitching ideas in social virtual reality settings such as AltSpaceVR is gaining popularity.

In situational settings like the one used by MIT, individuals consider possible scenarios, objectives and actions of other peers in the virtual setting. They also conduct self-reflection on decisions, which generally contributes to strategic thinking and behaviour that will assist them in achieving entrepreneurial success and create both economic and social impact on society. Furthermore, Schneider (2019) reports that virtual reality actively contributes to identity construction.

One initiative that utilises these implications has emerged within San Juan County, Utah, where Whitehorse High School has started to test its student entrepreneurship program. Using virtual reality to train students in new and marketable skills, the school aims to support entrepreneurial development in the region, where the unemployment rate stands at 40% (Kronk, 2019). By using various virtual reality settings, the program aims to support students in setting up their own businesses and boost the economic development of the impoverished region.

While service-based businesses require sharpening the vast array of soft skills, product-based business requires visualising projected outcomes. Virtual reality offers the possibility of familiarising the entrepreneur with product development through three streams: simulations, in which products can be tested virtually; skills training, where individuals can optimise the product development and realisation processes; and communication with other actors such as users, experts and customers. Individuals can interact with objects, test them in various settings and assess prototypes virtually. Virtual reality provides individuals with an opportunity to develop complicated and complex radical new products with insignificant costs (Ottosson, 2002). Furthermore, these products can be developed in an agile design manner (Choi & Chan, 2004) so that an early insight can be gained into how a particular product could function in various environments (Costa & Jongen, 2006). This contextualized experimentation can lower the fail factor (Delarue & Lageat, 2019), and these products can then be presented to other peers in either a decentralised social virtual reality setting or a teacher-led virtual reality class.

Conclusion

Outlining a handful of virtual reality educational settings, we have explored the potentials and possibilities in which virtual reality can enhance learning and knowledge transfer processes for entrepreneurship education. Existing literature indeed shows that virtual reality enables individuals to step into immersive environments, engage in social interactions with other peers, visualise their actions that are relevant to a particular learning outcome and reflect on their actions.

However, while virtual reality appears to have an underused potential, there are several drawbacks for broader adaptation of virtual reality technologies in entrepreneurship education. First, although virtual reality as technology has been developed for the last three decades (Bown, White, & Boopalan, 2017; Rosedale, 2016), it is still underdeveloped because virtual reality environments have functionality issues (Ke, Lee, & Xu, 2016). Second, while mobile virtual reality is developing at a relatively fast pace, making it more accessible for personal use (Oigara, 2018), it is still a costly solution for enhanced learning in group and teacher-led classes (Aebersold et al., 2018; Fernández & Alonso, 2015; Johnson, 2019). Third, reviewed literature shows that there is a lack of understanding on what to expect regarding the virtual reality experience within the education processes, making priority training of both learning staff and students a necessary pre-teaching process (Aebersold et al., 2018; Bertram et al., 2015; Foundry, 2014; Niebuhr & Tegtmeier, 2019).

Despite these drawbacks, virtual reality has significant potential and is ready for both classroom and personal use. There is a required seismic shift in education that will push the use of virtual reality tools forward in entrepreneurship education. Besides, new, more profiled and fully supported platforms and content will need to be developed in order to expand learners' engagement into virtual environments. Finally, the ongoing research effort will need to be expanded with empirical studies in order to support the effectiveness of incorporating virtual reality into the classroom. Learning possibilities in virtual reality environments are practically endless, and certainly entrepreneurship education could stand to benefit.

References

Aebersold, M., Voepel-Lewis, T., Cherara, L., Weber, M., Khouri, C., Levine, R., & Tait, A. R. (2018). Interactive anatomy-augmented virtual simulation training. *Clinical Simulation in Nursing, 15*, 34–41.

Al-Atabi, M., & DeBoer, J. (2014). Teaching entrepreneurship using massive open online course (MOOC). *Technovation, 34*(4), 261–264.

Altspacevr. (2019, August 6). Fail fast, fail forward – Entrepreneurship month meet-up. *AltspaceVR*. Retrieved from https://account.altvr.com/events/1080802322977652895

Bellotti, F., Berta, R., De Gloria, A., Lavagnino, E., Dagnino, F., Ott, M., … Mayer, I. S. (2012). Designing a course for stimulating entrepreneurship in higher education through serious games. *Procedia Computer Science, 15*, 174–186.

Bertram, J., Moskaliuk, J., & Cress, U. (2015). Virtual training: Making reality work? *Computers in Human Behavior, 43*, 284–292.

Bourne, J., Harris, D., & Mayadas, F. (2005). Online engineering education: Learning anywhere, anytime. *Journal of Engineering Education, 94*(1), 131–146.

Bown, J., White, E., & Boopalan, A. (2017). Looking for the ultimate display: A brief history of virtual reality. In J. Gackenbach & J. Bown (Eds.), *Boundaries of self and reality online* (pp. 239–259). Edmonton, Canada: Edmonton North Primary Care Network.

Childers, L. (2019, August 6). How VR enhances the business school experience. *U.S. News*. Retrieved from www.usnews.com/education/best-graduate-schools/top-business-schools/articles/2019-03-28/how-virtual-reality-enhances-the-business-school-experience

Choi, S. H., & Chan, A. M. M. (2004). A virtual prototyping system for rapid product development. *Computer-Aided Design*, *36*(5), 401–412.

Costa, A. I., & Jongen, W. M. F. (2006). New insights into consumer-led food product development. *Trends in Food Science & Technology*, *17*(8), 457–465.

Cruz, N. M., Rodriguez Escudero, A. I., Hernangomez Barahona, J., & Saboia Leitao, F. (2009). The effect of entrepreneurship education programmes on satisfaction with innovation behaviour and performance. *Journal of European Industrial Training*, *33*(3), 198–214.

Daly, S. P. (2001). Student-operated Internet businesses: True experiential learning in entrepreneurship and retail management. *Journal of Marketing Education*, *23*(3), 204–215.

Delarue, J., & Lageat, T. (2019). Conducting contextualized and real-Life product tests: benefits and experimental challenges. In H. L. Meiselman (Ed.), Context. *The effect of environment on product design and evaluation*. Cambridge, UK: Woodhead.

Faherty, A. (2015). Developing enterprise skills through peer-assessed pitch presentations. *Education+ Training*, *57*(3), 290–305.

Fernández, R. P., & Alonso, V. (2015). Virtual reality in a shipbuilding environment. *Advances in Engineering Software*, *81*, 30–40.

Foundry. (2014). *Is virtual reality set to replace real life experiences? A research report by Foundry*. London, UK: Author.

Hedberg, J., & Alexander, S. (1994). Virtual reality in education: Defining researchable issues. *Educational Media International*, *31*(4), 214–220.

Henry, C., Hill, F., & Leitch, C. (2005). Entrepreneurship education and training: Can entrepreneurship be taught? Part I. *Education+ Training*, *47*(2), 98–111.

Hill, R. C., & Levenhagen, M. (1995). Metaphors and mental models: Sensemaking and sensegiving in innovative and entrepreneurial activities. *Journal of Management*, *21*(6), 1057–1074.

Homitz, D. J., & Berge, Z. L. (2008). Using e-mentoring to sustain distance training and education. *The Learning Organization*, *15*(4), 326–335.

Huq, A., & Gilbert, D. (2017). All the world's stage: Transforming entrepreneurship education through design thinking. *Education+ Training*, *59*(2), 155–170.

Hynes, B. (1996). Entrepreneurship education and training-introducing entrepreneurship into non-business disciplines. *Journal of European Industrial Training*, *20*(8), 10–17.

Jack, S. L., & Anderson, A. R. (1999). Entrepreneurship education within the enterprise culture: Producing reflective practitioners. *International Journal of Entrepreneurial Behavior & Research*, *5*(3), 110–125.

Jiao, H., Ogilvie, D. T., & Cui, Y. U. (2010). An empirical study of mechanisms to enhance entrepreneurs' capabilities through entrepreneurial learning in an emerging market. *Journal of Chinese Entrepreneurship*, *2*(2), 196–217.

Johnson, D. M. (2019). *The uncertain future of American public higher education*. Cham: Palgrave Macmillan.

Jones, C., & English, J. (2004). A contemporary approach to entrepreneurship education. *Education + Training, 46*(8/9), 416–423.

Kantor, J. (1988). Can entrepreneurship be taught?: A Canadian experiment. *Journal of Small Business & Entrepreneurship, 5*(4), 12–19.

Karlsson, T., & Moberg, K. (2013). Improving perceived entrepreneurial abilities through education: Exploratory testing of an entrepreneurial self efficacy scale in a pre-post setting. *The International Journal of Management Education, 11*(1), 1–11.

Katz, J. A. (2014). Education and training in entrepreneurship. In R. Baum, M. Frese, & R. A. Baron (Eds.), *The psychology of entrepreneurship* (pp. 241–268). New York: Psychology Press.

Kaufmann, H., Schmalstieg, D., & Wagner, M. (2000). Construct3D: A virtual reality application for mathematics and geometry education. *Education and Information Technologies, 5*(4), 263–276.

Ke, F., Lee, S., & Xu, X. (2016). Teaching training in a mixed-reality integrated learning environment. *Computers in Human Behavior, 62*, 212–220.

Kira, D., & Saade, R. (2006). Factors affecting online learning. In *IADIS International Conference Cognition and Exploratory Learning in Digital Age 2006* (pp. 277–282). https://www.researchgate.net/profile/Raafat_Saade/publication/267692209_Factors_affecting_online_learning/links/54788aed0cf2a961e4877913.pdf

Kirby, D. A. (2004). Entrepreneurship education: Can business schools meet the challenge? *Education + Training, 46*(8/9), 510–519.

Kizilkaya, L., Vince, D., & Holmes, W. (2019, June). Design prompts for virtual reality in education. In S. Isotani, E. Millán, A. Ogan, P. Hastings, B. McLaren, & R. Luckin (Eds.), *International Conference on Artificial Intelligence in Education* (pp. 133–137). Cham: Springer. Retrieved from https://link.springer.com/chapter/10.1007/978-3-030-23207-8_25

Klein, P. G., & Bullock, J. B. (2006). Can entrepreneurship be taught? *Journal of Agricultural and Applied Economics, 38*(2), 429–439.

Krokos, E., Plaisant, C., & Varshney, A. (2019). Virtual memory palaces: Immersion aids recall. *Virtual Reality, 23*(1), 1–15.

Kronk, H. (2019, August 6). Navajo nation high schoolers receive VR and entrepreneurship training. *Elearning Inside*. Retrieved from https://news.elearninginside.com/navajo-nation-high-schoolers-receive-vr-and-entrepreneurship-training/

Lorenzo, C. M., Sicilia, M. Á., & Sánchez, S. (2012). Studying the effectiveness of multi-user immersive environments for collaborative evaluation tasks. *Computers & Education, 59*(4), 1361–1376.

Macpherson, A., Jones, O., & Zhang, M. (2005). Virtual reality and innovation networks: Opportunity exploitation in dynamic SMEs. *International Journal of Technology Management, 30*(1–2), 49–66.

Maffei, L., Masullo, M., Pascale, A., Ruggiero, G., & Romero, V. P. (2016). Immersive virtual reality in community planning: Acoustic and visual congruence of simulated vs real world. *Sustainable Cities and Society, 27*, 338–345.

Martín-Gutiérrez, J., Mora, C. E., Añorbe-Díaz, B., & González-Marrero, A. (2017). Virtual technologies trends in education. *EURASIA Journal of Mathematics Science and Technology Education, 13*(2), 469–486.

Matlay, H., Rae, D., Henry, C., & Treanor, L. (2012). Exploring entrepreneurship education within veterinary medicine: Can it be taught? *Journal of Small Business and Enterprise Development, 19*(3), 484–499.

Merchant, Z., Goetz, E. T., Cifuentes, L., Keeney-Kennicutt, W., & Davis, T. J. (2014). Effectiveness of virtual reality-based instruction on students' learning outcomes in K-12 and higher education: A meta-analysis. *Computers & Education, 70,* 29–40.

Mwasalwiba, E. S. (2010). Entrepreneurship education: A review of its objectives, teaching methods, and impact indicators. *Education+ Training, 52*(1), 20–47.

Nabi, G., & Holden, R. (2008). Graduate entrepreneurship: Intentions, education and training. *Education+ Training, 50*(7), 545–551.

Neck, H. M., & Greene, P. G. (2011). Entrepreneurship education: Known worlds and new frontiers. *Journal of Small Business Management, 49*(1), 55–70.

Niebuhr, O., & Tegtmeier, S. (2019). Virtual-reality as a digital learning tool in entrepreneurship: How virtual environments help entrepreneurs give more charismatic investor pitches. In R. Baierl, J. Behrens, & A. Brem (Eds.), *Interfaces between digital technologies and entrepreneurship* (pp. 123–158). Berlin and Heidelberg: Springer.

Oigara, J. N. (2018). Integrating virtual reality tools into classroom instruction. In J. Keengwe (Ed.), *Handbook of research on mobile technology, constructivism, and meaningful learning* (pp. 147–159). Hershey, PA: IGI Global.

Ottosson, S. (2002). Virtual reality in the product development process. *Journal of Engineering Design, 13*(2), 159–172.

Panoutsopoulos, H., Lykourentzou, M. A., & Sampson, D. G. (2011, July). Business simulation games as digital tools for supporting school entrepreneurship education. In *2011 IEEE 11th International Conference on Advanced Learning Technologies* (pp. 155–156). IEEE.

Perikos, I., Grivokostopoulou, F., Paraske, M. A., Kovas, K., & Hatzilygeroudis, I. (2018, March). Formulating an innovative training framework for STEM entrepreneurship. In *Proceedings of INTED2018 Conference* (pp. 9242–9246). INTED2018.

Perren, L. (2003). The role of e-mentoring in entrepreneurial education and support: A meta-review of academic literature. *Education+ Training, 45*(8/9), 517–525.

Pihie, Z. A. L., & Bagheri, A. (2011). Teachers' and students' entrepreneurial self-efficacy: Implication for effective teaching practices. *Procedia-Social and Behavioral Sciences, 29,* 1071–1080.

Piperopoulos, P., & Dimov, D. (2015). Burst bubbles or build steam? Entrepreneurship education, entrepreneurial self-efficacy, and entrepreneurial intentions. *Journal of Small Business Management, 53*(4), 970–985.

Premand, P., Brodmann, S., Almeida, R., Grun, R., & Barouni, M. (2016). Entrepreneurship education and entry into self-employment among university graduates. *World Development, 77,* 311–327.

Psotka, J. (1995). Immersive training systems: Virtual reality and education and training. *Instructional Science, 23*(5–6), 405–431.

Raposo, M., & Do Paço, A. (2011). Entrepreneurship education: Relationship between education and entrepreneurial activity. *Psicothema, 23*(3), 453–457.

Robinson, S., Neergaard, H., Tanggaard, L., & Krueger, N. F. (2016). New horizons in entrepreneurship education: From teacher-led to student-centered learning. *Education+ Training, 58*(7/8), 661–683.

Rogers, S. (2019, August 6). Virtual reality: The learning aid of the 21st century. *Forbes.* Retrieved form www.forbes.com/sites/solrogers/2019/03/15/virtual-reality-the-learning-aid-of-the-21st-century/#17198a17139b

Ronstadt, R. (1985). The educated entrepreneurs: A new era of entrepreneurial education is beginning. *American Journal of Small Business, 10*(1), 7–23.

Rosedale, P. (2016). Virtual reality: The next disruptor: A new kind of worldwide communication. *IEEE Consumer Electronics Magazine, 6*(1), 48–50.

Rubin, P. (2019, August 6). As social VR grows, users are the ones building its worlds. *Wired.* Retrieved from www.wired.com/story/social-vr-worldbuilding/

Rusko, R., Härkönen, K., & Liukkonen, S. (2016). Coopetition at elevator pitch events? A case study of micro-activities at a business innovation event. *Journal of Innovation Management, 4*(3), 79–100.

Sampson, D. G., Ifenthaler, D., Isaias, P., & Spector, J. M. (2014). Digital systems for open access to formal and informal learning. In D. G. Sampson, D. Ifenthaler, J. M. Spector, & P. Isaias (Eds.), *Digital systems for open access to formal and informal learning* (pp. 1–7). Cham: Springer. https://link.springer.com/chapter/10.1007/978-3-319-02264-2_1

Schneider, K. (2019). How to promote entrepreneurial identity through edutainment? *Journal of Entrepreneurship Education, 22*(3), 1–12.

Sheail, P. (2018). Temporal flexibility in the digital university: Full-time, part-time, flexitime. *Distance Education, 39*(4), 462–479.

Shen, J., & Eder, L. B. (2009). Intentions to use virtual worlds for education. *Journal of Information Systems Education, 20*(2), 225.

Singh, S., Corner, P., & Pavlovich, K. (2007). Coping with entrepreneurial failure. *Journal of Management & Organization, 13*(4), 331–344.

Taatila, V. P. (2010). Learning entrepreneurship in higher education. *Education+ Training, 52*(1), 48–61.

Tata, A., Laureiro-Martínez, D., & Brusoni, S. (2016). Don't look back? The effect of attention to time and self on startup funding. In *Academy of management proceedings* (2016, No. 1, p. 13926). Briarcliff Manor, NY 10510: Academy of Management.

Top, S., Çolakoğlu, N., & Dilek, S. (2012). Evaluating entrepreneurship intentions of vocational high school pupils based on self-efficacy concept. *Procedia-Social and Behavioral Sciences, 58*, 934–943.

Van de Ven, A. H., Sapienza, H. J., & Villanueva, J. (2007). Entrepreneurial pursuits of self-and collective interests. *Strategic Entrepreneurship Journal, 1*(3–4), 353–370.

Virvou, M., & Katsionis, G. (2008). On the usability and likeability of virtual reality games for education: The case of VR-ENGAGE. *Computers & Education, 50*(1), 154–178.

Wickens, C. D. (1992, October). Virtual reality and education. In *[Proceedings] 1992 IEEE International Conference on Systems, Man, and Cybernetics* (pp. 842–847). IEEE.

Wilson, F., Kickul, J., & Marlino, D. (2007). Gender, entrepreneurial self-efficacy, and entrepreneurial career intentions: Implications for entrepreneurship education. *Entrepreneurship Theory and Practice, 31*(3), 387–406.

Winn, W., & Jackson, R. (1999). Fourteen propositions about educational uses of virtual reality. *Educational Technology, 39*(4), 5–14.

Zhao, H., Seibert, S. E., & Hills, G. E. (2005). The mediating role of self-efficacy in the development of entrepreneurial intentions. *Journal of Applied Psychology, 90*(6), 1265.

Chapter 4

Mixed Reality applied theatre at universities

Joshua A. Fisher

Introduction

Educators have used applied theatre in classrooms throughout the 20th century (Prentki & Preston, 2013). Often taking the form of constructivist role plays, the pedagogical use of applied storytelling engages documentary evidence and personal narratives to develop knowledge by and for students. As part of this practice, educators have used visual media as motivational springboards and props. With the advent of contemporary Mixed Reality (MR)[1] headsets and capable mobile devices, educators can use new spatial and interactive affordances as part of an applied theatre pedagogy. Such pedagogy aligns with current trends in research into MR's pedagogical affordances (Garzón & Acevedo, 2019). However, while the use of MR in pedagogy has been proven to increase student motivation and engagement (Cheng, 2017), there is debate on whether the technology alone accomplishes this goal (Garzón & Acevedo, 2019) equally across subject domains (Sirakaya & Cakmak, 2018). Additionally, instructional concepts for using MR have not been fully explored by scholars (Barroso Osuna, Gutiérrez-Castillo, Llorente-Cejudo, & Valencia Ortiz, 2019) leaving some educators at a loss as to how to use the technology effectively. In response to these concerns, this chapter seeks to fill a knowledge gap and presents a lesson plan for MR applied theatre in a university classroom. The plan has been developed from insights derived from examples of an applied theatre method called Theater of the Oppressed. It was developed by the dramaturg Augusto Boal, who was inspired by the pedagogical tenets of Paulo Freire's Pedagogy of the Oppressed (Boal, 1993).

Applied theatre: a dramaturgical pedagogy

Applied theatre encompasses a wide range of performance practices that put the community first (Nicholson, 2011). The goals are twofold. The first is developing knowledge about a particular event or subject (Prentki & Preston, 2013). This process might include students sharing personal stories or bringing in subject matter material. Augusto Boal encouraged his students to construct scenarios from their communities. These scenes might include the seemingly mundane, such as waiting for a bus or having a family dinner. Boal's dramatic techniques for clarifying these moments helped participants generate knowledge upon which they could act.

The second goal of applied theatre is the use of information generated during role plays to motivate action (White, 2015). The kind of information developed determines the target of that motivation. For Augusto Boal, targets included corrupt and oppressive landlords (Boal, 1993). For dramaturgs in the League of Workers Theaters, applied performances sought systematic change in labour laws for worker empowerment (Cheng, 2017). Critically, the dramaturg only frames and directs the applied theatre process. Whatever action manifests is carried out by the participants themselves.

To reach these two goals, a process of critical reflection must occur. In order to achieve critical reflection, Augusto Boal relied upon observations made by his predecessor, pedagogist Paulo Freire (Boal, 1993). Freire sought to achieve *conscientizacao*, conscientization, an elevation of critical consciousness to the point of being able to see the world differently (Freire, 2005). From this new situated perspective, students can create knowledge and then can clarify a response. Augusto Boal relied upon his theatre practices to achieve this effect. His role plays enabled villagers to participate in unexpected situated perspectives. In line with work done by Brigit Schmitz, applied theatre methodologies can use interaction design patterns to scaffold immersive learning (Schmitz, Klemke, Walhout, & Specht, 2015). Specifically, building upon Freire and Boal, the spatial and interactive affordances of MR can be used to achieve a new kind of critical consciousness.

Using MR in a dramaturgical pedagogy

Within both applied theatre and Human-Computer Interaction literature, performance is commonly used as an analogy or metaphor to explore interactivity (Laurel, 2013; Stone, 1996; Turkle, 1997). MR extends these observations by instantiating three-dimensional content into physical reality, on the theatre's stage. The presence of an MR model fills a performance space (Fisher, 2019; Gandy et al., 2010; Holz et al., 2011). This non-physical presence is unique to reality media like MR. The physical space is both empty and full; it contains both nothing and a 3D model. For the user, it is an enticing dichotomy. It is the kind of structure that Boal believes a stage space needs for participants to engage in critical reflection (Boal, 1993).

Boal has a concept of gnostic space wherein two opposites can be contained within the same mutable performance space: activated participants or media artefacts perform these opposites (Boal, 2002). For example, one participant might portray those who believe in climate change, and another plays those who are science deniers. To explore the dichotomy, participants act out scenes through theatre games and activities (Boal, 2002). For example, participants may read or pantomime newspaper headlines about climate change. Each participant represents the opposite perspective. They enact one headline and then the opposing headline. Together, the participants critique and find similarities between the headlines. As they respond, the performance becomes a site for critical reflection.

Just as applied theatre uses embodied movement and dramatic techniques to motivate action, so too can the presence of MR. As participants create these MR representations, they create knowledge. The students learn about the subjects in their scene, how they as a group perceive those subjects and gain literacy in MR's affordances (Gifreu-Castells & Moreno, 2014). Interactive documentary scholar Sandra Gaudenzi (2013) has talked of these kinds of participatory, interactive experiences as living documentaries. Over time, as participants change the scene by adding content or modifying what exists, their experience evolves. As perspectives shift and participation continues, the process of critical reflection becomes more expansive and pluralist as new participants engage with the material. Boal's theatre games provide tactics to encourage this form of participation. MR adds a new route of inquiry and reflection to these tactics that are spatial, interactive, and embodied through digital materiality that has a tangible presence (Fisher, 2016).

Applied theatre tactics with MR

Applied theatre utilizes MR's digital materiality to co-create representations of subjects with one another in an educational setting. Such activities align with the current perspective that MR pedagogy is well suited to constructivist tactics (Gifreu-Castells & Moreno, 2014) as part of contextual, discovery-based and experiential learning (Wojciechowski & Cellary, 2013). Presented in this section are historical workshop tactics from Paulo Freire and Augusto Boal. These tactics are the foundation of the applied theatre lesson plan with MR. Freire provides general guidelines for participant engagement, and Boal's tactics are focused on the development of games.

Tactics from Paulo Freire

Paulo Freire's tactics from *Pedagogy of the Oppressed* address how practitioners should conduct themselves (Freire, 2005). Immediately applicable insights include critical reflection as a form of action, objectifying reality and problem-posing. Each tactic is meant to achieve conscientization. Teachers can use the tactics to help a student move from a naïve to a critical consciousness to reflect and act upon a subject. Freire's teachers were asked only to come with an authentic need within themselves to fight alongside their students. He framed this relationship between educators and their pupils as intersubjective: the educator as a teacher-student; the pupil as student-teacher.

A dialogic pedagogy in a participatory epistemological mode enables both the teacher and student to identify strengths within one another.

Objectifying reality and problem-posing dialogue

When talking about objectifying reality, Freire is referring to becoming objective regarding one's perception of reality. He observed that his students believed toxic myths about themselves and their reality. Freire recognized that these myths served those who had power over his students. In order to deconstruct these myths, a participant needs to be able to address them from an objective stance. To achieve this stance, a medium can be used (such as writing, painting or sculpture) to create a material artefact (Freire, 2005). Once materialized, the perspective exists both in and outside the individual. A student can locate themselves concerning the subject matter through the produced artefact (Freire, 2005). From this situated position, with the help of an educator and their peers, they can begin to deconstruct the subject through a problem-posing dialogue.

In a shared MR environment, students and teachers can expand their problem-posing dialogue with digital materiality. Such an approach uses MR's proven capacity to visualize and spatialize abstract concepts (Sirakaya & Cakmak, 2018). Further, the problems gain a social presence that is shared and felt in the physical space by the students (Fisher, 2019). Students enact the pedagogical tactic of a problem-posing dialogue through MR mediation and participatory activities. When a classroom of students can recognize abstract subjects and concretize them in MR, they can begin to critique and question them. Within the back-and-forth of dialogue, students may grasp their agency and pursue inquiries that they otherwise would not. Julie A. Delello recognized that AR extends this kind of curious motivation (2014). When working together, this pedagogical practice can help students gain a new sense of reality (Fleck, Simon, & Bastien, 2014; Gifreu-Castells & Moreno, 2014; Rosenbaum, Klopfer, & Perry, 2006).

Tactics from Augusto Boal

Augusto Boal takes Freire's tactics and modifies them specifically for performance to achieve embodied reflection and the rehearsal of future action. Boal's repertoire of games for achieving this work is quite extensive.[2]

Tactics for the classroom performance space

Boal sought to create a performance space where opposing ideologies and viewpoints could be interrogated simultaneously through embodied performance. Boal believed that in this state, anything is possible (1993). An aesthetic and didactic space embodies extreme creativity and freedom of expression because of its plasticity. It is where theatre becomes knowledge through student involvement. How participants work through the space to represent reality creates a plenitude of stories that can be explored to create knowledge.

Boal began perfecting his dramaturgical pedagogy with Newspaper Theater (Boal, 1993). Using the newspaper became a valuable way to identify and deconstruct knowledge in society. One of Boal's first tactics was to find two separate accounts of the same event from different papers. The participants in the scene would then take turns reading the articles sentence by sentence. Their co-created discordant oral text became the material for critical reflection. Activated spectators may ask why a particular newspaper published the story one way while another chose a different perspective. However, others may disagree with both newspaper accounts altogether. The community of learners itself has a story as well: one that may be more valid.

Image and Forum Theater tactics

Boal's more famous games include Image and Forum Theater.[3] For Boal, the use of the word image has two meanings. The first refers to the classic conception of a photograph or painting. A visual representation of an event via a medium, whether it be a Polaroid or a picture via a mobile phone does not matter. The second refers to a different kind of image entirely; the only medium is that of the activated participants' bodies engaged in various actions to create an image (Boal, 1993, 2002). This meaning of an image is an embodied representation. MR naturally extends this embodied representation (Jang, Wakefield, & Lee, 2017).

The goal of Image Theatre is to invite the spectators to interrogate the polysemy of the created images. Both a photograph and a scene composed of participants are reflective for Boal. Within them, each participant will find or imbue their memories, creativity and emotions to create a representation of a subject. The process of Image Theater is meant to externalize this internalized process of reflection for the group. This divulgence enables participants to identify the perceptions that they do or do not share regarding the subject in the scene. Participants are encouraged to understand the multiplicity of meanings surrounding these images, to engage in a critical reflection around them and expand their openness to new perspectives.

Take, for example, the Image Theatre tactic, Image of Transition. In this activity, participants begin by choosing a scene of oppression to represent. The group then develops the ideal model of the scene in which no one is experiencing oppression. After that, the actors re-enact the oppressive image as individuals. Their peers reflect upon these individual versions to clarify one another's perspectives on the subject. Through this re-presentation of the scene's transition from oppressive to freedom from oppression two effects result. First, students develop a pluralist understanding of the situation.

Second, the embodiment of the transition to the ideal becomes a rehearsal for future action (Boal, 1993). The visual, spatial and interactive affordances of MR can be designed to extend the possibilities of this process.

Practical articulations with interaction design

Applied theatre methodologies can be scaffolded to interaction design patterns that utilize the affordances of MR. As applied theatre relies on testimony and other evidence to construct its performances of subjects, theoretical insights from interactive non-fiction can be used to guide this scaffolding. Dayna Galloway's taxonomy for interactive documentary interaction paradigms, in Table 4.1, can be augmented to address how interactions in MR can engage with both physical and virtual reality, in Table 4.2 (Fisher, 2016; Galloway, McAlpine, & Harris, 2007; Holz et al., 2011). In Table 4.3, these domains of interactions pair with

Table 4.1 Dayna Galloway's interactions for interactive documentary.

Interaction	Definition
Expansive or Immersive (E or I)	Expansive interactions utilize networks of users to deliver non-fiction experiences. Immersive interactions are associated with fully embodied VR experiences. The experiences of applied theatre with MR move freely between the two.
Active-adaptive or Passive-adaptive (AA or PA)	The difference between active and passive adaptive inter-actions is tied to user agency. If a user feels like they are actively changing the scene, the interactions are active adaptive. If the interactions are based on data the user does not perceive, then they are passive adaptive. The user does not know how they are affecting the non-fiction material.

Table 4.2 Interaction domain summaries.

Interaction Domain	Definition
Physical or Virtual Presence (PP or VP)	The manner in which an experience is corporeally present: for example, MR shares a physical corporeal nature with its environment; VR is almost entirely virtual.
Physical or Virtual Interaction (PI or VI)	The way a user interacts with an experience, for example, a seated VR experience uses almost entirely virtual interactions through the controller. An MR experience using plane-detection on the street would have a range of physical interactions.

Table 4.3 Classifications of mixed reality interactions paired with participatory perform-ance methods.

Participatory Dramaturgical-pedagogical Tactics	Domain of Interaction	Family of Interactions	Example of Interaction
Warm-up Phases			
Get to Know Each Other	PP PI	PA & E	Students interview one another in the mode of a late-night TV show host and a guest.
Sociometry	PP & VP PI & VI	AA & I	Students move through space in relation to how they feel about subject matter. The students' movements are tracked by the device to create a spatial image in MR that represents the intersections between them-selves, their peers and the subject.
Practice Phase			
Image Theater	PP & VP PI & VI	AA & I	Scenes are sourced from the participants, re-presented using MR artefacts as tableaux and modified in a participatory mode.
Forum Theater	PP & VP PI & VI	AA & I	Scenes are sourced from the participants, re-presented using reality media artefacts and modified in a participatory mode through the direction of a lead student.
Newspaper Theater	VP PI & VI	AA & E	Newspaper headlines are sourced using an API, displayed using MR and modified in a participatory mode.
Cool Down Phase			
Monument Theater	PP & VP PI & VI	AA & I	Participants leave the workshop to con-struct an MR sculpture of their experience within the community.
Discussion	PP PI	AA & E	Participants sit in a fishbowl in the centre of the group and discuss how they felt during the workshop.

the tactics discussed in the last section. I have arranged them in the three phases for a lesson plan.

In Table 4.3, Passive-adaptive tactics are used primarily to source and implement subject material from the reality of the students. The same infor-mation is then used, through MR, to express one's perception of the subject in later phases. Participants implement the Active-adaptive affordances to this end. By way of example, an Image Theater exercise in which the leading participant has sourced documentary material via the *New York Times* API uses Passive-Adaptive and Expansive interactions that occur in the Virtual Domain. When the leading participant begins co-creating with the material through MR, they are engaging in Active-adaptive and Immersive interactions that have presence and interactions in both the virtual and physical domains. If a participant outside of the primary participant uses a device to view the constructed representation, they engage in an Immersive scene that is Active-adaptive.

Summary of dramaturgical-pedagogical tactics

These tactics, in tandem with those established by Boal and Freire, can be used in an applied theatre classroom.

- As part of the expansive process of gathering subject material, include APIs in the mobile app that utilizes the information that is representative of the community's social reality.
- Before beginning the workshop, develop an inventory of 3D models of objects and themes based on real-world objects in the community through photogrammetry to create representational scenes.
- Work with stakeholders within the school and community to ascertain enough mobile devices for use in the workshop. Do not assume that every student will come with a device capable of an app utilizing emerging media.
- Ensure that MR beacons and VR lighthouses frame the performance stages to create a media actuality (gnostic space). Ensure that participants have enough room for locomotion.
- In MR, materialized actualities must be shared, not individual, and mutable through the participation of other students. Critical reflection through emerging media is not possible unless the performance space is inclusive.
- MR consists not only of what is available outside of the workshop space but within it as well. The students should be able to record, manipulate and implement media documented during the workshop.
- MR should actualize outside of the workshop, just like the participants' actions. Applied theatre experiences with MR should move outside of the theatre space and extend its possibilities into the community.
- The affordances of the devices to track interactions and movement should be used to motivate participation in the dramaturgical-pedagogy.
- Whenever possible, experiences should move from the virtual end of the spectrum into the physical.

These tactics can be used in MR applied theatre as part of a dramaturgical-pedagogy. MR digital material is mutable, tangible and negotiable through the affordances of devices and participatory, constructivist activities. Used together, they result in representations of the subject matter. For the student, being able to interact with material through MR empowers them to express their perspective in new, potentially more critical ways (Sirakaya & Cakmak, 2018). When combined with the representations of their peers, students can identify and address a group's shared perspective on a particular subject.

The Our Reality Workshop

The concepts and theories discussed in this chapter were put into practice in an applied theatre class for students at the Georgia Institute of Technology. The series of classes were called The Our Reality Workshop, and they explored issues and concepts of safety on the university's campus. From 2015 through 2019, the campus experienced several student tragedies, including an increase in deaths (McCausland & Rosenblatt, 2017). To construct knowledge and better understand safety on campus, students employed their own experiences and non-fiction material in the form of anonymous testimonials from a public art campaign called, I Feel Safe When (IFSW) (Edwards, 2016). Students used this material along with a mobile app as part of the workshop activities.

Design of the our reality XR mobile app

The Our Reality XR mobile app was designed in Unity using the Placenote SDK and Apple's ARkit (Fisher, 2019). Students had access to over 100 models, including buildings from the university's campus. Further, they could change the colour, shape and texture of these objects. As part of the workshop, the students used a Ricoh Theta 360 camera to shoot 360 photos. These could be used as MR portals to create backdrops for their scenes at places on campus. Students could also draw in space using an interaction design pattern similar to Tiltbrush. Lastly, students could place human models into space and animate them in their scenes.

A unique aspect of the Our Reality XR App was that it enabled users to co-create with one another in MR. At the time of the workshop, collaborative MR was not included in ARKit or ARCore, the leading SDKs from Apple and Google. The novel system, made possible by Placenote and Photon Networking, allowed the students to create with one another in real time. It had a powerful effect on the students. During interviews after the workshop, many reported that this social aspect of the experience lent the MR its social presence in space.

Warm-up: sociometry

In the class, students began by sorting and exploring the testimonials from the IFSW campaign. These testimonials began with the phrase, 'I Feel Safe When' and then were filled in anonymously by students. Students in the class would then fill out their own cards, anonymously, and shuffle them in with the rest from the campaign. After that, they engaged in an applied theatre game called sociometry that allowed participants to see how they connected to those testimonials. In non-MR sociometry, the facilitator would read out a testimonial such as, 'I feel safe when I am with my family'. The facilitator then asked the students to move to one side of the room if they agreed, and to another side of the room if they did not. In this way, the students learned how they connected to specific ideas of safety and how their peers related to them as well.

In the MR version, sociometry has a spatial presence. As the students moved through space in response to the testimonials, they used the Our Reality XR app that allowed them to draw a trail as they moved. The interaction design pattern was similar to tilt-brush, but the app allowed all of the students to see one another's MR trails. What resulted was a network of MR trails representing the students' connections to feelings of safety. After reading through a number of the testimonials, the students were asked to step away, stop drawing and critically reflect on what they had constructed. MR enabled students to see where their feelings of safety intersected with those of their peers. The tighter knots in the MR trails, representing the students' commonly held feelings, prompted critical reflection and discussion.

Activity: Gallery of Images

After sociometry, students engaged in Boal's game, Gallery of Images (Boal, 2002). In this game, students created two lines facing one another. They each took turns sculpting one another into representations of the subject material. In the workshop, the students sculpted their peers into representations of safety written on the IFSW cards. Each pair of students utilized only a single card in the activity. In the non-MR version, students sculpted their peers into a representation using their hands or by pointing to how they should move their body. Students could not speak during this activity. After a set time, the student who was sculpting went back into line. Using the same IFSW card, the sculpted student became the sculptor and attempted to clarify what was written on the card by sculpting their peer. They built upon the way they were just sculpted. After a few rounds of this silent discourse, the image was settled upon by the pair of students. Other students in the line then critically reflected on how their peers had been sculpted to reflect the material of the activity.

In the MR-version, the procedure is very much the same. However, instead of only sculpting the student by directing them, the sculptor can use MR objects to add context and an immersive scene. For example, if the IFSW card said, 'I feel safe in bed', the student can add an MR bed or pillows into their image. Additionally, while students still stand in two lines, the MR only happens on one side. The students swap positions, from MR to non-MR in order to maintain the MR scene's presence in its physical space. Once the students have swapped positions, the new sculptor can modify the MR to clarify the image. After several rounds, students critically reflect on one another's MR scenes.

Activity: Image Theater

The last activity was Boal's Image Theater. In the non-MR version, students were split up into groups of three and four. As a group, they chose an IFSW card to turn into a representation of reality. One student sculpted the others into a scene that was identifiable with the story on the card. The students took turns, moving that image to the ideal representation. At this point, facilitators handed out dialogue cards and prompted the students to speak. Starting one at a time, the students began repeating, and completing, one of the phrases on the card from their point of view. It was a way of taking an internal reflection and externalizing it for others. The cards provided the following prompts:

* I want ... *or* I must ... *or* I need ...
* I fear ... *or* I do not want ...
* I think ...
* I feel ...

After students repeated these phrases out loud, filling them in with diegetic dialogue contextual to their scene, they were asked to improvise. They were to stop repeating the same phrases and move into a story. At this point, other student groups were brought around to view and reflect upon the scenes the students constructed. Students were then asked the following questions to spur reflection:

* What are you seeing?
* Where is the oppression?
* Where is the safety; where is the danger?
* Who is oppressed? Who is oppressing?
* Who is the witness?
* Is it realistic? What is real or false?

The MR version of Image Theater follows the same procedure but enables the students to use all of the affordances of the Our Reality XR app. This procedure enables them to make immersive scenes that utilizes not just their peers but the physical environment, their own MR props and the spatial drawing tool.

Student response to applied theatre with MR

Student response to the applied theatre with MR curriculum was generally positive. Fifteen students participated in the class. Six of the undergraduates were computer science majors, four were computational media majors, three were engineering majors and two were business majors. Nine of the students identified as male and six identified as female. The workshop's goal was to develop a critical consciousness about safety on campus through the participatory activities and the affordances of MR. An evaluative process of naturalistic inquiry was chosen. Semi-structured interviews, surveys and video recordings make up the qualitative information gathered. The interviews were completed within 24 hours of the final workshop and lasted on average 15 minutes. Short-answer surveys were taken immediately after the final workshop experience.

Critically, students felt that being able to use the physical environment, the IFSW material and AR objects in a shared real-time setting made the experience pedagogically valuable. For example, one participant stated, 'I think like augmented reality gave you the visual representation of everyone's choices but fit in the physical world. You can say 'Hey, like this person is choosing the same choices as I am. They might have the same interests as me'. So, you kind of notice it in both worlds'. Others felt this more strongly. Another participant said,

> When I looked through the phone it actually felt really like one of the biggest emotions I've felt. Like, oh – there's a lot of things going on here and then when I kind of looked away from it and then looked back I felt [...] all of the stuff going on actually looked like it belonged in the real world.

Ten of the fifteen students felt that the workshop activities helped to create knowledge about safety on campus and one another. Regarding the sociometry game, one participant said,

> When I saw those lines when we were doing walking back and forth activity (sociometry). I don't know what I felt but then it just felt alive. So, it's hard to describe – but then to see those different colored lines effectively delivered that everybody's different because each color was different and then each color had different lines. So, it was like a yeah, a good representation of how unique we are.

Many participants commented upon the constructivist nature of the knowledge. One participant put it succinctly, 'When my team members were creating it, it matched up with my views of how the scene should be, like how it should be related and conveyed'.

Participants succeeded at creating representations of reality about safety on campus. They utilized their memories and feelings as well as documentary source material. Half of the groups involved in the workshops felt like the representations they created counted as a form of knowledge about 'feeling safe' on campus. Critically, 60% of the participants believed that the representations they created could lead to some social action. This result is a positive indication that the workshop is a site of critical reflection that can reverberate throughout a community. Further, that the goals of applied theatre were accomplished and aided by MR.

Final insights

This chapter has sought to present instructional concepts for how MR can be used as part of an applied theatre pedagogy on a university campus. MR's capacity for interactive, spatial and visual representations of abstract and concrete ideas allows for a new avenue of critical reflection. This process is facilitated by the digital materiality of MR, which connects any pedagogical practice to both physical and virtual domains. Students can capably use the medium as a threshold to move abstract ideas into concrete reality. With this in mind, the lesson plan, derived from the tactics of Paulo Freire and Augusto Boal, effectively uses MR interaction design patterns with participatory tactics as part of a dramaturgical-pedagogy. The medium's affordance to be shared, in real time between students as they modify scenes and the physical environment, aids critical reflection. Further, it is heartening that the university students in the study felt that MR can be used in an applied theatre setting to effectively rehearse future actions. While more work and research are necessary, educators should feel encouraged to experiment with the medium to collectively explore and respond to local issues.

Notes

1 I use the term mixed reality as an umbrella term for a variety of emerging reality media including augmented and virtual reality (AR/VR).
2 There are many additional manuals for educators interested in implementing Boal's workshops from start to finish (Boal, 1993, 2002; Midha, 2010).
3 Forum Theater, an offshoot of Image Theater, utilizes the same tactics with one addition. Instead of constructing a still image on the stage, it moves and can be modified at any time by the participants. Both Image and Forum Theater are forms of simultaneous dialectic dramaturgy to identify all possible facets of an issue or subject.

References

Barroso Osuna, J., Gutiérrez-Castillo, J. J., Llorente-Cejudo, M. D., & Valencia Ortiz, R. (2019). Difficulties in the incorporation of augmented reality in university education: Visions from the experts. *Journal of New Approaches in Educational Research*, *8*(2), 126–141.
Boal, A. (1993). *Theatre of the oppressed*. New York, NY: Theatre Communications Group.
Boal, A. (2002). *Games for actors and non-actors*. New York, NY: Routledge.
Cheng, K.-H. (2017). Reading an augmented reality book: An exploration of learners' cognitive load, motivation, and attitudes. *Australasian Journal of Educational Technology*, *33*(4), 53–69.

Cherne, M. B. (2014, June 2). *Techniques for changing the world: The league of workers theatres/new theatre league.* University of Wisconsin Archive. Retrieved December 7, 2017 from https://minds.wisconsin.edu/handle/1793/69044?show=full

Delello, J. A. (2014). Insights from pre-service teachers using science-based augmented reality. *Journal of Computers in Education, 1,* 292–311.

Edwards, J. (2016). *I feel safe when.* Retrieved from Georgia Tech Arts. http://arts.gatech.edu/i-feel-safe-when

Fisher, J. A. (2016). Utilizing the mixed reality cube taxonomy for interactive documentary research. *Proceedings of the 1st International Workshop on Multimedia Alternate Realities* (pp. 9–14). Amsterdam: ACM.

Fisher, J. A. (2019). *Interactive non-fiction with reality media: Rhetorical affordances.* Atlanta: Georgia Institute of Technology.

Fleck, S., Simon, G., & Bastien, J. M. (2014). AIBLE: An inquiry-based augmented reality environment for teaching astronomical phenomena. *2014 IEEE International Symposium on Mixed and Augmented Reality – Media, art, social science, humanities and design* (pp. 65–66). Munich: ACM.

Freire, P. (2005). *Pedagogy of the oppressed.* New York, NY: Continuum.

Galloway, D., McAlpine, K. B., & Harris, P. (2007). From Michael Moore to JFK reloaded: Towards a working model of interactive documentary. *Journal of Media Practice, 8*(3), 325–339.

Gandy, M., Catrambone, R., MacIntyre, B., Alvarez, C., Eiriksdottir, E., Hilimire, M., … McLaughlin, A. C. (2010). Experiences with an AR evaluation test bed: Presence, performance, and physiological measurement. In *International Symposium on Mixed and Augmented Reality (ISMAR)* (pp. 127–136). Seoul: IEEE.

Garzón, J., & Acevedo, J. (2019). Meta-analysis of the impact of augmented reality on students' learning gains. *Educational Research Review, 27*(1), 244–260.

Gaudenzi, S. (2013). *The living documentary: From representing reality to co-creating reality in digital interactive documentary* (Doctoral thesis). Goldsmiths, University of London, London.

Gifreu-Castells, A., & Moreno, V. (2014). Educational multimedia applied to the interactive nonfiction area. Using interactive documentary as a model for learning. *Edulearn14: International Conference on Education and New Learning Technologies* (pp. 1305–1315). Barcelona: IATED.

Holz, T., Campbell, A. G., Ohare, G. M., Stafford, J. W., Martin, A., & Dragone, M. (2011). MiRA-mixed reality agents. *International Journal of Human Computer Studies, 69*(4), 251–268.

Jang, S.-A., Wakefield, G., & Lee, S.-H. (2017). Incorporating kinesthetic creativity and gestural play into immersive modeling. In *Proceedings of the 4th International Conference on Movement Computing* (pp. 1–8). New York, NY: ACM.

Laurel, B. (2013). *Computers as theatre.* Boston, MA: Addison-Wesley.

McCausland, P., & Rosenblatt, K. (2017). *NBC News.* Retrieved June 2019, from Georgia Tech Student-Activist Shot Dead by Campus Police. www.nbcnews.com/news/us-news/georgia-tech-student-activist-shot-dead-campus-police-n802146

Midha, G. (2010). *Theatre of the Oppressed a manual for educators.* Amherst, MA: University of Massachusetts Amherst.

Nicholson, H. (2011). Applied drama/theatre/performance. In S. Schonmann, *Key concepts in theatre/drama education* (pp. 241–245). Leiden: Brill | Sense.

Prentki, T., & Preston, S. (2013). Applied theatre: An introduction. In T. Prentki, S. Preston, T. Prentki, & S. Preston (Eds.), *The applied theatre reader* (pp. 9–17). New York, NY: Routledge.

Rosenbaum, E., Klopfer, E., & Perry, J. (2006). On location learning: Authentic applied science with networked augmented realities. *Journal of Science Education and Technology, 16*(1), 31–45.

Schmitz, B., Klemke, R., Walhout, J., & Specht, M. (2015). Attuning a mobile simulation game for school children using a design-based research approach. *Computers & Education, 81*(1), 35–48.

Sirakaya, M., & Cakmak, E. K. (2018). The effect of augmented reality use on achievement, misconception and course engagement. *Contemporary Educational Technology, 9*(3), 297–314.

Stone, A. R. (1996). *The war of desire and technology at the close of the mechanical age.* Cambridge, MA: MIT press.

Turkle, S. (1997). *Life on the screen: Identity in the age of the internet.* New York City, NY: Touchstone.

White, G. (2015). Introduction. In G. White, *Applied theatre: Aesthetics* (pp. 1–59). London: Bloomsbury.

Wojciechowski, R., & Cellary, W. (2013). Evaluation of learners' attitude toward learning in ARIES augmented reality environments. *Computers & Education, 68*, 570–585.

Chapter 5

Development of professional skills in higher education

Problem-based learning supported by immersive worlds

E. Fernández-Ahumada, J. Montejo-Gámez,
P. Sánchez-Zamora, M. Benlloch-González,
L. Ortiz-Medina, M. C. Beato and E. V. Taguas

Introduction

The knowledge society in which we are immersed has shifted the key learning process towards approaches focused on developing 'know-how', versus traditional teaching strategies based on gaining knowledge. As a result, the quality of teaching is becoming highly associated with the improvement of the labour insertion of the graduates. In this sense, there has been an emphasis on the need to provide students with a wide range of skills and knowledge beyond those merely technical such as communication skills, the ability to work in multidisciplinary teams, entrepreneurship, global and collaborative solving problems approaches, and a respectful sensitivity for the cultural, social and economic environment (Ohland, Frillman, Zhang, & Miller, 2004).

Under this context, the European Higher Education Area aims to promote the acquisition of professional competences by working on real problems in such a way that students acquire a leading role (Sáiz-Manzanares, Montero-García, González-Fernández, Aguilar-Romero, & Peláez-Vara, 2010). Andersson and Andersson (2010) define 'competence' as a series of knowledge, skills and attitudes, which allow the students to know how to act under professional conflicts and the consequences of their choice. The hope is that they become able to judge and understand their actions in a wide social-professional context. Consequently, the development of professional competences is achieved through learning experiences in which the teacher must encourage students' attributes such as creativity, autonomy, exploration and critical analysis that are associated with common scenarios or real situations that may arise in future professional scenarios (Redel, Castillo, Aguilar, Polo, & Taguas, 2014; Rodríguez-Donaire & Amante, 2012; Taguas, Falconer, & Tarquis, 2014). The use of interactive training methods that encourage the interest in the profession, promote an efficient acquisition of knowledge, include participation and interaction with external professional agents, form behavioural patterns and provide high motivation and a team-work conscience is necessary (Yakovleva & Yakovlev, 2014).

There are various strategies for designing learning activities based on role-playing games. All of them involve the experimentation of typical situations of the professional reality and are focused on gaining a deeper and more complex knowledge than that provided by other methodological approaches. These approaches allow students to work and interact collaboratively, as well as to become aware of attitudes that are not usually addressed. In this sense, virtual reality and immersive worlds ease the creation of versatile scenarios at a low cost and eliminate social and behavioural barriers that might eventually hinder learning. The success of these tools in the service of learning has been well documented in the literature (see, for example, Bouras & Tsiatsos, 2006; Grunwald & Barak, 2001; Kickmeier-Rust, Bull, & Meissl-Egghart, 2014; Lorenzo, Sicilia, & Sánchez, 2012; Mamo et al., 2011; Mathers, Goktogen, Rankin, & Anderson, 2012; Sumners, Reiff, & Weber, 2008), in particular for the application of role-playing games (Deshpande & Huang, 2011; Sancho, Moreno-Ger, Fuentes-Fernández, & Fernández-Manjón, 2009). For this reason, virtual reality and immersive worlds have been identified as some of the early 21st-century technological elements that will most dramatically change the way we live, particularly in the areas of education (Schmorrow, 2009).

As emphasized by Gisbert, Esteve, and Camacho (2011), the benefits of using 3D worlds as a tool for teaching are multiple. They provide a unique learning and knowledge exchange environment, which offers opportunities for group interactions and shared reflections on the learning process. They improve collaboration and communication skills, in such a way that students have an easier time transferring knowledge from the classroom to the real-life context. They promote the resolution of problems and negotiation skills that facilitate the development of social experience in the understanding of other cultures and people. Finally, they constitute a support for creativity, exploration and identity development through open ways for learning. As a consequence, the combination of role-playing strategies and immersive virtual worlds become an enormous potential tool for the recreation of scenarios in which students can temporarily assume identities and tasks without facing their consequences in the real world. In this sense, both academic and professional scopes have recognized the learning possibilities offered by 3D virtual worlds as spaces to create and collaborate during the learning process (Gisbert et al., 2011). Therefore, from a multi-user domain software, each participant can be represented in specific created three-dimensional environment through an 'avatar' or figurative individual. Avatars allow the selecting of attributes such as gender, age or appearance to play different professional roles, which enhances the experience of emulating real situations (Baker, Wentz, & Woods, 2009).

All these ideas led to the development of a series of learning experiences that place students of different degrees in key scenarios of their future professional activity. The aim of this proposal was to develop students' professional competences of engineering and mathematics teaching areas from real tasks proposed by professionals. Environments recreated in immersive worlds paid special attention to the importance of interactions, both with professionals from different sectors and with peers. In particular, the aim of this project was two-fold:

1) The design of a specific case set of role-playing games for the participation in public contracts, technical assistance and curricular designs. Students interact as different stakeholders in the process and work interactively on the corresponding documentation depending on the professional role played.
2) The implementation of these role-playing games in higher education classrooms and the evaluation of the development of this experience, paying special emphasis to the attitude shown by the students.

This chapter is devoted to explaining the experiences carried out, as well as their evaluation. In this way, the following section explains the design of the project while the next includes the implementation and evaluation of the proposal in each of the disciplines in which it was applied. Finally, the last section summarizes the main conclusions obtained after the experience.

Design of the experiences

The project was addressed from a multidisciplinary teaching approach between Engineering and Teacher Education Faculties at the University of Córdoba (Spain). In particular, teaching proposals were carried out for three courses: 'Sociology and Forest Policy', a second year course of the forestry engineering degree studies; 'Engineering Projects', of the third year of the agricultural engineering degree studies; and 'Didactics of Numbers, Operations and Measurement', of the second year of the elementary school teacher's degree studies.

The proposed professional tasks related to each of these courses were the following: planning of rural development under a regional scope and the design of forest strategies, public biddings and curricular design, respectively. The tasks were proposed within key scenarios that were emulated in an immersive world. Concretely, these e-scenarios were recreated in a 3D-virtual environment by using OpenSim (http://opensimulator.org/).

In order to coordinate the teaching proposals, 6 work packages were designed:

1. Design of the role-playing games, content and milestones linked to the time schedule and the syllabus of each course.
2. Presentation of the real tasks proposed by professionals in the context of the course, detailing the objectives pursued and the professional competencies

to be acquired, team building and overview of the relationships between agents.

3. Introduction to ICT tools for the development of real tasks (immersive virtual platform, websites, legislation and other applications).

4. Tutoring and mentoring sessions with external professionals who provided guidance on the strategies to be followed by the teams. Students' work on videos and deliverables in accordance with their role.

5. Evaluation of the teaching experience in each subject focused on the students' learning results and their assessment.

6. Joint analysis of all participating teachers on the experience: strengths, weaknesses, recommendations and potential lines of improvement.

Table 5.1 displays the main organizational aspects of these packages, including scenario requirements for the immersive world, design of activities and group interaction, material used and aspects of the evaluation.

In order to evaluate the proposal, the attitudes shown by the students before and after the implementation of the experiences were analysed. To reach this goal, a 4-block questionnaire was prepared for each course. It was intended to assess the degree of confidence of the student to carry out the different tasks associated with each of the blocks, according to his/her current abilities; the degree of motivation to perform the proposed tasks; the degree of anxiety that the proposed tasks could cause; and the degree of success he/she thought he/she could achieve in the proposed tasks. A scale from 0 to 100 was used. The minimum value '0' indicated 'I expect a bad result or a mediocre work'; '50', 'I expect a moderately good result'; and '100', 'I expect to develop excellent work'. An analysis of the mean with the t-Student test was carried out to compare the answers before and after the teaching experiences. Excel software within Microsoft Office was used for all calculations.

Implementation

Details on the classroom experiences as well as the evaluations are provided below.

Classroom experiences

Sociology and Forest Policy – forestry engineering degree studies

The development of the activities took place for six weeks with a total of 21 hours including the award session in which the association of farmers and consumers 'Organic Subbética' participated (Table 5.2).

Seminars and theoretical discipline were performed in lectures with the whole group, made up of a total of 29 students who agreed to participate in

Table 5.1 Summary of the main aspects of the project.

	Sociology & FP	Engineering Projects	Didactics N, O & M
Requirements of the immersive world to recreate (scenarios)	Environment Natural Park/office	Work on the sewage system (real case of the public company)/office	Teacher's room/office or meeting room
Activity and interaction of working groups and external agents and roles	*Planning for the Sustainable Development of a Natural Park.* On the one hand, students with the role of different agents constituted a sectorial committee to diagnose the state of the Natural Park (phase 1). Then, students acted as technicians who prepared action strategies (phase 2). The application of these strategies and the role of the participants in the discussions were evaluated. The final result of each team was a Sustainable Development Plan that was evaluated by an external agent responsible for the Administration.	*Public bidding.* The manager of the public company provided documentation in relation to a real bidding for the replacement and improvement of a sanitation network. The teacher selected the necessary information so that the teams of students who assumed the role of technicians could prepare the technical specifications, following a real example. Other teams of students assumed the role of bidding companies and worked on the documentation, according to the interpretation of the received specifications. Finally, the teams of technicians decided the bid award. As support during the process, the manager of the public company and an infrastructure technician of the Regional Government gave seminars on the new Law of Public Sector Contracts and its application. They	*Didactic Proposal.* An elementary school teacher raised various contents within the block 'Number and Operations' for the 1st year of Primary school. Students' teams acquired, on one hand, the role of tasks designers. Their proposal was to facilitate the learning of those contents. On the other hand, they played the role of evaluators to determine the quality and usefulness of each task proposal for the acquisition of the competences indicated by the teacher. Performances of the different groups were evaluated in terms of the work presented.

Working material: documentation prepared and used according to the designed activity	Presentation on rural planning process. Guide to the Natural Park 'Sierras Subbéticas'. Readings on consensus and conflicts in the Natural Park 'Sierras Subbéticas' Working document on roleplaying in environmental education Basic manual for the organization of a work meeting in the virtual world	also tutored the evaluation of the actions of the different groups in terms of documentation and explanatory videos. Specifications and plans of the work. Presentation of the updated Contract Law. Work script for each session, specific for each role.	Presentations on the didactics of natural numbers List of content to work in a fortnight A teacher's workbook with activity planning and design
Aspects of evaluation and discussion of results	Evaluation of the impact of the experiences with pre-test and post-test analysis, based on the principles of self-efficacy (Carberry, Lee, & Ohland, 2010), applied to each case.		

Table 5.2 Time planning and student groups for the activities carried out in the subject of Sociology and Forest Policy.

Tasks	Time	Group
0. Presentation of the teaching innovation project, its fit with the practical section of the subject and explanation of the Sustainable Development Planning of a Natural Park.	Week 1	All (29)
1. Team building and assignment of roles: representative of environmentalist group; representative of entrepreneurs; representative of farmers; representative of hunters' association; representative of civil society and political actors.	Week 2	Teams
2. Characterization of the avatar according to the chosen role		
3. Work on the diagnosis (description, analysis and interpretation) of the Natural Park based on the role played and identification of the main problems.	Week 3	Teams
4. Recording teamwork meetings (diagnostic phase)		
5. Work on formulation (design of objectives, strategies and activities) and application of policy instruments	Week 4	Teams
6. Recording teamwork meetings (formulation phase)		
7. Seminar: teams present the Sustainable Development Plan	Week 5	All
8. Delivery of documents and recordings		
9. Seminar given by 'Organic Subbética'. Award ceremony for the best planning works.	Week 6	All
Total (hours)	**21 h**	

the project. For activities associated with the use of ICTs, students were divided into six teams (5 teams of 5 students and 1 team of 4 students).

The activity corresponded mainly to the second and third issues of the course syllabus, dedicated to the analysis of forests as renewable natural resources and to the study of principles, objectives and instruments of Forest Policy, respectively. That was the first time that students of this degree tackled these issues. For the teaching of these topics, 9 hours of lectures were dedicated, distributed over 3 weeks to allow the establishment of the conceptual base to sustain the activity.

As shown in Table 5.2, after a first introductory session on the teaching innovation project, its fit with the practical section of the subject and the explanation of the sustainable development planning of a natural park (0), the work teams were formed and the roles assigned (1). After that, students had a first contact with the immersive worlds and the management and characterization of the avatars according to the chosen role (2). For this purpose, 6 teams of 4 or 5 members each were established, and each member of the team developed one of the following roles: representative of an environmentalist group; representative of entrepreneurs; representative of farmers; representative of hunters' association; representative of civil society and political actors. The assignment of different roles was fundamental in this experience, since the number of agents involved in the management of forest areas has given rise to conflicts of interest of several types: conflicts between different sectors of the local population according to their relationship with the parks; conflicts between new or traditional users who take advantage of the protected area for different and sometimes conflicting purposes (tourist, hunting, economic, etc.); and conflicts between public actors in charge of applying the different conservation measures and the interests of different actors. Thus, the design of the Sustainable Development Plan should take into consideration the position of all the actors involved in the process, so that its legitimacy was valued.

In the third week, the members of each team searched for the main problems existing in the natural park from the point of view of the role played (3). Then, through a recorded session in the immersive worlds, participated with the rest of their team in a discussion table that ended with a diagnosis agreed upon by all parties (4). In the following week, members of each team acted as administration technicians and, based on the diagnosis made in the previous phase, jointly designed objectives, lines of action and measures of the park's sustainable development plan (5). During this formulation phase, a recording was made of one of the discussion sessions held in the virtual worlds (6). Once all the planning work was done, in about the fifth week, each team presented the results of their work in a seminar (7) and delivered the corresponding documentation and recordings (8). Finally, in the last week, after the review of the work by the teaching staff and the external evaluator (Head of Singular Projects of the Agency of Agrarian and Fishing Management of Andalusia), a session on solidarity economy given by 'Organic Subbética' was presented and the award ceremony took place (9).

Engineering Projects – agricultural engineering degree studies

A total of 62 students were enrolled in this course and agreed to participate in the project. They were divided into three small groups of 20–22 students for the practical sessions where the acquisition of ICT skills was promoted; theoretical lectures and seminars were carried out in sessions with all students. Within the small groups, different teams were set up. In each small group, there were 1 team of 5 to 6 students with the role of technicians of a public institution and 3 teams of 5 to 6 students with the role of engineers of a private company. The teaching activities were developed along 6 weeks and a total of 31 hours (Table 5.3), including the award ceremony. The context of the activity corresponded to the fifth issue, dedicated to Contracting. This topic develops the differences in management between public and private projects and studies the particularities of the contracting of public projects included in the law. That was the first time that students of this degree tackled these issues. Eight hours distributed over four weeks were devoted to lectures, a group dynamic on private project contracting, two seminars given by experts in rural public works bidding and a test on the most important legislative aspects on Public Sector Contracts.

According to the details displayed in Table 5.3, an introductory practical session was held to allow the students to become familiar with the interpretation of the specifications of a real bidding (0) in the context of a project about the repair of a sanitation network. All students adopted the role of a manager of a company interested in the preparation of the documents and budget demanded by the public institution for awarding projects. In this activity, students had to check the documents, legal terminology and economic calculations to bid for the public contract.

For the second session and following, the designed game aimed at experiencing the complete approach of preparation and awarding of public projects. The

Table 5.3 Time planning and student groups for the activities carried out in the subject of Engineering Projects.

Tasks	Time	Group
0. Reading and interpretation of the bidding documents corresponding to a project about the replacement and improvement of a sanitation network. Preparation of offers and work schedule of the project.	Week 1	All (62)
1. Team building and role assignment: company managers and public technicians (presidents-secretaries-chairpeople).	Week 2	All (62)
2. Personal characterization of the avatar, according to the chosen role.		
3. Exploration of the scenarios for planning the work and the representation of the professional situation.	Week 3	All (62)
4. Preparation of the legal and technical specifications by the group of technicians.		Teams of Public technicians
5. Preparation of the general administrative documentation to be presented by the companies.		Teams of Companies
6. Recording of scenes by the group of technicians in the virtual world.	Week 4	Teams of Public technicians
7. Preparation of economic offer and schedule of the construction work by companies.		Teams of Companies
8. Evaluation of the documents presented by the companies and award of the public contract.	Weeks 5-6	Teams of Public technicians
9. Recording of scenes by the members of the companies.		Teams of Companies
10. Awarding of prizes and projection of the best works.	Week 7	All (62)
Total (hours)	**31 h**	

project consisted of the replacement of a pipeline in a rural area. Three teams (of 5 to 6 students) played public employees and nine teams performed as managers of private companies (three companies for each public institution). Then, a tutored session to gain a handle on immersive worlds took place (1–2). The aim of this session was that the students became familiar with the role to be played as technicians of the public entity or company workers.

Next, each team of technicians worked simultaneously with three teams of companies. This design allowed for the interaction in the work of the teams and allowed for the cycle of preparation of bidding documents, preparation of bids and adjudication.

Thus, during sessions of the third week, the teams of technicians prepared the documentation of the public contract supervised by the teacher and the professionals, while the companies prepared the general administrative documentation usually demanded (tasks 3–5).

In the fourth week, the technicians prepared the scene and the script for recording the video in the virtual environment (6), while the teams of companies calculated the offers and the temporal schedule of the construction work (7). Finally, the public technicians evaluated the documentation and the offers and eventually awarded the contract. In parallel, the companies prepared the script and the staging of the bidding (8-9).

During the following month, the teacher prepared a detailed evaluation of the work delivered, whose feedback was sent to each team through the Moodle platform. This same platform was used both for the delivery of the work and for accessing to the work material of each practical session, as can

Details of the work: Replacement of general drainage pipe in the municipality Helion

The project consists of the installation of 1000 m of ductile iron pipe C40, buried in a trench 0.8 m wide and 1.20 m medium deep. It will be installed on a 10 cm thick sand bed and covered up to 10 cm above the pipe. Next, aggregates derived from the excavation to cover (0.60 m) will be selected and finally a 15 cm layer of concrete will be added where the hydraulic floor tiles will be supported.

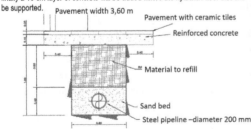

MEASUREMENTS AND MATERIAL: DETAILS

Figure 5.1 Samples of the material used and the result work of the students: layout, measurements and work units of the project of replacement of the pipeline and representation in the virtual world and works of technicians and companies available in the Moodle platform.

be seen in Figure 5.1, which comprises the composition of images that show the basic information of the tendered work, a sketch and details of the measurements and their recreation in the immersive world.

Didactics of Numbers, Operations and Measurement – elementary school teacher's degree studies

A total of 22 students participated in this course and agreed to participate in the project. The development of all activities took place over four weeks and a total of 18 hours (Table 5.4). The presentation of the project, the seminar with the teacher and the lectures for explanation of theoretical basics were carried out in sessions with all students. Activities associated with the use of ICTs were developed during sessions with small groups, where different teams were set up: 4 teams of teachers who designed a proposal of activities and 4 teams of teachers who evaluated these proposals.

Table 5.4 Time planning and student groups for the activities carried out in the subject of Didactics of Numbers, Operations and Measurement.

Tasks		Time	Group
0.	Presentation of the teaching innovation project, planning of activities linked to the project and orientation talk by the elementary school teacher on planning, design of activities and evaluation. Choice of contents on which to design the proposal and evaluation	Week 1	All (22)
1.	Team building, role assignment (teachers who design a proposal for activities, teachers who evaluate the proposals)		
2.	Familiarization with the immersive world, characterization of avatars and choice of work scenario.		
3.	Work on the proposal of activities according to the selected contents, choice and design of activities, planning.	Week 2	Team of Designers
4.	Work on the rubric for evaluation		Team of Evaluators
5.	Recording of group work meetings for the elaboration of didactic proposals.	Week 3	Team of Designers
6.	Evaluation of proposals		Team of Evaluators
7.	Recording of group work meetings for the evaluation of proposals		Team of Evaluation
8.	Video projections and project closure	Week 4	All (22)
Total (hours)		**18 h**	

The context of the activities chosen corresponded to the third issue of the course syllabus, dedicated to the didactics of natural numbers. The teaching of this topic was carried out during 9 hours of lectures, distributed over three weeks, with the intention of providing the fundamentals of the teaching-learning process of natural numbers, necessary for the development of the activity. Students had taken a course on planning activities in the previous semester.

As can be seen in Table 5.4, the activity began with an introductory session on the teaching innovation project, its fit with the practical section of the subject and the explanation carried out by the elementary school teacher, who summarized her experience in planning and designing activities (0). She also proposed the following list of contents, on which the activities of each group should be developed: (a) Additions with numbers up to 19, counting from the first addend; (b) Reading, writing and representation of tens; (c) Use of equivalences between tens and units; (d) Reading, writing, representation and decomposition up to 29; (e) Subtraction with numbers up to 10; (f) Resolution of addition and subtraction problems; (g) Interest in mathematically solving everyday situations of addition or subtraction. In the following session of the same week, the work teams were set up and roles were assigned (1). After that, contact was initiated with the immersive worlds and the handling and characterization of avatars (2). For this purpose, eight teams of 2 and 3 members each were established. Four teams acquired the role of designing a proposal of activities and the other four teams focused on the evaluation of these proposals.

In the second week, the members of design teams selected 2 or 3 items from the list proposed by the teacher and started with the elaboration of the activities, indicating resources to be used and time planning in the classroom (3). Team 1 worked on (a) Additions with numbers up to 19, counting from the first addend and (b) reading, writing and representation of the tens. Team 2 focused all its activities on (f) Solving addition and subtraction problems. For its part, team 3 developed activities around (a) Additions with numbers up to 19, counting from the first addend, (c) Use of equivalences between tens and units and (f) Resolution of addition and subtraction problems. Team 4 focused its proposal on (d) Reading, writing, representation and decomposition up to 29 and (f) Resolution of addition and subtraction problems. The four teams with the role of evaluators worked in the elaboration of a rubric constituted by different items and different levels of attainment of these items (4).

During week 3, teams with the role of proposal designers recorded coordination meetings among 'teachers' to establish the activities to be carried out on the selected content (5). Simultaneously, the rest of the teams began their evaluation task, making use of the ready-made rubric (6). Later on, the evaluation sessions of each assigned proposal were recorded (7). During this week, each team delivered the documents and videos generated by their own work. Finally, in the last week, sessions with all students were dedicated to the visualization of videos, the exchange of opinions and concerns between teachers and students and the closing of the project.

Results of the evaluation

Tables 5.5, 5.6 and 5.7 show the results of the questionnaires answered by the students in order to evaluate their learning experiences. All questionnaires were printed out, and students were voluntarily asked to fill them out.

Sociology and Forest Policy – forestry engineering degree studies

For the course 'Sociology and Forest Policy', although 29 students participated in the project, only 28 and 24 completed the pre- and post-tests, respectively. Results from this course showed that both the degree of confidence (section i) and the degree of success (section iv) in carrying out the proposed tasks, improved significantly ($P<0.05$), as shown in Table 5.5.

Engineering Projects – agricultural engineering degree studies

In this case, although 62 students participated in the project, only 31 and 32 completed the pre- and post-tests, respectively. Results from this course showed that only the degree of confidence (section i) for the performance of the proposed tasks improved significantly ($P<0.05$) as can be seen in Table 5.6. The motivation sections reached, before and after the experience, rates close to 76%, the degree of anxiety associated was about 39% and the degree of success expected was close to 77%. Regardless of the figures, the work produced by the students was considered excellent, with expressed congratulations from the participating professionals. This is especially notable when compared to the deliveries of sheets and offers from previous years. The improvement of the material provided to the students (by the professionals and adapted by the teacher) and the work schedule (class hours dedicated to the activity have been doubled) have been the main factors that contribute to the improvement of learning.

Didactics of Numbers, Operations and Measurement – elementary school teacher's degree studies

In this course, although 22 students participated in the project, only 20 and 19 completed the pre- and post-tests, respectively. In this case, in the four

Table 5.5 Descriptive statistics associated with the degree of confidence and degree of success for the accomplishment of tasks in the subject of Sociology and Forest Policy.

Sociology and Forest Policy – Planning a Natural Park	Pre (n = 28)		Post (n=24)	
i) Please, evaluate your degree of confidence to perform the following tasks, according to your current abilities. Use a scale from 0 to 100	M	Sd	M	Dd
1. Characterising a Natural Park with a view to its subsequent planning (describe the main aspects).	53.57	24.22	79.6	19.4
2. Analysing a Natural Park on the basis of its weaknesses, threats, strengths and opportunities (SWOT matrix)	58.93	27.53	82.1	17.7
3. Identifying and interpreting the main problems and needs of a Natural Park (elaboration of a problem tree).	54.64	27.69	81.3	16.5
4. Identifying objectives that respond to the needs of a Natural Park (elaboration of an objective tree).	51.43	24.30	80.8	16.7
5. Designing and analysing strategies or lines of action to achieve a main objective.	46.43	27.78	82.5	15.9
6. Developing a planning matrix based on the logical framework	38.93	26.01	76.7	16.1
7. Establishing a productive discussion under a specific role, presenting arguments and preparing a joint proposal.	56.79	32.78	82.5	18.2
8. Preparing a professional document, making a presentation to an expert audience.	43.70	30.27	80.0	19.1
ii) Please, evaluate the degree of success you would reach performing the following tasks. Use a scale from 0 to 100				
1. Characterising a Natural Park with a view to its subsequent planning (describe the main aspects).	65.36	20.09	79.17	16.92
2. Analysing a Natural Park on the basis of its weaknesses, threats, strengths and opportunities (SWOT matrix)	67.14	22.09	82.08	18.65
3. Identifying and interpreting the main problems and needs of a Natural Park (elaboration of a problem tree).	65.36	21.17	82.08	18.65
4. Identifying objectives that respond to the needs of a Natural Park (elaboration of an objective tree).	65.00	21.34	81.25	17.52
5. Designing and analysing strategies or lines of action to achieve a main objective.	63.21	19.26	79.58	16.01
6. Developing a planning matrix based on the logical framework	60.36	20.99	78.33	17.61
7. Establishing a productive discussion under a specific role, presenting arguments and preparing a joint proposal.	69.64	24.72	84.58	18.17
8. Preparing a professional document, making a presentation to an expert audience.	67.14	25.94	82.92	19.44

'M' refers to Mean; 'Sd' refers to Standard Deviation.

Table 5.6 Descriptive statistics associated with the degree of confidence for the accomplishment of tasks in the subject of Engineering Projects.

Engineering Projects – Bidding	Pre (n=31)		Post (n=32)	
i) Please, evaluate your degree of confidence to perform the following tasks, according to your current abilities. Use a scale from 0 to 100	M	Sd	M	Sd
1. Reading and interpreting the content of the economic and administrative specifications for a public bidding.	67.4	15.7	78.8	13.6
2. Identifying the design needs and economic constraints associated with work on a bidding.	68.1	16.4	74.4	15.0
3. Investigating what type of documentation should be included in the bidding of a work.	69.7	16.0	77.5	17.4
4. Developing appropriate strategies according to the role in the bidding (technicians and companies).	67.1	17.4	75.0	13.2
5. Identifying the key items for the preparation of an adequate offer.	68.1	16.6	76.3	14.1
6. Identifying the key items to proceed with the award.	68.4	18.5	76.6	14.3

'M' refers to Mean; 'Sd' refers to Standard Deviation.

Table 5.7 Descriptive statistics associated with the degree of confidence for the accomplishment of tasks in the subject of Didactics of Numbers, Operations and Measurements.

Didactics of Numbers, Operations and Measurement – Proposal of activities	Pre (n=20)		Post (n=19)	
Please, evaluate your degree of confidence to perform the following tasks, according to your current abilities. Use a scale from 0 to 100	M	Sd	M	Sd
1. Knowing and knowing how to apply the basic mathematical concepts that make up the Primary Education curriculum, referring to blocks of Numbers, Operations and Measurement.	66.0	12.3	70.0	11.5
2. Implementing teaching and learning processes associated with the transmission of knowledge of Numbers, Operations and Measurement.	62.5	12.1	65.8	13.0
3. Knowing and incorporating resources and materials of didactic use for the teaching and learning of numerical operations and measurement.	61.5	15.0	67.4	14.5
4. Analysing and evaluating the curricular content of activities and exercises proposed in the Primary Education Mathematics textbooks.	60.0	11.2	64.7	13.9
5. Organizing curricular contents and defining methods and criteria of evaluation for the educational processes linked to the knowledge of Numbers, Operations and Measurement in Primary Education.	60.0	13.4	64.7	16.5

'M' refers to Mean; 'Sd' refers to Standard Deviation.

aspects evaluated, improvements were registered between the pre-test and the post-test but none of them became significant (P<0.05). Table 5.7 shows the results obtained for the degree of confidence.

Conclusion

This chapter shows an interdisciplinary teaching proposal with a main goal of the development of students' professional competencies. Such competencies are crucial for the education of reflective engineers and elementary teachers, who are intended to tackle the challenges of the knowledge society in which we are immersed. Taking advantage of virtual reality tools, such as immersive worlds, allowed implementing three teaching experiences. These facilitated not only the students' first insight in their future responsibilities, but also the peer interactions in higher education.

The work done by students during these experiences went beyond solving the usual learning tasks. Participants provided ideas and proposals that are valuable for carrying out forthcoming projects. In addition to the development of professional skills, students exhibited creativity in their videos, which leads one to believe they enjoyed the experience. Moreover, results from evaluations indicated that the project had a positive impact on their confidence in carrying out complex professional tasks. This effect was shown to be significant in some cases.

Related to the teaching and external professional agents, these experiences contributed to building an interdisciplinary working group between university lecturers and professionals. As a consequence, a shared space was created for mutual enrichment and the generation of new projects. Likewise, using immersive worlds has been integrated as part of the different courses, and new development paths are being explored to improve the learning experience.

Acknowledgments

This work was partially supported by the University of Cordoba (Teaching Innovation call 2017–2018). Authors would especially like to thank Subbética Ecológica, Francisco J. Taguas Ruiz, Luis Moya and Mª Teresa García, who collaborated as the external agents providing their help, seminars and documentation. Authors also appreciate the valuable work carried out by the students of the courses 'Sociology and Forest Policy' of the forestry engineering degree studies, 'Engineering Projects' of the agricultural engineering degree studies, and 'Didactics of Numbers, Operations and Measurement' of the elementary school teacher's degree studies.

References

Andersson, N., & Andersson, P. (2010). Teaching professional engineering skills - industry participation in realistic role play simulation, In *Proceedings of the 6th CDIO Conference*. Montréal: École Polytechnique de Montréal.

Baker, S. C., Wentz, R. K., & Woods, M. M. (2009). Using virtual worlds in education: Second life® as an educational tool. *Teaching of Psychology, 36*(1), 59–64. doi:10.1080/00986280802529079

Bouras, C., & Tsiatsos, T. (2006). Educational virtual environments: Design rationale and architecture. *Multimedia Tools and Applications, 29*(2), 153–173.

Carberry, A. R., Lee, A. S., & Ohland, M. W. (2010). Measuring engineering design self-efficacy. *Journal of Engineering Education, 99*(1), 71–79.

Deshpande, A. A., & Huang, S. H. (2011). Simulation games in engineering education: A state-of-the-art review. *Computer Application in Engineering Education 2011, 19*(3), 399–410.

Gisbert, M., Esteve, V., & Camacho, M. (2011). Delve into the deep: Learning potential in Metaverses and 3D worlds. *eLearning Papers, 25*, 1–8.

Grunwald, S., & Barak, P. (2001). The use of VRML for virtual soil landscape modeling. *Systems Analysis, Modelling, Simulation, 41*, 755–777.

Kickmeier-Rust, M. D., Bull, S., & Meissl-Egghart, G. (2014). Collaborative language learning in immersive virtual worlds: Competence-based formative feedback and open learner modeling. *International Journal of Serious Games, 1*(2), 67–74.

Lorenzo, C. M., Sicilia, M. A., & Sánchez, S. (2012). Studying the effectiveness of multi-user immersive environments for collaborative evaluation tasks. *Computers & Education 2012, 59*, 1361–1376.

Mamo, M., Namuth-Covert, D., Guru, A., Nugent, G., Phillips, L., Sandall, L., ... McCallister, D. (2011). Avatars go to class: A virtual environment soil science activity. *Journal of Natural Resources and Life Sciences Education, 40*, 114–121.

Mathers, N., Goktogen, A., Rankin, J., & Anderson, M. (2012). Robotic mission to Mars: Hands-on, minds-on, web-based learning. *Acta Astronautica, 80*, 124–131.

Ohland, M. W., Frillman, S. A., Zhang, G., &Miller, T. K., III. (2004). NC state's engineering entrepreneurs program in the context of US entrepreneurship programs. In *Education that works: The National Collegiate Inventors and Innovators Alliance (NCIIA) 8th Annual Meeting* (pp. 155–164). San Jose, CA.

Redel, M. D., Castillo, C., Aguilar, C., Polo, M. J., & Taguas, E. V. (2014). Development of a virtual tool for learning basic organization and planning in rural engineering projects. *European Journal of Engineering Education, 39*(5), 507–517.

Rodríguez-Donaire, S., & Amante, B. (2012). Collaborative environments, a way to improve quality in higher education. *Procedia – Social and Behavioral Sciences, 46*, 875–884.

Sáiz-Manzanares, J., Montero-García, E. L., González-Fernández, E., Aguilar-Romero, M. J., & Peláez-Vara, F. (2010). An analysis of the meta-cognitive approach and support for information skills with industrial engineering students. Ways to the convergence of European higher education. In *Proceedings of the 1st International Conference on European Transnational Education (ICEUTE 2010)* (pp. 18–25). Burgos (Spain): University of Burgos.

Sancho, P., Moreno-Ger, P., Fuentes-Fernández, R., & Fernández-Manjón, B. (2009). Adaptive role playing games: An immersive approach for problem based learning. *Educational Technology & Society*, 2009, *12*(4), 110–124.

Schmorrow, D. D. (2009). Why virtual?*Theoretical Issues in Ergonomics Science*, *10*(3), 279–282.

Sumners, C., Reiff, P., & Weber, W. (2008). Learning in an immersive digital theater. *Advances in Space Research*, *42*, 1848–1854.

Taguas, E. V., Falconer, R., & Tarquis, A. M. (2014). Engineering education on geosciences in a changing world.*European Journal of Engineering Education*,*39*(5), 463–466.

Yakovleva, N. O., & Yakovlev, E. V. (2014). Interactive teaching methods in contemporary higher education. *Pacific Science Review*, *16*(2), 75–80.

Chapter 6

Virtual reality and augmented reality in educational programs

Tomas Blazauskas and Daina Gudoniene

Introduction

Traditional educational programs are delivered by using video, text and a virtual learning environment, but the next generation is engaged in using virtual reality (VR) and augmented reality (AR) in education, which might increase engagement and effectiveness. Technological advancements and mobile devices opened new ways for educators to use VR and AR in practice and ensure successful learning. Westlake (2019) indicated that the new generation of students is technology savvy with a high knowledge of and interest in social media, mobile technologies and strategy games. Ibáñez and Delgado-Kloos (2018) claim that some of the media characteristics of AR, namely, sensory immersion, navigation and manipulation, seem to work as promoters of positive emotions while learning and help to achieve more efficiency and better learning outcomes. Barrow, Forker, Sands, O'Hare, and Hurst (2019) note that AR has the opportunity to be a challengeable technology in the delivery of educational materials at all levels, from public outreach activities to expert level teaching at undergraduate and postgraduate levels.

In this chapter, the method of literature review is employed to find out the key points of using VR and AR in educational programs. The authors will provide the most popular examples for using VR and AR in medicine, sport, military and history by using the following methods: simulations, games, staging and exercises related to learners' engagement. Expert evaluation method was selected to evaluate the methods mentioned, and conclusions were provided by reviewing the effectiveness of the mentioned methods and ideas related to VR and AR in educational programs.

Literature review

There is a lot of research about VR and AR in education. However, not much is related to VR and AR relating to the effectiveness of mental and physical educational.

Dunleavy and Dede (2014) claim that AR is primarily aligned with situated and constructivist learning theory, as it positions the learner within a real-world physical and social context while guiding, scaffolding and facilitating participatory as well as such metacognitive learning processes as authentic inquiry, active observation, peer coaching, reciprocal teaching and legitimate peripheral participation with multiple modes of representation.

Kim, Park, Lee, Yuk, and Lee (2001) state that the technological features of VR and simulations are highly interactive and include a computer-based multimedia environment in which the user becomes the participant in a computer-generated world. The key feature of VR is real-time interactivity in which the computer is able to detect user input and instantaneously modify the virtual world in accordance with user interactions.

Garrett, Anthony, and Jackson (2018) indicate some health educational programs where one of the ways to learn is through structured mobile learning (or 'm-learning') that offers a constructivist approach in which educators can provide AR activities using heuristic learning strategies. This provides students with alternative ways to engage with content and thereby promotes more active learning and enhancing the learning experience.

Kamarainen et al. (2018) discuss how augmentation allows students to 'see the unseen' in concepts such as photosynthesis and respiration as well as to apply the causal reasoning patterns that they learned about in the classroom while using an inquiry-based immersive virtual environment.

Masmuzidin and Aziz (2018) indicate how the features of the technology enable students to: (1) learn content in 3D perspectives, (2) engage in ubiquitous, collaborative and situated learning, (3) identification of learners' senses of presence, immediacy and immersion, (4) visualize the invisible and (5) bridge formal and informal learning. With these features, AR has created a new way of learning and making the learning experience more fun and engaging. One of the biggest advantages of such technology can be seen from the perspective of motivation, especially in terms of: (1) fun, interest and enjoyment; (2) engagement; (3) satisfaction; (4) willingness to learn; (5) positive attitude; (6) attention and (7) level of confidence.

The existing research reveals that the value of VR and AR is increasing especially because of the improvements in computational power and advances in visual and haptic display technologies. Virtual surgical environments can now offer potential benefits for surgical training, planning and rehearsal in a safe, simulated setting.

Ibáñez and Delgado-Kloos (2018) in their systematic review on AR for Science, Technology, Engineering and Mathematics (STEM) learning identified the general characteristics of AR applications in terms of building tools, type of application and AR features included. They also identified the science domain, educational level and educational context as well as building tools, AR features, type of activity (e.g. simulation, game and exploration) and assets (e.g. text, images, 3D model, animation, video, 3D objects and audio).

Simulation allows learners to see a situation in a safe way and thus is usually used to gain new skills in professions that include risks, especially where the risk could become an obstacle for achieving the desired learning goals. Scholars recognize that the design and implementation of an immersive VR surgical simulator requires expert knowledge from many disciplines.

Gunn, Jones, Bridge, Rowntree, and Nissen (2018) found that VR simulation learning tools facilitated technical skill acquisition equal to or slightly better than traditional laboratory training. Many authors (Fisher et al., 2018, Hartney et al., 2019, Mirghani et al., 2018) analysed simulation based on VR in medicine. Fire sector professional training is also helped by simulation in VR: Many authors (Rossler et al., 2019, Shen et al., 2018, Cakiroglu & Gokoglu, 2019, Han et al., 2018) analysed Virtual Reality Simulation of Fire Control and the effectiveness of simulation in VR for fire sector professional training. Fire-training simulators provide the general public as well as inexperienced firefighters or commanders with wide-ranging second-hand experience so that they can make prompt decisions together with safe and organized responses in actual fire situations.

Simulation scenarios are used as a teaching strategy complementing the existing curriculum. They have been found to be effective in meeting learning objectives. Games are popular means among young learners, who grew up in the technology age and are engaged in learning STEAM subjects. A competitive gaming approach conducted in a real-world field trip found that elementary students assigned to the gaming approach outperformed students in the non-gaming approach. The research of Pallavicini et al. (2019) shows effectiveness in the assessment of the executive functions using a new type of interactive content, VR games, which combine the advantages of VR with those of commercial video games.

Wang et al. (2018) concluded that the VR immersive learning mechanism designed in their research can effectively trigger the motivation of learners to gain new knowledge and to improve learning results.

Another important aspect of VR and AR is engagement. Yoip et al. (2019) discuss improving the quality of teaching and learning in classes by using AR videos. They conducted a study on engagement, which contributes to enhancing students' learning experience and increasing their understanding of complex issues. An AR mobile application (i.e. an app) in which a threading task was carried out was incorporated into a sewing workshop to facilitate better learning relative to a conventional approach. All educational games and videos that can be used in educational programs can positively affect the learning process related to gaining new skills. The main findings of study say that normal videos may achieve similar outcomes; the use of AR videos definitely provided convenience to students in learning; thus, the advantages of the pedagogical design should not be neglected. The study focused on the evaluation of an AR application in education and showcased the pedagogical design. However, effectiveness depends on the training program's aims, objectives and possibility to use mental and mental-physical methods.

Mental and physical methods of using VR and AR in educational programs

In this chapter, the authors discuss VR and AR are related to the learners' mental and physical interactions based on VR technologies and educational approach. VR merges physical and digital worlds in real time. AR is related to tracking information from the physical world. Factors such as the learners' involvement, inclusion and engagement are very important in the success of the educational process. The participants of the educational process also have different roles and can work in different ways (i.e. as single students or teams that have different tasks and exercises).

This chapter discusses several methods for using VR and AR in education that engage the learners to participate in the different educational programs: virtual inclusion and participation, simulations, mind-fight, competition, games, physical tasks and exercises and tasks that include events and reconstructions of events (Figure 6.1).

The practical implementation of VR and AR in education stems from the needs of the learners and can be integrated into different educational programs.

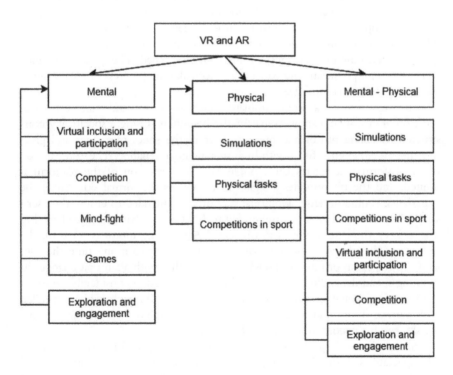

Figure 6.1 Methods for using VR and AR in education.

Below the authors provide an experience of the Virtual Reality Technologies Laboratory at Kaunas University of Technology, Lithuania, where VR projects are developed and integrated into educational programs (https://vimeo.com/ktuvrlab). The university staff work close with the teachers in Lithuania and the need for the VR projects is expressed by the teachers interested in having these items in educational programs. The laboratory works closely with the business sector by implementing many business orders. However, some examples provided below are directly 'for fun' (Cherniack, 2011) (i.e. to engage learners at the start of some longer or deeper educational program).

Mental-physical educational method in VR and AR

Mental-physical educational method based on simulation

Mental-Physical educational based on simulation is one of the possible educational activities connected to VR. One of the practical examples is Abili VR based on physical simulation, used for health. Abili VR is a gamified VR application for a balancing platform. The platform is used for various training exercises and rehabilitation. In the game, the player is placed on top of a wooden log in a river. The player's main objective is to try to avoid as many logs flowing towards him/her as possible. The player moves the log that s/he is standing on by simply providing an impulse to the platform towards the left or right side, depending on where the player wants to move. The player can also change the difficulty of the game by increasing or decreasing the incoming log speed. The game is designed to help to train physicians and patients and to make the progress in rehabilitation by gaining skills to control deep muscles.

Activities based on a skiing simulator, such as Snow Land, can be used in sport programs or in a snow arena for the beginners. Using a specifically constructed balancing platform it puts the user in the shoes of a skier and gives him/her an experience filled with high speeds and adrenaline. The construction has a platform that rotates on a single axis. The rotation of the platform is limited, and the tilt provides a signal that controls the virtual skis. Since the experience is quite intense, additional supports are included to ensure the user's safety. The user is always recommended to hold onto a bar and spread his/her legs to keep the base of the platform stable. A vibrating motor is fitted on the bottom of the platform and a signal to vibrate is sent to it any time the user lands from a jump or hits an obstacle. This, together with a fan that changes its spinning speed depending on the speed of the skis, adds a considerable amount of immersion. The experience takes the user to a long ski track, which is riddled with various jumps and obstacles. The skier must avoid these obstacles while the skis reach a maximum speed of 144 km/h.

An experimental spectator mode was also developed for this application. The spectator sees the skier's progress throughout the track from various fixed and dynamic angles. The goal of this spectator mode is to provide a view of the experience to people who have not yet experienced the simulator without showing the first-person view, which could spoil the first-hand experience.

Mental-physical method of using VR in rowing competitions

VR is used in rowing competitions in educational programs at sport schools. The aim was to design an exercise machine as a natural input device for a VR application. Concept 2 rowing erg was chosen as such a device. The user's goal in the application is to reach the finish line in a 250-meter long track. The user can do this alone or against other users that are connected locally. The virtual environment is modelled by replicating a Lithuanian town of Trakai, which is the biggest base for such water sport. It is also a place where a lot of academic rowing events are organized. Both the practical activities and educational purposes are effective. VR assures accuracy and physical relevance for the learning process.

Physical method of VR for virtual paragliding

An educational program based on VR is presented at the aviation museum. Virtual paragliding's construction has two inputs: the tilt of the paraglider harness and the pulling force of left and right brake handles. Such an amount of control immerses the user and provides him/her with a realistic feel of the paraglider. Moreover, immersion is achieved by using a fan to simulate the ambient wind that is felt when paragliding. The speed of the fan changes depending on the speed of the virtual paraglider.

Users experience paragliding above a virtual recreation of the student campus of Kaunas University of Technology. As the user is placed high above the ground and can see a lot of the area, further surroundings of the student campus had to be also modelled. A tremendous effort was made to realistically convey the landscape and all the main buildings of the student campus, including the Santaka Valley, the Design Faculty and the Electronics Hall. The total area covered by the virtual environment is 4 km^2.

Physical exercises based on VR for shooting practices

In general, educational exercises based on VR can be used for military training. Shooter games for VR are no longer an innovation. Typically, these games use standard VR input devices called motion controllers. The controllers allow the player to control the flow of the game, to pick up and shoot various weapons as well as to interact with the rest of the environment. However, such experience lacks the feeling of holding a real weapon in one's hands.

Gunplay VR was an attempt to bring a 'real' gun into VR. This required a replica of the desired gun and its photo-realistic 3D model, a Vive Tracker and some small tinkering. In the current implementation, a Vive Tracker was fitted onto an airsoft replica of an SR–13 assault rifle with a 3D printed mount. The pogo pins on the Vive Tracker were wired to the weapon's trigger to synchronize it with the virtual trigger of the rifle. Finally, a model was prepared to bring it all together in VR.

The result is interesting for learners and a highly immersive VR experience. The real and the virtual rifles match perfectly, the weight and the grip make users feel like they are really holding guns and pulling triggers. Currently, the system including scenario creation tools for military educators is being developed for military training.

Mental educational method of using VR and AR

Exercises related to history educational programs based on VR

One use of AR is for practical exercises for learning history through participation in the events of a particular time. My Street Story 360 (mental method) is presented at Vincas Kudirka Library and is based on VR. The purpose of this solution is to present Kaunas district history by using 360 panorama images taken by the participants of the project. Around 100 high-quality panorama pictures were taken, mostly in the forts of Kaunas' fortress. These panoramic images were used to create the four following products: virtual tour around the district, the web-based game, the game for Windows operating system and the VR game to be used on the Oculus platform devices (see Figure 6.2).

These products are exhibited and used in educational programs at the library. The resources were used for scientific research as well. The educational

Figure 6.2 An example of the educational game based on VR.

game (a cropped version of the game designed for a library) was created to test the impact of immersive learning. The aim of the game is to find historical objects scattered around real environments. In order to proceed a learner has to read information and find out the right answers to the questions that appear at certain moments. Some results were published in the article 'Virtual reality in education: new ways to learn'.

Mental method in educational programs based on AR is used for engagement of learners

The mental method following is used to gain new skills in history and virtually participate in an event. The method presents historical airplanes in AR, and they are exhibited in Vytautas the Great War Museum and Lithuanian Air Forces. The purpose of this application is to present historical Lithuanian airplanes created in independent Lithuania during the period between the two world wars (i.e. 1919–1939). The application contains six historical airplanes (ANBO I, ANBO IV, ANBO VII, DOBI I, DOBI II, DOBI III), the legendary airplane 'Lituanica' and the first Lithuanian tank 'Slibinas'.

By using this application, one can place these vehicles on the ground and inspect them. Some vehicles are interactive: one can start the engine of the airplane or make the tank shoot. All vehicles can be scaled from the original size to the ratio 1:16. One can also take a photo with people standing beside the historical vehicles in order to share it on social networks. The application can be used on Android and iOS devices (see Figure 6.3).

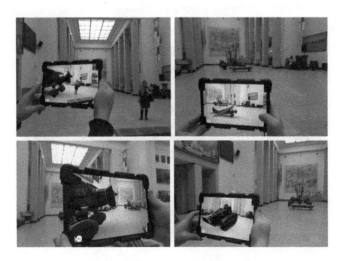

Figure 6.3 Mental method of learning history based on AR.

The mental educational method based on simulation

The simulation method is based on 3D objects and environments that deliver immersive and engaging learning experiences. The Battle of Salakas VR historical game is exhibited in Vytautas the Great War Museum. Its purpose is to depict the battle of Salakas from the first person point of view and to allow the user to familiarize him/herself with a real weapon that was actually used in that battle. It makes use of the HTC Vive system and its trackers as well as a replica of the Mauser firearm, which serves as the controller. The VR game depicts the battle scene in which the Lithuanian military defended a city against advancing enemies. The player is located in the ruins of a destroyed house and endeavours not to allow advancing enemies to get close. The game finishes after the player fails to protect the building or when one succeeds to protect it for 5 minutes. It is exhibited as part of a World War I and independence battles exhibition where a big painting of the Salakas battle and historical firearms are located.

Another example related to the mental educational based on VR is provided at the history learning program and suggests a flight over the Atlantic in the airplane 'Lituanica'. It is an educational game with many different activities allowing learners to participate in a team or individually. It engages learners to learn and read more about the event. The game is exhibited at Vytautas the Great War Museum. It covers a story of two Lithuanian pilots, Steponas Darius and Stasys Girėnas. In 1933, they set out to fly over the Atlantic Ocean in a modified plane they called 'Lituanica'. They took off in New York and sadly met their tragic fate right before reaching their final destination – landing in the city of Kaunas (Figure 6.4).

Figure 6.4 A wreckage of the plane depicted in a game.

Many exercises related to the historical event are provided to the learners, who must follow the flight and do the intended educational exercises (Figure 6.5). These educational exercises include searching information in the real environment. Figure 6.4 shows a real situation with wreckage of the airplane and Figure 6.5 shows exhibited objects by inspecting airplane in AR and solving the tasks mentally.

A game consists of 9 mini-games. Each mini-game is assessed by points collected at the end of the game. This game can be played by teams or individuals competing with each other.

The mental method related to engagement

Staging and participation in real events by using VR allow the learners to acquire new skills. An additional history learning example gives learners the possibility of participating in the Battle of Saule using a 'live picture' movie. 'Live' means that the point of view of the battle changes according to the position of the viewer.

The Battle of Radviliskis, based on a VR solution, is another example of a history educational program related to the mental method and engagement. This VR movie depicts one of the main independence battles fought in Radviliskis city. The battle was fought against numerous Bermontian forces, which were located in the city. This battle raged for several days. Bermontians turned mills into strongholds. During the battle, mills changed hands several times. The solution makes use of the VR systems supporting 6 degrees of freedom (6DoF) tracking. The person who watches the movie in VR can relive a scene of capturing a mill by the Lithuanian military forces. The person can walk around on the battlefield, but the movie is not interactive.

Figure 6.5 Real historical objects to drag and drop in a game.

Engagement into educational programs by using VR and AR

Scientific research (Allcoat & von Mühlenen, 2018, Collins et al., 2018, Reger et al., 2019) identifies engagement as the major factor involving learners in educational programs and inviting them to learn more not only in the VR environment. It is also mentioned by many scholars that VR and AR engage learners to learn more about different topics after participation in the VR experiences.

One of the examples of how to engage participants in knowing more about aircraft is an Anti-aircraft shooting game based on VR that is exhibited at Vytautas the Great War Museum. The purpose of this VR game is to showcase WW I anti-aircraft weapons that are exhibited nearby. The player is located in the trenches and fires an anti-aircraft gun. One must shoot enemy targets and avoid hitting friendly aircraft and deliverables. The game is suitable for Samsung Gear VR and compatible devices (Oculus Go and similar).

Another example is virtual tour-based Vehicles of Lithuanian Armed Forces that can be presented to the young learners at Vytautas the Great War Museum. Its aim is to present the vehicles that are now used in the Lithuanian armed forces. The technology includes a virtual tour for the web, a virtual tour for VR (Oculus platform) and a 3D shooting game created for VR (Oculus platform). Virtual tour (for both web and VR) includes the M113 armoured personnel carrier, a helicopter and a military airplane (Spartan). High-quality panoramic images were taken using stereoscopic photography so that the depth is sensible when viewing in VR application. A virtual tour for the web is accessible here at www.virtualivizija.lt/projek tai/muziejus/. The 3D VR game depicts a present-day training session. The environment is modelled to be a generic shooting range for training. The player shoots from an M3 Browning machine gun mounted on an M113 armorer personnel carrier. The game turned out to be very successful. Its mobility allows the museum to take it on various trips. Moreover, the look and feel of the game as well as the ability to compete for the highest score are attractive both to young learners and adults.

Conclusions

There are still many discussions on the effectiveness of the implemented VR- and AR-based mental and physical methods in educational programs. Looking to the future of educational content based on VR, we should draw attention to the application of technologies in context. The main criteria for the evaluation of the mental and physical methods in education are effectiveness and functionality. However, educational games should not be based just on mental exercises. Educational games mixed with practical and physical exercises are functionally more effective and engaging.

The literature analysis of the existing methods in VR and AR showed the new ways of using VR and AR in educational programs and let the authors identify different mental and physical methods as well as learning forms. The provided VR examples can be integrated into school programs and used in educational environments like museums, sport schools and schools. The presented games can be integrated into the virtual learning environments like Moodle, where learners can have communication and collaboration tools. Moreover, they can be used for learning process of the groups and supported online.

Acknowledgment

The authors are thankful to the Virtual Reality Technologies Laboratory at Kaunas University of Technology for the ideas related with VR and AR implementation into educational process (https://vimeo.com/ktuvrlab).

References

Allcoat, D., & von Mühlenen, A. (2018). Learning in virtual reality: Effects on performance, emotion and engagement. *Research in Learning Technology, 26*, 9.

Barrow, J., Forker, C., Sands, A., O'Hare, D., & Hurst, W. (2019, March). Augmented reality for enhancing life science education. In W. Hurst, J. Moores, & V. Brun (Eds.), *VISUAL 2019-The Fourth International Conference on Applications and Systems of Visual Paradigms* (pp. 7–12). Rome, Italy.

Çakiroğlu, Ü., & Gökoğlu, S. (2019). Development of fire safety behavioural skills via virtual reality. *Computers & Education, 133*, 56–68.

Cherniack, E. P. (2011). Not just fun and games: Applications of virtual reality in the identification and rehabilitation of cognitive disorders of the elderly. *Disability and Rehabilitation: Assistive Technology, 6*(4), 283–289.

Collins, M. K., Ding, V. Y., Ball, R. L., Dolce, D. L., Henderson, J. M., & Halpern, C. H. (2018). Novel application of virtual reality in patient engagement for deep brain stimulation: A pilot study. *Brain Stimulation: Basic, Translational, and Clinical Research in Neuromodulation, 11*(4), 935–937.

Dunleavy, M., & Dede, C. (2014). Augmented reality teaching and learning. In *Handbook of research on educational communications and technology* (pp. 735–745). New York, NY: Springer.

Fisher, N., Nesichi, L., Negrin, E., Zaslavski, M., & Slepnev, S. (2018). U.S. Patent Application No. 15/720143.

Garrett, B. M., Anthony, J., & Jackson, C. (2018). Using mobile augmented reality to enhance health professional practice education. *Current Issues in Emerging eLearning, 4*(1), 10.

Gunn, T., Jones, L., Bridge, P., Rowntree, P., & Nissen, L. (2018). The use of virtual reality simulation to improve technical skill in the undergraduate medical imaging student. *Interactive Learning Environments, 26*(5), 613–620.

Han, Y., Liu, H., Tian, Y., Chen, Z., & Nie, Z. (2018, November). Virtual reality oriented modeling and simulation of water-dropping from helicopter. In *Proceedings of the 2018 International Conference on Artificial Intelligence and Virtual Reality* (pp. 24–29). ACM.

Hartney, J. H., Rosenthal, S. N., Kirkpatrick, A. M., Skinner, J. M., Hughes, J., & Orlosky, J. (2019, March). Revisiting virtual reality for practical use in therapy: Patient satisfaction in outpatient rehabilitation. In *2019 IEEE Conference on Virtual Reality and 3D User Interfaces (VR)* (pp. 960–961). IEEE.

Ibáñez, M. B., & Delgado-Kloos, C. (2018). Augmented reality for STEM learning: A systematic review. *Computers & Education, 123*, 109–123.

Kamarainen, A. M., Thompson, M., Metcalf, S. J., Grotzer, T. A., Tutwiler, M. S., & Dede, C. (2018, June). Prompting connections between content and context: Blending immersive virtual environments and augmented reality for environmental science learning. In *International Conference on Immersive Learning* (pp. 36–54). Cham: Springer.

Kim, J. H., Park, S. T., Lee, H., Yuk, K. C., & Lee, H. (2001). Virtual reality simulations in physics education. *Interactive Multimedia Electronic Journal of Computer-Enhanced Learning, 3*(2).

Masmuzidin, M. Z., & Aziz, N. A. A. (2018). The current trends of augmented reality in early childhood education. *The International Journal of Multimedia & Its Applications (IJMA), 10*(6), 47.

Mirghani, I., Mushtaq, F., Allsop, M. J., Al-Saud, L. M., Tickhill, N., Potter, C., … Manogue, M. (2018). Capturing differences in dental training using a virtual reality simulator. *European Journal of Dental Education, 22*(1), 67–71.

Pallavicini, F., Pepe, A., & Minissi, M. E. (2019). Gaming in Virtual Reality: What Changes in Terms of Usability, Emotional Response and Sense of Presence Compared to Non-Immersive Video Games?. *Simulation & Gaming, 50*(2), 136–159.

Reger, G. M., Smolenski, D., Norr, A., Katz, A., Buck, B., & Rothbaum, B. O. (2019). Does virtual reality increase emotional engagement during exposure for PTSD? Subjective distress during prolonged and virtual reality exposure therapy. *Journal of Anxiety Disorders, 61*, 75–81.

Rossler, K. L., Sankaranarayanan, G., & Duvall, A. (2019). Acquisition of fire safety knowledge and skills with virtual reality simulation. *Nurse Educator, 44*(2), 88–92.

Shen, B., Liu, Y., & Cai, G. (2018, August). Message transfer in virtual reality simulation of fire control. In *2018 3rd International Conference on Control, Automation and Artificial Intelligence (CAAI 2018)*. Atlantis Press.

Wang, P., Wu, P., Wang, J., Chi, H. L., & Wang, X. (2018). A critical review of the use of virtual reality in construction engineering education and training. *International journal of environmental research and public health, 15*(6), 1204.

Westlake, J. (2019). Exploring the potential of using augmented reality and virtual reality for STEM education. In *Learning Technology for Education Challenges: 8th International Workshop, LTEC 2019*, July 15–18, 2019, Proceedings (p. 36). Zamora, Spain: Springer.

Yip, J., Wong, S. H., Yick, K. L., Chan, K., & Wong, K. H. (2019). Improving quality of teaching and learning in classes by using augmented reality video. *Computers & Education, 128*, 88–101.

Chapter 7

An exploration of the impact of augmented and Virtual Reality within compulsory education

Oli Howson

Introduction

First, a caveat: The author has experience within the UK educational system and while many of the concerns and suggestions noted within this chapter will have international application, the investigation is framed within the UK.

Teachers hate buzzwords (Secret Teacher, 2014) and it is the author's experience that buzzwords will often be ignored at every opportunity, but there is one inescapable buzzword – impact. The Office for Standards in Education (Ofsted) themselves see the phrase impact as being synonymous with curriculum quality (Ofsted, 2018). When questioning what impact an action has upon a learner, we are questioning what change we are bringing to that learner. Some read this as 'Can I hold you to account; is what you are doing measurable?' (Burton, 2018). It is a reality that if tangible, positive impact upon final results can be shown then a new technology, methodology or pedagogy is more likely to be taken on board by senior leaders.

In this chapter we will explore what evidence there is of measurable impact upon learning when using augmented, virtual or mixed reality – what we will refer to as XR – within the age range for which, in the United Kingdom, it is compulsory for children to be in education: 5 to 18 years old. For those unused to the system this is up to but not including university degrees.

Teachers work long hours; the UK self-reported average in 2016 was 54.4 hours a week (Higton et al., 2016) and the author is aware of many excellent teachers routinely working more hours than this in a week. The author, like many colleagues, was regularly conducting action research as a classroom teacher. However, time to write up findings was difficult to find and of questionable use when a thread on a Facebook group could share discoveries with others quicker and potentially to a wider, more interested audience; formal peer review was seen as little benefit. The second part of this chapter, then, will review a number of interesting case studies that may otherwise not see the light of day.

Curriculum focus

Traditionally, Her Majesty's inspectors have focussed heavily on exam results when carrying out an OFSTED review of a school. However, the Chief Inspector has recently stated that 'our inspections have looked hardest at outcomes, placing too much weight on test and exam results when we consider the overall effectiveness of schools' (Spielman, 2019), and indeed the section has been removed from the latest inspection framework as applied from September 2019. However, the ultimate line within the quality of education section of the inspection handbook (a much more substantial, reference document) still reads 'inspectors will consider the outcomes that pupils achieve as a result of the education they have received (we call this the "impact")' (Ofsted, 2019).

It has not been suggested that schools will focus less on results than they are currently. This is partially because there is no easier way to measure impact and quality of education provided by an educational establishment than looking at what numbers come out of the other end and depending on the governmental decisions of the day comparing that to the learner's starting point. This method has changed four times since 2002 (Leckie & Goldstein, 2016). For reference, the current method in brief is to take the best English grade (doubled as long as literature and language are both studied), the Mathematics grade (doubled), best three grades from sciences, Geography, History and French, Spanish or German, and then the best three of any other subjects deemed worthy in that academic year. These grades are added up to give an attainment 8 score. The student's attainment 8 score is then divided by 10, compared with every other child in the country that achieved the same grade at age 10 (end of year 6), and if they are above they have a positive progress 8 score and if below they have a negative progress 8 score.

What does this mean for the child? Well let's take an average child that studies the bare minimum eight subjects (often more are included at least initially for a backstop). Some quick and dirty calculations suggest they have 143 hours of teaching per subject, or less than 37 hours per hour of assessment (Howson, 2019) to do better than students deemed to be as intelligent/able as they are, just to get above average. But of course, all those other students are trying to do the same thing.

But where is the relevance to exploring the use of XR in education? Well, there is a very limited amount of time for learners to gain sufficient knowledge to pass their exams, and teachers feel this pressure. This means there is limited opportunity to extend learning beyond the curriculum. As an A-level (16–18) Computer Science teacher, the author was regularly asked – or even begged – to teach artificial intelligence, machine learning, neural networks and other exciting, modern technologies, technologies learners may well quickly find an enormous part of their working lives. AI – and by extension data science – are incredibly fast growing fields (Furman & Seamans, 2018). In 2018 there were 4.5 times the amount of jobs requiring AI in the US as in 2013 (Shoham, Perrault, Brynjolfsson, & Openai, 2017). Due to the limited amount of time to get through the curriculum the author had to turn down these requests and refuse the learner's thirst for new knowledge. So the take home thought is that if educators want to use XR within their learning, it is essential that it tie in with and enhance the curriculum rather than offering add-on or even ad-hoc opportunities.

Overview of curricula

The curriculum approach varies around the world, as does assessment method and technique. The author has only limited experience within the international curriculum provision but in-depth experience of the UK curriculum, which at least towards the higher end, is highly restrictive and widely thought of as too prescriptive (Ward, 2015).

Where the UK curriculum becomes most limiting is at key stages 4 and 5. Key stage 4 runs from ages 14–16 and culminates with the large number of GCSE (General Certificate of Secondary Education). Learners should then enter into education or training, possibly alongside employment, until the age of 18. 86% of the population (as of 2017) entered into sixth form or further education (Department for Education, 2018) which, in most cases, leads to three courses that are generally assessed by further education.

But what does this curriculum actually look like? There are five examination boards within the UK that build a qualification around a Department for Education subject content document. These qualifications are published in the form of specifications that specify how the qualification will be assessed and what the assessment will cover. As an example, the GCSE Computer Science subject content document has three bullet-pointed pages of content (Department for Education, 2015). However, by the time this had been approved by the Office of Qualifications and Examinations Regulation (Ofqual) in terms of a teachable, deliverable specification, it was 24 pages of individual points of learning. One learning point, in the AQA specification, is 'Discuss the benefits and risks of computer networks' (2016), which in itself or with associated points may lead to one or many lessons. Within the specification is also a breakdown of assessment objective weightings that must be met in every series of examinations. In the aforementioned GCSE Computer Science specification, this is 35–40% *demonstration* of knowledge and understanding of key concepts and principles. 45–50% is *application* of knowledge and understanding of key concepts and principles, and 15–20% is analysing problems in computational terms. Within this 35–40% of demonstration, a maximum of 15% (a maximum of 6% of the total marks) may be allocated to demonstration of knowledge in isolation (Ofqual, 2019).

So far this chapter has set the scene in compulsory education within the UK at higher secondary and post-16, what is officially referred to as key stages 4 and 5. Education is still formal, though less restrictive, at key stages 1 (5–7 years old), 2 (7–11 years old) and 3 (11–14 years old). A national curriculum is issued by law (Department for Education, 2014) that outlines what subjects must be taught and what areas of the subject should be taught at which key stage. However, this is much less prescriptive than the later key stages; for example, key stage 2 children must learn about (amongst other topics) changes in Britain from the Stone Age to the Iron Age. However, the content within that subject is merely indicative; teachers are not restricted and are able to vary what and how they teach. They are also not constrained by external national examinations in the subject.

Difficulties with embedding XR within current curricula

Challenges

With luck you have gained an insight into the UK educational system and the restrictions within with teachers have to work; while there are significant differences with other educational systems around the world, no doubt at least some of the restrictions will apply internationally. What has this to do with embedding XR? The key word here is embedding – it is feasible though difficult to find time to run a short time-scale investigation into using XR in a classroom. However, to *embed* this within the curriculum means that it must be of benefit to the delivery of the curriculum.

Within this chapter we have already looked at the limitations on teaching in terms of time, both in the classroom for delivery and for planning and development. The author perceives introducing XR could eat into teachers' time by;

- Requiring time to plan lessons with the technology,
- Requiring time to learn how to use the technology,
- Requiring time to develop resources for the technology,
- Requiring time to setup and disassemble the technology.

Some of these problems can be solved simply; some less so. Lesson plans can be provided, and although they may require adjustment, they are a good time saver. Learning to use the technology is a bigger problem; 20,000 (UK) teachers now work in schools with absolutely no budget for continued professional development (Weston, 2017). This budget covers not only the cost of the training, but also the cost of covering their normal teaching time. As governments come and go money becomes less and more available (Belfield, Crawford, & Sibieta, 2019), but if this expense can be reduced/nullified by simplicity and methods of introduction then this is all to the good. Many teachers, the author included, enjoy making and developing resources. While talking to teachers interested in using XR, and more specifically virtual reality (VR), within education, the software CoSpaces is referred to regularly. This is 'intuitive educational technology enabling students and teachers to easily build their own 3D creations, animate them with code and explore them in Virtual or Augmented Reality' (CoSpaces, 2019). This is a wonderful resource for the more basic (mainly passive) modes of XR but higher levels of interaction; higher quality of graphical output is still the reserve of more complex systems.

From the author's experience, software such as Unity 3D (https://unity.com/) has a significant learning curve, and it would be a non-starter to expect teachers to have to develop all of their own content, although it is certainly not something they should be blocked from. There is already a number of large libraries of XR resources on the likes of Steam (https://steampowered.com/), although this is centred around games with some educational content and an opportunity is open to form a repository of resources. A challenge still as-yet unanswered is how to develop resources in such a way as to be available for teaching without incurring a large cost to the educational establishment.

A more practical challenge is that of equipment preparation. Part of the problem with solving this challenge is we do not yet know what the typical infrastructure will look like. Presently the author has experienced three main infrastructures within schools;

- Fixed computer laboratory,
- Portable laptop 'trolley' system,
- Bring your own device (BYOD).

Much XR used within education currently uses relatively low-powered devices (mobile telephones or similar) and can be used (sometimes with some tweaking) with a BYOD model or an adaption of the trolley system where dedicated headsets are provided in a mobile caddy of some form. However, this will not be so applicable if and when higher-end equipment moves into education. Both of the current high-end systems, the Oculus Rift (www.oculus.com/) and HTC Vive (www.vive.com/), use remote sensors to determine position. This is becoming less of an issue with the current trend towards untethered inside-out tracking headsets (although they have their own issues in terms of content-access difficulties). A current high-end system needs a powerful PC, the headset, and two or more sensors all set up in a space (at least 2m square seems to be the minimum needed), all connected via wires, and all needing power supplies. This is not exactly portable and is closest to the fixed computer laboratory structure.

Another setup problem is that of accessing relevant software (and areas of that software). Some existing systems leverage the strengths of Google

Expeditions (https://edu.google.com/products/vr-ar/expeditions/) to have a 'guide' that can jump student devices to particular areas of an expedition. Unfortunately, this does not work for (for example) steam applications in high-end VR. This is a design issue for which there is still no simple solution and will require further investigation.

We have discussed the cost of teacher development, but the single biggest factor blocking the author when discussing implementing XR – and particularly high-end VR – into schools is that of cost. The cheapest model currently available is marrying the power of systems such as Google Expeditions and similar technologies with BYOD. In fact, this system can be effectively free although the addition of cheap (or not so cheap) Google Cardboard (https://vr.google.com/cardboard/get-cardboard/) or similar production headsets starts to have things add up. This is exacerbated if devices need to be provided either due to some students not having (suitable) devices available or if for policy or other reasons BYOD is a model that cannot be followed.

At the other end of the scale, high-end VR equipment is expensive. Add the cost of a gaming PC (the graphics capabilities are equivalent to the VR needs) to the purchase cost of the VR headset and things quickly get very expensive. At the time of writing, the cost of a VR system as a proportion of a teachers' wage is roughly equivalent to the cost of putting in a BBC Micro into a school in the early 1980s, or an Acorn Archimedes in the early 1990s, both of which were seen as substantial and risky investments. Thankfully, technology capabilities continue to increase, and costs decrease over the long term. With the increasing capability of disconnected headsets such as the Oculus Quest, we may be approaching a period when a class set of high-end VR may not be beyond reasonable expectations.

The author finds VR in particular absolutely fascinating and merrily spends many hours flying around hunting space pirates in full emersion. It is too easy to forget that not everyone can enjoy the same level of enjoyment. Significant numbers of children have some form of vision impairment (National Center for Children's Vision & Eye Health, 2016), and a proportion of these will not be able to engage with XR. While teachers of heavily visually impaired students may already be used to dealing with the particular challenges this brings, many visual impairments may have (relatively) negligible impact on every day learning but make some aspects of XR partially or totally inaccessible. Stereoscopic vision, or lack of, is one example.

Furthermore we have the problem of cyber sickness (La Viola, 2000). La Viola describes a number of factors that contribute to cyber sickness (akin but separate to motion sickness), and the author has noted that the majority of these are solved or at least reduced by the use of high-end VR systems with sufficient resolution, frame-rate and field of view, alongside properly designed software to reduce conflicting illusions of self-motion. Unfortunately, these benefits are less apparent in the low-end equipment used in the likes of Google Expeditions, and there is a risk of causing a dislike or distrust of XR as a whole, which may have knock on effects in terms of lack of willingness to invest time and money in future systems.

There's no debate that children are easily distracted. Discussions with colleagues at the VR workshop provider Prime VR (www.primevr.co.uk/) suggests that students are less distracted by the 'wow factor' of using their VR equipment if they visit for two or more sessions, in comparison to the first time they pick up and use a VR headset. The author has plenty of anecdotal evidence of any new technology being initially engaging due to this wow factor that, while the engagement is a positive thing, can in itself detract from the learning that should be happening. However, again anecdotally, technologies that become the norm will generally reduce in wow factor; hence, the distraction of having something new should be minimalised. Indeed, a recent investigation suggests that an immersive learning experience can have 'massive impact' on students that struggle with concentration or sensory issues (Mannion, 2019). Other studies suggest that the high perceptual demands found within an XR learning experience, and in particular the immersion of high-end VR, may reduce the impact of multi-sensory distractors and allow learning to happen at a higher rate (Matusz et al., 2015). One of the earliest studies into VR use in education the author considers still valid argues that 'computer games, Egypt, and field trips to the museum are all very popular with this age group' and that 'all of the test subjects would be so excited that the added thrill of visual immersion would not make a measurable difference' (Jacobson, 2008). Further work may be needed over a long period of time to ascertain whether the 'newness' of XR learning does hold the key to some of the improvements that are seen in the research and whether this might reduce over an extended period of time.

Identified impact

Earlier in this chapter we discussed the need to demonstrate impact for XR technology to stand a chance of being adopted on more than an ad-hoc basis. Unfortunately, there is not an enormous body of knowledge that focusses on compulsory-age education and curriculum focussed impact; the author has no doubt that more work needs to be done in investigating this area. That being said, the evidence to date argues that the impact is likely to be significant.

Chang *et al.* conducted a study in 2013 using mobile augmented reality to contextualise learning of socioscientific issues that showed significant improvement on the conceptual gains shown between the pre-tests and the post-tests (Chang, Wu, & Hsu, 2013). This was further evidenced with a larger study by Ibáñez et al. in 2013 that focussed on using AR to deliver learning on the subject of electro-magnetism (a topic more likely to be found in curricula nationwide than the socioscientific issues covered in the other study we looked at). This study engaged 64 learners from 4 schools. Although the learning covered a number of weeks, the AR (or non-AR for the control group) intervention lasted only 10 minutes. Again, however, students were shown to perform significantly higher using the AR-based learning system compared to the more common web-based learning system (Ibáñez, Di Serio, Villarán, & Delgado Kloos, 2014).

Moving into Virtual rather than Augmented reality, a 2009 doctoral study used the CAVE and Earth Theatre system to immerse learners within a 3D ancient Egyptian temple. This is particularly interesting as one of the first applications that led the author to see potential within VR for educational purposes was *Nefertari: Journey to Eternity*, which allows the user to 'step inside Nefertari's tomb and immerse yourself in the story of its art, history, construction, and mythology through interactive elements' (Experius VR, 2018). History is common to most curricula, and ancient Egypt features within the UK national curriculum. The immersive study found significant improvements in learning when using a VR game *of some sort* but showed an inability to differentiated between the efficacy of screen-based VR and that of immersive VR (Jacobson, 2008). This was put down to a lack of ability within the testing to differentiate deep learning opportunities. It may also be a factor of the CAVE-based system used making use of a wrap-around projection rather than the head-mounted displays currently used in high-end VR.

Other studies, however, have shown that immersive head mounted display (HMD)- based VR can have a significant difference upon learning. It has been shown that '3D IVR [immersive virtual reality] environment would create the best conditions enhancing learning of analogical reasoning' (Passig, Tzuriel, & Eshel-Kedmi, 2016: 305). Furthermore, staying within the historical curricula but moving on to a more specific local history investigation, it was found that 'headset-based virtual reality systems stimulate young pupils' interest in learning history more than screen-based virtual reality systems' (Fabola & Miller, 2016).

Pervasiveness within the curriculum

The author has looked at a large number of studies of XR in education. One thing has become glaringly obvious: The approaches taken so far are for the large part ad-hoc or one-off studies with little or no obvious intent to repeat the delivery year in and year out. Additionally, there is little evidence of more than one project being run in a single learning establishment; there is a minimal level of pervasiveness.

This could be perceived as having a number of knock-on effects. Because learners are exposed to this new technology only briefly, we have no data as to the impact of the 'newness' effect of excitement upon the student engagement and the efficacy of the learning during this period or whether the effects noted by Fabola and Miller (2016), amongst others, may tail off after this honeymoon period. We also don't have enough data to identify whether the use of XR over an extended period will have a positive or negative impact on the most precious of teacher resources: time. If the impact on learner understanding is increased but the time taken to deliver using XR is also increased, this could come at a cost of other areas of the subject matter not being taught to a sufficient depth and negating any gains. There is also the ethical question of continual offering: Picking on Fabola and Miller again, their equipment was set up in a school for a period of one week. Therefore, it was not available to students in the following year groups who now miss out on this opportunity that has been proved to enhance their learning. While in this case the impact is relatively low as the topic is not one examined at a national level, if we are to prove impact in a high-stakes scenario such as delivering GCSE material, it has to be considered whether not offering the material and technology to future cohorts is ethically acceptable.

Case studies

Wolsey Hall Oxford

Wolsey Hall Oxford (https://wolseyhalloxford.org.uk) has been offering distance education since 1894. Learning material was delivered originally via post but is now primarily online via the Canvas platform. Students are home schooled through Wolsey Hall Oxford for a range of reasons; they may live abroad (or be travelling) but prefer a British education. They may find accessing a traditional educational setting difficult due to travel times, psychological or neurological conditions, interpersonal problems or a host of other reasons. Home schooling allows flexibility in a way that a traditional school cannot.

However, home schooling does come with some disadvantages. The literature is at odds as to the effect home schooling may have on the socialisation of the learners. Feelings of 'restriction and isolation [can be] intense' (van Schalkwyk & Bouwer, 2011) while other sources suggest that home schooled children have 'higher scores on self-concept measures, appear socially and emotionally well-adjusted, and have opportunities for interaction with other children and adults' (Grubb, 1998).

The team at Wolsey Hall Oxford, however, perceived a need for a different way of interacting with learners. At present, all learners will have an initial video call meeting with their tutors, and from then onwards the majority of communication is via e-mail or through the on-line learning environment. It was perceived that e-mail alone can lead to feelings of isolation whereas video calling can feel over-formal, difficult to arrange and, due to tutors being paid on a time basis, relatively expensive. Their particular concern was a supposed lack of socialisation from home schooling.

Recently the team at Wolsey Hall Oxford have been developing a customised version of VirBela (www.virbela.com) a desktop-based VR system. Within this system learners can navigate an island as an avatar (a 3D humanoid figure). The island provides a range of opportunities to enhance learning and the learning experience, as well as opportunities for social engagement including an interactive owl hunt, movie nights in a virtual cinema and a planned interactive chess club.

VirBela includes a gallery in which students can share their work. While this is a common event, both formally in terms of showcases and informally in terms of classroom displays in traditional schools, it is something that is considered less within a home-schooling environment. Along with the multi-user nature of VirBela, this adds a feeling of community to the application and, it is hoped, will give learners a feeling of belonging.

There are open and private teaching areas within the island. Allowing tutors to teach via VirBela has a lot of the strengths of using video calls but reduces the social anxiety that many students may feel from being in front of a video camera and/or having to communicate through a microphone (avatars can communicate either through voice or through typed commands). Given the make-up of the school's students, including many who home school due to anxiety issues in main stream schools and many who are have English as an additional language and may not feel comfortable with the clarity of their spoken communication, this is perceived as a strong benefit. This also avoids overuse of forums, which the author has seen within adult online learning environments such as the Open University, but Wolsey Hall Oxford have identified as less appropriate to young learners.

There are also added opportunities for learners to work interactively, with virtual rooms available not only for learners to meet and communicate, but also with virtual smart whiteboards and built-in web browsers to allow collaboration.

The opportunity to tutor a number of students at once reduces the financial impact for the school (and hence for the students). It also increases the potential for group learning opportunities and opens up more avenues for students to collaborate. Currently this is primarily through a forum infrastructure which is very adult-oriented in comparison to the instant communication that many are used to and is the norm in traditional educational environments.

PrimeVR

PrimeVR (www.primevr.co.uk/) is a British company providing VR workshops to schools. The equipment used are low-end (and so cost-effective) head mounted displays running on mobile phone type technology. The workshops are focussed primarily on Key Stage 2 (7–11 years old) and link in with the National Curriculum.

PrimeVR saw the opportunities provided by Google Expeditions and similar software along with low-cost headsets. They are firm believers that experiencing something first-hand is the best way to learn about it, but that when this is not possible VR can provide a close second. The workshops are designed as multi-area experiences, with related discussion topics and on-going lesson plans to extend the learning outside of the workshop.

One workshop offered is entitled 'climate change'. Learners will have the opportunity to visit the Arctic and Antarctic and experience the impact of melting ice caps on the flora and fauna both locally and world-wide. From there students will take a journey under water, experiencing the impact of raising sea temperatures on sea creatures, learn about coral bleaching and see the wide-ranging impacts. Finally, students will travel to the Borneo rainforest and see the impact of deforestation.

As mentioned elsewhere in this chapter, permeation through the curriculum has not yet happened. PrimeVR believe that 'for VR to have a meaningful impact, it should be planned alongside the requirements of the national curriculum and embedded into your scheme of work'.

There is a tendency for VR to be used in a primarily experiential way. If students are studying World War 1, VR could be used to show students what the trench warfare system looked like. However, PrimeVR have gone one step further by linking the experiences with specific learning intentions and opportunities. The World War 1 bundle they provide is developed into a literacy lesson, including example letters from the front, writing checklists, and other useful links to encourage the teacher to focus on learning and use the VR as a tool, rather than focussing on the VR and using the learning as a reason to use the VR.

Caroline Chrisholm School

One of the most exciting case studies the author has come across was run by a school in Northampton, UK, and spearheaded by their faculty lead teacher for Computing and IT, Kay Sawbridge. The school applied for and received a partnership grant from the Royal Society (https://royalsociety.org/grants-schemes-awards/grants/partnership-grants) to investigate whether Computer Science could be made more engaging with the use of VR. Working in partnership with a University partner, the students (in Year 12, 16–17 years old) developed and produced a VR application using the Unity 3D software environment. The application was devised to introduce the CPU cycle, showing how different clock speed and RAM can affect the speed of processing and how the data flows through the components on the motherboard.

The application was trialled on 100 students in Year 8 (12–13 years old) who were queried before and after the trial. Some of the qualitative comments received were heart-warming:

- 'It's cool because you can see all the parts and it feels real'.
- 'It's awesome, it would help teach classes a lot and everyone would be able to engage'.
- 'It's the coolest thing ever, it's a fun way to learn since kids of our age have a lot of interest in devices like XBoxes. The technology would therefore be an appropriate way of learning'.
- 'It really shows you how things work that you do not get in normal lessons'.

The final comment in particular resonates with the feelings of the author; XR has the potential to not just teach what is already being taught; it also has the potential to extend teaching to a new level and teach things in a whole new way that is not currently possible. This could then extend what it is possible to teach.

The quantitative data was through self-assessment and was collected by the students and analysed along with their class teacher. The VR system improved the enjoyment of Computer Science for all students, but the most impressive gain was a change from 6% to 24% of girls 'really enjoying' Computer Science.

Other improvements were seen in perceived difficulty of the subject with an improvement of 20% for boys and 16% for girls not perceiving Computer Science as difficult as they did before the trial. An incredible 38% of both boys and girls found Computer Science interesting post-trial (up from 16% of boys and just 2% of girls).

Thinking back to some of the challenges the author has made earlier in this chapter, the author is delighted to see that the department are thinking ahead; as they ran the investigation, the school is able to keep the equipment and are hoping for future grants to purchase more. Future year 8 students will continue to use the application in its current form, but the Year 12s will continue to develop it further, increasing the pervasiveness within the current curriculum. Planned improvements include adding new hardware to the model (such as a network card and hard drive), showing interactions between hardware components (such as simulating network interaction, printing, CPU/RAM interaction), and adapting the application to become an 'escape room' game to enhance engagement.

What next?

XR is still relatively new. Although initial explorations into digital VR started in the 1960s with the Ultimate Display (Sutherland, 1965), and the term XR itself can be traced back to the work of Wyckoff in the 1960s, VR as we know it is a child of this century; the first high-end HMD, the Oculus Rift, was released commercially in 2016 and AR became accessible in about 2008 with the G1 Android phone and Wikitude AR travel kit, although it could be argued it came of age with the release of Pokémon Go, again in 2016.

As already discussed, we do not know enough about the potential XR has to impact education in general and compulsory-age education in particular. Uptake of new technology has never been fast in this stage of education; it wasn't until the early 1980s that computers became a common sight in schools, and it took another 25–30 years before schools had the 1:1 student/ computer ratio that is now common in many countries.

One thing the author has noted about the introduction and use of technology, anecdotally and from personal experience, is a tendency to base lessons on the technology; a French teacher declaring 'today we are going to have a computer lesson', or using technology for the sake of using technology rather than an enhancement to learning. This is the so-called 'PowerPoint lesson' where a teacher tells students to make a PowerPoint presentation on a subject they are studying. The same method was used pre-technology as 'poster lessons'; this approach can be highly effective but (again anecdotally) is often used as a filler lesson or when a teacher cannot think of a way to engage students in a subject, without the emphasis and planning needed to develop deep learning. It is to be preferred that the route XR technology takes when introduced into teaching is to use the potential it offers as a route to enhance learning. In short, the author desires to hear 'today we are learning about X and we are going to use the XR equipment to support that learning' rather than 'today we are going to have an XR lesson on X'.

We have already seen how one school has used their own students and support from Higher Education to build an interactive system to learn about the inner workings of a computer, and this is an excellent example of the kind of creativity needed to drive XR learning forwards. Google expeditions are a way of getting learners into situations they cannot normally access, and by extension to this the immersive VR experiences explored by Jacobson (2008) and demonstrated in Nefertari could be used to bring to life historical experiences in such a way as to not just enhance the experience but develop deeper learning across subjects. The power of interactive VR with 6 degrees of freedom means that learners can handle objects they cannot touch in real life, due to risk of harm, scarcity or cost. The high resolution now available allows learners to see more detail than they otherwise could; the VR Museum of Fine Art (www.wearvr. com/developers/finn-sinclair/apps), for example, allows a close-up view of the Mona Lisa that one would not get on even the quietest day at the Louvre. Gaining this experience for a whole host of artworks stored in different museums all across the world would bring to the fingertips of the teacher something that is not currently feasible.

Possibilities abound, and as we saw with the transition of traditional computing devices, from Colossus to main-frames to micro-computers to the computing power available in our mobile telephones, it is impossible to predict with any form of certainty where XR technology will be in ten or twenty years' time. However, with the reducing cost and increasing capability comes an opportunity for educators to embody this exciting technology into learning at the ground level. Who knows, learning in XR could become the norm and lead to some incredible developments outside of the classroom when the amazing young people become amazing adults.

The author would like to leave you with one final thought: 'For a bunch of hairless apes, we've actually managed to invent some pretty incredible things' (Cline, 2012).

Acknowledgements

Thanks go to PrimeVR, Wolsey Hall Oxford and Kay Sawbridge at Caroline Chrisholm School for their support and assistance in writing the case studies. The author's time is funded by the Office for Students, through the Institute of Coding.

References

AQA. (2016). *GCSE COMPUTER SCIENCE (8520) specification for teaching from September 2016 onwards for exams in 2018 onwards get help and support.* Manchester: Author. Retrieved July 25, 2019 from https://filestore.aqa.org.uk/resources/computing/specifications/AQA-8520-SP-2016.PDF

Belfield, C., Crawford, C., & Sibieta, L. (2019). *Long-run comparisons of spending per pupil across different stages of education.* J. Payne (Ed.). London: The Institute for Fiscal Studies. Retrieved from www.ifs.org.uk

Burton, L. (2018). *'Impact' is just another meaningless educational buzzword.* Retrieved July 12, 2019, from www.teachwire.net/news/impact-is-just-another-meaningless-educational-buzzword

Chang, H.-Y., Wu, H.-K., & Hsu, Y.-S. (2013). Integrating a mobile augmented reality activity to contextualize student learning of a socioscientific issue. *British Journal of Educational Technology, 44*(3), E95–E99. doi:10.1111/j.1467-8535.2012.01379.x

Cline, E. (2012). *Ready player one.* London: Arrow Books.

CoSpaces. (2019). *CoSpaces Edu: About the innovative EdTech platform.* Retrieved July 26, 2019, from https://cospaces.io/edu/about.html

Department for Education. (2014). *National curriculum in England: Framework for key stages 1 to 4 – GOV.UK.* Retrieved July 25, 2019, from www.gov.uk/government/publications/national-curriculum-in-england-framework-for-key-stages-1-to-4

Department for Education. (2015). *Computer science GCSE subject content.* Retrieved July 25, 2019 from https://assets.publishing.service.gov.uk/government/uploads/system/uploads/attachment_data/file/397550/GCSE_subject_content_for_computer_science.pdf

Department for Education. (2018). *Destinations of key stage 4 and key stage 5 students, England, 2016/17.* Manchester. Retrieved July 25, 2019 from https://assets.publishing.service.gov.uk/government/uploads/system/uploads/attachment_data/file/748199/Destinations_Main_Text_2017.pdf

Experius VR. (2018). *Nefertari: Journey to eternity on steam*. Retrieved July 30, 2019, from https://store.steampowered.com/app/861400/Nefertari_Journey_to_Eternity/

Fabola, A., & Miller, A. (2016). Virtual reality for early education: A study. In *Immersive Learning Research Network Second International Conference* (pp. 59–72). Switzerland. doi:10.1007/978-3-319-41769-1_5

Furman, J., & Seamans, R. (2018). AI and the Economy (No. 24689). Cambridge, MA. Retrieved July 25, 2019 from https://aiindex.org/2017-report.pdf

Grubb, D. (1998). *Homeschooling: Who and why?* Annual meeting of the Mid-South Educational Research Association, New Orleans, LA. Retrieved July 25, 2019 from https://files.eric.ed.gov/fulltext/ED427138.pdf

Higton, J., Leonardi, S., Richards, N., Choudhoury, A. R., Dr., Sofroniou, N., & Owen, D. (2016). *Teacher Workload Survey 2016*. Retrieved July 25, 2019 from https://assets.publishing.service.gov.uk/government/uploads/system/uploads/attachment_data/file/592499/TWS_2016_FINAL_Research_report_Feb_2017.pdf

Howson, O. (2019). *What exams are we inflicting on our young people?* Retrieved July 31, 2019, from https://badllama.net/what-exams-are-we-inflicting-on-our-young-people/

Ibáñez, M. B., Di Serio, Á., Villarán, D., & Delgado Kloos, C. (2014). Experimenting with electromagnetism using augmented reality: Impact on flow student experience and educational effectiveness. *Computers and Education*, *71*, 1–13. doi:10.1016/j.compedu.2013.09.004

Jacobson, J. (2008). *Ancient architecture in virtual reality does immersion really aid learning?* University of Pittsburgh. Retrieved July 25, 2019 from http://d-scholarship.pitt.edu/7499/1/JacobsonDissertationSpring2008.pdf

La Viola, J. J., Jr (2000). A discussion of cybersickness in virtual environments. *SIGCHI Bulletin*, *32*(1), 47–51. Retrieved July 25, 2019 from www.eecs.ucf.edu/isuelab/publications/pubs/cybersick.pdf

Leckie, G., & Goldstein, H. (2016). *The evolution of school league tables in England 1992–2016: "Contextual value-added", "expected progress" and "progress 8"* (2016 No. 02). Retrieved July 25, 2019 from www.bristol.ac.uk/media-library/sites/education/documents/bristol-working-papers-in-education/The-evolution-of-school-league-tables-in-England-1992–2016.pdf

Mannion, J. (2019). *Growth headset? Exploring the use of virtual reality and augmented reality in schools | impact.chartered.college*. Retrieved April 24, 2019, from https://impact.chartered.college/article/growth-headset-exploring-virtual-reality-augmented-reality-schools/

Matusz, P. J., Broadbent, H., Ferrari, J., Forrest, B., Merkley, R., & Scerif, G. (2015). Multi-modal distraction: Insights from children's limited attention. *Cognition*. doi:10.1016/j.cognition.2014.11.031

National Center for Children's Vision & Eye Health. (2016). *Children's Vision and Eye Health: A snapshot of current national issues*. Retrieved July 25, 2019 from www.preventblindness.org/sites/default/files/national/documents/Children%27s_Vision_Chartbook.pdf

Ofqual. (2019). *GCSE (9 to 1) Subject level guidance for computer science*. Coventry. Retrieved July 25, 2019 from https://assets.publishing.service.gov.uk/government/uploads/system/uploads/attachment_data/file/811066/Subject-level_guidance_for_GCSE_computer_science.pdf

Ofsted. (2018). *An investigation into how to assess the quality of education through curriculum intent, implementation and impact.* Manchester. Retrieved July 12, 2019 from https://assets.publishing.service.gov.uk/government/uploads/system/uploads/attachment_data/file/766252/How_to_assess_intent_and_implementation_of_curriculum_191218.pdf

Ofsted. (2019). *School inspection handbook.* Manchester. Retrieved July 25, 2019 from www.gov.uk/government/publications/education-inspection-framework-draft-for-consultation

Passig, D., Tzuriel, D., & Eshel-Kedmi, G. (2016). Improving children's cognitive modifiability by dynamic assessment in 3D immersive virtual reality environments. *Computers & Education, 95,* 296–308. doi:10.1016/j.compedu.2016.01.009

Secret Teacher. (2014). *Secret teacher: Jargon is ruining our children's education | Teacher Network | The Guardian.* Retrieved July 12, 2019, from www.theguardian.com/teacher-network/teacher-blog/2014/aug/09/secret-teacher-jargon-education-pupils

Shoham, Y., Perrault, R., Brynjolfsson, E., & Openai, J. C. (2017). *Artificial intelligence index: 2017 annual report.* Retrieved July 25, 2019 from https://aiindex.org/2017-report.pdf

Spielman, A. (2019). *Speech to the SCHOOLS NorthEast summit – GOV.UK.* Retrieved July 16, 2019, from www.gov.uk/government/speeches/amanda-spielman-speech-to-the-schools-northeast-summit

Sutherland, I. E. (1965). The ultimate display. In *Information Processing 1965: Proceedings of IFIP Congress 65. Vol. 1* (pp. 506–508). London: Macmillan and Co. Retrieved April 26, 2019 from http://worrydream.com/refs/Sutherland%20-%20The%20Ultimate%20Display.pdf

van Schalkwyk, L., & Bouwer, C. (2011). Homeschooling: Heeding the voices of learners Lizebelle van. *Education as Change, 15*(2), 179–190. Retrieved July 25, 2019 from https://repository.up.ac.za/bitstream/handle/2263/18334/VanSchalkwyk_Homeschooling(2011).pdf?sequence=1

Ward, H. (2015). *Teachers condemn the `joyless' new curriculum | Tes News.* Retrieved July 24, 2019, from www.tes.com/news/teachers-condemn-joyless-new-curriculum

Weston, D. (2017). *21,000 Teachers in Schools Reporting No CPD Budget.* Retrieved July 25, 2019, from https://tdtrust.org/press-release-21000-teachers-schools-reporting-no-cpd-budget-says-teacher-development-trust-study

Part II

Concepts of virtual reality

Chapter 8

Transcendent learning spaces

Neus Lorenzo Galés and Ray Gallon

Terminology

Something is *transcendent* when it exceeds or surpasses usual limits or extends beyond the limits of ordinary experience; it can also mean being universally applicable or significant (Merriam-Webster, 2019).

Augmented reality (AR) is the result of adding layers of digital information onto the real world in real time, 'an enhanced version of the physical, real-world reality of which elements are superimposed by computer generated or extracted real-world sensory input such as sound, video, graphics or haptics' (Schueffel, 2017). Eventually, AR can even include olfactory and somatosensorial input.

Virtual Reality (VR) is the computer-generated simulation of a three-dimensional image or environment that can be interacted with in a seemingly real or physical way by a person using special electronic equipment (Oxford English Dictionary, 2019). The result is a sensorial experience that allows a person to use equipment such as a helmet with a screen inside or gloves fitted with sensors to interact with the images in a seemingly experiential or physical manner as with the real world.

Context and relevance

Human society is experiencing a major global change, which can be described as the fourth industrial revolution. Thanks to the combination of the Internet and emerging technologies such as artificial intelligence (AI) and the Internet of Things (IoT), objects are now autonomously connected and interact independently of humans. Smartphones have rendered people and their data into ubiquitous and deterritorialised meta-beings. Our meta-selves exist on an abstract, invisible plane, in parallel with our physical selves, built around a digital identity that we are obliged to manage carefully. We live in an always-on, always-connected universe where, for the first time in human history, machines are making decisions in our place, without human involvement. This fourth industrial revolution, also known as Industry 4.0, is already part of our lives, and its impact will grow exponentially during the next decades. We interact in hybrid human-machine ecosystems on a daily basis, and in the near future we will be able to intervene directly in distant locations, even on other planets, transcending space and time.

This transcending of space and time, coupled with the hybridisation of our communication paradigms, implies significant changes to our perceptual frameworks. We cannot yet measure the full impact of these changes, but it seems clear that they imply a shift towards a more abstract conception of the world around us. For example, industries are now working with 'digital twins', digital models of industrial equipment or processes. The digital twin is, in effect, a virtual representation of the physical production apparatus. Humans and machines apply requirements or modifications to the digital twin, which models the effects of these operations. Once these operations are validated, the digital twin is then authorised to apply them to the physical elements that it represents. An operator of heavy machinery has acquired an enormous database of knowledge based on experiential physical information: vibrations, sounds, levels of resistance and so forth. The shift to a digital twin is likely to make the operator's job safer and more comfortable, but it also means that such physical knowledge, acquired through experience, will be lost unless the digital twin has sensors that capture similar data and algorithms to interpret it. The role of the operator, therefore, will also change. S/he will be interacting with a digital entity, probably including an AI agent, and will be concerned with parameters that have nothing to do with the direct feedback of physical interaction.

This is just one scenario illustrating how abstraction and hybrid interactions can embed themselves pervasively in any aspect of human activity. As educators, we have a responsibility to anticipate these developments. We must prepare youngsters to grow up in hybrid virtual environments, and we must help adults with a different set of perceptions about reality to adjust and adapt so they can continue to grow and prosper. We must also do this in the context of growing urgency around questions such as global warming and threats to biodiversity.

The emerging technologies of virtual reality (VR) and augmented reality (AR) have been used in a wide variety of situations, to create immersive games, enhance perception, provide instructions for complex procedures and train people for professions in which life and safety can be at risk, such as airline pilots or surgeons. They can also be used to model the kinds of daily life situations that learners will have to face as the fourth industrial revolution progresses. They can provide powerful educational experiences that go beyond traditional classroom scenarios, provided there be a sound pedagogical basis for their use. The focus must be on giving learners an experience that enhances their knowledge and understanding. The potential of mindful use of these technologies to reveal hidden relationships and provide appropriate emotional feedback to anchor new knowledge can lead to true transcendence – taking the learner significantly beyond traditional learning experiences.

Alternative realities and transcendence in education

It is possible to embed real world elements within VR scenarios and vice versa, creating a potent mixed reality that provides a very rich environment for exploring communication, cultural expression and learning processes. The added information has the potential to enhance and enrich existing information, but it can also distort the learner's perception and mask the original intention. This type of perception transcends normal sensorial reconstruction of the external world and alters consciousness, in an amplified experience similar to that reported by shamans. This means that if we want to enhance learning with these approaches, we also need to understand how to guide learners through this sensitive process.

Neural Science has shown us that this altered hybrid reality affects the human brain with the same intensity as a real-world sensorial experience and can activate the same neurotransmissions that produce feelings and emotions in the real world. Learning experiences in a virtual world can produce the same effects as their counterparts in physical reality (Riva et al., 2007). Space, time and contextualized understanding become part of a singular, non-transferrable personal learning experience.

The concept of an abstract world of ideas is present in occidental culture at least since Ancient Greece and possibly farther back. The first use of the expression 'virtual reality' in modern times comes to us directly out of the illusory nature of literature and theatre. In a collection of essays by French playwright Antonin Artaud (1938), who was also interested in cinema and literary immersive environments, theatre is seen as a *VR* that evolves through interaction of the characters, objects, images and atmosphere created on the stage. This artificially generated mind space provides infinite possibilities to learn, exchange and create alternative situations that will never be interpreted twice in exactly the same way. In a direct analogy, modern VR headsets offer a virtual context that combines with the user's gestures and movements to create an individual holistic experience.

For Artaud, the immersive theatre concept generated 'a conflagration of feelings at a given point, of human sensations, creators of suspended situations, but expressed in concrete gestures' (Artaud, 1938). He found affinity with the Dada movement, centred on ideas of multisensory stimulation and disruption of audience expectations (Galacticgabby, 2014). He also followed the evolution of some Dadaists into Surrealism, in which cinematographic technology helped create ludic alternative realities, and provided visual playfulness (Grossman, 2004). Both approaches used immersive virtuality to stimulate the audience's spontaneous creativity and favour actors' engagement and professional development.

When real world and conceptual space are combined, learning becomes an active co-creation and reinterpretation, in a collective exploration of processes and meanings. Instead of passively integrating a given input, learners participate in a social constructivist building process where social exchange and emotional interaction play a major role (Davydov, 1995).

In 1959, John Cocke and Harwood G. Kolsky used the term 'virtual' for the first time tied to computer science. It was in a paper on 'The Virtual Memory in the STRETCH Computer' (Cocke & Kolsky, 1959) and referred to the additional memory that could come from using temporarily empty space on the hard drive to increase computer speed (Kelly, 2016). In 1979, the term 'virtual reality' was used by IBM in an announcement of a powerful operating system 'to enable the user to migrate to totally unreal systems' (Kelly, 2016). The invention of the first data glove capable of fine-grained finger movement sensing, by Thomas Zimmerman, Jaron Lanier, and Young Harvill in the mid-1980s, provided a serious human–machine interface that propelled VR into the world of gaming, albeit very expensive gaming (Wikipedia, 2019a). Transcending human literary abstraction, this digitally created VR represents a major new technological universe that has steadily grown in its power, popularity and variety of experiences. It has been used to treat war veterans, helping them to overcome post-traumatic shock syndrome; by surgeons to learn how to perform complex operations; by paraplegics wanting to feel the sensation of flight; and as an environment for prototyping almost every car made in the last 20 years, and other vehicles as well (Wikipedia, 2019b).

Thus, as a learning environment, it goes beyond the acquisition of objective knowledge and enters the realm of the senses and of feelings and emotions. In such an environment, learners have a high possibility of experiencing intense moments of understanding and awareness of transcendence, the so-called 'aha moment', propelled by the immersive nature of the learning space.

While VR can completely substitute for a real-world environment, AR acts to combine digital elements with objects in the real world. In doing so, it alters the usual perceptions of that world. It can add to existing reality, enriching or enhancing it (Schueffel, 2017), or it can be subtractive, removing detail to simplify real images, for example in order to better understand a fundamental principle of how a machine works (Rosenberg, 1992).

Both AR and VR provide an environment and a context in which hybrid interactions with non-human agents occur. They follow a progression through three specific domains of socio-cognitive development that correlate with the three main competency levels of the OECD PISA evaluations (OECD, 2016):

- An explicit information acquisition domain
- An implicit knowledge development domain
- A meta-domain of abstract reflection

It is important to note that in the VR/AR context, machine-machine inter-actions almost always involve human moderators, and even human-human interactions can be considered hybrid, since the message passes through the filter of the device and the software environment and so is moderated by them.

Figure 8.1 shows that in VR and AR, most interactions occur at the higher socio-cognitive levels.

This is where real transcendence in education takes place most often. In meta-reflection learners can integrate current learning with existing know-ledge, construct new abstract models and make new connections that reveal new relationships (Lorenzo Galés & Gallon, 2018, pp. 30–42).

Transcendence of VR and AR as virtual learning spaces

The rapid evolution of human-machine interfaces is going to make it difficult for the brain to distinguish between physical and digital realities. The chal-lenge for education will be how to use this ambiguity in a positive manner.

The authors take the position that at this time, enhancing physical reality using AR provides a richer field of possibilities with more complex results than the full contextual substitution provided by VR. In a further development, IBM has begun talking about extended reality (XR) to include VR, AR and a variety of mixed situations, where 'XR combines the insight you receive

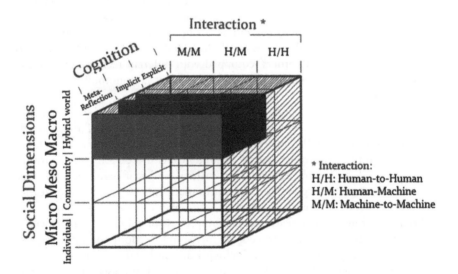

Figure 8.1 Hybrid interactions in VR and AR involve higher-level regions of the socio-cognitive learning space.

Source: The Transformation Society, used with permission.

from AI and the real-time data stream you get from IoT with the overlay of work instructions created by AR' (Ortiz, 2019). This Industry 4.0 scenario can provide humans with an immersive, three-dimensional, ubiquitous, enriched learning space that can transform formal and informal education.

Smart learning spaces: expanding educational concepts

While teaching and learning have traditionally been seen as the province of specialised disciplines such as philosophy, pedagogy, and educational psychology (De Corte, 2010), people from many diverse disciplines have contributed their ideas and theories to the notion of learning spaces in our modern hyper-connected global culture (Lorenzo & Gallon, 2019):

- Architecture
- Landscaping and gardening
- Psychiatry and medicine
- Anthropology and ethnology
- Education
- Neurobiology
- Engineering

In parallel, ideas about what should go on in the classroom have evolved towards an active learning paradigm (e.g. Dewey, Montessori, Rosa Sensat, etc.). Other theorists, following that paradigm, have reorganised physical classrooms into specialised technological spaces with a scenario for each. Freinet (1927) used printing machines to offer a creative space where students could develop both professional skills and critical thinking. He also gave students specialised corners, equipped with different technologies of different professions, where they could experiment autonomously (Freinet, 1993, pp. 371, 379).

The classroom space needs to accommodate the intended teaching and learning function, and technology is selected as a function of those needs (Lorenzo & Gallon, 2019). A consequence of this approach is that as technologically equipped learning spaces become ever more complex, learning activities need to be increasingly personalised and self-regulated, to offer advanced learning strategies and procedures that promote autonomous learning processes (Heo & Joung, 2004).

Student autonomy is usually seen as the process of gaining a certain learning maturity, but it is also a process for increasing freedom and attaining the responsibility to choose their own lifelong learning itineraries independently. If teachers are able to help students connect personal interests with common needs and social welfare, we can start to develop a smart pedagogy that transcends individual process (Lorenzo & Gallon, 2019). This opens opportunities not only for traditional academic domains, but for engineering disciplines as well. It presents new challenges, which are clearly connected to the UN sustainable development goals (SDGs) for 2030, and it raises ethical and epistemological questions that can't be addressed without involving the most advanced technologies.

A pedagogy that is capable of blending the Industry 4.0 ecosystem with SDGs requires new literacies, especially transliteracy, as learning clearly needs to take place in a transmedia context. Development of such a pedagogy means we need a greater understanding of how students perceive physical, virtual and augmented realities and how they integrate each type of information.

VR, AR and transmedia cognition

VR/AR learning tasks move us away from local teaching and into a new 'trans-local' form, where processes jump across different platforms, software-tools and cognitive contextual interpretations. The virtual world gives students the possibility to disconnect from their physical environment and practice with digital/virtual objects that respond to their eye movements, their hand gestures or their voice. The anticipation that youngsters will grow up immersed in these virtual transmedia environments and use them for learning, entertainment, work and other daily activities presents us with a complex set of unknowns related to perception and cognition.

Human capacity to perceive information is related not only to human senses, but also to the cultural biases that shape our interpretation of reality with collective shared filters and the asynchrony of consciousness (Zeki & Bartels, 1998b).

It seems clear that culture, individual experiences and personal somatic markers affect differences in how we react in front of an image, but we still don't know why, as a species, we all react differently to a real baby's face than to a picture of one. The modular doctrine of vision (Zeki & Bartels, 1998a, 1998b; Aleksander & Dumall, 2000) proposes that the visual brain consists of many distributed perceptual systems, each one responsible for the processing of different visual attributes. We teach our students that they see the lightning before they hear the thunder because light travels at a faster speed than sound, but we forget to tell them that what we call *seeing* is also a compound perception of different parameters like movement, colour and shape (Zeki & Bartels, 1998a). Research shows that colour is perceived slightly earlier than form and processed almost simultaneously, but they can feed back on each other when we try to focus on specific visual tasks. If we are in highly task-oriented mode, we relegate peripheral vision to a lower perceptual level of consciousness. As neurons in the early visual cortex can be highly context-dependent, both in their identification and interpretation processes, our final understanding of a scene is highly personalised and singular (Rentzeperis, Nikolaev, Kiper, & van Leeuwen, 2014, p. 31). Studies have also demonstrated that movement is perceived slightly delayed from form, by about 50 milliseconds (Viviani & Aymoz, 2001), but all that our eyes perceive at different speeds is interpreted and merged together by our brain for operational reasons during task-focussed activities.

Learning to identify and interpret AR (with images that might – or might not – be similar to the real objects in the field of vision) is a completely new experience for human beings. What we know already of humans' cognitive capacity to perceive and imagine should be re-tested and analysed to understand how humans perceive pictures, holograms or VR scenes. We already know that spatial binding is separate from, and subsequent to, stimulus processing and that it is an attribute-dependent and post-conscious process (Zeki & Bartels, 2006). We also know that deeper understanding of a situation (e.g. consequences or implications of it) comes from a sequence of separate processes that take place in the cortex after the different zones in the brain have converged their modular information to make up the complex whole. However, awareness (or belief) about the reality of an object can itself disrupt our perceptual channels and alter the way we perceive, integrate and interpret a situation. The feedback loop created by the interaction of these phenomena demonstrates the importance of the iterative practice of alternating action-research with reflection on practice.

We still don't know much about why our brain activates secretion of saliva and gastric juices when perceiving an orange, but it seems obvious that previous knowledge about an image can affect our interpretation of what we see. How will we respond when a VR experience includes not only the image of the orange, but also its odour and maybe even its texture in a virtual tactile stimulus? More research is needed to understand how our senses and brain identify reality produced with 'physical things' versus digitalised representations in both VR and AR.

Human cognitive capacity to perceive and imagine is not only context-dependent, but also personally affected by the previous digital experience of the protagonist. Our final understanding of an image is different if we perceive it as 'a real physical scene' or a photo of a real scene or a painting of the scene. The levels of possible cognitive misdirection become truly complex if we imagine a painting of a non-real object that we may or may not have experienced in VR. Research is now trying to identify the exact visual components that trigger specific identification of AR or VR images: aerial perspective influences depth; shadows in VR scenes simulate the shadows created when light interacts with physical objects; shading models used to render a virtual object influence its perceived spatial properties (Diaz, Walker, Szafir, & Szafir, 2017).

Digital information provides an alternative ecosystem that gives humans the opportunity to have experiences not possible in the real world, and it equips them with the possibility to see objects, places and situations that can't be visited in reality. VR and AR offer high-level multi-sensory learning experiences that can bring changes not only to everyday life, but also to people's cognitive capacity to perceive and interpret images. It changes the entire field of education, affecting the way students learn and the way they build knowledge. Consequently, urgent changes need to be made in the way knowledge is taught and learning is assessed in formal educational environments where AR and VR are going to be developed and applied.

For VR/AR educational experiences, we need significant transformations related to the treatment of input, process and output. On the input side, we need to examine criteria such as who decides the sequence of data acquisition, how decisions are made about timing and content planning, the role of teachers and students in selecting resources to access information and the criteria for including self-access and personalized input in the group or class.

We also need meaningful transformations of teaching and learning processes when using VR/AR devices, such as how to include collaborative tasks, how to enrich flipped classrooms with collective reflection on self-regulation and digital dependencies and how to help students develop personal criteria for driving their own learning autonomy and building their own personal learning networks.

Finally, we need important transformations connected to expression, dissemination and information sharing, leading to the creation of new values. Immersive VR/AR learning tasks will change identity-building processes, social interaction, conceptualisation of reality and contextual perception of the real world, among other cultural constructs. Education will need to focus on how these tools and pedagogical approaches are implemented, their lifelong applicability and their capacity to aid transition processes at different stages of life.

New educational networks will be created in virtual communities and learning spaces, partially transforming both the informal socialisation process and the formal learning environment. They, in turn, will bring new challenges and solutions to the teaching and learning process. Education can weave a transformative path through these in-between spaces, from traditional literacies to new competences, at the frontier of formal and informal education and in the transition zone between the defined physical classroom and the ongoing expansion of the virtual universe. These fragmented spaces, where disruption and creativity grow together, can be clearly included in the enriched organic ecosystems that Zygmunt Bauman defined as *liquid modernity* and about which he brilliantly diagnosed: 'what unites them all is precisely their fragility, temporariness, vulnerability and inclination to constant change' (Bauman, 2012, p. x).

What are now perceived as immersive games will one day soon become enablers for people who need to work in faraway places, manipulate objects in dangerous environments or otherwise function in the most challenging working contexts. These complex digital workspaces require not only the traditional literacies that we develop at school (mostly academic) but also others that have been commonly seen as marginal abilities or soft skills such as relational abilities, global communicative competences and strategic executive skills.

The role of transmedia and transliteracy

Even prior to the coinage of the word 'transmedia' by Marsha Kinder in 1991, educational approaches and pedagogical methods employing multiple communication channels had been developed: the Total Physical Response (TPR) approach, rooted in gestures (Asher, 1969); Suggestopedia, built around audial sensitivity (Lozakov, 1971) and new ideas of textuality (both oral and written) that completely revise translation methods, emphasising the social and communicative constraints of complex linguistic objects (Neubert & Shreve, 1992). They all have in common the intention to add alternative educational narratives to traditional linear teaching and learning instructional processes. They also emphasise the relational skills that help develop social cohesion at school (e.g. empathy, engagement and other emotional appreciations). They give importance, as well, to mental associations and cultural filters (analogy, correlation, context awareness, or synthesis) that are indispensable for integrating and combining fragments of meaning into the global comprehension of a situation.

The evolution and generalisation of radio and television production techniques have made evident that content fragmentation is a characteristic of mass media (McLuhan, 1964). Fragmentation has also become a central interest for research on reactions to and understanding of gamification, marketing and publicity (Steinberg, 2012). In entertainment, interaction among multiple digital channels, coupled with increasingly complex storytelling, has created a shared concept of 'transmedia universe' that is now relevant for education, sociology and economics (Dena, 2009). The definition of *transmedia storytelling* – 'where integral elements of a fiction get dispersed systematically across multiple delivery channels for the purpose of creating a unified and coordinated entertainment experience' (Jenkins, 2007) seems almost directly applicable to AR.

Transliteracy, on the other hand, is among the most strategic of human learning skills, as it *bridges* and integrates fragmented knowledge acquired through multiple competences. Transliteracy is seen as 'the ability to read, write and interact across a range of platforms, tools and media from signing and orality through handwriting, print, TV, radio and film, to digital social networks' (Thomas, 2005). It means that the traditional four skills (listening, speaking, reading and writing) broaden their descriptors to include new competences such as interaction and mediation (both in physical and digital channels), enhancing communication with a kind of global human competence that experts are still trying to define. This complexity is even more tangled when adding variables to deal with cultural differences and social filters for interpreting meanings, messages and situations in a global context, where virtualising technology increases the impact of media products from far-off lands. The OECD definition of 'global competence' already emphasises the importance of the social factor and intentional executive purposes:

Global competence is the capacity to examine local, global and intercultural issues, to understand and appreciate the perspectives and world views of others, to engage in open, appropriate and effective interactions with people from different cultures, and to act for collective well-being and sustainable development.

(2018, p. 7)

The Council of Europe has recently published a Companion Volume to the *Common European Framework of Reference for Languages* (CEFR), adding new descriptors and abilities that are essentially relational, social and context-dependent (2018).

Case studies: VR/AR when reality is not available

These case studies are of training experiences in two very different educational contexts, both targeting similar goals:

- A workshop on serious games with AR/VR for students with a high risk of exclusion, in closed educational centres in Catalonia (Spain), to experience an outside reality that is unavailable to incarcerated students.
- A university level workshop to restore a past that no longer exists to a virtual present, in order to make an archaeological site live for young visitors.

In both situations, students are building an alternative present following a transversal co-creational activity that includes strong horizontal interaction – collaborating in the design of virtual games: one for a collective jam session and one to propose to a cultural institution.

These case studies involve student populations at opposite extremes of the educational system (youngsters at risk versus university architecture students), but both groups benefitted from similar collaborative digital learning projects involving similar educational processes:

- *Student collaborative learning:* in both cases, teamwork was indispensable to the completion of the assignment, with results to be shared after an action-research challenge. This approach fostered interaction among students, some of whom were not used to working in teams with strangers.
- *Exploratory AR/VR teaching techniques:* The rich perceptual experience in AR/VR and the ludic nature of the activity offered supplementary emotional and sensorial reinforcement that anchored learning through the experience.
- *Enriched digital institutional development:* Introducing AR/VR game jam strategies in environments as diverse as prisons and universities provides an example of how digital development is affecting every single educational context.

Case study 1: serious games with AR/VR

A 2019 Summer School Workshop for fighting against exclusion

Overview

Within the panorama of transforming education towards the UN SDGs, this Workshop offered participants the possibility of exploring the changes to healthcare resulting from digital transformation. After a short presentation in which the main session rules were established, students were able to experiment with different serious games, VR headsets and co-creation technologies:

- *MomentosVR Clinic:* immersive VR experience to improve stress and anxiety in oncology patients
- *Training Dravet:* serious immersive VR game to facilitate the social inclusion of children with epilepsy
- *Premis Muncunill augmented reality app:* tool to create simple AR games from basic components

Students were asked to negotiate and design, in teams, the external settings, protagonists and type of goal in a health-related game. A final game jam to share their productions served to recognise their work and publicly celebrate their collective results, while also commenting on errors in a ludic manner.

Organisation

The main elements and key players in this workshop were the following:

- **Type of activity:** Serious games workshop with AR/VR techniques
- **Levels:** Entry level, secondary, vocational, and adult learning
- **Duration:** One four-hour session (30 minutes of instruction; 45 minutes of technology trials; 165 minutes of game jam)
- **Attendees:** Young adults in nine closed educational centres in Catalonia, Spain (adult schools in penitentiaries)
- **Organiser:** Sub-directorate General for Educational Transformation in the Directorate General for Innovation, Research and Digital Culture (Department of Education), coordinated with the Department of Justice (Generalitat de Catalunya)
- **Provider:** *Humantik*, coordinated through Department of Education in Catalonia, Spain
- **Language of instruction:** Catalan and Spanish
- **Objective:** 'To obtain a general perspective on how serious games and new technologies are beginning to revolutionise the education sectors, training and health, and practical training experience with a *Game Jam*'

- **Co-ordinator**: Frank del Àguila Espejo
- **Dates:** 1–31 July 2019
- Included in the *2019 Summer School Workshops* for adult schools in penitentiaries (Catalonia, Spain)

Professionals' involvement

This workshop was designed to be both a training session in creating games and a practice experience with digital AR/VR. The trainer involved in this case study participated in the workshop design, the instructional sessions and the final assessment of the experience. His involvement was initially related to the possible improvement of the AR/VR tools and the training session itself, but in the final assessment form, he definitely was more impressed by the emotional relationships created during the sessions and his own feelings of success and discovery when the participants enjoyed the activities and shared their ideas.

Students' involvement

The activities were designed for the students to work in small groups and share their ideas, feelings and suggestions. After the first instructional steps, they become fully engaged without showing any behavioural conflict, and they were clearly involved in their own discoveries. Playfulness and relaxed relational climate were common among the youngest participants, sharing humour while developing their game. One of the imprisoned young adults, impressed with the AR/VR images on his head mounted display, asked the teacher, 'Sir, can you put my girlfriend inside here?'

Transferability

This experience has elements that can be generalised into different educational environments and provides useful methods to help develop digital skills, relational competences and collaborative strategies. For vulnerable communities and people at risk of exclusion, AR/VR workshops are highly engaging training resources. In this particular case study, sessions were also useful in promoting participants' reflection and encouraging meta-cognition on their own future challenges and needs. One of the attendees, imprisoned for more than ten years, came to the teacher after having used a head-mounted display with AR/VR images, saying, 'Now I really can see that the world outside has changed a lot: I won't know how to navigate when I go back there, if we cannot learn how to use these tools of yours!'

Impact

This workshop provided a combination of immersive learning and ludic experience that was highly motivating and very efficient in engaging students. As a result, several participants asked to attend classes in the next round of the same workshop, wherever it took place.

Case study 2: Empuries game jam with AR/VR

A university workshop to find AR or VR representations for empowering younger students to understand cultural heritage

Overview

After a successful first trial in 2014 around promoting innovative tourist services, the architecture school of the Polytechnic University of Catalonia (UPC) and the Museum of Archaeology of Catalonia signed a framework agreement for continued collaboration. Under this agreement, additional workshops were held in 2016, 2018 and 2019. Eight professors, 35 students, and four invited professors participated in 2019. One of the authors of this chapter, Ray Gallon, was there as an invited professor.

Five teams spent the workshop time preparing projects built around different types of architectonic representation: 3D modelling, photogrammetry and virtual and augmented reality, using tablets, mobiles, 360° cameras, drones, etc. The project assignment was to create a proposal that could actually be used by the museum to create an application or game that would bring the site of the Greek and Roman cities located at Empuries, Catalonia, Spain, to life for young visitors who tended to see the site as a 'pile of stones'.

During the workshop, teams drawn from diverse student populations (e,g, architecture, video game design, programming) worked together to gather data *in situ*. They then worked to create at least a partial prototype that shows how their solution would function and what it would offer young visitors from a pedagogical and ludic perspective.

Organisation

The main characteristics and educational agents involved in in this workshop were the following:

- **Type of activity:** Workshop with AR/VR, on archaeological site
- **Level:** University and adult learning
- **Duration**: A 2.5-day session (alternating informational presentations and game jam in teams)

- **Attendees:** Students and professors in architecture, art and animation, programming and video game design
- **Organisers:** *Departament de representació arquitectònica, Escola Tècnica Superior d'Arquitectura de Barcelona (ETSAB)–Universitat Politècnica de Catalunya (UPC)*, together with the *Museu d'Arqueologia de Catalunya (MAC), Seu d'Empúries de L'Escala* (Catalonia, Spain) and the *Escola de Noves Tècnologies Interactives (ENTI), Universitat de Barcelona*
- **Providers:** *Labs4 Reality* (private company), participant universities and attendees provided the equipment used (BYOD – 'Bring Your Own Device' – was encouraged)
- **Language of instruction:** Catalan and Spanish
- **Objective:** To obtain viable proposals for an application that could provide engagement for young children with the archaeological site in Empuries, usable in place without guidance
- **Co-ordinators:** Isidro Navarro, Lluís Giménez, Ernest Redondo, all from ETSAB
- **Dates**: 10–12 May 2019
- Optional excursion in the annual university programme

Professionals' involvement

Professors' roles varied. Some were the students' usual teachers, there to provide technical and conceptual advice as projects advanced. Others were from related disciplines or invited specialists, who had more of a questioning role. Some professors also participated in generating project ideas. Professors were fully engaged and were there to learn as well as to facilitate the project.

Students' involvement

This workshop was something students looked forward to for many weeks before it took place. Once on site, they were completely engaged. Some students went to the museum library and worked as late into the night as they were allowed. Students who brought drones sent them on photogrammetry runs on their own time, when the museum site was closed to the public, to obtain quality images to use in the AR and VR experiences.

Transferability

This workshop had academic objectives at several levels:

- Training students directly in skills needed as part of their professional education

- Collaborating with, and assisting, a major cultural institution in order to improve the attractivity of their site for visiting tourists
- Giving students experience in applying professional tools and technology to a real-world use for an outside (i.e. non-professional) public
- Understanding how these technologies can be integrated into a pedagogical objective and provide a ludic learning situation.

The workshop process used could easily be transferred to different subject matter and different collaborations between academia and the outside world. Most especially, it can be applied in a teacher-training situation to help show the educational value of AR and VR learning spaces and how to construct a sound pedagogical plan.

Impact

The museum already had a VR application to show reconstructions of certain sites, which participants could experience before beginning their projects. This application, while carefully executed, presented a safety problem as users needed to wear a head-mounted display and could not see their actual surroundings. A museum staff person had always to be on hand to prevent users from walking into a wall or falling off a platform. For this reason, most of the projects presented focussed on AR solutions. It was also felt, from a pedagogical point of view, that it was important that visitors see the real site at the same time that they experience reconstructions or other synthesised images.

Many of the projects involved memory games to help visitors remember the important points learned through the application. Question sets were often geared for different age groups so that all visitors could participate.

At the conclusion of the workshop, the museum archaeologists were impressed with the results, saying they would study the propositions seriously with an eye to possibly implementing one of them.

Conclusion

AR and VR, when incorporated into a solid pedagogical plan, offer enormous opportunities for developing inclusive techniques for at-risk student populations, for using digital spaces in situations in which physical reality is not available or for training for professions in which life, health or safety can be at risk. Educational institutions and associations have a responsibility to collaborate with civil society to ensure that such powerful technologies are used to benefit social cohesion, equity and inclusion. The intense stimulus offered by these activities provides a transcendent experience that anchors learning and helps promote their engagement in digital lifelong learning for all types of students.

The case studies demonstrate the extent of student engagement when using AR/VR to explore realities unavailable to them. Beyond executing the defined work plans for these experiences, they were willing to contribute new ideas, enhancing the educational design and executing unexpected sequences. Without knowing about each other's' activities, teachers in both workshops designed sessions that stepped from learning about the tools (AR/VR) to using the tools to learn. Moreover, both workshops ended up as learning-by-doing sessions and encouraged students to explore how AR/VR can be effectively used in real situations. These case studies provide clear examples of how AR and VR can act as emotional amplifiers for teachers' and students' opinions, feelings and attitudes.

Both workshops profited from the fact that several institutions, administrations and professional agents were interested in collaborating for mutual benefit. As the UN 2030 Agenda defends in its SDG 17, successful partnerships between institutions, the private sector and civil society require projects built upon a shared vision and common principles that place people at the core of their goals at local, regional and global levels.

References

Aleksander, I., & Dumall, B. (2000, January 22). An extension to the hypothesis of the asynchrony of visual consciousness. (R. Society, Ed.) *Proceedings of the Royal Society*, 267(1839), 197–200. doi:10.1098/rspb.2000.0987

Artaud, A. (1938). *Le Théâtre et son double*. Paris: Gallimard. Retrieved August 12, 2019, from https://fr.wikisource.org/wiki/Le_théâtre_et_son_double/Texte_entier

Asher, J. J. (1969). The total physical response approach to second language learning. *The Modern Language Journal, 53*(1), 3–17.

Bauman, Z. (2012). *Liquid modernity*, 2012 ed. Cambridge, UK: Polity Press. Retrieved September 1, 2019, from https://leseprobe.buch.de/images-adb/ca/39/ca398fc8-0c78-4ce3-ba48-adf44ed1c7c9.pdf

Cocke, J., & Kolsky, H. G. (1959). The virtual memory in the STRETCH computer. *The Joint IRE-AIEE-ACM Computer Conference*, 81–93. Boston, MA. The 1959 Eastern Joint Computer Conference for the National Joint Computer Committee. Retrieved August 12, 2019, from www.textfiles.com/bitsavers/pdf/ibm/7030/1959_fallJCC.pdf

Council of Europe. (2018). *Common European framework of references for languages: Learning, teaching assessment. Companion volume with new descriptors*. Council of Europe, Education Policy Division, Education Department. Strasbourg: Language Policy Programme, Council of Europe. Retrieved from https://rm.coe.int/cefr-companion-volume-with-new-descriptors–2018/1680787989

Davydov, V. (1995). The influence of L. S. Vygotsky on education theory, research, and practice. *Educational Research, 24*(3), 12–21. Retrieved August 12, 2019.

De Corte, E. (2010). Historical developments in the understanding of learning. In H. Dumont, D. Istance, & F. Benavides (Eds.), *The nature of learning: Using research to inspire practice* (pp. 35–68). OECD Publishing. Retrieved April 6, 2018, from www.

keepeek.com/Digital-Asset-Management/oecd/education/the-nature-of-learn
ing_9789264086487-en#page1

Dena, C. (2009). *Transmedia practice: Theorising the practice of expressing a fictional world across distinct media and environments.* Sydney: University of Sydney. Retrieved from http://dl.dropbox.com/u/30158/DENA_TransmediaPractice.pdf

Diaz, C., Walker, M., Szafir, D. A., & Szafir, D. (2017). Designing for depth perceptions in augmented reality. In *Proceedings of the IEEE International Symposium on Mixed and Augmented Reality (ISMAR 2017), Nantes, France.* Boulder, CO: University of Colorado. Retrieved September 1, 2019, from www.danszafir.com/papers/ISMAR17-Szafir.pdf

Freinet, C. (1927). *L'imprimerie à l'école.* Boulogne: E. Ferrary Éditeur.

Freinet, C. (1993). *L'Education du Travail.* (J. Sivell, Trans.). Lewiston, NY: Edwin Mellen Press.

Galacticgabby. (2014, February 23). *The defiance of logic: Avant-Garde theatre in the modern period.* Retrieved August 6, 2019, from Transnational Modernism Blog https://transnationalmodernism.wordpress.com/2014/02/23/the-defiance-of-logic-avant-garde-theatre-in-the-modern-period/

Grossman, E. (2004). *Antonin Artaud, œuvres.* Paris, France: Éditions Gallimard. Retrieved August 12, 2019.

Heo, H., & Joung, S. (2004). *Self-regulation strategies and technologies for adaptive learning management systems for web-based instruction.* Retrieved April 6, 2019, from ERIC https://files.eric.ed.gov/f

Jenkins, H. (2007, March 21). *Transmedia storytelling 101. Confessions of an Aca-Fan.* Retrieved from The Official Weblog of Henry Jenkins http://calendar.google.com/calendar/r/day/2019/9/10?tab=mc

Kelly, J. (2016, April 1). *Why is it called "Virtual Reality"?* Retrieved August 12, 2019, from Mashed Radish Everyday Etymology https://mashedradish.com/2016/04/01/why-is-it-called-virtual-reality/

Lorenzo, N., & Gallon, R. (2019). Smart pedagogy for smart learning. In L. Daniela (Ed.), *Didactics of smart pedagogy* (pp. 41–69). Cham: Springer Nature.

Lorenzo Galés, N., & Gallon, R. (2018). A social constructionist model for human-machine ecosystems. In L. Daniela (Ed.), *Learning strategies and constructionism in modern education settings* (pp. 25–50). Hershey, PA: IGI Global.

Lozakov, G. (1971). *Suggestology and outlines of suggestopedy.* New York, NY: Routledge, Taylor and Francis Group.

McLuhan, M. H. (1964). *Understanding media: The extensions of man.* New York, NY: McGraw Hill.

Merriam-Webster. (2019, August 5). *Transcendent.* Retrieved August 12, 2019, from Merriam-Webster Dictionary www.merriam-webster.com/dictionary/transcendent

Neubert, A., & Shreve, G. M. (1992). *Translation as text.* Retrieved from www.scribd.com/document/251117849/Translation-As-Text-pdf

OECD. (2016). *PISA 2018 draft analytical frameworks, May 2016.* Retrieved June 14, 2017, from OECD www.oecd.org/pisa/data/PISA-2018-draft-frameworks.pdf

OECD. (2018). *Preparing our youth for an inclusive and sustainable world. The OECD-PISA global competence framework.* Directorate for Education and Skills OECD. Paris: OECD. Retrieved from www.oecd.org/education/Global-competency-for-an-inclusive-world.pdf

Ortiz, A. (2019, March 14). *Welcome to extended reality: Transforming how employees work and learn.* Retrieved from IBM Web www.ibm.com/blogs/services/2019/03/14/welcome-to-extended-reality-transforming-how-employees-work-and-learn/

Oxford English Dictionary. (2019). *Virtual reality.* Retrieved September 1, 2019, from Lexico www.lexico.com/en/definition/virtual_reality

Rentzeperis, I., Nikolaev, A. R., Kiper, D. C., & van Leeuwen, C. (2014, October 27). Distributed processing of colour and form in the visual cortex. *Frontiers in Psychology, 5*(932), 23–36. doi:10.1016/S0042-6989(01)00160-2. Retrieved September 1, 2019.

Riva, G., Mantovani, F., Capideville, C. S., Preziosa, A., Morganti, F., Villani, D., & Alcañiz, M. (2007). Affective interactions using virtual reality: The link between presence and emotions. *CyberPsychology & Behavior, 10*(1). doi:10.1089/cpb.2006.9993. Retrieved September 1, 2019.

Rosenberg, L. B. (1992, September). *The use of virtual fixtures as perceptual overlays to enhance operator performance in remote environments.* Retrieved August 12, 2019, from Defense Technical Information Center https://apps.dtic.mil/dtic/tr/fulltext/u2/a292450.pdf

Schueffel, P. (2017). *The concise FINTECH compendium.* Retrieved August 12, 2019, from School-of-Management-Fribourg www.heg-fr.ch/FR/HEG-FR/Communi cation-et-evenements/evenements/SiteAssets/Pages/patrick-schuffel/Schueffel%20 (2017)%20The%20Concise%20FINTECH%20COMPENDIUM.PDF

Steinberg, M. (2012). *Anime's media mix: Franchising toys and characters in Japan.* Minneapolis, MN: Univerity of Minnesota Press. Retrieved from https://ijoc.org/index.php/ijoc/article/download/3171/1216

Thomas, S. (2005). Transliteracy – Reading in the digital age. *Higher Education Academy English Subject Centre Newsletter.* (November). Retrieved September 30, 2015, from www.english.heacademy.ac.uk/explore/publications/newsletters/newsissue9/thom

Viviani, P., & Aymoz, C. (2001, October 1). *Colour, form, and movement are not perceived simultaneously.* Retrieved September 1, 2019, from Science Direct. doi:10.1016/S0042-6989(01)00160-2

Wikipedia. (2019a, August 10). *Wired glove.* Retrieved August 12, 2019, from Wikipedia https://en.wikipedia.org/wiki/Wired_glove

Wikipedia. (2019b, August 12). *Jaron Lanier.* Retrieved August 12, 2019, from Wikipedia https://en.wikipedia.org/wiki/Jaron_Lanier

Zeki, S., & Bartels, A. (1998a). The autonomy of the visual system and the modularity of conscious vision. (R. Society, Ed.) *Philosophical Transactions of the Royal Society, B, 353,* 1911–1914. Retrieved from www.ncbi.nlm.nih.gov/pmc/articles/PMC1692424/pdf/9854263.pdf

Zeki, S., & Bartels, A. (1998b). The asynchrony of consciousness. *Proceedings of the Royal Society, B, 265,* 1583–1585. London. Retrieved September 1, 2019, from https://pdfs.semanticscholar.org/aaf6/c2d41699c1e2608fb58565dd4601ddb362d8.pdf

Zeki, S., & Bartels, A. (2006, August). The temporal order of binding visual attributes. *Vision Research, 46*(14), 2280–2286. Retrieved September 1, 2019, from www.scien cedirect.com/science/article/pii/S0042698905005997

Chapter 9

Enhancing trust in virtual reality systems

Davide Salanitri, Glyn Lawson and Brian Waterfield

Introduction

Virtual Reality

Virtual Reality (VR) is a technology that has seen recent increase in interest, both in academia and among the general public, mainly thanks to the decrease in cost and increase in quality (Young, Gaylor, Andrus, & Bodenheimer, 2014). The potential of VR has been known for decades, and this technology is nowadays applied in several fields. VR has been seen as effective in fields including industry (Lawson, Salanitri, & Waterfield, 2016), healthcare (Ma, Jain, & Anderson, 2014), training (Borsci, Lawson, Salanitri, & Jha, 2016) and education (de Faria, Teixeira, Júnior, Otoch, & Figueiredo, 2016). Thanks to the aforementioned decrease in cost and increase in quality, the studies on VR systems have increased significantly, and the advantages that VR offers compared to other technologies are now clearer. The improved sense of immersion and the possibility to explore objects and environments not accessible in real life are among the most valuable characteristics in VR technology.

VR in education

Several VR systems have been developed for teaching and learning over the years. Twenty-four years ago, Psotka (1995) highlighted the advantages of VR applied to the educational field. The author stated that the immersive power of VR could pave the way for VR as an effective and widely used system. Since then, important advancements have been put in place in the field of VR, and more systems have been developed. For instance, Kaufmann, Schmalstieg, and Wagner (2000) developed a system called Contruct3D to help teach mathematics and geometry. The system, composed of a stereoscopic Head Mounted Display (HMD) and a two-handed 3D control tool, was developed to help the visual representation of geometric shapes and to improve the spatial abilities of children. Odor (2009) developed a 3D system to teach Sign Language. The author stated that the 3D representation and the possibilities of varying speed and position and choosing an avatar can improve the process of learning Sign Language. de Faria et al. (2016) analysed the effectiveness of VR for medical and anatomical education. The authors found that there was a statistically significant improvement in students' results when learning through VR systems compared to learning by conventional methods. Other than single cases, several literature reviews were performed on the field of VR in education (e.g. Hew & Cheung, 2010; Lee, 2010 Sitzmann, 2011; Vogel et al., 2006). These reviews all found that VR, simulations and games increase the effectiveness of learning. Some negative impact was also found, such as the negative attitude of students on using simulation for learning when left without guidance on how to use the system and the reduced effectiveness when the user is not in control of the system. One of the most complete literature reviews was made by Merchant, Goetz, Cifuentes, Keeney-Kennicutt, and Davis (2014). The analysis focused on Desktop-VR used for K-12 (kindergarten to 12th grade in the U.S. school system) and higher education and included games, Virtual Words and simulations. The authors explored a total of 69 studies and found that various types of VR are effective in improving learning outcomes (Merchant et al., 2014). The results of the analysis found that desktop-VR is a very effective method in teaching and that, in general, games are more effective than simulations and virtual worlds.

Trust in VR

Despite the positive outcomes reported above, in order for VR systems to be used effectively there is an important aspect that has to be taken into consideration: the trustworthiness of the system. Various research has highlighted that the perception of trust influences the interaction between the user and the technology and it can be a turning point in the decision to use (or not) the system. Technologies like e-commerce (Ba, Whinston, & Zhang, 1999; Kim & Peterson, 2017), social networks (Lankton & McKnight, 2011) and automated systems (Muir & Moray, 1996) have been seen to require users' trust to be effective and actually used at all. However, there is still discussion in the literature on the factors influencing people's trust in technology and especially the factors influencing trust in VR. Lippert and Michael Swiercz (2005) theorised different types of determinants of trust in technology: organisational, technological and user.

The model of trust created by McKnight et al. (2011) explains that trust in technology is given, in general, by three factors: trust in a specific technology (functionality, reliability and helpfulness), propensity to trust and institution-based trust. While propensity to trust and institution-based trust are more related to personal and organisational characteristics (same as the 'organisational' and 'user' characteristics described by Lippert & Michael Swiercz, 2005), functionality, reliability and helpfulness are more related to the technology characteristics and can, therefore, be improved in the technology design.

While these models usefully frame our understanding of trust in technology, there is not yet a complete model of factors that could influence trust in VR systems, which may differ from other technologies for their possibility to immerse the user and the different type of interaction involved (e.g. the use of stereoscopic view, the use of seamless interaction devices).

Trust in VR education

In education, the trust people have in the technology they are using is a key factor for the effectiveness of the system. Wang (2014) highlighted how, for instance, e-learning causes more doubts than face-to-face education, because the potential risks of using a technology (e.g. privacy, technology failure) have to be taken into account by students when deciding to study remotely. These risks and doubts cause a higher number of dropouts in e-learning course than in face-to-face courses (Bell & Federman, 2013; Patterson & McFadden, 2009; Tyler-Smith, 2006). Understanding how to increase users' trust in the VR system they are using could therefore be a key factor for the success of this technology in the educational field.

The model

The literature suggested three main factors influencing trust in VR systems: technology acceptance, usability and presence, which were used to build a model to investigate trust in VR. Key findings from each area follow.

Technology acceptance

Various studies (Gefen, Karahanna, & Straub, 2003; Hernandez-Ortega, 2011; Wu, Zhao, Zhu, Tan, & Zheng, 2011) demonstrated the relationship between technology acceptance and trust. Davis (1985) first theorised the concept of technology acceptance and developed the Technology Acceptance Model (TAM). According to Davis (1985), there are two factors of technology acceptance: perceived usefulness and perceived ease of use. Perceived usefulness is defined as the users' belief that the technology will improve their performance. Perceived ease of use refers to the effort needed to use the technology (Davis, 1985). Technology acceptance explains 40% of the users' intention to use the system (Venkatesh & Davis, 2000). Studies in the literature investigate the relationship between technology acceptance and trust. Trust has been related to technology acceptance in online purchasing (Gefen et al., 2003), online gaming (Wu et al., 2011) and e-banking (Suh & Han, 2003). In a meta-analysis, Wu et al. (2011) found that trust is positively correlated with both factors of technology acceptance. Hernandez-Ortega (2011) demonstrated that perceived ease of use is one of the factors influencing trust.

Usability

Usability is extensively studied in human factors and is based on whether technology satisfies users' needs (Bevan, 2009). Bevan, Kirakowski, Maissel, and Maissel (1991) defined usability as

> *the ease of use and acceptability of a system or product for a particular class of users carrying out specific tasks in a specific environment; where "ease of use" affects user performance and satisfaction, and "acceptability" affects whether or not the product is used.*

(p. 652)

The choice of usability was made following studies in the literature on the relationship between usability and trust (Bevan, 2009; Roy et al., 2001) and the fact that usability was included as a factor of trust in some previous studies (e.g. Lippert & Michael Swiercz, 2005).

Presence

One of the best known definitions of presence is the sensation of being in a place, while situated in another (Witmer & Singer, 1998). Therefore, if a VR system induces enough presence, the users will develop the belief that they actually are present in the virtual environment instead of the 'real' one. Expansion of the definition of presence was given by Slater (2009). The author argued that presence is composed of two orthogonal concepts: Place Illusion (PI) and Plausibility illusion (PSI). PI corresponds to the sensation of being there. That is the classic definition. PSI is the illusion that what it is happening in the virtual world, is actually happening.

The choice of presence as a potential factor influencing trust in VR was due to the importance this concept has in the VR field; it is one of the most studied and important factors in VR (Sanchez-Vives & Slater, 2005; Slater & Wilbur, 1997; Witmer & Singer, 1998).

Method

An experimental study was designed to further investigate the model of trust in technology described previously. The study was part of a PhD project co-funded by Jaguar Land Rover (JLR). The company was particularly interested in the investigation of the factors influencing trust as they could be important in the vehicle development process. A total of 19 participants (Mean age= 30.21, SD=13.67; 13 Males) were recruited among the staff at JLR. Certain characteristics that have been seen to increase the possibility of cybersickness symptoms (e.g. suffer from migraines or epilepsy or being pregnant) were listed as exclusion criteria.

It is important to note that the aim of this study was not to understand the system effectiveness for training, and this was not measured. The investigation aimed at the factors enhancing users' trust in the system in order to guide the design of future VR technologies for educational and other purposes.

Materials

VR

The participants interacted with the JLR CAVE. The JLR CAVE projects images on four different walls (left, right, front and ceiling) with eight 4K Sony projectors (SRX-t105) (two per wall). The CAVE is powered by 16 computers (4 per screen) each with dual core CPU (Intel Xeon ES-2690). For 3D representation, the participants wore a pair of tracked glasses. The tracking permitted the model to adjust to the position of the participant's head, ensuring that the model (and occlusion effects) matched the participant's perspective. This was particularly important for realism, because the perspective of the object would feel less artificial, and for cybersickness, since the movement in the virtual environment was the same as the participants' head, avoiding contrast of senses, one of the possible cause of cybersickness (LaViola, 2000). The controller used was a joystick. The joystick was tracked, thus the participants had to move it in order to move the pointer on the screen. An example of the CAVE is showed in Figure 9.1.

QUESTIONNAIRES

The questionnaires were divided into pre-interaction questionnaires (given before the interaction with the VR system) and post-interaction questionnaires (given after the interaction questionnaire).

Figure 9.1 Example of a car model displayed in the JLR CAVE.

Pre-interaction questionnaires:

Demographic Questionnaire:

A demographic questionnaire was built to gather information about the participants (e.g. age, gender, VR experience).

Post-Interaction questionnaires

ITC-Sense of presence inventory (ITC-SOPI) (Lessiter et al., 2001):

The ITC-SOPI has been used to assess the level of presence perceived by the participants.

System Usability Scale (SUS) (Brooke, 1996):

The SUS has been seen as a useful tool to assess people's perceived usability.

Technology Acceptance Questionnaire (Hernandez-Ortega, 2011; Venkatesh & Davis, 2000):

The technology acceptance questionnaire has been used in the literature to understand the level of technology acceptance of the users.

Trust in Technology measure (McKnight et al., 2011):

The questionnaire has been used to assess the level of users' trust in the specific system.

Tasks

The participants had to perform six assembly and disassembly tasks on a car model already loaded into the CAVE.

Procedure

The entire procedure lasted approximately 45 minutes. The participants were invited into the room and asked to read the information sheet and complete the consent form. If the participants decided to take part in the study, the pre-interaction questionnaires were given. After the questionnaires were complete, a trial phase started. In the trial phase, the researcher first explained the main features of the CAVE and the controller buttons. Then, the participants watched an explanatory video on a laptop for each task and performed the task straight away inside the CAVE. In the trial phase, the participants could ask questions and ask for help to complete the task. After the trial, the participants started the experiment. The participants had to perform the task within 3 minutes in the same order as during the trial. In accordance with guidance from the Engineering Faculty Ethics Committee at the University of Nottingham, the participants were interrupted after every two tasks to complete a cybersickness assessment. The participants had to verbally confirm when and if they thought the task was completed. If the participants did not complete the task in time, the task would be considered failed. In the experimental phase, no help was given to the participants. After the interaction, the participants were invited to complete the post interaction questionnaires. The maximum exposition time to VR was 18 minutes.

Data analysis

In order to understand the nature of the sample, frequencies were performed with the data from the demographic questionnaire. All the analyses were performed with SPSS®. To understand the relationship between the three factors and trust, four regression analyses were performed: three with each factor as an independent variable and trust as a dependent variable and a regression analysis with all the factors as independent variables and trust as a dependent variable.

Results

Demographic

Table 9.1 shows the frequencies of the demographic questionnaire data.

Regressions

In order to understand the relationship between the three factors and trust, four regressions were performed. In addition, two regressions were performed to investigate the influence of pre-interaction trust on final trust. Table 9.2 describes the independent and dependent variables of each regression.

Usability and trust

The first regression was performed to investigate the relationship between usability and trust. First of all, a scatter-dot plot was created to visually investigate the relationship between the two variables (Figure 9.2).

Table 9.1 VR experience demographic data.

VR experience	Number	Percentage
I have never heard of VR.	0	0%
I have heard of it but do not know what it is.	0	0%
I have some idea of what VR is.	2	10.5%
I know what VR is but have never seen or used it.	6	31.6%
I have seen a VR system in use.	6	31.6%
I have used a VR system once or twice.	4	21.1%
I have often used VR.	0	0%
I use VR almost every day.	1	5.3%

Table 9.2 List of regression performed.

Regression	Independent variable	Dependent variable	Aim
Regression 1	Usability		To investigate the relationship between usability and trust
Regression 2	TAM		To investigate the relationship between TAM and trust
Regression 3	Presence		To investigate the relationship between presence and trust
Regression 4	Usability, Technology acceptance, Presence	Trust	To investigate the relationship between the three factors and trust
Regression 5	Pre-interaction trust		To investigate the relationship between pre-interaction trust and trust
Regression 6	Pre-interaction trust, usability, technology acceptance, presence		To investigate the influence of pre-interaction trust on the complete model.

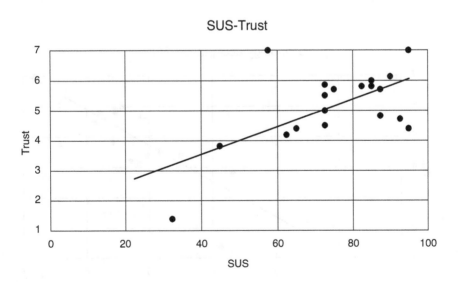

Figure 9.2 Scatter-dot plot of the interaction between SUS and trust.

The regression was significant [F(1,17)= 10.730, p=.004], with usability accounting for 35.6% of trust (Adj. R^2 =.356).

Technology acceptance and trust

The second regression was performed with technology acceptance as an independent variable and trust as a dependent variable and was used to investigate the possible relationship between these two factors. A scatter-dot plot was created to investigate the relationship between the two factors (Figure 9.3).

The regression was significant [F(1,17)= 22.44, p<.001], with technology acceptance accounting for 54.4% of trust (Adj. R^2 =.544).

Presence and trust

The third regression was performed to investigate the relationship between presence and trust. Figure 9.4 shows a scatter-dot plot created in order to have a visual representation of the relationship.

The regression was not significant [F(1,16)= 3.39, p=.084].

Technology acceptance, usability, presence and trust

The fourth regression is the first attempt at the validation of the framework. Even though this was the first experiment, it could be useful to understand if there is the base for confirming the framework as explained in the introduction.

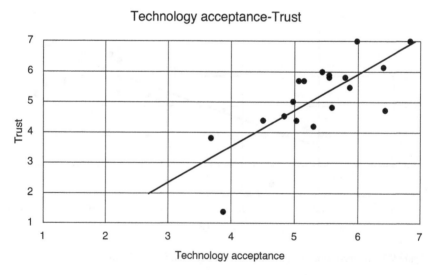

Figure 9.3 Scatter-dot plot of the interaction between technology acceptance and trust.

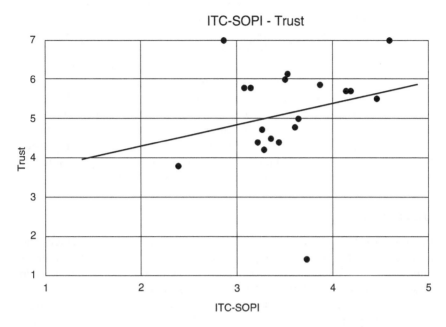

Figure 9.4 Scatter-dot plot of the relationship between ITC-SOPI and trust.

The regression included all three factors (usability, technology acceptance and presence) as independent variables and Trust as a dependent variable.

Participant 2 was removed from the analysis as the leverage value (.44) and Cook's value (1.68) were high and the leverage and influential points assumptions were not respected.

The regression was significant [$F(3,14)=5.467$, p=.011] with the model accounting for the 52% of trust (Adj $R^2 = .518$).

The coefficients of each independent variable are shown in Table 9.3.

Table 9.3 Coefficients of the regression with usability, technology acceptance and presence as independent variable and trust as a dependent variable.

Regression SUS, Technology acceptance, ITQ-SOPI – Trust				
	R^2	Adj R^2	Beta	Sig.
SUS			0.179	0.458
Technology acceptance	0.599	0.518	0.655	0.014
ITQ-SOPI			-0.056	0.756

However, as the table shows, the only variable that significantly added to the model was technology acceptance. This result could be interpreted in various ways depending on the factor under consideration. Usability, for instance, had a significant influence on trust when analysed alone, but it lacked significance when included in the last regression. This could be interpreted as an indirect influence of usability on trust. Presence, on the other hand, was not significant when analysed alone or when included with the other factors. This could mean that presence does not have any influence on trust. However, there were some methodological issues (discussed in the following section) that could have influenced the results of this regression. Regarding technology acceptance, both regressions were significant. This could be the first step for confirming the relationship with trust.

Discussion

In order for VR systems to be effective and correctly implemented, they have to be trustworthy. This applies in every field in which VR systems are implemented, but special attention should be given to systems built for educational purposes. As Wang (2014) argued, trust in educational technology can be the turning point for the decision to actually use it and could influence the dropout rate in online courses. This may also be more relevant as digital technologies become more pervasive within face-to-face education. To improve users' trust in a VR system, it is fundamental to investigate the factors enhancing trust. For this purpose, a model was built, and this chapter describes the first pilot study in the validation of the model. The model, developed following literature on trust in technology and on VR systems, theorised that usability, technology acceptance and presence are among the factors influencing trust in VR.

The results show that when analysed singularly, usability and technology acceptance have an influence on trust, with technology acceptance having a bigger effect. Even though the regression between usability and trust is significant, the effect is low. This could be interpreted as a sign of an indirect relationship. This interpretation is confirmed by the last regression, where all three factors are included together. The results of this regression show that usability does not have a significant influence on trust. The short tasks and the continued interruption of the interaction with the VR system (as stated in the procedure section, the participants were interrupted every two tasks for the cybersickness assessment) could have affected the measurement of usability. Another study assessed the relationship between usability and trust and found similar results (Salanitri et al., 2015). The third factor studied was presence, which was not found to have an influence on trust. In fact, both when taken singularly and when added in the last regression, the results were not significant. These results could mean that presence does not have any type of influence (direct or indirect) on trust in VR. However, some experimental design characteristics may have influenced this result. For example, the interruption of the participants' interaction with the technology could have impacted the immersion the users felt. Another possible explanation could be the type of questionnaire used. In later studies, with adjustments on the questionnaires used and the experiment design, the effect of presence was found to be significant (Salanitri, Lawson, & Waterfield, 2016).

Limitation

As said in the introduction, this study was an initial investigation of the trust in the VR model. Therefore, some methodological limitations may have influenced the results of the study. The first one regards the sample size. The number of participants, even though sufficient for a pilot study, does not permit a conclusive demonstration of the model. However, it gives enough evidence to move forward with the model. Another limitation is given by the study design. As stated in the method section, the participants had to be assessed for cybersickness symptoms every 2 tasks; this could have interrupted the flow of the environment, decreasing the sense of presence (Lessiter et al., 2001).

Conclusion

VR in education has been seen as an effective method, improving users' learning skills. This is because of some technology characteristics, like the possibility of immersion and the 3D visual representation. However, as demonstrated in studies on e-learning technologies, the users have to rely on the system they are using in order for it to be used and used properly. Lack of trust can negatively influence the advantage VR gives over other technology and can provoke some 'side effects' such as higher dropout rates (Wang, 2014). Therefore, it is important to study the factors that could influence trust in VR systems, in order to help the design of better, more trustworthy technologies. This chapter analysed a pilot study to validate a theoretical model where usability, presence and technology acceptance are thought to be determinants of trust in VR systems. The study had conflicting results. While technology acceptance and usability were found to be related to trust, presence was not. Moreover, usability seemed to have a weaker effect on trust. As stated in the discussion section, these results could be given from methodological and design issues but can also mean that the relationship is actually more complicated than initially theorised. The results are a good starting point on the validation of the model, even though more in-depth studies should be done. Future steps of this model are already included in other works such as Salanitri et al. (2015 and 2016). However, this study was the first to include all of the factors together.

References

Ba, S., Whinston, A., & Zhang, H. (1999). Building trust in the electronic market through an economic incentive mechanism. *ICIS 1999 Proceedings 19,* 208-213.

Bell, B. S., & Federman, J. E. (2013). E-learning in postsecondary education. *The Future of Children, 3(1),* 165–185.

Bevan, N. (2009, July). Extending quality in use to provide a framework for usability measurement. In *International Conference on Human Centered Design* (pp. 13–22). Berlin and Heidelberg: Springer.

Bevan, N. K., Kirakowski, J., Maissel, J., & Maissel, J. (1991, September). What is usability. In *Proceedings of the 4th International Conference on HCI, Stuttgart, Germany* (pp. 1–6). Elsevier Science.

Borsci, S., Lawson, G., Salanitri, D., & Jha, B. (2016). When simulated environments make the difference: The effectiveness of different types of training of car service procedures. *Virtual Reality, 20(2),* 83–99.

Brooke, J., 1996. SUS-A quick and dirty usability scale. *Usability evaluation in industry,* 189(194), pp. 4–7.

Davis, F. D. (1985). *A technology acceptance model for empirically testing new end-user information systems: Theory and results* (Doctoral dissertation). Massachusetts Institute of Technology.

de Faria, J. W. V., Teixeira, M. J., Júnior, L. D. M. S., Otoch, J. P., & Figueiredo, E. G. (2016). Virtual and stereoscopic anatomy: When virtual reality meets medical education. *Journal of Neurosurgery, 125(5),* 1105–1111.

Gefen, D., Karahanna, E., & Straub, D. W. (2003). Trust and TAM in online shopping: An integrated model. *MIS Quarterly, 27(1),* 51–90.

Hernandez-Ortega, B. (2011). The role of post-use trust in the acceptance of a technology: Drivers and consequences. *Technovation, 31(10–11),* 523–538.

Hew, K. F., & Cheung, W. S. (2010). Use of three-dimensional (3-D) immersive virtual worlds in K-12 and higher education settings: A review of the research. *British Journal of Educational Technology, 41(1),* 33–55.

Kaufmann, H., Schmalstieg, D., & Wagner, M. (2000). Construct3D: A virtual reality application for mathematics and geometry education. *Education and Information Technologies, 5(4),* 263–276.

Kim, Y., & Peterson, R. A. (2017). A meta-analysis of online trust relationships in E-commerce. *Journal of Interactive Marketing, 38,* 44–54.

LaViola Jr, J.J., 2000. A discussion of cybersickness in virtual environments. ACM Sigchi Bulletin, 32(1), pp. 47–56.

Lankton, N. K., & McKnight, D. H. (2011). What does it mean to trust Facebook?: Examining technology and interpersonal trust beliefs. *ACM SIGMIS Database: The DATABASE for Advances in Information Systems, 42(2),* 32–54.

Lawson, G., Salanitri, D., & Waterfield, B. (2016). Future directions for the development of virtual reality within an automotive manufacturer. *Applied Ergonomics, 53,* 323–330.

Lee, E. A. L., Wong, K. W., & Fung, C. C. (2010). How does desktop virtual reality enhance learning outcomes? A structural equation modeling approach. *Computers & Education, 55(4),* 1424–1442.

Lessiter, J., Freeman, J., Keogh, E. and Davidoff, J., 2001. A cross-media presence questionnaire: The ITC-Sense of Presence Inventory. Presence: Teleoperators & Virtual Environments, 10(3), pp. 282–297.

Lippert, S. K., & Michael Swiercz, P. (2005). Human resource information systems (HRIS) and technology trust. *Journal of Information Science, 31*(5), 340–353.

Ma, M., Jain, L. C., & Anderson, P. (2014). Future trends of virtual, augmented reality, and games for health. In *Virtual, augmented reality and serious games for healthcare 1* (pp. 1–6). Berlin and Heidelberg: Springer.

Mcknight, D.H., Carter, M., Thatcher, J.B. and Clay, P.F. (2011). Trust in a specific technology: An investigation of its components and measures. *ACM Transactions on management information systems (TMIS), 2(2)*, pp. 1–25.

Merchant, Z., Goetz, E. T., Cifuentes, L., Keeney-Kennicutt, W., & Davis, T. J. (2014). Effectiveness of virtual reality-based instruction on students' learning outcomes in K-12 and higher education: A meta-analysis. *Computers & Education, 70*, 29–40.

Muir, B. M., & Moray, N. (1996). Trust in automation. Part II. Experimental studies of trust and human intervention in a process control simulation. *Ergonomics, 39*(3), 429–460.

Odor, A. (2009). High resolution 3D models for the teaching of American sign language. *Annual Review of Cybertherapy and Telemedicine 2009: Advanced Technologies in the Behavioral, Social and Neurosciences, 144*, 82.

Patterson, B., & McFadden, C. (2009). Attrition in online and campus degree programs. *Online Journal of Distance Learning Administration, 12*(2), 1–8.

Psotka, J. (1995). Immersive training systems: Virtual reality and education and training. *Instructional Science, 23*(5–6), 405–431.

Roy, M.C., Dewit, O. and Aubert, B.A., 2001. The impact of interface usability on trust in web retailers. *Internet research*.

Salanitri, D., Hare, C., Borsci, S., Lawson, G., Sharples, S., & Waterfield, B. (2015, August). Relationship between trust and usability in virtual environments: An ongoing study. In *International Conference on Human-Computer Interaction* (pp. 49–59). Cham: Springer.

Salanitri, D., Lawson, G., & Waterfield, B. (2016, September). The relationship between presence and trust in virtual reality. In *Proceedings of the European Conference on Cognitive Ergonomics* (p. 16). ACM.

Sanchez-Vives, M. V., & Slater, M. (2005). From presence to consciousness through virtual reality. *Nature Reviews Neuroscience, 6*(4), 332.

Sitzmann, T. (2011). A meta-analytic examination of the instructional effectiveness of computer-based simulation games. *Personnel Psychology, 64*(2), 489–528.

Slater, M. (2009). Place illusion and plausibility can lead to realistic behaviour in immersive virtual environments. *Philosophical Transactions of the Royal Society B: Biological Sciences, 364*(1535), 3549–3557.

Slater, M., & Wilbur, S. (1997). A framework for immersive virtual environments (FIVE): Speculations on the role of presence in virtual environments. *Presence: Teleoperators & Virtual Environments, 6*(6), 603–616.

Suh, B. and Han, I., 2002. Effect of trust on customer acceptance of Internet banking. *Electronic Commerce research and applications*, 1(3-4), pp. 247–263.

Tyler-Smith, K. (2006). Early attrition among first time eLearners: A review of factors that contribute to drop-out, withdrawal and non-completion rates of adult learners undertaking eLearning programmes. *Journal of Online Learning and Teaching, 2*(2), 73–85.

Venkatesh, V., & Davis, F. D. (2000). A theoretical extension of the technology acceptance model: Four longitudinal field studies. *Management Science, 46*(2), 186–204.

Vogel, J. J., Vogel, D. S., Cannon-Bowers, J., Bowers, C. A., Muse, K., & Wright, M. (2006). Computer gaming and interactive simulations for learning: A meta-analysis. *Journal of Educational Computing Research, 34*(3), 229–243.

Wang, Y. D. (2014). Building student trust in online learning environments. *Distance Education, 35*(3), 345–359.

Witmer, B. G., & Singer, M. J. (1998). Measuring presence in virtual environments: A presence questionnaire. *Presence, 7*(3), 225–240.

Wu, K., Zhao, Y., Zhu, Q., Tan, X., & Zheng, H. (2011). A meta-analysis of the impact of trust on technology acceptance model: Investigation of moderating influence of subject and context type. *International Journal of Information Management, 31*(6), 572–581.

Young, M. K., Gaylor, G. B., Andrus, S. M., & Bodenheimer, B. (2014, August). A comparison of two cost-differentiated virtual reality systems for perception and action tasks. In *Proceedings of the ACM Symposium on Applied Perception* (pp. 83–90). ACM.

Chapter 10

Simulation data visualization using mixed reality with Microsoft HoloLens™

Michael Spitzer, Manfred Rosenberger and Martin Ebner

Introduction

With the growth of technology, new possibilities are arising to improve the learning process. In the last years several smart glasses emerged on the market for a reasonable price. One of these devices is the HoloLens. Microsoft released their Head-Mounted Display (HMD) as a Development Edition in March 2016 (Tsunoda, 2016). The HoloLens is a see-through head-mounted device. Microsoft defines their HMD as a Mixed-Reality (MR) device.

MR defines a very broad spectrum in the Reality-Virtuality Continuum between real environment and virtual environment. A MR environment visualizes real-world and virtual-world entities within a single display (Milgram, Takemura, Utsumi, & Kishino, 1995). Within the HoloLens display, real-world objects are shown as they are because of the see-through display; virtual objects are displayed as holograms.

In this chapter, we follow the idea of using this technology to visualize complex processes in the field of vision to make those processes more efficient. Smart glasses were used in several studies to explain complex processes and to improve the learning outcome. The studies are listed and analysed in the Overview of the state of the art section.

We strongly adhere to two main concepts of successful learning: learning by doing and interaction (Dewey, 1916) and learning through visualization (Holzinger & Ebner, 2003; Vygotsky, 1978). Holograms or 2D planes such as browser windows or other 2D applications can be pinned to world space at specific locations in the room. Figure 10.1, a screen shot made with HoloLens, shows a pinned browser window above the test bed. This feature can be used to add context-based information to the learning situation.

The HoloLens can be used as an untethered solution; hence, no infrastructure is necessary. All functionality can be programmed into the app. This is very useful because our experiences showed that the IT infrastructure in the educational domain often lags far behind the state-of-the-art (Spitzer & Ebner, 2015). In this chapter, we describe how to use the HoloLens for

Figure 10.1 Pinned browser window above the test bed.

learning purposes. We developed a HoloLens app with two modes: VR and AR to support learners in various states of the test bed design and implementation process. The app concept is described in the Prototype section. The main purpose of the app is to show invisible processes such as temperature and pressure changes in the field of view of the user to make it easier to understand the test bed functionality.

Overview of the state of the art

This chapter provides an overview of current trends and uses of wearable enhanced learning relevant to MR. Smart glasses open new possibilities for learning scenarios. With smart glasses, many issues of other hardware solutions are solved. Smart phones and tablets can use AR technology, but they must be carried by hand during the learning scenario. Tablets are often large and heavy, which could influence the learning experience, particularly when learners need their hands free (Leighton & Crompton, 2017).

We have already used smart glasses in education and have developed a prototype to support distance learning. Users of smart glasses, in that case the ReconJet (Recon, 2018), were able to establish a real-time video/audio stream and the instructor drew shapes to mark objects in the video stream. The prototype was tested in two use-cases. The first was an industrial use-case:

a maintenance procedure of a production machine. It is comparable to the test bed use-case described in this chapter. To be able to maintain a machine or a thermodynamic test bed, the functionality of such a device must be clear. With the distance learning approach, we gave live support during the process. With the HoloLens app, we provide a solution to enable unsupervised learning. The second use-case of the distance learning approach was a generic fine-motor-skills task: to assemble a wooden toy without any *a priori* information. The experiments showed supporting the subject during assembly of the toy by displaying information in the smart glasses was very effective (Spitzer, Nanic, & Ebner, 2018). Additionally, we developed a scenario for learning knitting while using smart glasses. Learners need both hands to perform the task of knitting; therefore, smart glasses were used (Spitzer & Ebner, 2016).

Smart glasses were used in several other educational scenarios: In the medical domain, Google Glass was used to solve communication and surgical education challenges (Moshtaghi et al., 2015). Additionally, in context-aware learning scenarios, smart glasses were used to give support during a physics experiment of visualizing invisible processes (frequency of sound) (Kuhn et al., 2016). This learning scenario faced challenges similar to those of our use-case.

AR technology not only supports the learning scenario in educational settings; it also raises the motivation of the learners by providing descriptive visualizations of context-based information (Freitas & Campos, 2008). AR technology has the potential to engage and motivate learners and help them to understand real-world challenges more efficiently by providing additional context-based information during the learning scenario (Lee, 2012).

Use-case and learning scenario

In this chapter, a further practical example will be carried out. The department of thermodynamics is finding it difficult to transport their domain-specific knowledge to other departments or customers. This knowledge-related problem can be solved by providing additional information such as learning material and descriptive visualizations. Additionally, they face the challenge of training and teaching new researchers or students the use of thermodynamics test beds. In this chapter, the following questions are addressed:

- RQ1: Are MR applications suitable for supporting learning scenarios in which students or new employees learn how to use thermodynamic test beds?
- RQ2: Can MR applications be used to foster the transfer of domain-specific knowledge to experts of other domains or to customers?

This section describes the life cycle of a thermal test bed, beginning with the Computer-Aided Design (CAD) construction, followed by the assembly and start up procedure of such a test bed. The main motivation of using a MR application in a learning scenario is that new employees or students can already train to use the test bed during the design phase of the test bed. Usually, they must wait until the whole test bed is built and operational. The research idea is that during the assembly phase the missing parts can be placed as holograms in the field of view to verify the correct position and to get a better understanding of how the test bed will be operational when it is finished. Additionally, basic training scenarios such as localization of the parts within the test bed can be performed in early stages. Figure 10.2 shows a comparison between the usual learning approach and the MR learning scenario. Usually, in the CAD phase there is no learning material available since the test bed is in the construction phase; the only available data is the CAD, which is improved iteratively. During the assembly phase, some changes can be made to the test bed. In the usual learning approach, the learner can only perform learning scenarios while using the test bed in the operational state. In the MR scenario, the learner should be able to walk through simulated test-bed experiments in VR mode. The two modes of the HoloLens app are explained in detail in the Prototype section. For the VR mode, one reasonable state of the CAD is sufficient to create a VR learning environment. The learner is able to train in VR mode even if no physical test bed has been

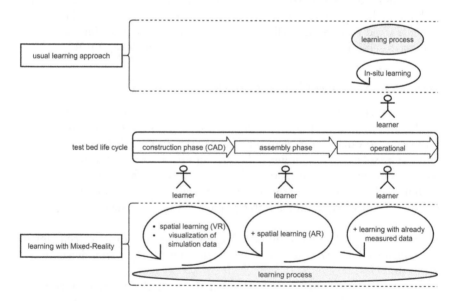

Figure 10.2 Learning approaches.

built. During the assembly phase, more and more parts are physically available. The missing parts can be placed as hologram overlays, and the learner can perform spatial learning (location of parts) in AR mode.

Additionally, simulation data can be visualized to train already simulated learning situations. During operational phase already performed test runs can be displayed to train learning situations even if the test bed is not in service. In our new learning approach learners can perform learning and training situations in all the three states of the test bed life cycle.

Design of the learning scenario

A learning scenario should always reference a clearly defined objective. In the validation method, the context and the learner influence the design of the learning scenario (Airasian et al., 2001; Bloom, Englehart, Furst, Hill, & Krathwohl, 1956; Starr, Manaris, & Stalvey, 2008; Weidenmann, 1993). The design of such a learning scenario can be compared to the requirements of the engineering phase for product development. There is a need for detailed pre-examination and requirements analysis (Meyer, 2003; Ross & Schoman, 1977).

Additionally, aspects of learning psychology have to be considered (Schulmeister, 2004). The learning objective can be separated into knowledge and competences. Knowledge can be grouped into conceptual, procedural and declarative knowledge. Knowledge is the basis for acquiring competences. The acquired competences can be transferred to other domains (Heyse & Erpenbeck, 2004; Hudson & Miller, 2005; North, 2011). We use a context-based approach to support the learner, by showing location-based information of parts, temperature and pressure. Several learning methods use location to help learners remember content. One of these methods is called *Loci*, a method of memory enhancement using spatial memory to recall information. This method was developed in ancient Rome and Greece to support learning large numbers and texts (Yates, 1966). The *Loci* method has already been implemented in a mobile app called Loci Spheres. The app has been evaluated in an in-the-wild study. Visual stimuli such as spatial and panning loci provide higher perceived system support (Wieland, Müller, Pfeil, & Reiterer, 2017).

Research method

This section describes the method we used to develop the Software. We used the prototyping approach we already used in another learning scenario (Spitzer et al., 2018). Prototyping is very effective when new technology is introduced, in our case, the HoloLens. The prototyping approach is necessary for learning the working of the device, which features are available and the sophistication of the features before developing a full-scale system (Alavi, 1984).

First, we identified the basic requirements: to show invisible, physical conditions. Then we built the prototype and tested it with key users. We improved the prototype iteratively to follow agile software development principles (Cockburn, 2001). The prototyping approach was necessary for quickly evaluating a functional software artefact.

The prototype was tested with subjects from the target group in a qualitative evaluation (thinking aloud) to gather early feedback. This feedback was then considered for improving the app iteratively. We have followed this approach in other studies (Spitzer & Ebner, 2015, 2017). After the thinking-aloud test, the users answered the following questions:

- Do you understand the functionality of the thermodynamic test bed?
- What are the risks of operating the test bed?
- Please describe the parts of the test bed and their functionality.

The purpose of these questions was to identify issues with the learning situation in a very early stage. When the prototype reaches a more mature state, a final evaluation will take place to verify the success of the learning situation compared to other learning materials such as paper-based manuals and video instructions. The target group for the MR test bed is made up of new employees or students in the mechanical engineering domain who are not yet familiar with real-world simulations and test beds. They can train and learn how to use a thermodynamic test bed without being at risk.

Prototype

We implemented a MR application to visualize the temperature and pressure of a car air conditioning unit test bed. The first step was to create a CAD model of the test bed. The test bed consists of the following components:

1. Frame
2. Compressor
3. Condenser
4. Filter
5. Expansion Valve (EXV)
6. Vaporizer
7. Measuring probes
8. Analogous gauges
9. Emergency switch
10. Pipes

The test bed model is shown in Figure 10.3.

The next step was to define measurement points, which were then used to visualize measurement and simulation data. At first, we implemented the

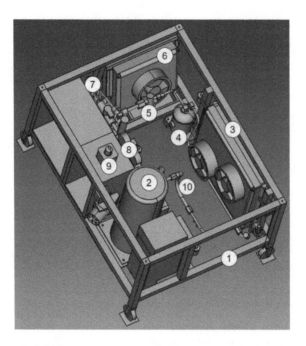

Figure 10.3 Test bed CAD.

VR mode. The advantage of providing a VR mode is that learners are able to see the 3D model as a hologram even though the test bed is not physically built yet.

Figure 10.4 shows the test bed in a VR mode. The whole test bed is displayed as a hologram without any related real-world context. The cursor is used as pointing area, which is controlled by the HoloLens user's head movement. Instead of a mouse or other pointing devices, head movement (direction of view) is used to determine the region of interest. The cursor is always centred in the direction of view of the user. This kind of user interaction was unfamiliar for all subjects, but they adapted to this input technique quickly. When the cursor hits a part of the model, the part is highlighted gray. Figure 10.4 shows the VR mode with highlighted condenser. A video of the VR mode is available (Spitzer, 2018b). All parts of the model are augmented with a text description and title. When the user air taps the part, the information is displayed in 3D space.

The part information is not implemented within the HoloLens application itself. All text information is accessed from a web server. The advantage of this approach is that the text can be easily adapted to various training and learning situations without reprogramming the HoloLens application. The

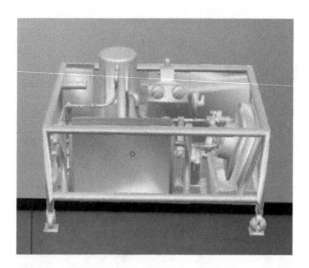

Figure 10.4 VR mode of the test bed.

part information is shown as a text plane in 3D space, which adapts to the user's distance and rotation automatically.

The vaporizer is selected and the current pressure from a simulation or already performed test run is displayed. The white button below (show description) opens a more detailed description of the selected part. A pole connects the part with the corresponding text information to create the appropriate context. Users can freely move the text information within the 3D space.

This functionality (VR mode and part description) can be used in the early test-bed development stage to train and teach students or new employees. They learn the exact 3D position of parts in the test bed and can connect the related context information (part descriptions) more efficiently.

When the user taps on the tubes, the animation of temperature or pressure distribution in the test bed for a simulated or already performed test run is displayed. White rings indicate the flow direction of the coolant. Every measurement point is coloured according to the measured or simulated value. The lowest value of the simulation is coloured blue and the highest value is coloured red. For the visualization of the tubes between the measurement points, we use colour interpolation. Figure 10.5 shows VR mode placed above the real-world test bed. The next step was to connect the Software prototype with the simulation data. We exported the simulation data from a simulation tool as comma-separated values. To visualize current measurements of an ongoing test run, we connected the measurement software with the HoloLens app via a web service.

Figure 10.5 VR mode placed above the real-world test bed.

The red and blue airflow indicate hot and cold air. This information is useful for safety reasons. Operators should stay away from hot sections of the test bed. A lot of information is transferred to the learner with the VR mode even though the test bed does not physically exist yet. During the assembly (second) phase, users can switch to the AR mode. Figure 10.6 shows a screen shot of the AR mode. A video capture of the HoloLens app is available (Spitzer, 2018a). The blue cursor indicates the view of the user. The compressor hologram is shown and can be tapped to show the description. The same functionality is provided in the VR mode. The major difference is that part holograms are shown only when the cursor hits part of the model. Since all parts were already physically available, this approach was obvious. We decided not to implement occlusion (hidden sur-face detection) because it seemed better to show the simulation regardless of whether other parts are located between the tubes and the line of sight. We decided to implement the visualization of the AR mode similarly to the VR mode to provide a continuous learning experience in all test-bed phases.

The visualization process and workflow are shown in Figure 10.7. At first, we created the CAD model of the test bed. Then we calculated simulations of different learning scenarios for several test-run types. The values for the simula-tion (temperature and pressure) were provided via a Representational State Transfer web service. This web service was also used to access stored measure-ment data of real test runs. The next step was to create a visualization of the temperature and pressure distribution. We decided to colour the tubes accord-ing to the simulated or measured values. This process is a general approach, independent of the used device. The same process can be used to display the learning scenario on a tablet or smart phone. Only the last step is adapted to the HoloLens. The focus of the used process was to create generic architecture for multiple learning scenarios.

Figure 10.6 AR mode.

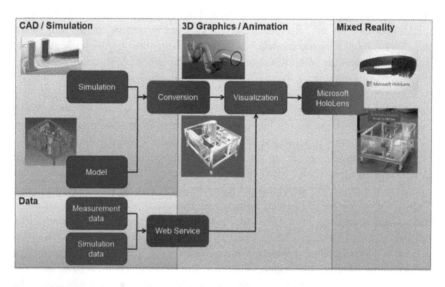

Figure 10.7 Information visualization with mixed reality.

Discussion and conclusion

With our prototype, we addressed two research questions. First, we investigated whether MR applications are suitable for supporting learning in the thermodynamic domain. The app was very helpful even for non-experts. We tested the learning situation with five internal test people in a qualitative evaluation. Additionally, we tested the learning situation with external audiences at several public events (open houses) without performing formal evaluations. The test users did not get any *a priori* detailed information of the test bed. They explored the HoloLens app mainly in AR mode with the physical test bed on site. We used a thinking-aloud approach to validate their understanding of the test bed and the running simulations.

The main purpose of the qualitative evaluation was to identify major flaws in our design. We are now improving the app according to the feedback and will perform thorough evaluations of the app and the learning scenario after the prototype reaches a more mature state. We are now implementing the following improvements:

- The highlighting of the parts in the field of view is sometimes confusing when users look around quickly. This issue is fixed by delaying the highlighting until the user stops looking around and focuses on a certain part.
- The poles and part information stay in the field of view even though the user has already selected another part. This issue is fixed by closing all open text fields and poles after the user selects another part. In this way, only the currently selected part is displayed.
- The user interface is in a very early stage. Since the Microsoft HoloLens is very new, it is very challenging to design and implement a sophisticated user interface. There are no long-term guidelines and experiences in building UIs in 3D space for smart glasses. We are now improving the UI iteratively. We are considering more accurate algorithms for adapting label size according to the distance of the user so that label placement will not block the field of view. The most challenging part is to show only as much information as is needed for learning context; we do not want to pollute the field of view with unnecessary information that could distract and confuse the user.

All test users understood the functionality quickly. It was very helpful that various simulations could be executed to show different results to the user. It took some time to become familiar with the input techniques of the device, but it was very intuitive for most of the users, even wearers of regular glasses did not have problems. One issue was that placing virtual content in a room had to be thoroughly considered. The more content was added, the more confusing it was for users. Hence, only context-based content should be displayed; all unrelated content should be hidden. Another issue was that users were able to move the description labels freely in the room without any restrictions. After some time, they forgot where they had put the labels in the room. The poles connecting parts to their descriptions were very helpful in that case. In general, all users enjoyed watching the MR content with the HoloLens and were very motivated to investigate the test bed. Since motivation is a key factor in increasing the learning effectivity, technology is very useful in this learning scenario (Dickinson, 1995) (RQ1). We further investigated how this technology can be used to foster the transfer of domain-specific knowledge to experts of other domains or to customers. The feedback of the target group was very promising. With such technology, it is easier to compare different settings of a certain machine, test bed or other devices and the effects of the adaptions can be visualized efficiently without understanding the device fully. This makes it easier to justify decisions of parameterizing the test bed. By visualizing invisible content in the field of view of the user, even non-technical experts could better understand complex processes (RQ2).

The introduced learning prototype should also be evaluated according to the aspects mentioned in this section and compared with alternative learning methods or learning support. Table 10.1 compares possible alternative learning approaches. This incomplete comparison also provides an outlook on further evaluations of different learning approaches in the described learning context. Since our focus in this work was a prototypical implementation, further research will be performed in the evaluation of this approach compared with other approaches.

The costs of the implementation of the different types of learning support must be considered. In our case, the effort was justified by the fact that it could be very dangerous and expensive if students or employees make mistakes while using the test bed (e.g. due to high temperature and pressure). In other learning situations, the outcome in relation to the effort and costs should be discussed and considered.

Acknowledgements

This chapter was written at VIRTUAL VEHICLE Research Center in Graz, Austria. The authors would like to acknowledge the financial support of the COMET K2 – Competence Centers for Excellent Technologies Programme of the Federal Ministry for Transport, Innovation and Technology (bmvit), the Federal Ministry for Digital, Business and Enterprise (bmdw), the Austrian Research Promotion Agency (FFG), the Province of Styria and the Styrian Business Promotion Agency (SFG).

Table 10.1 Alternative learning support.

Alternative learning support	features/drawbacks (±)
Test bed process description performed by an expert on site	(+) questions are answered by the expert (+) the expert can explain coherences that are not documented anywhere (+) existing learning material can additionally be used (-) support from an expert can be expensive and time consuming (-) invisible/audible signals cannot be perceived by the learner
Test bed simulation with a domain specific tool on a PC off-site	(+) when the user learns how to use the software, a lot of training and learning situations can be simulated and tested without any further help (-) domain-specific software often is difficult to use (-) very time consuming to become familiar with such highly specialized software (-) information is completely decoupled from the test bed
Previously recorded learning situation or simulation.	(+) acceptable effort to create learning content (-) nearly no interactive participation of the user except for browsing/ repeating sections of the video (-) not every detail can be covered by video (-) a video has a fixed viewing angle (-) information is completely decoupled from the test bed
Infra-red goggles	(+) easy to use, easy to use for other learning situations (-) show only current temperature in pipes, no simulation (VR) mode, test bed must already be built and must be activated and running while observed by the learner (-) no additional context-based information available
Mixed reality glasses (HoloLens)	(+) augmentation of invisible/auditable processes (+) spatial awareness, objects are placed/attached to the real test bed (+) context related information can be displayed directly on the test bed (+) intuitive navigation in 3D space (zoom/pan/context information) (+) effective learning/recognition effort because of the usage of real-world context in AR mode

(Continued)

Table 10.1 (Cont.)

Alternative learning support	features/drawbacks (±)
	(-) high implementation effort (-) expensive hardware (smart glasses) (-) infrastructure (WLAN, server) necessary to display simulations and measurement values with HoloLens

References

Airasian, P. W., Cruikshank, K. A., Mayer, R. E., Pintrich, P. R., Raths, J., & Wittrock, M. C. (2001). *A taxonomy for learning, teaching, and assessing. A revision of Bloom's taxonomy of educational objectives.* L. W. Anderson & D. R. Krathwohl (Eds.), (2nd ed.). New York, NY: Allyn & Bacon.

Alavi, M. (1984, June). An assessment of the prototyping approach to information systems development. *Communication of the ACM, 27*(6), 556–563. doi:10.1145/358080.358095. Retrieved from.

Bloom, B. S., Englehart, M., Furst, E. J., Hill, W. H., & Krathwohl, D. R. (1956). *Taxonomy of educational objectives: Handbook I. Cognitive domain.* New York, NY: David McKay.

Cockburn, A. (2001). *Agile software development* (Vol. 177). Cary, NC: Addison-Wesley Professional.

Dewey, J. (1916). *Democracy and education. An introduction to the philosophy of education (reprint 1997).* Rockland, NY: Free Press.

Dickinson, L. (1995). Autonomy and motivation a literature review. *System, 23*(2), 165–174. doi:10.1016/0346-251X(95)00005-5. Retrieved from www.sciencedirect.com/science/article/pii/0346251X95000055

Freitas, R., & Campos, P. (2008). Smart: A system of augmented reality for teaching 2nd grade students. In *Proceedings of the 22nd British HCI Group Annual conference on People and Computers: Culture, creativity, interaction – Volume 2* (pp. 27–30). Swindon, UK: BCS Learning & Development Ltd. Retrieved from http://dl.acm.org/citation.cfm?id=1531826.1531834

Heyse, V., & Erpenbeck, J. (2004). Kompetenztraining. *Informations-und Trainingsprogramme, 2.* Retrieved from www.ciando.com/img/books/extract/3799263675_lp.pdf

Holzinger, A., & Ebner, M. (2003). Interaction and usability of simulations & animations: A case study of the flash technology. In *Proceedings of the human-computer interaction interact 2003* (pp. 777–780). Amsterdam: IOS Press.

Hudson, P., & Miller, S. P. (2005). *Designing and implementing mathematics instruction for students with diverse learning needs.* Boston, MA: Pearson/Allyn and Bacon.

Kuhn, J., Lukowicz, P., Hirth, M., Poxrucker, A., Weppner, J., & Younas, J. (2016, October). gPhysics – Using smart glasses for head-centered, context-aware learning in physics experiments. *IEEE Transactions on Learning Technologies, 9*(4) 304–317. doi:10.1109/TLT.2016.2554115

Lee, K. (2012, March 01). Augmented reality in education and training. *TechTrends*, *56*(2), 13–21. doi:10.1007/s11528-012-0559-3. Retrieved from https://link. springer.com/article/10.1007/s11528-012-0559-3.

Leighton, L. J., & Crompton, H. (2017). Augmented reality in k-12 education. In G. Kurubacak & H. Altinpulluk (Eds.), *Mobile technologies and augmented reality in open education* (pp. 281–290). Hershey, PA: IGI Global. doi:10.4018/978-1-5225-2110-5.ch014. Retrieved from www.igi-global.com/gateway/chapter/178247

Meyer, H. (2003). Zehn Merkmale guten Unterrichts. *Pädagogik*, *10*(2003), 36–43.

Milgram, P., Takemura, H., Utsumi, A., & Kishino, F. (1995). Augmented reality: A class of displays on the reality-virtuality continuum. In *Telemanipulator and telepresence technologies* (Vol. 2351, pp. 282–293). International Society for Optics and Photonics. Doi:10.1117/12.197321. Retrieved from https://www.researchgate.net/publication/228537162_Augmented_reality_A_class_of_displays_on_the_reality-virtuality_continuum

Moshtaghi, O., Kelley, K. S., Armstrong, W. B., Ghavami, Y., Gu, J., & Djalilian, H. R. (2015). Using google glass to solve communication and surgical education challenges in the operating room. *The Laryngoscope*, *125*(10), 2295–2297. doi:10.1002/lary.25249 Retrieved from https://onlinelibrary.wiley.com/doi/abs/10.1002/lary.25249

North, K. (2011). Wissen in Organisationen. In *Wissensorientierte Unternehmensführung: Wertschöpfung durch Wissen* (pp. 35–68). Wiesbaden: Gabler. doi:10.1007/978-3-8349-6427-4_3. Retrieved from https://rd.springer.com/book/10.1007/978-3-8349-6427-4.

Recon. (2018). *ReconJet*. Retrieved 2018-03-26, from www.reconinstruments.com/products/jet/

Ross, D. T., & Schoman, K. E. (1977, January). Structured analysis for requirements definition. *IEEE Transactions on Software Engineering*, *SE-3*(1), 6–15. doi:10.1109/TSE.1977.229899

Schulmeister, R. (2004). Didaktisches Design aus hochschuldidaktischer Sicht – ein Plädoyer für offene Lernsituationen. In U. Rinn & D. M. Meister (Eds.), *Didaktik und Neue Medien* (Vol. 21, pp. 19–49). Münster: Waxmann. Retrieved 2018-01-08, from www.zhw.uni-hamburg.de/pdfs/Didaktisches_Design.pdf

Spitzer, M. (2018a). *Test bed – AR mode*. Retrieved 2018-02-10, from https://youtu.be/LB7SiJKzHc8

Spitzer, M. (2018b). *Test bed – VR mode*. Retrieved 2018-02-10, from https://youtu.be/Bx-lmA9pc_E

Spitzer, M., & Ebner, M. (2015). Collaborative learning through drawing on iPads. In *EdMedia: World conference on educational media and technology* (pp. 806–815). Vancouver, BC: Association for the Advancement of Computing in Education (AACE).

Spitzer, M., & Ebner, M. (2016, 6 29). Use cases and architecture of an information system to integrate smart glasses in educational environments. In *Proceedings of edmedia: World conference on educational media and technology 2016* (pp. 51–58). Vancouver, BC: AACE.

Spitzer, M., & Ebner, M. (2017, 6 19). Project based learning: From the idea to a finished Lego technic artifact, assembled by using smart glasses. In *Proceedings of edmedia: World conference on educational media and technology 2017* (pp. 196–209). United States: Association for the Advancement of Computing in Education.

Spitzer, M., Nanic, I., & Ebner, M. (2018, 1 27). Distance learning and assistance using smart glasses. *Education Sciences, 8*(1), 18. doi:10.3390/educsci8010021

Starr, C. W., Manaris, B., & Stalvey, R. H. (2008, March). Bloom's taxonomy revisited: Specifying assessable learning objectives in computer science. *SIGCSE Bulletin, 40*(1), 261–265. doi:10.1145/1352322.1352227. Retrieved from https://dl.acm.org/doi/abs/10.1145/1352322.1352227.

Tsunoda, K. (2016, February). *Introducing first ever experiences for the Microsoft HoloLens development edition.* Retrieved 2018-01-17, from https://blogs.windows.com/devices/2016/02/29/introducing-first-ever-experiences-for-the-microsoft-holo lens-development-edition/

Vygotsky, L. (1978). Interaction between learning and development. *Readings on the Development of Children, 23*(3), 34–41.

Weidenmann, B. (1993). *Instruktionsmedien (Arbeiten zur Empirischen Pädagogik und Pädagogischen Psychologie nr. 27.).* München: Hochschule der Bundeswehr.

Wieland, J., Müller, J., Pfeil, U., & Reiterer, H. (2017). Loci spheres: A mobile app concept based on the method of loci. In M. Burghardt, R. Wimmer, C. Wolff, & C. Womser-Hacker (Eds.), *Mensch und Computer 2017 – Tagungsband* (pp. 227–238). Regensburg: Gesellschaft für Informatik e.V. doi:10.18420/muc2017-mci-0235. Retrieved from https://dl.gi.de/handle/20.500.12116/3265

Yates, F. A. (1966). *The art of memory.* Chicago, IL: University of Chicago Press.

Chapter 11

A+Ha!

Combining tactile interaction with augmented reality to transform secondary and tertiary STEM education

Gregory Quinn and Fabian Schneider

Introduction

The benefits of active learning are well documented (Prince, 2004) and widely accepted. Integrating active learning in science, technology, engineering and mathematics (STEM) subjects has seen many successes, but 'traditional' learning still dominates the clear majority of STEM education across all tiers of learning. Even when the benefits of active learning are known, the implementation thereof is usually *easier said than done*. This is due, in part, to educators' lack of access to suitable training or resources.

The advent of augmented reality technologies often promises great potential in improving education, and slowly some validation for such claims is beginning to emerge (Ibáñez, Di Serio, Villarán, & Delgado Kloos, 2014). It is generally accepted however that the potential strengths of augmented reality technologies in education lie in 'facilitating collaborative, experiential inquiry in and out of the classroom' (Dunleavy & Dede, 2014).

STEM subjects typically involve complex concepts and theory but in practice relate to very tangible and visible physical phenomena. The task of STEM educators is to effectively bridge the gap between the two and help students not only to develop an understanding of the subject matter but also to gain an intuition for it. In the case of structural mechanics, attempts to illustrate structural systems with tangible or accessible models are as old as structural design itself.

The work presented here provides a state-of-the-art review of existing physical and digital aids used to assist in the education of structural mechanics. This review and the shortfalls identified within it inform the development of a novel technology that is presented and detailed within. This novel technology is called Augmented Haptics or A+Ha! for short and combines explorative design with tactile interaction and augmented reality to facilitate a new type of analogue-digital hybrid learning that, it is claimed, could provide significant improvements to STEM learning. The novel technology, the realisation of a fully functional prototype and a scope of future work is presented.

State of the art

Educators of structural mechanics (and many other subjects) have long exploited physical props in the classroom. The most common examples of these include sponge blocks marked with a grid to communicate visually the compression and expansion of beam under bending and physical models to demonstrate the buckling loads of differently supported columns or hanging chains to illustrate the significance of a catenary. Educators will typically also task their students with building scaled structures (such as trussed bridges) and testing them to failure. Sometimes full-scale demonstrators are built (Vrontissi, 2015). A good review of common physical teaching aids is provided by De Oliveira (2008). Despite their strengths, physical props are not used by most educators, as they tend to be prohibitively impractical but also because they cover only singular topics as opposed to a spectrum thereof. Beyond simple physical props, teaching aids to assist in the education of engineering mechanics tend to fall into two main categories: laboratory equipment and software.

Comparison

This chapter (and within it Figure 11.1 and Table 11.1) provide a state-of-the art review of popular and/or significant examples of teaching aids used in the education of structural mechanics for discussion and contextualisation. The selected examples are representative of the state-of-the-art, but this list is not without omissions such as *CASDET* (Computer Assisted Structural Design Education Tool) (Piccolotto & Rio, 1996), *DEFLECT* (MacCallum & Hanna, 1996) and *EasyStatics* (Pedron, 2006) as detailed, in part, by Alalade (2017).

As detailed in Table 11.1 *TecQuipment*, founded in 1958, is the oldest establishment still selling tools for the teaching of structural mechanics (and many more disciplines) providing customers with precision engineered equipment predominantly for use in educational laboratories. *GUNT*, established later in 1977 in Germany, is the primary competitor in this space with very similar products. These well-established brands are popular choices for engineering laboratories in higher education across the world. Their numerous products typically facilitate investigations into a single, or set of, pedagogic learning objectives such as calculating bending moments in a beam or axial forces in a truss and typically will include a custom kit of components fixed to a 2D frame of extruded aluminium, equipment to measure results (e.g. forces and deflections) and complementary learning material such as worksheets. Typically, separate physical kits must be purchased for each individual topic or learning objective, and the custom reassembly of components into different structural systems is neither encouraged nor catered for. Furthermore, these products are designed to complement the pedagogical nature of laboratory exercise (i.e. with great focus on data gathering and analysis), which, it is

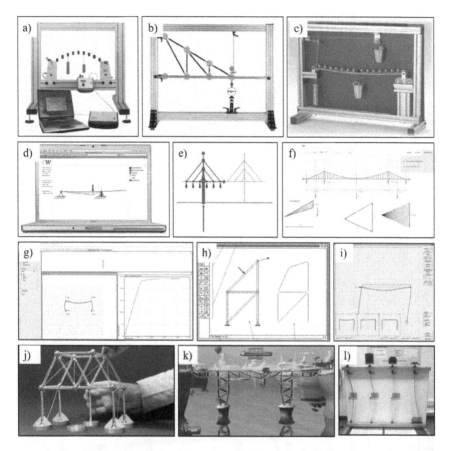

Figure 11.1 State-of-the-art review of teaching aids for structural mechanics. See Table 11.1 for references. a) TecQuipment, b) GUNT, c) TechnoLab, d) push me pull me, e) Active Statics, f) eQUILIBRIUM, g) Arcade, h) Dr Frame (3D), i) STIFF, j) mola, k) Bridge Builder, l) assorted physical teaching props.

argued, can detract from the primary learning objective at hand. The truss and beam products from *GUNT* shown in Figure 11.2 illustrate this point. These set examples are highly prescriptive and make use of precision equipment to measure deflections that are barely visible to the naked eye. While small deflections are a fundamental principal of structural mechanics and a desirable characteristic of built structures, it is in fact deformations that determine the flow of forces; exaggerating them is generally more effective in helping recipients to develop an intuition for a given structural phenomenon. These precision-engineered products tend to be very expensive, which limits their markets to wealthier higher education institutes and companies.

Table 11.1 State-of-the-art review of teaching aids for structural mechanics.

Image	Name	Medium	Description	Pedagogical focus / technical strength	Caveats	Origin year	Author / institution	Approx. cost (USD)	Website
a	TecQuip-ment	Physical Paper Specialist	The oldest and most estab-lished firm for engineering education lab equipment and tools originating in the UK.	High-quality equipment for hands-on laboratory experiments predom. in higher educa-tion with focus on precision.	Heavy focus higher educa-tion and pre-cision engin-eering limits accessibility.	1958	Prof Joseph Pope Nottingham University	$5000–$20,000	www.tec quipment. com
b	GUNT	Physical Paper Specialist	The oldest and most estab-lished firm for engineering education lab equipment, software and tools originating in Germany.	High-quality engineered products. High QTY of prod-ucts and disciplines.		1977	G.U.N.T. Geraetebau GmbH Hamburg	$3000–$15,000	www.gunt. de
c	TechnoLab	Physical Paper Specialist	A smaller, cheaper set of kits for labora-tory experi-ments in higher education.	As above but smaller (desk-top sized) kits with less pre-cise engineered parts.	Sole focus on structural mechanics and some dynamics.	1996	Nicholas Haritos	$2000–$7000	www.techno lab.net.au

d	push me pull me	Web PC	Web-based interactive demos of structural systems, factsheets and an interactive design & analysis tool programmed in processing.	(Interactive) force diagrams for pre-set examples of structural systems + 3D design & analysis tool. Focus on force flow and structural systems.	GUI limitations in 3D design / analysis software.	2011	Gennaro Senatore Daniel Piker Expedition Engineering / Think Up	free	https://expeditionworkshed.org/workshed/push-me-pull-me/
e	Active Statics	Web	Eight flash-based interactive set demos of common structures (mostly trusses) showing internal and external force flow.	Internal and external force flow for set demos for structures only.	Discontinued service and heavily limited scope.	2003	Simon Greenwold Edward Allen Massachusetts Institute of Technology	free	https://acg.media.mit.edu/people/simong/statics.html
f	eQUILIBRIUM	Web	Java-based interactive pre-set tutorials to learn about structural systems via graphic statics which complements	Structured lesson plans on structural design with complementary case studies using the software that helps	Exclusive focus on graphic statics.	ca. 2010	Block Research Group ETH Zurich	free	http://block.arch.ethz.ch/eq/

(Continued)

Table 11.1 (Cont.)

Image	Name	Medium	Description	Pedagogical focus / technical strength	Caveats	Origin year	Author / institution	Approx. cost (USD)	Website
			the ETH online syllabus structural design study unit.	to explain structural performance.					
g	Arcade	PC	Written in C++ with OpenGL, this executable software uses an explicit dynamic solver allowing users to design and analyse 2D structural systems within constraints.	Simplified and pedagogically oriented FEM incl. physics-based failure animations.	Discontinued service. Limited GUI.	2002	Kirk Martini University of Virginia	free	http://web.arch.virginia.edu/arcade/about.html
h	Dr Frame (3D)	PC	Developed as a learning software for the design and analysis of quasi-static linear problems.	Primary focus on structural frames and beams.	Discontinued service. Limited GUI.	1998	Michael Rucki Dr Software LLC	$899 (professional) $99 (educational)	http://www.drsoftware-home.com (inactive)

		Platform	Description	Approach	Notes	Year	Developer	Price	URL
i	STIFF	PC	Comparatively more sophisticated FEM design & analysis tool for education including (2nd and 3rd order) non-linear analysis.	This tool is intended for use by advanced higher education engineering students to encourage theoretical learning. All theory and formulations are accessible to users.	Limited GUI. Advanced users only.	1999	Prof. Dr.-Ing. K.-U. Bletzinger Technical University of Munich	free	https://www.st.bgu.tum.de/en/software/education/stiff/
j	mola	Physical	mola is a kit of physical components that represent, and look somewhat similar to, structural components to be assembled and physically interacted with.	Physical interaction with and design exploration of simple structural systems in 2D and 3D.	Physical components only approximate intended behaviours.	2014	Marcio Sequeira Universidade Federal De Ouro Preto	$135	www.molamodel.com
k	Bridge Builder	PC Mobile Console	Physics-based bridge building games are popular and	Heavily focused on fun over education with typical gameplay speed and	Physics engines typically prioritise speed and	ca. 2000 and onwards	var.	var.	http://bbg.bridgebuilder-game.com/

(Continued)

Table 11.1 (Cont.)

Image	Name	Medium	Description	Pedagogical focus / technical strength	Caveats	Origin year	Author / institution	Approx. cost (USD)	Website
			numerous across multiple platforms. Typically, the aim is to build and test trussed bridges for crossing live loads.	reward mechanisms.	visuals over reality.				https://www.coolmathgames.com/0-build-the-bridgehttp://www.physicsgames.net/game/Bridge_Builder.html
I	assorted physical teaching props	Physical	To help illustrate specific phenomena of structural behaviour, university lecturers may often use physical props such as sponge blocks or buckling column models.	Typically larger props for specific learning objectives accompanying taught units.	Large, not readily available.	NA	NA	var.	NA

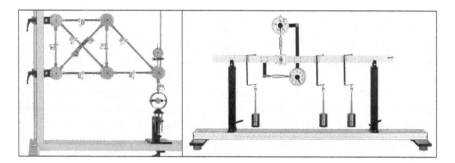

Figure 11.2 'Over-engineered' and pre-set kits for individual learning objectives.
('GUNT – Engineering mechanics and engineering design', n.d.).

TechnoLab follows the same approach as *TecQuipment* and *GUNT* (i.e. with aluminium frames and pre-set systems) but does so at a smaller desktop scale and slightly less expensively.

At quasi-regular intervals over the past 30 years, acclaimed academic institutions in the fields of structural and/or architectural design have released software designed with the intention to simplify and improve students' learning of structural mechanics and usually with the promise of a greater 'fun factor' too. The software programs are typically associated with a notable academic (or academics) in the field.

Some software packages are standalone programs (*Arcade, STIFF, Dr Frame*) while others are web-based (*push me pull me, Active Statics, eQUILIBRIUM*). Some focus on graphic statics (*eQUILIBRIUM, Active Statics*) while most focus on general structural performance and force flow; *STIFF*, developed by Professor Bletzinger at the University of Munich, is advanced enough to perform 2nd and 3rd order non-linear structural analysis and is designed to give its users access to and insight in the mathematical formulations it uses. Unlike most programs in this comparison, *push me pull me* was developed by a consortium (consultancy firm *Expedition Engineering* with *Think Up* from the *Useful Simple Trust*), and its ambitions and resources reflect this with web content covering interactive structural simulations, videos, factsheets and exercises targeting an industry-wide repository for structural engineering. *eQUILIBRIUM* (Mele, Lachauer, Rippmann, & Block, 2012) is similarly broad in its attempted reach but with a stronger focus on structured learning modules linked to the software with a focus entirely on graphic statics.

Bridge-building computer games have also been included in this state-of-the-art review because they represent an end of the spectrum that prioritises the enjoyment factor over engineering precision or education. Gamification refers to 'the use of game design elements in non-game contexts' (Deterding, Dixon, Khaled, & Nacke, n.d.) and has documented successes (Groh, 2012). Lessons can be learned from an industry that excels in harnessing and maintaining users' attention. The ubiquity of games and high-quality media nowadays is further justification for striving towards executing teaching tools to similarly high standards of visual and interactive fidelity; successful examples have been documented (Drea, Tripp, & Stuenkel, 2005).

Active Satics, Dr Frame (Rucki, Miller, & Cooper, 1998) and *Arcade* are discontinued or no longer maintained. We may assume that the cessation of these programs is related to a failure in gaining traction or producing an income and to the unsustainable dependency on a single (or small group of) developer(s). In contrast, *GUNT* and *TecQuipment* have enjoyed sustained longevity in the same field, one may presume due to their focus on physical products and to their more diversified assets (e.g. multiple disciplines and mediums).

While the standalone software programs detailed here have provided various degrees of technical innovation and have enjoyed some success in terms of dissemination and adoption, all have failed to gain real traction and make a widespread (global), significant impact on the education of structural mechanics. Limiting education technologies to single platforms (particularly personal computers) or single disciplines is shown by their discontinuation to be a recipe for almost guaranteed stagnation, and ultimately, failure.

2D abstraction

Abstraction is a fundamental tenet of the engineering discipline and the education thereof. Various means of abstraction are essential for effective learning of complex concepts and theories (Yasar & Maliekal, 2014). 2D abstraction of structures on a plane is the default approach to teaching structural mechanics (as well as most other STEM subjects). Abstraction on a 2D plane is compatible with the vast majority of structural designs in which drawings reference orthogonal elevations or sections, and 2D systems provide, pedagogically, a more accessible gateway to structural mechanics.

Almost all of the systems listed in Figure 11.1 are based on 2D abstraction except for *Dr Frame 3D, push me pull me 3D, mola* structural kit and some student-made models. Expanding an educational tool to 3D is associated with substantially greater development and/or computational requirements, and no evidence has been found pointing to a significant advantage in learning outcomes or intuition gained through 3D systems.

A novel approach

We present a novel teaching tool for structural mechanics and other STEM subjects such as physics, mechatronics and dynamics. This novel teaching aid consists of two major innovations:

1) Physical components that closely resemble the graphic symbols used in their pedagogy and can be joined together into assemblies representing (e.g. structural) systems that can, in turn, be physically interacted with by the user(s).
2) Automatic or scripted generation of digital twins of the user-made assemblies for which a simulation depicts the same deflections as induced by the user; they can optionally display additional information (e.g. internal forces or enhancing visual cues) via a projected image, thereby augmenting the learning experience.

Educational software programs commonly fail to convey important information in an accessible, fun or effective way. Furthermore, not all educational software programs exploit the benefits of the 'haptic bond' between visual and auditory stimuli, which has well-established cognitive and pedagogical value (Fredembach, de Boisferon, & Gentaz, 2009). The physical teaching props that do (e.g. sponge blocks, hanging chains) are generally prohibitively impractical and narrow in their scope of concepts covered. The innovations presented here promise to deliver potentially disruptive technological solutions in the space of educational tools for STEM subjects, a field so fundamental and pervasive that almost every child on the planet encounters it. The general concept of this novel method (A+Ha!) is to facilitate both free and scripted learning, enhanced by haptic interaction and augmented via digital simulations. This patent-protected technology aims to make the learning of STEM concepts more effective, more accessible and more fun. The embodiments described in this chapter are representative of a fully functioning prototype of the A+Ha! system. It should be noted that significant further developments are planned and therefore not fully represented by this early, albeit fully functional, prototype.

Physical components

The main physical components of the novel system comprise

*   a back panel that doubles as a projection surface featuring an array of cross-shaped orifices to facilitate the docking of physical nodal components,
*   physical **nodal** components such as pinned or rigid connectors as well as various types of supports that can be docked at 90° orientations into the back panel by means of an elastic cross-shaped buckle and
*   physical **linear** components such as beams, struts and cables that connect the nodal components.

In contrast to the pre-set configurations of typical lab equipment (e.g. from *GUNT* or *TecQuipment*), this system grants the user to engage in explorative design with the freedom to generate a plethora of assemblies, to experiment with them physically and to iteratively explore variations thereof, thereby broadening understanding of structural behaviour (Figure 11.4). Such an explorative task could, for example, involve the student being prompted to assemble a reticulated frame (i.e. such that it is unstable and collapses as a mechanism) and then the student is tasked with finding ways to stabilise the frame by adding bracing or by changing support conditions and connections, see Figure 11.3. The solutions that the student finds can of course be interacted with physically and augmented digitally.

A key innovation is that the physical components closely resemble their schematic symbols used in pedagogy. In structural mechanics, this relates to the geometric shapes (triangles, circles and lines) used to represent such items as pinned or rigid connections as well as pinned, sliding or rigid supports – see Figure 11.5.

Digital augmentation

The digital augmentation software can be divided into two primary functions:

1. A physics solver that simulates deflections and resultant forces of the digital twin
2. An interface that facilitates user interaction with the physical construct and the digital augmentation synchronously

By monitoring how the finite elements deform under user-induced deformations, internal forces can be generated and plotted (Figure 11.6).

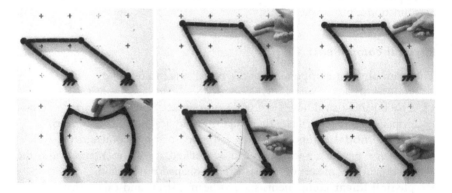

Figure 11.3 The physical components of the system are assembled to represent (e.g. structural) systems that are removably docked into a back panel-cum-projection surface. Here the user is iteratively exploring various ways to stabilise a frame.

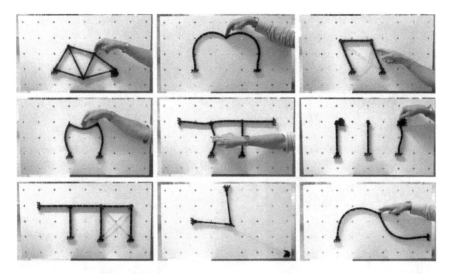

Figure 11.4 A plethora of custom assemblies can be created by the user facilitating explorative design and problem solving.

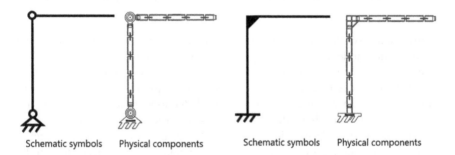

Schematic symbols   Physical components   Schematic symbols   Physical components

Figure 11.5 A key innovation is that the physical components closely resemble their schematic symbols used in pedagogy.

Dynamic relaxation physics simulation

A fundamental innovation of this technology is simulating a digital twin of the physical assembly that deforms synchronously with it upon user-induced deformation. This has been achieved with an underlying physics simulation using a projection-based dynamic relaxation solver; initial prototypes were completed using Kangaroo (Piker, 2013).

The dynamic relaxation (DR) method for solving physical simulations was first developed in the 1960s (Day, 1965) and has since become established in

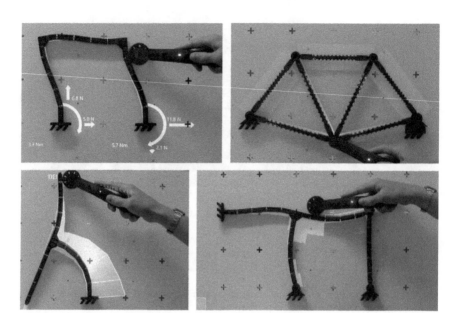

Figure 11.6 Four different assemblies displaying four different layers of augmentation. From top left clockwise: reactions, axial forces, shear forces & bending moments.

many fields. In the built environment, DR is most commonly associated with stiffness-independent (purely force based) membrane form-finding. In structural engineering, implicit integration methods are more common that can accurately describe mechanical stresses and displacements in a discretised continuum under the assumption of small deflections. If equilibrium is being sought in a system where deflections are large, the stiffness matrix must be updated over multiple iterations in a non-linear analysis that can be computationally demanding and often unstable. Generally, a prerequisite for implicitly integrated methods is that the systems must be statically determinate or indeterminate. Mechanisms can cause numerical instability and are more difficult to solve. DR on the other hand does not require the computation and inversion of a global stiffness matrix, but instead seeks equilibrium in each node explicitly and simultaneously by assigning mass, acceleration and a method of damping to the nodes. As highlighted by Martini (2006), this means that DR methods are insensitive to the static determinacy of the structural system such that mechanisms and large deformations are not an issue, provided the solver is able to remain stable. This insensitivity to static determinacy and large deformations is highly suitable and forgiving in an experimental and interactive design environment such as this one. Imposing large deformations on the fly and observing the immediate impact they have on structural performance (e.g. deflections, internal forces and reactions) is an illuminating experience for the user.

In order to achieve a digital twin that behaves synchronously with the physical construct, the following technical features were developed:

• The physical components are represented by corresponding objects and matching topological connectivity in the digital twin (see Figure 11.7 left).
• The discretisation of the finite elements is similarly embodied in the physical components (see Figure 11.7 right).

Matching the design of the physical components with the discretisation logic of the underlying finite element model presents two significant advantages:

• The matching ensures a close correlation between the digital and physical deflections. In effect, this means that the plotting of internal forces per finite element corresponds to the segmentation of the elements (i.e. beam, strut or cable).
• For more advanced users, the matching provides an added pedagogical value by providing a physical abstraction of finite element discretisation, a fundamental aspect of structural engineering analysis.

Previous and less advanced prototypes of this technology (Quinn, Galeazzi, & Gengnagel, 2017; Quinn, Geleazzi, Schneider, & Gengnagel, 2018) were implemented with a DR solver based on three degrees of freedom and subsequently were handicapped in the types of systems and constraints that could be modelled. The prototype presented here exploits finite elements

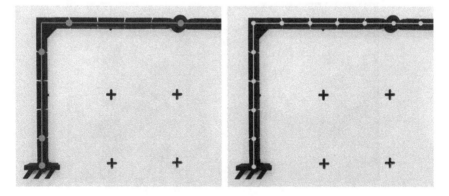

Figure 11.7 Left: The object bodies as defined by the digital twin correlate with the physical components. Right: the finite element discretisation of the digital twin is also replicated in the physical components.

featuring six degrees of freedom, without which the accurate representation of rigid supports (and more) would not be feasible.

User interface

Since users interact with both the physical construct and the digital twin, this presents some interesting interface design challenges. There should be a consistent and fluid duality between the physical assembly and its digital twin, not just visually but also through sensory interactions.

The working prototype allows the user to navigate a basic digital UI to select one of the exemplary learning objectives. Once a learning objective has been selected, the user is tasked with building a structural assembly, which is presented graphically by means of the relevant schematic symbols (Figure 11.8). Further augmentative information can be added to the UI, such as images referencing real-world equivalent structures or embedded data on material performance or cost. This ability to customise and carefully curate the amount and type of complementary data or visuals is a unique strength of augmented reality.

Wand & tracking

User interaction with the physical components must be emulated precisely in the simulation of the digital twin. To achieve this, a physical hand-held wand device was developed (Figure 11.9), which ensures that the user interacts with the physical components in a way that can be replicated in the simulation. This was realised with two separate modes:

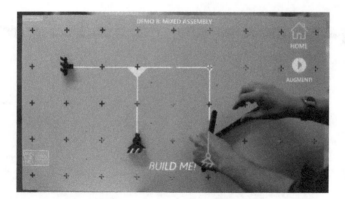

Figure 11.8 The system facilitates pedagogically scripted learning objectives (e.g. with 'build me' scenarios).

Figure 11.9 The hand-held wand ensures simple and deliberate interaction with the physical components; this is accurately replicable in the simulation. The wand is tracked via IR LED.

1) **Beam push mode**

    When physically interacting with beam elements, the wand is equipped with a spinning wheel attachment. This wheel ensures an effectively frictionless collision with the beam element, which is duplicated in the simulation by means of a collision force between a circular object and the segments of the beam.

2) **Node pull mode**

    When interacting with strut assemblies such as trusses, it is not desirable or effective for the user to push the struts along their lengths; it is better to pull at the nodes and to observe the induced compression and tensions in the members. For this mode, the wheel is simply removed from the wand revealing a peg that is the right size to dock inside a cylindrical cavity in every pinned nodal component. The simulation replicates this behaviour by applying an attraction force to the node in question.

The location of the wand is tracked by means of infrared LEDs embedded in the wand and computer vision algorithms using a camera that filters out visible light. The tracking is computationally lightweight, robust and fast. To facilitate interface navigation, the wand can be used as a point-and-click device. This essentially turns the board into a big touchscreen. An important and novel feature of the interface design is its ability to augment sensory experience; it does so by displaying the actual magnitude of force the user exerts on the structure promoting intuition for what a unit of force actually 'feels' like. The authors are also investigating object recognition on the fly, removing the need for a hand-held wand altogether.

Multi-platform learning

A failure of other educational tools can be traced to their limitation to a single platform. The apps *Active Statics*, *Dr Frame* and *Make a Scape* are no longer available because, presumably, their development was no longer sustainable and/or they didn't gain enough traction to merit maintenance. The lack of web activity and publications relating to *Arcade, Stiff, eQUILIBRIUM* and *push me pull me* seem to suggest that these platforms have not gained traction or that they have not become widely used outside the academic institutions in which they were created. *GUNT* and *TecQuipment*, on the other hand, have survived the test of time, and they are still sought after. This is undoubtedly attributable not only to their high-quality products but also to the fact that they feature predominantly physical embodiments that are complimented by a multitude of learning mediums (e.g. software, testing equipment, machine tools etc.). Diversifying assets have proven a valuable ingredient for success with these firms.

While there is clearly a business case for a learning platform covering multiple mediums, it is argued that if teaching, sharing and collaborating are well facilitated then learning will be more effective. We believe that the multi-platform approach described here is novel in this context.

References

Alalade, G. M. (2017). *The pedagogy of architectural structures in selected universities in Southwest Nigeria*. Ota, Nigeria: Covenant University.

Day, A. S. (1965). An introduction to dynamic relaxation. *The Engineer* 219, 5688, (pp. 218–221) https://www.scopus.com/record/display.uri?eid=2-s2.0-0000015224&origin=inward, https://en.wikipedia.org/wiki/The_Engineer_(UK_magazine).

Deterding, S., Dixon, D., Khaled, R., & Nacke, L. E. (n.d.). *Gamification: Toward a definition*. In CHI 2011 Gamification Workshop Proceedings, Vancouver, BC, Canada (p. 4).

Drea, J. T., Tripp, C., & Stuenkel, K. (2005). An assessment of the effectiveness of an in-class game on marketing students' perceptions and learning outcomes. *Marketing Education Review, 15*(1), 25–33. doi:10.1080/10528008.2005.11488887

Dunleavy, M., & Dede, C. (2014). Augmented reality teaching and learning. In J. M. Spector, M. D. Merrill, J. Elen, & M. J. Bishop (Eds.), *Handbook of research on educational communications and technology* (pp. 735–745). New York: Springer. doi:10.1007/978-1-4614-3185-5_59

Fredembach, B., de Boisferon, A. H., & Gentaz, E. (2009). Learning of arbitrary association between visual and auditory novel stimuli in adults: The "bond effect" of haptic exploration. *Plos One, 4*(3), e4844. doi:10.1371/journal.pone.0004844

Groh, F. (2012). Gamification: State of the art definition and utilization. In N. Asaj, B. Konings, M. Poguntke, F. Schaub, B. Wiedersheim, & M. Weber (Eds.), *Research trends in media informatics* (Vol. 4, pp. 39–46). Ulm: Ulm University.

GUNT – Engineering mechanics and engineering design. (n.d.). *Engineering design*. (p. 195) Norderstedt, Schleswig-Holstein, Germany: G.U.N.T. Gerätebau GmbH.

Ibáñez, M. B., Di Serio, Á., Villarán, D., & Delgado Kloos, C. (2014). Experimenting with electromagnetism using augmented reality: Impact on flow student experience and educational effectiveness. *Computers & Education, 71*, 1–13. doi:10.1016/j.compedu.2013.09.004

MacCallum, C., & Hanna, R. (1996, September 12–14). DEFLECT: A computer aided learning package for teaching structural design. In J. af Klercker, A. Ekholm, & S. Fridqvist (Eds.), *Education for practice [14th eCAADe Conference Proceedings / ISBN 0-9523687-2-2]* (pp. 253–262). Lund, Sweden. Retrieved from http://papers.cumincad.org/cgi-bin/works/Show?8832

Martini, K. (2006). A new kind of software for teaching structural behavior and design. In D. Oakley & R. Smith (Ed.), *Building Technology Educators' Symposium* (pp. 279–288). College Park, MD.

Mele, T. V., Lachauer, L., Rippmann, M., & Block, P. (2012). Geometry-based understanding of structures. *Journal of the International Association for Shell and Spatial Structures, 53*(4), 11.

Oliveira, M. S. D. (2008). *MODELO ESTRUTURAL QUALITATIVO PARA PRÉ- AVALIAÇÃO DO COMPORTAMENTO DE ESTRUTURAS METÁLICAS.* (p. 186).

Pedron, C. (2006). An innovative tool for teaching structural analysis and design. vdf Hochschulverlag AG.

Piccolotto, M., & Rio, O. (1996). A computer-based teaching tool for structural design. *Automation in Construction, 5*(3), 233–242. doi:10.1016/0926-5805(96)00143-4

Piker, D. (2013). Kangaroo: Form finding with computational physics. *Architectural Design, 83*(2), 136–137. doi:10.1002/ad.1569

Prince, M. (2004). Does active learning work? A review of the research. *Journal of Engineering Education, 93*(3), 223–231. doi:10.1002/j.2168-9830.2004.tb00809.x

Quinn, G., Galeazzi, A., & Gengnagel, C. (2017). Augmented and virtual reality structures. In *Proceedings of the IASS Annual Symposium 2017*. Presented at the Interfaces: architecture. engineering. science.

Quinn, G., Geleazzi, A., Schneider, F., & Gengnagel, C. (2018). StructVR virtual reality structures, In *Proceedings of the International Association for Shell and Spatial Structures (IASS) Symposium 2018* (p. 9). Boston, MA, 2018.

Rucki, M. D., Miller, G. R., & Cooper, S. C. (1998, June 28). *Direct manipulation visualization of the behavior of framed structures in the Dr. Frame+R[33]C Environment.* 3.215.1-3.215.5. Retrieved from https://peer.asee.org/direct-manipulation-visualization-of-the-behavior-of-framed-structures-in-the-dr-frame-r-33-c-environment

Vrontissi, M. (2015). *The physical model in structural studies within architecture education: paradigms of an analytic rationale?.* In Proceedings of IASS Annual Symposia International Association for Shell and Spatial Structures (IASS). pp. 1–12.

Yasar, O., & Maliekal, J. (2014). Computational pedagogy: A modeling and simulation approach. *Computing in Science & Engineering, 16*(3), 78–88. doi:10.1109/MCSE.2014.60.

Chapter 12

The use of fuzzy angular models and 3D models on a construction method assessment on The Great Wall of China in Jinshanling as a case study of the history and heritage of civil engineering in education

Jin Rong Yang, Fabian Hadipriono Tan and Adrian Hadipriono Tan

Introduction

This chapter introduces a scientific technique tailored to recreating the construction method of the Great Wall of China, using a combination of fuzzy logic and the 3D modelling software SolidWorks. Both of these are employed to create a virtual reality (VR) model of the structure. One of the main objectives of recreating the construction of the Great Wall was to use it as a teaching aid in undergraduate courses such as History of Ancient Engineering (ENGR 2361) and History of Construction Engineering (CE 5860H: Sustainable Ancient Constructed Facilities) at Ohio State University, where limited textbooks are offered on the construction engineering aspects of the structures. While this chapter uses the Great Wall of China as a case study, the technique described may be used to teach the history and heritage behind the civil engineering of other ancient structures as well. The knowledge acquisition (on-site visits, fuzzy logic, etc.) and display results (3D models and VR) may be used to teach ancient engineering courses in different settings, such as primary, secondary and/or university education. Whereas traditional photos capture the authenticity of the ancient structure, 3D models and VR show hidden components that traditional photos could not capture. On-site walkthroughs with students remain the most effective way to explain the knowledge and concepts involved in a structure's construction, but such field trips are costly and often infeasible. VR offers an immersive virtual environment using the Oculus Rift headset, enabling walkthroughs of the structure without requiring students to be on site. Furthermore, the 3D models and VR can be adapted to the instructor's teaching style. Namely, the technique allows the instructor to control the movement speed, the way construction methods are displayed, what information is displayed (e.g. original versus current conditions) and many other features. The content of this chapter is derived from the first author's dissertation (Yang, 2018).

In the field of construction engineering, construction methods and sequences are often created based on decades' worth of experience and practice, combining construction expertise, engineering logic and computations and common sense. In a typical blueprint or plan, a construction sequence is presented as a guide for building a structure after being created by the engineers in the 'office'. While the engineers do have the opportunity to conduct on-site visits and investigations, the plans are typically made prior to the implementation phase of construction; therefore, they are often more a theoretical than a hands-on type of implementation. The sequences may need to be changed due to unexpected factors, such as lack of workers, availability of construction material and equipment and unforeseen weather conditions. The field engineers or contractors may request the change of the construction sequences, and any changes made during construction of the project can be submitted as an 'as-built' plan in today's construction. Therefore, the 'as-built' blueprint or plan is a more practical practice.

The same principles no doubt held true for the construction of ancient structures and monuments. The example used in this chapter is the Great Wall of China in Jinshanling, which, approximately 700 years ago, was built primarily on the ridge of the terrain. Three construction methods for building the Great Wall are proposed in this chapter. The first method was derived from positive and engineering-based contributing factors, such as a sufficient number of workers, material availability and good soil condition. Conversely, the second method was derived from negative contributing factors, such as deficient numbers of workers, lack of material availability and hard soil condition, among others. The third method is similar to the second except for the opposite sequence of erecting the structure. Notice also that a method may involve any combination of these contributing factors. The three methods evaluated in this chapter are assumed to contain the most plausible combinatorial sets of these factors. In addition, the sequences discussed in this chapter were demonstrated using SolidWorks 3-D images. The advantages and disadvantages of the sequences were taken into account, and fuzzy set evaluation was performed to assess which method would have been more feasible to implement during the construction of the Wall in the Ming Dynasty. However, despite the site observations, data collections, extensive literature search and interviews, detailed information about these methods is limited and fragmented. The current standards for construction practices, albeit useful as guidelines of past practice, may not be able to determine which method would have been most likely adopted by the ancient Chinese authorities during the construction of the wall. This may be attributable to the innumerable renovation processes throughout the centuries as well as the involvement of various parties in the construction and reconstruction of the structure, even if the area to be studied is limited to the Jinshanling section during the Ming Dynasty. Consequently, the research in this chapter resorts to the non-deterministic, non-probabilistic approach – the fuzzy logic concept – that capitalizes on the abundance of subjective assessments and variables when making decisions, in this case associated with the most likely method the ancient Chinese would had selected to their advantage on building their wall in Jinshanling. Where appropriate and reasonable, basic present construction erections and sequences were employed as references for recreating the past methods.

Scope and limitation of the study

As the Ming Dynasty's Great Wall spans over 8800 kilometres, this study covers the Jinshanling section of the monument, consisting of the towers and the wall connecting them, which was originally built at the beginning of the dynasty in AD 1368 and was renovated later in this dynasty, around AD 1567 (the historical dates of these events were displayed on site). Because Beijing was the capital of China during the Ming Dynasty (Luo, Dai, Wilson, Drege, & Delahaye, 1981), and because this section of the wall was only 150 km away from that city (Beijing, China to Jinshan Ridge Great Wall [Map], 2017), fortification against invasion by the Mongolians, Japanese pirates and Manchus was essential. The structure of the Jinshanling section is therefore quite complex, with foundation stones and bricks covering the outer layer of the wall and rubble with rammed earth confined inside. This study was built upon the authors' earlier studies (Yang, Hadipriono Tan, & Tan, 2017; Yang, Hadipriono Tan, Tan, & Parke, 2017; Yang, Tan, Tan, Parke, & Yang, 2016); it focuses primarily on reasonable and feasible construction sequences. An example comparison is between the sequence of the initial installation of stones diagonally from the four corners of the building and placing them at one corner for the foundation layout of the building. Either one is a feasible sequence, depending on the different contributing factors such as the unevenness in the bedrock elevation. Some construction stages have little relevance to this research, such as the process of constructing Roman-influenced arches and vaults for the openings and ceilings of the towers, having already been elaborated in an earlier study (Yang, Hadipriono Tan, & Tan, 2017). In order to install brickwork for the arch and vault in such circumstances, a temporary framework must be used to hold the bricks and mortar in place until the mortar is cured to full strength. Other sequences not discussed in this chapter include trivial processes, such as the bottom-up erection of the timber columns. In this example, the plinth must be placed first before the column can be erected.

Method 1

The first method introduced in this section, Method 1, takes the following factors into account:

- Adequate amounts of labour
- Available construction materials and equipment on site during the start of a sequence
- Favourable soil condition or existing structure
- Ease of access to the outside of the structure and temporary storage of construction materials inside the structure were unlikely to have been required during construction

First, the levelled placement of the foundation stones and bricks would have to be constructed on bedrock or existing structure in order to be structurally sound, as shown in Figure 12.1a and b. Next, the foundation stones and bricks for the outer layer and the rubble and rammed earth would be installed in a hill shaped for the inner core. Next, the initial phase of the stonework for the towers would be placed diagonally starting from the four corners of the building, eventually forming a square shape. For the superstructure of the brick towers, the brick interior and exterior walls would be constructed simultaneously. For the superstructure of the wood column towers, the erecting columns and stacked exterior wall would be built simultaneously. Lastly, the installation of brickwork and stonework for the battlement of the second floor would be completed after the construction of the exterior wall of the first floor (for both towers). Table 12.1 summarizes the major proposed sequence of construction and its advantages. The detailed version of the proposed first construction sequence of the Wall can be found in the authors' earlier research (Yang, Hadipriono Tan, & Tan, 2017; Yang et al., 2016).

Method 2

The factors considered in Method-2 include:

- Inadequate amounts of labour
- Lack of construction materials and equipment on site during the start of a sequence
- Unfavourable soil conditions
- Ease of access to the outside of the structure and temporary storage inside of the structure during construction

The main sequence of Method 2 involves constructing the structure inside out.

During the excavation stages of construction in which the hard bedrock was difficult to excavate or level, the placement of the foundation stones could be unlevelled, as shown in Figure 12.1c. The bricks were then cut to be level with the ground. This method also increased workability and productivity compared to that of workers trying to excavate the foundation or stones to level. In one specific instance, shown in Figure 12.1d, both the stones and the bricks were installed at an angle according to the slope of the

Figure 12.1 On-site photos of the Great Wall in Jinshanling.

Table 12.1 Method 1 of the Great Wall in Jinshanling construction.

Phase of Construction	Sequence of Construction	Advantages of Sequence
Excavation (for both towers and the Wall)	Levelled placement of the foundation stones and bricks	Structurally sound
Substructure	Install foundation stone and bricks for the outer layer and rubble and rammed earth in a hill shaped for the inner core simultaneously	Mortars are set at the same rate
Substructure	Install diagonally from the four corners of the building and eventually form a square shape	Less surveying and checking
Superstructure (for bricks and arched towers)	Install bricks for interior and exterior walls simultaneously	Easier to integrate interior and exterior wall
Superstructure (for wood column towers)	Erect columns and stacked exterior wall simultaneously	Ensure proper installing of the columns from bricks
Superstructure (for bricks and arched towers)	Erect columns and stacked exterior wall simultaneously for the mini towers	Ensure proper installing of the columns from bricks
Superstructure (for both towers)	Install brickwork for the battlement of the second floor consecutively from the construction of the exterior wall of the first floor	Does not require higher scaffolding; could use the second floor for standing

ridge of the terrain. The next step for constructing the wall was to work on the outer layer and inner core consecutively, moving between them regularly and integrating them with any natural or existing material, if possible. This would be especially feasible when bedrock was too hard to cut; therefore, the workers built the structure along the natural rock, as shown in Figure 12.1e. If the existing structure was still in good condition (for renovation), they would integrate the structure by keeping the existing material and adding material to it for expansion. At the time, this would have saved construction material. For the towers, workers would have had to install the foundation stones in a one-way direction starting from one corner and continuing in a completely square pathway. This is feasible if the bedrock is too difficult to cut and cannot be made into a levelled (in elevation) square foundation.

For the superstructure of the brick towers, workers would have installed bricks for the interior and exterior walls separately, either by constructing the interior wall first (as shown in Figure 12.2a) and then working toward the exterior wall, or by constructing the exterior wall first before working toward the interior wall (as shown in Figure 12.2b). For the mini-tower on

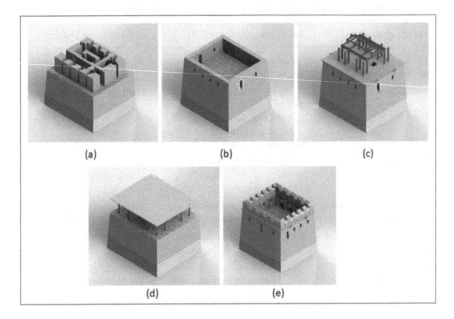

Figure 12.2 Construction sequence of the towers.

the brick towers, workers would erect the columns and stack the bricks for the exterior wall consecutively, as shown in Figure 12.2c. For the superstructure of the wood column towers, the second or third method would be to erect columns and the stacked exterior wall separately, as shown in Figures 12.2d or 12.2e. Lastly, for both types of towers, the brickwork and stonework for the battlement would be set in place by installing both on the second floor concurrently, such that the exterior wall of the first floor would have been constructed as shown in Figure 12.2e. This would require high scaffolding and integration of the second floor. Table 12.2 summarizes the major proposed methods for the second and third sequences of construction and their corresponding advantages (Yang, 2018).

Method 3

This method is in many ways similar to Method 2, except for the critical sequence in which the structure was built from the outside in. In this method, the construction sequence opposite to Method 2 warrants a different method category altogether. The contributing factors, such as the inadequacy of workforce, construction materials, equipment and soil conditions are relatively similar in the two methods. In addition, this method also has the advantage of workers having easy access to the construction site and materials (outside of the tower or

Table 12.2 Second and third construction methods on the Great Wall in Jinshanling.

Phase of construction	Sequence of construction	Additional information (step) on sequence	Conditions for sequence	Advantages of sequence
Excavation	Unlevelled placement of the foundation stones and bricks		Suitable for hard bedrock foundation where excavation is impossible	Increase workability and productivity
Substructure	Install construction material for the outer layer and inner core consecutively to each other		Too hard to cut in the foundation; lack of material availability during stage of construction; lack of workers	Use of existing structure or natural material
Substructure	Install in a one-way direction at one corner and come back in a complete square direction		Bedrock too hard to cut or form into a levelled (in terms of elevation) square	Use of natural material
Superstructure (for bricks and arched towers)	Install bricks for interior and exterior walls separately	Interior wall first, then exterior	Lack of workers and construction materials	Easy access coming in and out
		Exterior wall first, then interior	Lack of workers and construction materials	Layout of the structure, which would reduce mistakes from brickwork
Superstructure (for wood column towers)	Erect columns and install exterior wall separately	Wood column first, then exterior wall	Lack of workers and construction materials	Easy access coming in and out to ensure bricks are neatly installed around the timber columns
		Exterior wall first, then wood column	Lack of workers and construction materials	Provides a layout of the tower for storage
Superstructure (for the mini towers of the bricks and arched towers)	Erect columns and install exterior wall consecutively	Wood column first, then wall	Lack of workers and construction materials	Would ensure bricks are neatly installed around the timber columns

(Continued)

Table 12.2 (Cont.)

Phase of construction	Sequence of construction	Additional information (step) on sequence	Conditions for sequence	Advantages of sequence
		Exterior wall first, then wood column	Lack of workers and construction materials	Would provide a layout of the mini-tower for storage
	Install brickwork for the battlement of the second floor simultaneously to the construction of the exterior wall of the first floor		Must have high scaffolding and would require integration of the second flooring	Would provide layout of the structure

walls) and temporary material storage (inside of the structure). Except for the direction of the sequence, the construction phases and advantages of this method are the same as in Method 2, and are described in Table 12.2.

Fuzzy angular models

Due to innumerable contributing factors to the construction methods of the wall and towers of the Great Wall of China at Jinshanling, as elaborated, along with the scarcity of information, selecting the most likely method is not straightforward. Nonetheless, this knowledge base combined with fuzzy set and fuzzy logic approach (i.e. the *modus ponens deduction* (MPD)) technique, may lead to a reasonable conclusion. Ever since Zadeh (1965) introduced the concept of fuzzy sets over a half century ago, various fuzzy set models, such as translational, triangular and rotational models, have been employed in the domain of construction engineering (Al-Humaidi & Hadipriono Tan, 2010a, 2010b; Al-Humaidi & Tan, 2005; Hadipriono, 1985, 1995; Yang, Hadipriono Tan, Tan, et al., 2017). These models were then used in MPD in various construction-engineering areas (Al-Humaidi & Tan, 2005, 2013a, 2013b; Hadipriono, 1985, 1995).

Fuzzy angular models were used for the fuzzy logic operations in this study. The choice of these models was substantiated by the fact that they closely represent the actual behaviour of the occurrence of an event (Hadipriono & Sun, 1990). The results of the angular model reflect the general observation from on-site visits, construction experience and engineering reasoning. For instance, the overall result of the fuzzy set analysis on the wall was not clear (*undetermined*) about which methods were implemented during the construction of the Jinshanling wall and towers. Moreover, the result aligned with the on-site visits where evidence of the first construction method, such as the levelled foundation stones, presented in some sections of the wall, while in other sections of the wall, the second or third method had been used, such as with the installation of the angled foundation stonework. Note that the universe of discourse (collection of fuzzy sets) in this chapter gravitates to the **likelihood** of the implementation of a construction method on the Great Wall at Jinshanling. The angular fuzzy sets represent the values (variables) of this likelihood, such as *likely, unlikely, fairly likely* and *very unlikely*.

Using the tangent property of the triangle shown in Figure 12.3, $f_A(a)$ is defined as follows (Hadipriono & Sun, 1990):

$$f_A(a) = a \tan A, \text{where } A \subset A; \forall a \in A \qquad (Eq.12.1)$$

Where $f_A(a)$ is the membership value, a is the fuzzy element and tan A is the fuzzy set. For example, the value of *likely* is represented by the angular model of tan A = 1 or A = 45°.

There are three operations in the MPD technique: the Inverse Truth Functional Modification (ITFM), the Lukasiewicz Implication Rule (LIR) and the Truth Functional Modification (TFM) (Blockley, 1980). The MPD was necessary and the equation is shown below:

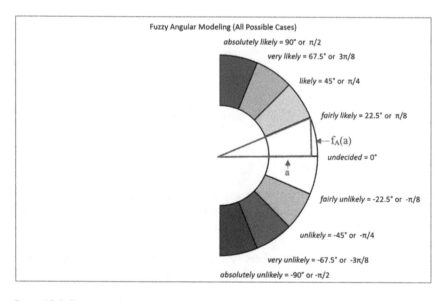

Figure 12.3 Fuzzy angular model.

$$A \Rightarrow B$$
$$\frac{A'}{(A \text{ is } T) \Rightarrow (B \text{ is } T')}$$
$$\therefore B'$$

(Eq.12.2)

By the triangular property shown in Figure 12.3 and Eq. 12.1, the truth value (T) in ITFM can be defined as follows:

$$\tan T = \frac{\tan A'}{\tan A}$$

(Eq.12.3)

By LIR:

$$\tan T = \frac{\tan T'}{(1 - \tan T')}, \tan T' = \frac{\tan T}{(1 + \tan T)}$$

(Eq.12.4)

By TFM:

$$\tan B' = \tan B \times \tan T'$$

(Eq.12.5)

Substituting the variables from ITFM and LIR equations (Eqs. 12.3 and 12.4) to TFM (Eq. 12.5) and yields the following:

$$\tan B' = \frac{\tan B \times \tan A'}{\tan A + \tan A'}$$

(Eq.12.6)

where $\tan A \neq - \tan A'$

And from (Eq. 12.6), the solution or the output B' can be defined as follows:

$$B' = \text{arc} \tan \left(\frac{\tan B \times \tan A'}{\tan A + \tan A} \right)$$

(Eq.12.7)

Rules for the MPD

The rules for the MPD for the fuzzy set assessment were derived from the authors' on-site visits, including investigations, construction experience and engineering-based logic. These rules are as follows:

- If there were enough workers (45°), then the proposed first method was *likely* (45°) to be implemented during construction of the Great Wall in Jinshanling.

- If all the construction methods were available on site (45°), then the proposed first method was *likely* (45°) to be implemented.
- If the levelling on the bedrock was feasible (45°), then the proposed first method was *very likely* (67.5°) to be implemented.
- If there was need of easy access coming in or out during the construction of the towers (45°), then the proposed first method was *unlikely* (-45°) to be implemented.
- If there was a need of temporary storage (in the towers) during the construction of the towers (45°), then the proposed first method was *unlikely* (-45°) to be implemented.

Note that the truth value of the rules (and information) may vary from expert to expert, and therefore that the degree of belief can be altered based on the experts' subjective judgment.

Fuzzy MPD of the towers

The information for the MPD (input for the fuzzy sets evaluation) was gathered on site, and some of the input was derived from the authors' knowledge base and their subjective judgment.

- There were *likely* (45°) enough workers.
- All the construction methods were *fairly likely* (22.5°) to have been available on site.
- The levelling on the bedrock is a little more than *likely* (50°) feasible.
- There was a *fairly likely* (22.5°) need of easy access coming in or out during the construction of the towers.
- There was a little more than *fairly likely* (25°) a need of temporary storage (in the towers) during the construction of the towers.

Table 12.3 shows the output of MPD, which was calculated with Eq. 12.7; a sample calculation of the result for workers is shown in Eq. 12.8. The mean (average) of the conditions is 12.32°.

Table 12.3 The likelihood of the first proposed construction sequence on the towers.

Condition	Likelihood of Implementation of Method 1 Sequence
Enough workers	26.56°
Material availability	16.32°
Bedrock excavation feasibility	52.70°
Ease of access in the towers (during construction)	-16.32°
Temporary storage in the towers (during construction)	-17.64°

$$B'(\text{for workers}) = \text{arc } \tan\left(\frac{\tan B \times \tan A'}{\tan A + \tan A'}\right)$$

$$= \text{arc } \tan\left(\frac{\tan 45° \times \tan 45°}{\tan 45° + \tan 45°}\right) = 26.56°$$

(Eq.12.8)

Fuzzy MPD of Walls

The information related to the Wall for workers, material availability and ease of access was similar to that of the towers. However, based on the on-site inspections, the levelling on the bedrock was deemed to be *undecided* to *fairly unlikely* at -5° feasibility; therefore, the likelihood of the first sequence changed to -13.03° using Eq. 12.7. The overall (mean) value for the Wall is 3.38°. Table 12.4 shows the likelihood of the first proposed construction sequence on the Wall.

Discussion of the fuzzy sets evaluations and results on the construction methods

The angular model was appropriate for this evaluation, based on the likelihood that the first construction method was implemented instead of the other two sequences, because this model can produce a quantifiable solution when the conditions in the rule (A in Eq. 12.2) and in the information (A' in Eq. 12.2) are opposite. For instance, if there were a *likely* need of easy access in or out of the construction area, then the proposed first method would be *unlikely* to have been implemented during construction. The information can be on the negative side of the scale, such as a need of easy access during construction being *unlikely*. This cannot be done using other fuzzy models such as Baldwin's rotational model. In this instance, the output of Baldwin's model would always produce an *undecided* solution if A' is opposite of A. Furthermore, the characteristics of the angular model remove

Table 12.4 The likelihood of the first proposed construction sequence on the walls.

Condition	Likelihood of Implementation of Method 1 Sequence (for the Wall)
Enough workers	26.56°
Material availability	16.32°
Bedrock excavation feasibility	-13.03°
Ease of access in the Wall (during construction)	-16.32°

some of the fuzziness from the system to produce a crisper solution. As such, it is a more appropriate choice with which to analyse the data in this chapter, since many of the fuzzy data were derived from the evidence of the on-site visits (i.e. as previously shown in Figure 12.1d for the angled foundation stones). Therefore, in general, the angular model is more suitable for examining data that is less subjective. However, the advantages of the angular model can also become limitations, such as when data is heavily subjective and reliant on the experience of experts. In such cases, other types of fuzzy model, such as the translational model in the authors' earlier research (Yang, Hadipriono Tan, Tan, et al., 2017), are more suitable for the assessment when compared to the angular model.

While the overall results fell within the *undecided* rating, the result for the towers was closer to *fairly likely* with regards to having been preferred and implemented, and the results for the Wall fell within the positive range. Because of this and some fuzziness in the angular model, it was viable to bump the results up to the next rating. This also led the authors to believe that Method 1 was *fairly likely* to have been preferred and implemented but would have been combined with either Method 2 or Method 3 where conditions were not feasible. The standalone Method 2 or Method 3 could have been used as well in some areas where soil conditions were deemed unfavourable.

Methodology (fuzzy logic, 3D models and VR) from an educational perspective

The methodology used in this chapter can be used in any classroom setting. The use of 3D models in VR, without presenting the complexity of fuzzy logic, may be implemented in primary and secondary education history courses or undergraduate university history courses, as illustrated in Figures 12.4a and 12.4b. The display of fuzzy logic, similarly to the display shown in Figure 12.3, may be implemented in VR for graduate university courses related to computer science and the history of engineering.

One of the advantages of presenting the information display in the form of VR is that the programmer can program the VR application to fit the instructor's teaching style. For instance, instructors may display the information in the order of the instructor's syllabus, align the movement speed in the VR model with the instructor's lecture and/or create games to test students' knowledge retention after the lecture. Therefore, a customized VR application, similar to what is shown in this chapter, can accommodate instructors' individual teaching methods.

One disadvantage of VR is cybersickness, but earlier research study offers recommendations to reduce or eliminate it, such as not using the Oculus Rift headset, controlling the movement speed and using the Omni Treadmill (Yang & Tan, 2018). Furthermore, as technology advances, *augmented reality* (AR) may prove a feasible solution to digital motion sickness. State-of-the-art

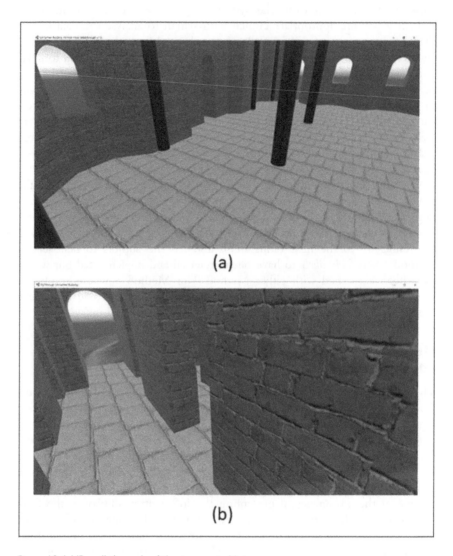

Figure 12.4 VR walkthrough of the towers in Unity.

AR headset displays, such as the Microsoft HoloLens, have been found to have a positive impact on cybersickness issues (Vovk, Wild, Guest, & Kuula, 2018). The Microsoft HoloLens 2 may enhance this impact further. However, IRB testing, similarly to the authors' earlier work on VR, should be performed to ensure that the findings are conclusive. The Microsoft HoloLens 2 is yet to be released. Another limitation of the AR headset is the cost of innovative AR headset technology. Currently, the initial cost for the Holo-Lens is $3000 (USD) (Warren, 2017), and the upcoming HoloLens 2 is priced at $3500 (USD) (Bohn, 2019). Nevertheless, based on the price trends of technology, the price of the AR headset may drop as AR headset technology advances. A decrease in costs would make it feasible for the authors to perform IRB testing on AR with students as test subjects.

Conclusions

The research results of this study reveal that Method 1 for the towers was *fairly likely* to have been preferred and implemented compared to Method 2 or Method 3. However, where the conditions were not feasible for Method 1 alone, the other two methods or a combination of Method 1 and the other two methods were executed. Additionally, while the fuzzy sets result showed that the preference for Method 1 was not clear (*undecided*) for the Wall, it was in the positive direction (in degree). Therefore, it can be interpreted as *fairly likely* for Method 1 to have been implemented, which also applies to the towers. However, the standalone method or a combination of construction methods was *likely* to have been implemented during the construction of the Wall. Furthermore, the authors believe that the first method had been included in the blueprint or plan because it was an engineering-based design and theoretical practice in the pre-plan and planning phase of construction. The standalone, or a combination of the sequences, may have been applied during the implementation phase of construction because it is a more practical way of proceeding. The authors hope that the application of the fuzzy sets angular model introduced in this chapter can be implemented for decision-making processes such as in creating, recreating and comparing the construction sequences in both current and ancient structures.

As previously noted, the technique described in this chapter used to recreate the construction sequence of the Great Wall could be replicated for other ancient structures for which data are limited and dependent on expert subjective judgment. This method of knowledge acquisition may be used in primary, secondary and undergraduate university education regarding the history and heritage of engineering. Fuzzy logic may be used to evaluate knowledge acquisition and to teach university graduate-level courses. The 3D models and use of VR make teaching more efficient because of the ability to display information virtually. While digital motion sickness does occur in VR, future AR headsets such as the Microsoft HoloLens 2 may be a solution to prevent cybersickness. It is hoped that this chapter will inspire future research and set standards to acquire knowledge, such as ancient construction methods, using fuzzy logic. The chapter has aimed to showcase how a cutting-edge display, made possible with VR or AR, can enable further knowledge acquisition for students in courses on the history and heritage of civil engineering.

References

Al-Humaidi, H., & Tan, F. H. (2013a). New approach to model material-related problems contributing to project delays using rotational fuzzy set. *Journal of Performance of Constructed Facilities, 26*(3), 279–286.

Al-Humaidi, H., & Tan, F. H. (2013b). Using fuzzy failure mode effect analysis to model cave-in accidents. *Journal of Performance of Constructed Facilities, 26*(5), 702–719.

Al-Humaidi, H. M., & Hadipriono Tan, F. (2010a). A fuzzy logic approach to model delays in construction projects using rotational fuzzy fault tree models. *Civil Engineering and Environmental Systems, 27*(4), December 2010, 329–351.

Al-Humaidi, H. M., & Hadipriono Tan, F. (2010b). A fuzzy logic approach to model delays in construction projects using translational models. *Civil Engineering and Environmental Systems, 27*(4), 353–364.

Al-Humaidi, H. M., & Tan, F. H. (2005). A fuzzy logic model to avoid electrocution during mobile crane operations. In *Proceedings of the Tenth International Conference on Civil, Structural and Environmental Engineering Computing in Rome*. Italy, 30 August–2 September 2005.

Beijing, China to Jinshan Ridge Great Wall [Map]. (2017). In *Google Maps*. Retrieved January 19, 2017, from Beijing, China to Jinshan Ridge Great Wall.

Blockley, D. I. (1980). *The nature of structural design and safety*. New York, NY: Halsted Press div. of Wiley Press.

Bohn, D. (2019). *Microsoft's HoloLens 2: A $3,500 mixed reality headset for the factory, not the living room*. Retrieved July 17, 2019, from www.theverge.com/2019/2/24/18235460/microsoft-hololens-2-price-specs-mixed-reality-ar-vr-business-work-features-mwc-2019

Hadipriono, F. C. (1985). Assessment of falsework performance using fuzzy set concepts, structural safety. *International Journal on Integrated Risk Assessment for Constructed Facilities, 3*(1), 47–57.

Hadipriono, F. C. (1995). Fuzzy sets in probabilistic structural mechanics. *Probabilistic Structural Mechanics Handbook*, 280–316. doi:10.1007/978-1-4615-1771-9_13

Hadipriono, F. C., & Sun, K. (1990). Angular fuzzy set models for linguistic values. *Civil Engineering Systems, 7*(3), 148–156. doi:10.1080/02630259008970583

Luo, Z., Dai, W., Wilson, D., Drege, J., & Delahaye, H. (1981). *The Great Wall*. London: M. Joseph.

Vovk, A., Wild, F., Guest, W., & Kuula, T. (2018). Simulator sickness in augmented reality training using the Microsoft HoloLens. In *2018 CHI Conference*, 1–9. doi:10.1145/3173574.3173783

Warren, T. (2017). *Microsoft's HoloLens successor reportedly arriving in 2019*. Retrieved July 17, 2019, from www.theverge.com/2017/2/20/14667306/microsoft-hololens-v2-rumors-2019

Yang, J. (2018). *The application of fuzzy logic and virtual reality in the study of ancient methods and materials used for the construction of the Great Wall of China in Jinshanling* (Electronic Dissertation). Retrieved from https://etd.ohiolink.edu/

Yang, J., Hadipriono Tan, F., & Tan, A. (2017). The ancient construction materials and methods: The Great Wall of China in Jinshanling as a case study. *KICEM Journal of Construction Engineering and Project Management, 7*, 37–50. doi:10.6106/JCEPM.2017.3.30.037

Yang, J., Hadipriono Tan, F., Tan, A., & Parke, M. (2017). Sustainability evaluation of the Great Wall of China using fuzzy set concepts by incorporating leadership energy and environmental design. *Civil Engineering and Environmental Systems*, 1–33. doi:10.1080/10286608.2017.1293662

Yang, J., Tan, A., Tan, F., Parke, M., & Yang, F. (2016). Computer-aided construction of the Great Wall of China in Jinshanling. In *Proceedings of the 17th International Conference on Geometry and Graphics*. Beijing, China: Beijing Institute of Technology.

Yang, J. R., & Tan, F. H. (2018). Classroom education using animation and virtual reality of the Great Wall of China in Jinshanling: Human subject testing. *Didactics of Smart Pedagogy*, 415–431. Springer International Publishing, doi:https://doi.org/10.1007/978-3-030-01551-0_21

Zadeh, L. A. (1965). Fuzzy sets. *Information and Control, 8*(3), 338–353.

Virtual reality in sciences and medical education

Part III

Chapter 13

Virtual Reality for teaching clinical skills in medical education

Charles Hand, Raphael Olaiya and Mohamed Elmasry

It is the convention within medical education that clinical skills are taught using traditional teaching methods such as didactic lectures, text books, photographs, images and more dynamic learning methods such as video and manikin-based physical simulation. Clinical skills are defined within health-care as any discrete and observable act within the overall process of patient care including communication skills (AAMC, 2005). A subset of clinical skills are procedural skills that involve an actual physical manoeuver or intervention that may or may not require specific equipment and may be undertaken for either investigative/diagnostic or therapeutic/management purposes. Their execution requires both psychomotor skills and background knowledge. When undertaken each procedure should be underpinned by sound clinical reasoning.

Over the past 20 years the medical profession has moved from text book and lecture based teaching methods towards simulation training due to increasing emphasis upon patient safety, limited resources, consensus of unpreparedness among junior doctors, a shortage of clinical placement opportunities and increased time pressures on clinical educators. Increasing amounts of published academic research on simulation training mostly concerned with high and low fidelity manikin-based simulation has been followed by subsequent increasing adoption and investment by medical education establishments in manikin-based simulation training. The significant monetary cost of resources needed for manikin-based simulation training is an attributed reason for the drive for robust research into effectiveness of this form of simulation; nonetheless, this form of simulation training is an expected and standard resource of western world medical schools (Willis & Van Sickle, 2015).

Simulation allows medical students the chance to practice clinical skills in a controlled environment with no risk to patients (Myers, 1998). Simulation training can take many different forms and structures, each having its own profile of advantages and disadvantages concerning practicalities and learning. Broad headings of simulation-based training types used in healthcare are artificial manikin low and high fidelity simulation training, human actor based simulation training and VR-assisted simulation training.

Simulation has long been used in the military, aviation and formula one industries (Helmreich, Merritt, & Wilhelm, 1999; Loftin, 2002). They are able to produce huge quantities of performance data using high-fidelity simulations to inform their research and development. This high level of simulation has previously been prohibitively expensive for other industries; however, in recent years hardware costs have significantly fallen whilst software technologies (such as graphics and gameplay) have improved considerably, allowing high-fidelity computerised environments to be created at relatively low cost. This, alongside increasing computer literacy, has heralded the viability of VR as a teaching tool in medical education (Cohen, 1999; Drake, 1998; Forrest & Taylor, 1998; Rosen, 2008; Ryall, Judd, & Gordon, 2016; Strachan, 2016).

VR is defined as 'a three-dimensional, computer generated environment which can be explored and interacted with by a person' (Virtual Reality Society, 2017). It is regarded as having started in the 1950s with the advent of the 'Sensorama', an interactive theatre device invented by Morton Heilig. VR with CGI interaction as we define it today surfaced publically in the 1980s with Jaron Lanier coining the term 'virtual reality' in 1987 (Virtual Reality Society, 2017). Today, the use of VR systems in medical education is in its infancy with only a handful of serious and successful attempts to introduce VR educational programs into curriculums of medical education. For example, Case Western Reserve University Medical School internally continue to confirm VR's effectiveness as a teaching tool, thus replacing cadaver-based teaching models with fully integrated virtual holographic systems in their 2019 new campus build (Case-Western-Reserve-University, 2013). In the UK in 2017, Boston Pilgrim hospital integrated (courtesy of Medigage Ltd and Olaiya et al. 2017) VR clinical skills basic life support simulation modular training for junior doctors and nurses to support the transition stage from the university to the ward and to combat the unpreparedness among juniors. Other advanced simulations are available, such as the da Vinci skills simulator, but these have not to our knowledge been integrated into educational programmes.

The field for VR in medical education is rapidly advancing, particularly with sophisticated lifelike VR interactions with medical apparatus, real-time responsive patients and immediate feedback to learner choices and actions. Modern VR technology is usually delivered through a wearable VR headset or glasses with accessory additions of haptic pressure feedback apparatus and motion sensing to increase immersion in the virtual world.

VR can be used in medical education for simulation training, theory learning and assessment. VR and simulation offer effective solutions to the modern problems of training a medical workforce in a cost-effective, measurable and transparent manner (Ryall et al., 2016). A number of key advantages make VR an excellent medical educational tool.

Firstly, VR provides a safe environment where students can practice their clinical skills without any risk to patients, themselves or equipment and can increase the proficiency of students above that of traditional teaching alone, as demonstrated by De Oliveira, Glassenberg, Chang, Fitzferald, & McCarthy (2013).

Secondly, VR can improve outcomes by providing superior feedback to students. Jasinevicius, Landers, Nelson and Urbankova (2004) and Engum, Jeffries and Fisher (2003) demonstrated that through VR, students can gain objective and reproducible feedback that can be accessed repeatedly. A student could use this to review clinical skills techniques, identify weaknesses and proactively take steps to improve skills wherever and whenever they wish. This ease of access extends to faculty members as well, making it possible to evaluate a student's work remotely and out of normal working hours. Consequently, VR offers a potentially more efficient method of teaching clinical skills, as students can oversee their own psychomotor learning without having to rely upon the availability of faculty members, which is often limited.

Lastly, as VR is a digital medium, individual software can be downloaded to common hardware such as iPhones or iPads. De Oliveira Jr et al. (2013) used free software in their study, making it easily accessible worldwide. With this sort of access, the latest VR would be available to many students at any one time, a clear advantage over traditional methods such as text books that are slow to update and require the physical text to learn from. VR therefore offers a more efficient method of teaching that allows the student to take control of their own learning, bridges the gap between theory and practical application of clinical skills and provides a solution to the modern problem of training medical staff within restricted working hours.

Despite these potential advantages, VR is yet to be widely taken up within medical education. The reasons for this are multifactorial, including financial costs and availability of hardware to deliver a VR experience. Another likely factor is a lack of high-quality evidence demonstrating that VR is superior to traditional methods for teaching clinical skills. See Table 13.1 . Only a handful of high-quality papers exist (i.e. using randomised controlled trials and robust research design). Before there can be a wide uptake of VR as a medical educational tool, this lack of high-quality evidence will need to be addressed.

Additionally, those papers that had adequate design demonstrated that VR was at least as good as traditional methods, but weren't able to demonstrate an advantage for VR over traditional methods. We propose this is due to two key amendable fundamental factors as opposed to any intrinsic quality of VR as a teaching platform.

1. The specific limitations of the fidelity and sophistication of the VR software and hardware used
2. The degree of optimisation of the learner journey learning dynamics, gamification metrics and immersion

The studies cited meet the criteria of VR, as they are in 'a three-dimensional, computer generated environment which can be explored and

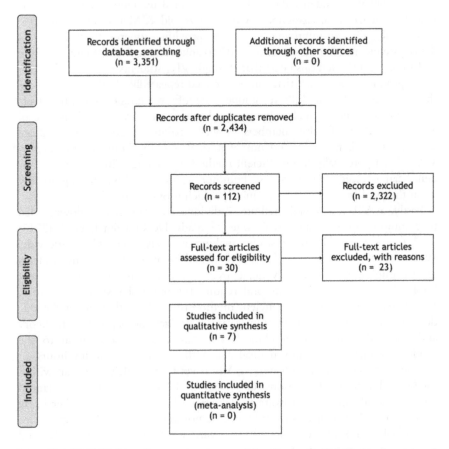

Figure 13.1 PRISMA flow diagram showing number of records identified, screened and deemed eligible and the final number of papers included in the analysis.

interacted with by a person' (Virtual Reality Society, 2017); however, most use monoscopic two-dimensional viewing formats as low-fidelity simulations. By today's modern standards, a consumer would expect to have a far more immersive experience, one in which a headset was used, graphics were high quality and there was an element of gamification with scores and performance feedback. A 2017 qualitative phenomenological study by Olaiya et al. compared the use of immersive stereoscopic VR headsets to traditional manikin teaching for basic life support skill training for primary care general practice multidisciplinary staff members including the secretary, nurse and general practitioner physicians. Table 13.2 shows feedback from study participants and demonstrates how the limitation of VR revolves around technical issues that are attributable to hardware and software errors.

Table 13.1 Studies found searching PubMed, Embase, ERIC, CINAHL, Web of science and Scopus using search terms: virtual reality", "education", "teaching" and "simulation" and whether they demonstrated a difference between traditional teaching methods and VR.

Study	Results summary
William et al., 2016	No significant differences between traditional and VR groups
Ingrassia et al., 2015	No significant differences between traditional and VR groups, both groups improved equally significantly.
Jasinevicius et al., 2004	No significant differences between traditional and VR groups
Scerbo et al., 2006	No significant differences between traditional and VR groups for pre-test scores, post-test scores higher in traditional group
Engum et al., 2003	No significant differences between traditional and VR groups for outcomes, however higher satisfaction in traditional group
Kanumuri et al., 2008	No significant differences between traditional and VR groups, both groups reached proficiency
De Oliviera Jr et al., 2013	No significant differences between traditional and VR groups; however, more failed attempts in the traditional group

Table 13.2 User written feedback comments from a qualitative study conducted by Olaiya et al 2017.

User	Positive	Negative
GP1	Virtual reality is new to me and I think it's the future frontier for education. It helped make the experience closer to reality. Course was very unique; I've never seen anything like it.	At one point the headset I used showed an overheating warning and a spare headset was needed whilst the other cooled down.
GP2	Course was very unique; I've never seen anything like it.	I really struggled with the controls. The touch pad was tricky to use and this made the whole simulation difficult to advance.
Receptionist 1	It was like nothing I've ever seen, the scenario was fun and the teaching was thorough.	I felt a bit dizzy and nauseous when I first put the headset on.
Receptionist 2	Easy to use once I got my finger on the touch pad correctly. The headset really exciting to put on.	Two hours was a bit long and we overran a bit when I needed to get back to the front desk.
Practice Nurse	This felt just like a recent event where a patient collapsed in the waiting room and we did CPR on her. It's really useful to be able to practice it in a simulation.	There was a glitch where the character couldn't advance and the program had to be restarted.

The quality of the VR systems used in the literature review studies can be assessed by ease of use, realism, level of immersion, optimisation of the learning journey and cost-effectiveness (Virtual Reality Society, 2017). Although the authors of this chapter cannot comment upon the cost-effectiveness of the VR programmes used, the quality of the included studies was nonetheless poor when judged upon the remaining criteria. The low quality of the VR is therefore highly likely to have confounded results. Another potential confounding factor is the type of clinical task to which VR is being applied. We suggest that VR is best applied to complex procedural tasks to which students are less often exposed in clinical practice, whereas three of the seven studies focused upon phlebotomy, a relatively simple clinical task commonly undertaken by medical students. Where simple tasks are used, both groups are likely to reach high success rates; thus, there is likely to be no difference observed between VR and traditional methods. To combat this, Jasinevicius et al. (2004) measured not only success rates but time taken to acquire proficiency of the taught skill. The studies should also use real patients instead of part task trainers or manikins (where possible) when comparing proficiency of learning so that the findings can be translated to real healthcare scenarios (Jasinevicius, 2004).

None of the seven studies included used VR that was immersive enough to create an accurate representation of real life, as discussed by Engum et al. (2003). Future research should use VR of higher quality, with immersive environments and complex procedural tasks to determine the potential of VR as a teaching tool over traditional methods.

Additionally, several other factors that may impact the results of any VR system need to be explored and controlled for in future research. Some potential areas for study are the effects of computer literacy, age (which may link to computer literacy), optimisation of the learning journey, previous exposure to VR, learning style and quality of VR (Gluch, Stewart, Buchanan, & Hammrich, 1999).

Finally, the available literature on VR as a teaching method for medical students is small, and many of the papers that do exist were excluded from this review as they had major limitations. Examples include groups that were not directly comparable due to heterogeneous subjects (surgeons of differing levels alongside medical students) or were not randomly assigned and methods that did not clearly detail the traditional or VR teaching methods involved. In these cases, excessive variables could have accounted for the differences seen between groups, making it impossible to draw any reliable conclusions; hence, they were rejected from the review.

Currently, neither traditional nor VR teaching methods can perfectly simulate clinical skills scenarios. While traditional methods have long since reached their ceiling of capabilities, VR is in its infancy and has huge potential as technology continues to advance rapidly. The medical education field is a major stakeholder in VR as it offers the chance to optimise ever-stretched faculty time, immerse students in an engaging but safe environment, facilitate self-directed learning and modernise the teaching of clinical medical skills. As such, early investment from the medical education field is vitally important: to explore and discern the priorities of research concerning how to optimise VR as a medical education learning medium and in high quality, immersive VR software and hardware to take advantage of the technological advancements of the twenty-first century. This means conducting high quality research and improving the computer literacy of the medical work force, as well as faster migration away from traditional to the novel, embracing high-quality, immersive VR as a key technology of medical education.

Conclusion

VR offers students an environment to practice clinical skills that is engaging, safe and has easy access to in-depth feedback. This allows for effective self-directed study; students can take control of their own learning, and it offers a solution to the problem of restrictive time constraints placed upon trainees in modern medicine. The current literature uses VR of low quality and does not clearly evidence the potential benefits of VR over traditional methods. The medical education industry should invest in modernising medical education by conducting research of robust study design and developing high quality, immersive VR.

References

AAMC, A. o. (2005). *Recommendations for clinical skills curricula for undergraduate medical education*. Washington, DC: Association of American Medical Colleges.

Case Western Reserve University. (2013, January 01). *Building the future of medicine*. Retrieved July 20, 2017, from http://case.edu/think/fallwinter2013/future-of-medical-education.html

Cohen, L. (1999). Medical simulation is the wave of the future, U of O doctors say. *Canadian Medical Association Journal, 160*, 557.

De Oliveira, G. J., Glassenberg, R., Chang, R., Fitzferald, P., & McCarthy, R. (2013). Virtual airway simulation to improve dexterity among novices performing fibreoptic intubation. *Anaesthesia, 68*(10), 1053–1058.

Desender, L. I. V. H., Lachat, M., Rancic, Z., Duchateau, J., Rudarakanchana, N., & Group, P. S. (2016, July). Patient-specific rehearsal before EVAR: Influence on technical and nontechnical operative performance. A randomized controlled trial. *Annals of Surgery, 264*(5), 703–809.

Drake, J. (1998). *Commercial simulation market drives industry's future growth*. Retrieved August 15, 2016, from *National Defense Magazine* www.nationaldefensemagazine.org/

Engum, S., Jeffries, P., & Fisher, L. (2003). Intravenous catheter training system: Computer-based education versus traditional learning methods. *The American Journal of Surgery, 186*(1), 67–74.

Forrest, F., & Taylor, M. (1998). High level simulatiors in medical education. *Hospital Medicine, 59*, 653–655.

Gluch, J., Stewart, C., Buchanan, J., & Hammrich, P. (1999). Virtual reality technology in preclinical laboratory: Differential student responses based on learning styles. *Journal of Dental Education, 63*(1), 58.

Helmreich, R., Merritt, A., & Wilhelm, J. (1999). The evolution of crew resource management training in commercial aviation. *International Journal of Aviation Psychology, 9*, 19–32.

Ingrassia, P., Ragazzoni, L., Carenzo, L., Colombo, D., Gallardo, A., & Corte, F. (2015). Virtual reality and live simulation: a comparison between two simulation tools for assessing mass casualty triage skills. *European Journal of Emergency Medicine, 22*(2), 121–127. 2015.

Jasinevicius, T., Landers, M., Nelson, S., & Urbankova, A. (2004). An evaluation of two dental simulation systems: Virtual reality versus contemporary non-computer-assisted. *Journal of Dental Education, 68*(11), 1151–1162.

Kanumuri, P., Ganai, S., Wohaibi, E., Bush, R., Grow, D., & Seymour, N. (2008). Virtual reality and computer-enhanced training devices equally improve laparoscopic surgical skill in novices. *Journal of the Society of Laparoendoscopic Surgeons, 12*(3), 219–226.

Loftin, B. (2002). Med school 1.0: Can computer simulation aid physician training. *Quest, 5*, 16–19.

Myers, B. (1998). A brief history of human computer interaction technology. *ACM Interactions, 5*, 44–54.

Olaiya, R. (2017) *The VR Doctor: The world's first accredited VR assisted emergency life support course.* Retrieved December 10, 2017, from VR focus. www.vrfocus.com

Rosen, K. (2008). The history of medical simulation. *Journal of Critical Care, 23*(2), 157–166.

Ryall, T., Judd, B., & Gordon, C. (2016). Simulation-based assessments in health professional educations: A systematic review. *Journal of Multidisciplinary Healthcare, 9*, 69–82.

Scerbo, M., Bliss, J., Schmidt, E., & Thompson, S. (2006). The efficacy of a medical virtual reality simulator for training phlebotomy. *Human Factors, 48*(1), 72–82.

Strachan, I. (2016, August 15). *Technology leaps all around propel advances in simulators.* Retrieved August 15, 2016, from *National Defense Magazine* www.nationaldefense magazine.org/

Virtual Reality Society. (2017, January 01). *Virtual reality society.* Retrieved June 22, 2017, from www.vrs.org.uk/virtual-reality/what-is-virtual-reality.html

William, A., Vidal, V., & John, P. (2016). Traditional instruction versus virtual reality simulation: A comparative study of phlebotomy training among nursing students in Kuwait. *Journal of Education and Practice, 7*(9), 1.

Willis, R., & Van Sickle, K. (2015). Current status of simulation-based training in graduate medical education. *The Surgical Clinics of North America, 95*(4), 767–779.

Chapter 14

Virtual photoreality for safety education

Hai Chien Pham, Anh-Tuan Pham-Hang and Thi-Thanh-Mai Pham

Introduction and background

Construction plays a significant role in economic development all over the world, contributing $8.7 trillion and accounting for 12.2% of the world's economy (Perspectives & Economics, 2013). Despite its important contribution to the Gross Domestic Product (Raheem & Hinze, 2014), the construction sector accounts for 31% of all fatalities all over the world (Hämäläinen, Saarela, & Takala, 2009; Lingard et al., 2013). The high rate of construction accidents and fatal injuries causes many serious issues such as cost overruns and time delays (Le, Lee, & Park, 2014), which negatively affects project performance (Hussain, Pedro, Lee, Pham, & Park, 2018). To promote safety at construction jobsites, safety education at the tertiary level plays a very important role in providing sufficient safety knowledge and skills before graduates enter construction workplaces (Park & Kim, 2013). However, safety curricula have been considered low priority (Le, Pedro, Pham, & Park, 2016). Moreover, safety courses are isolated and learning methods have not engaged learners (Pedro, Le, & Park, 2015). As a result, learners feel bored and distracted, and safety education has failed to impart sufficient safety knowledge and professional skills to learners (Pedro, Pham, Kim, & Park, 2018).

With the emergence of state-of-the-art technology, Virtual Reality (VR) has proven advantageous in various disciplines such as life sciences (Adedokun et al., 2012), factories (Rahim et al., 2013), geography (Krakowka, 2012), and education (Sampaio, Henriques, & Martins, 2010). VR is created by computer-based 3D models to develop virtual environments in which learners can interact with 3D worlds (Pedro, Chien, & Park, 2018). For construction safety management, scholars have applied VR to provide interactive and experiential learning environments for students, such as the Design-for-Safety-Process system (Hadikusumo & Rowlinson, 2002), Cave Automatic Virtual Environments (Perlman, Sacks, & Barak, 2014), System for Augmented Virtuality Environments (Albert, Hallowell, Kleiner, Chen, & Golparvar-Fard, 2014), the Visualized Safety Management System (Park & Kim, 2013) and the Multiuser Virtual Safety Training System (Li, Chan, & Skitmore, 2012). For construction safety education, a small amount of research has adapted VR technology, including VR-based learning framework (Le, Pedro, Lim, et al., 2015), a social VR-based construction safety education system (Le, Pedro, & Park, 2015) and a pilot study for a 3D game environment (Lin, Son, & Rojas, 2011). However, a 3D-VR limitation is the lack of real-world visibility (Pham, Pedro, Le, Lee, & Park, 2019). To overcome this issue, VP has emerged as an innovative pedagogic method, which provides a real-world environment (Pham, Dao, Pedro, et al., 2018). The rationale behind VP technology is a projection of spherical images to render the surroundings, where a camera view is positioned to realize human-eye behaviour. There has not been a lot of research on applying VP to construction training (Eiris, Gheisari, & Esmaeili, 2018). One example is that Jeelani et al. developed an immersive personalized training environment for construction workers using VP technology (2017). Moreover, VP has been proven an energy-efficient tool for education and training (Pham, Dao, Kim, Cho, & Park, 2018). Despite its many advantages, more research is needed to adapt VP as a potential for improving construction safety education.

This chapter proposes an innovative learning approach for construction safety education using the VP platform. A VP-based learning framework is developed, consisting of three modules: Construction Accident Learning (CAL), Construction Hazard Investigation (CHI) and Construction Safety Performance (CSP). A VP prototype is proposed, derived from accident case studies that are common on construction jobsites. Then, validation of this VP platform is explored by educators, construction managers and students, and learning outcome effectiveness is reviewed. Findings reveal that VP would be a potential pedagogic method for enhancing construction safety education.

Research methodology

The main objective of this chapter is to propose an innovative learning approach for construction safety education using VP technology. To achieve this objective, this chapter begins with a literature review to investigate the importance of safety education for reducing construction accidents at the workplace. The literature review reveals that even though VP has been applied and proven beneficial in many disciplines, it has not been considered potential pedagogy in safety education. Therefore, it motivates the development of VP-based learning framework for safety education. A VP prototype is developed based on common accident case studies on real construction sites. After that, validation is implemented by participants through interviews and exams. Finally, discussion and recommendations reveal the advantages and limitations of a VP-based learning approach as well as recommend future work (see Figure 14.1).

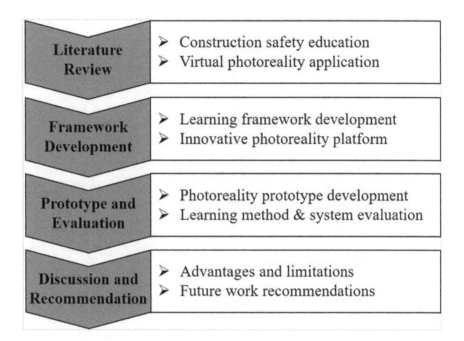

Figure 14.1 Research methodology.

VP-based learning framework

This section describes an innovative VP-based learning framework for improving construction safety education. As depicted in Figure 14.2, the framework consists of three (CAL, CHI and CSP) modules assisted by a unique VP platform throughout the teaching–learning activities. The innovative learning approach emphasizes the importance of positioning students in the centre of safety learning and promotes the interaction and engagement of learners.

Firstly, CAL aims to provide construction accident lessons through case-based learning. The educator disseminates common construction accident cases to students. Following educator instruction, students carry out online discussions through a chatroom in the VP platform. During discussions, learners can easily upload or share e-materials (images, videos, animation and e-documents) related to accident case being analysed. This function supports online learning. Students can raise questions to educators and classmates in the classroom or in the chatroom on the VP platform. Then, the educator explains and synthesizes each accident case to ensure students thoroughly understand the lesson before moving to the next step.

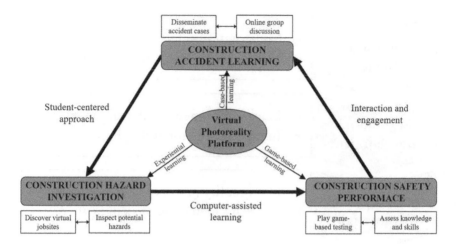

Figure 14.2 VP-based learning framework.

To apply the knowledge obtained in CAL, students are required to investigate and inspect potential hazards in virtual jobsites in CHI. CHI provides an experiential learning environment using the VP platform (see Figure 14.3). Students play the role of safety manager to explores a virtual jobsite, identify dangerous scenarios and recognize potential hazards, assigned by hotspots. As

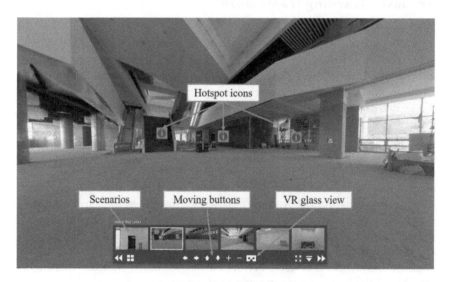

Figure 14.3 Photoreality prototype application.

depicted in the CHI module in Figure 14.4a, each hotspot includes hazard information and safety e-materials to assist learners in identifying potential hazards. During hazard recognition and safety knowledge reflection, the online chatroom in the VP platform supports students in raising question and having discussions with classmates and educators. As in CAL, users can easily upload or share e-materials through the chatroom. In addition to knowledge dissemination, CHI is designed to help learners improve safety skills before entering a real construction workplace.

To assess knowledge and skills obtained from previous modules, students take part in CSP to play simulation testing games (see Figures 14.4a and 14.4b). Taking on the role of safety manager, students search a virtual construction jobsite and tag potential hazards with exclamation signs. After hazard identification, students are required to complete a Job Hazard Analysis (JHA), including type of accident, element, accident description, root causes of hazard, etc. After correctly analysing a hazard, students move on to the next. Wrong answers result in negative scores. Due to the importance of prevention methods for eliminating hazards at workplace, students must submit sequence steps for safe practice in JHA. The VP platform automatically records game-based test results to assess the safety performance of the learner.

Photoreality

A spherical panorama is an image format that represents the whole real surrounding space, covering a 360-degree horizontal angle and a 180-degree vertical angle from the reference point of projection. Generally, spherical panoramas are created with omnidirectional cameras specialized for 360 panorama images or multiple-angle images based on stitching techniques.

 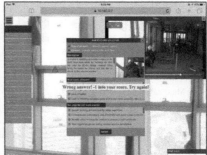

(a) Investigate and inspect potential hazards   (b) Game-based testing and job hazard analysis

Figure 14.4 Construction Hazard Investigation (CHI) and Construction Safety Performance (CSP) modules.

Two main spherical formats are the cubic (6 cube faces (i.e., 6 separate images) to display the whole sphere around the projection point) and the equirectangular (a single 2:1–ratio image covering 360 x 180 degrees) (Arth, Klopschitz, Reitmayr, & Schmalstieg, 2011). To improve the correction of the stitching result, there must be some amount of overlap (e.g., 25%) among pairs of neighbouring images within a unique parallax (Guan, Shark, Hall, & Deng, 2009).

Prototype

Prototype development

Figure 14.5 describes the development of a VP system. Although a spherical panorama is able to present the whole surrounding space, it is not user-friendly in terms of gathering information. Fortunately, the emerging digital projection techniques can completely address this problem. The webGL framework supports smoothly rendering multiple images to form a wide-eye screen. JavaScript code provides more rich features for the user to interact on the screen, such as control functions (e.g. moving around, interchanging scenarios, multimedia resources), supplemental explanation materials (e.g. text, files, links) and management privileges (e.g. system access control, user group) (Ventura & Höllerer, 2013).

On the virtual scenarios, each educational object is marked by a hotspot icon; information appears when the mouse hovers on it. A learner can click to obtain more detailed knowledge (e.g. images, specifications, videos of the

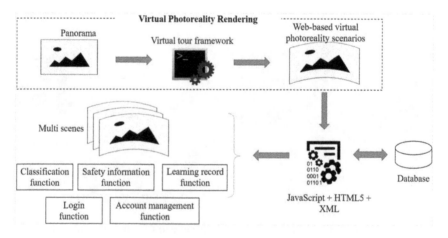

Figure 14.5 VP prototype development.

installation process and additional material). The VR glass view ability will be ready after the external VR glass detection.

Case study

To identify the advantages and limitations of the new learning framework, case studies deriving from real construction accidents are developed for the VP prototype. According to the Occupational Safety and Health Administration (OSHA), the 'Fatal Four' (i.e. falls, being struck by an object, electrocution and caught-in cases) are the most common accidents in reality (OSHA, 2019). Thus, the Fatal Four are chosen for designing the 20 VP case studies. They include a fall from a mobile scaffold on the first floor, a worker being struck by a falling object due to the lack of safety nets; electrocution when using hand tool; a worker caught between a truck and concrete due to toppling over of precast concrete building unit, etc.

The educator and students log into the VP system and click CAL functions to learn accident lessons. After thoroughly understanding the 'Fatal Four', they continue to experience a virtual high-rise building jobsite in CHI (see Figure 14.4a). The building construction consists of a basement and 14 floors. Students are required to navigate the whole virtual building to investigate potential hazards. Learning activities of students are hazard identification and inspection. Finally, students click the CSP function (see Figure 14.4b) for game-based testing to assess their safety knowledge and skill after using this VP-based learning approach.

Evaluation

Evaluation scheme

To determine the proposed tool's pedagogic effectiveness and limitations, an evaluation scheme has been designed, depicted in Figure 14.6. The first evaluation stage applies a traditional learning approach: Thirty four-year students participated in a lecture-based lesson led by a construction professor in the classroom. They were asked to complete a before-exam questionnaire.

All students then moved on to the second evaluation stage, which featured adapting the new VP-based learning approach. All students, ten professors and ten safety managers experienced the VP system using their own mobile devices (e.g. ipad, laptop). After the VP experience, all participants evaluated the VP system and new VP-based learning approach through interviews and questionnaires. Likert scales (1 point for strongly disagree to 5 points for strongly agree) were used for these subjective evaluations. The evaluation criteria (Pedro et al., 2015; Usoh, Catena, Arman, & Slater, 2000; Virvou & Katsionis, 2008) for evaluating VP system were 1) Sense of being in real construction workplaces (to what degree users feel they are in a real

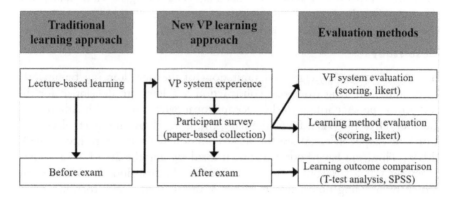

Figure 14.6 Evaluation scheme

construction workplace); 2) Ease of navigation (how easily users can navigate the virtual construction jobsite); 3) Comfort of using mobile devices (how comfortable the participant is using the VP system); 4) Close to reality (how well the VP system can provide real-world visibility) and 5) Computer-assisted learning (how well the VP system can support a new learning approach). To validate the new learning method, the evaluation criteria (Le et al., 2016; Park, Le, Pedro, & Lim, 2015;) are 1) Learner-oriented approach; 2) Spatial and experiential learning; 3) Learning engagement; 4) Motivation and 5) Improvement of professional skills.

In the final evaluation stage, the thirty students were required to take a final examination after using the VP platform. A comparison of the before-exam and after-exam results was made to evaluate the learning effectiveness of the new VP-based approach. A paired sample T-test analysis determined whether the difference between the two exam mean scores was statistically significant. A null hypothesis is that the two exam mean scores are equal, while the alternative hypothesis is that two exam mean scores are not equal. SPSS.20 statistic software was used for this paired sample T-test analysis at the 5% significance level.

Result

Figure 14.7 depicts the results of evaluating the VP system, focusing on five aforementioned criteria. All participants responded that they had the feeling of being in a real construction workplace. Moreover, users highlighted that the VP design is intuitive and that they could easily navigate the virtual construction jobsites by using their fingers or a mouse to interact with the system. Since VP system can run based on individual mobile devices, participants felt

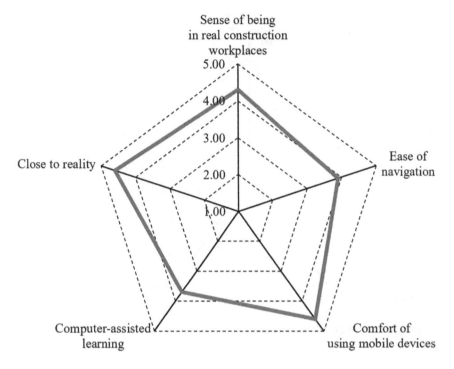

Figure 14.7 System evaluation

very comfortable learning anywhere and anytime. They agreed that the proposed system using VP technology provided real-word visibility better than
the common 3D-VR. Learners emphasized the importance of computer-
assisted learning to overcome the limitations of the traditional approach.

The new learning method evaluation focused on five criteria as illustrated in
Figure 14.8. All participants emphasized that the learner-oriented approach
prominent in the VP-based method could benefit the learning outcome. Moreover, they emphasized that the VP platform provides good spatial and experiential learning and that the VP-based learning method motivated and engaged
them in learning safety knowledge better than the lecture-based traditional
method. Due to their acting as safety managers inspecting hazards and promoting work safely, learners agreed that their safety professional skills could be
improved by obtaining safety knowledge through the VP system.

Table 14.1 provides average results of both exams, taken by thirty construction students before and after using the VP system. According to Table 14.2,
since the Sig. (2-tailed) value of 0.001 is less than the significance level of

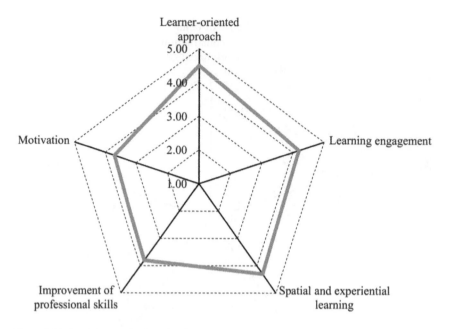

Figure 14.8 Learning method evaluation

Table 14.1 Learning outcome results.

		Mean	N	Standard Deviation
Pair	Before exam	75.17	30	3.592
	After exam	80.33	30	4.749

Table 14.2 Paired samples test.

		Paired Differences					t	df	Sig. (2-tailed)
		Mean	Standard Deviation	Std. Error Mean	95% Confidence Interval of the Difference				
					Lower	Upper			
Pair	Before exam & After exam	-5.666	6.530	1.192	-8.105	-3.228	-4.753	29	0.001

0.05, the null hypothesis was rejected. Therefore, it is concluded that there is a statistically significant difference between the mean scores of the two exams. The evaluation results of learning outcome effectiveness in Table 14.1 reveal that learners using the VP-based method would have higher scores (80.33) than those who learn based on traditional method (75.17). Therefore, it is proven that the proposed VP-based learning approach can assist learners in improving safety knowledge and skills.

Discussion and conclusion

Safety education is very important for promoting safety performance at construction workplaces. However, safety curricula have not been given attention by universities, and programs have failed to provide students with sufficient safety knowledge and professional skills. Therefore, construction graduates cannot recognize hazards and safely perform construction. Thus, worksite accidents are increasing. To improve construction safety education, this chapter proposes an innovative VP-based learning approach, which will provide an interactive and experiential learning environment. A learning framework and VP prototype are developed to evaluate the proposed pedagogic method. Preliminary findings reveal that a VP-based pedagogy approach can significantly help learners acquire safety knowledge and professional skills, thus improving construction safety education.

Although the VP-based pedagogic method provides improvements in safety education, future research needs to investigate the application of new wearable devices (e.g. head-mounted-displays, Microsoft Hololens, Google glass, etc.) to develop an immersive learning environment. Since the VP prototype focuses on a virtual high-rise building, it is necessary to conduct an in-depth investigation of learning outcome effectiveness in cases of experiencing different types of construction (e.g. bridges, tunnels, damps). Moreover, a full-scale VP system should be developed to evaluate the VP application in training workers and engineers at real jobsites before working.

References

Adedokun, O. A., Hetzel, K., Parker, L. C., Loizzo, J., Burgess, W. D., & Robinson, J. P. (2012). Using virtual field trips to connect students with university scientists: Core elements and evaluation of zipTrips™. *Journal of Science Education and Technology*, *21*(5), 607–618.

Albert, A., Hallowell, M. R., Kleiner, B., Chen, A., & Golparvar-Fard, M. (2014). Enhancing construction hazard recognition with high-fidelity augmented virtuality. *Journal of Construction Engineering and Management*, *140*(7), 04014024.

Arth, C., Klopschitz, M., Reitmayr, G., & Schmalstieg, D. (2011, October). Real-time self-localization from panoramic images on mobile devices. In *2011 10th IEEE International Symposium on Mixed and Augmented Reality* (pp. 37–46). IEEE.

Eiris, R., Gheisari, M., & Esmaeili, B. (2018). PARS: Using augmented 360-degree panoramas of reality for construction safety training. *International Journal of Environmental Research and Public Health, 15*(11), 2452.

Guan, X., Shark, L. K., Hall, G., & Deng, W. (2009, September). Distortion correction for immersive navigation in spherical image environment. In *2009 International Conference on CyberWorlds* (pp. 96–101). IEEE.

Hadikusumo, B. H. W., & Rowlinson, S. (2002). Integration of virtually real construction model and design-for-safety-process database. *Automation in Construction, 11*(5), 501–509.

Hämäläinen, P., Saarela, K., & Takala, J. (2009). Global trend according to estimated number of occupational accidents and fatal work-related diseases at region and country level. *Journal of Safety Research, 40*, 125–139.

Hussain, R., Pedro, A., Lee, D. Y., Pham, H. C., & Park, C. S. (2018). Impact of safety training and interventions on training-transfer: Targeting migrant construction workers. *International Journal of Occupational Safety and Ergonomics*, 1–13.

Jeelani, I., Han, K., & Albert, A. (2017). Development of immersive personalized training environment for construction workers. *In Computing in Civil Engineering, 2017* 407–415.

Krakowka, A. R. (2012). Field trips as valuable learning experiences in geography courses. *Journal of Geography, 111*(6), 236–244.

Le, Q. T., Lee, D. Y., & Park, C. S. (2014). A social network system for sharing construction safety and health knowledge. *Automation in Construction, 46*, 30–37.

Le, Q. T., Pedro, A., & Park, C. S. (2015). A social virtual reality based construction safety education system for experiential learning. *Journal of Intelligent & Robotic Systems, 79*(3–4), 487–506.

Le, Q. T., Pedro, A., Pham, H. C., & Park, C. S. (2016). A virtual world based construction defect game for interactive and experiential learning. *International Journal of Engineering Education, 32*(1), 457–467.

Le, Q. T., Pedro, A. K. E. E. M., Lim, C. R., Park, H. T., Park, C. S., & Kim, H. K. (2015). A framework for using mobile based virtual reality and augmented reality for experiential construction safety education. *International Journal of Engineering Education, 31*(3), 713–725.

Li, H., Chan, G., & Skitmore, M. (2012). Multiuser virtual safety training system for tower crane dismantlement. *Journal of Computing in Civil Engineering, 26*(5), 638–647.

Lin, K. Y., Son, J. W., & Rojas, E. M. (2011). A pilot study of a 3D game environment for construction safety education. *Journal of Information Technology in Construction (Itcon), 16*(5), 69–84.

Lingard, H. (2013). Occupational health and safety in the construction industry. *Construction Management and Economics, 31*, 505–514. doi:10.1080/01446193.2013.816435

OSHA. (2019). *United States Department of Labor.* Retrieved July, 2019 from www.osha.gov/oshstats/commonstats.html

Park, C. S., & Kim, H. J. (2013). A framework for construction safety management and visualization system. *Automation in Construction, 33*, 95–103.

Park, C. S., Le, Q. T., Pedro, A., & Lim, C. R. (2015). Interactive building anatomy modeling for experiential building construction education. *Journal of Professional Issues in Engineering Education and Practice, 142*(3), 04015019.

Pedro, A., Chien, P. H., & Park, C. S. (2018). Towards a competency-based vision for construction safety education. In *IOP Conference Series: Earth and Environmental Science* (Vol. 143, No. 1, p. 012051). IOP Publishing. Hochiminh city, Vietnam.

Pedro, A., Le, Q. T., & Park, C. S. (2015). Framework for integrating safety into construction methods education through interactive virtual reality. *Journal of Professional Issues in Engineering Education and Practice, 142*(2), 04015011.

Pedro, A., Pham, H. C., Kim, J. U., & Park, C. (2019). Development and evaluation of context-based assessment system for visualization-enhanced construction safety education. *International Journal of Occupational Safety and Ergonomics*, 1–33.

Perlman, A., Sacks, R., & Barak, R. (2014). Hazard recognition and risk perception in construction. *Safety Science, 64*, 22–31.

Perspectives, G. C., & Economics, O. (2013). *Global Construction 2025. A global forecast for the construction industry to 2025* (pp. 28–325). Global Construction Perspectives and Oxford Economics. United Kingdom.

Pham, H. C., Dao, -N.-N., Kim, J.-U., Cho, S., & Park, C.-S. (2018). Energy-efficient learning system using web-based panoramic virtual photoreality for interactive construction safety education. *Sustainability, 10*(7), 2262.

Pham, H. C., Dao, -N.-N., Pedro, A., Le, Q. T., Hussain, R., Cho, S., & Park, C. S. (2018). Virtual field trip for mobile construction safety education using 360-degree panoramic virtual reality. *International Journal of Engineering Education, 34*(4), 1174–1191.

Pham, H. C., Pedro, A., Le, Q. T., Lee, D. Y., & Park, C. S. (2019). Interactive safety education using building anatomy modelling. *Universal Access in the Information Society, 18*(2), 269–285.

Raheem, A. A., & Hinze, J. W. (2014). Disparity between construction safety standards: A global analysis. *Safety Science, 70*(Supplement C), 276–287.

Rahim, E. E. A., Dünser, A., Unsworth, K., Mckinnon, A., Billinghurst, M., Gostomski, P., & Herritsch, A. (2013, August). Visiting a milk factory without gumboots: Students' attitudes towards a virtual field trip. In *Proceedings of 2013 IEEE International Conference on Teaching, Assessment and Learning for Engineering (TALE)* (pp. 423–428). IEEE.

Sampaio, A. Z., Henriques, P. G., & Martins, O. P. (2010). Virtual reality technology used in civil engineering education. *The Open Virtual Reality Journal, 2*, 1.

Usoh, M., Catena, E., Arman, S., & Slater, M. (2000). Using presence questionnaires in reality. *Presence: Teleoperators & Virtual Environments, 9*(5), 497–503.

Ventura, J., & Höllerer, T. (2013). Structure and motion in urban environments using upright panoramas. *Virtual Reality, 17*(2), 147–156.

Virvou, M., & Katsionis, G. (2008). On the usability and likeability of virtual reality games for education: The case of VR-ENGAGE. *Computers & Education, 50*(1), 154–178.

Chapter 15

Encouraging immersion in the Soil Sciences through virtual conferences where ideas are shared among avatars to improve the educational background of young scientists

E.V. Taguas, E. Fernández-Ahumada, L. Ortiz-Medina, S. Castillo-Carrión, M.C. Beato, P. Alarcón Ramírez, J.J. Martínez Molina, C. Pérez Martínez, M.C. del Campillo, A.M. Tarquis, J. Montejo-Gámez and J.E. Guerrero-Ginel

Introduction

Currently, social networks and other innovations involving millions of people all over the world are revolutionizing the traditional paradigms of communication and creation of knowledge (Moedas, 2015). Virtual immersive environments are a relevant tool for eliciting distance, real-time interactions. A virtual immersive word consists of an interactive platform connecting participants from all parts of the world. Dionisio, Burns and Gilbert (2013) recommended taking into account four factors when designing a virtual space: i) realism: the virtual space should be realistic enough to allow users to feel psychologically and emotionally immersed in this world; ii) accessibility: the virtual spaces should be accessible on any existing digital device (e.g. desktop computers, tablets or mobile devices) and ensure that the virtual identity of the user or group user remained throughout the transitions in the Metaverse; iii) interoperability: the virtual spaces should comply with standards compatible with being modified and created using other software and later imported. Users should also be able to move around smoothly during their experience of immersion; iv) scalability: the server architecture should provide sufficient resources to allow a large number of users to occupy the virtual space without compromising system efficiency and user experience. Rodríguez García and Baños González (2011) emphasized that the experiences based on an immersive world should reproduce the essential characteristics of a forum for face-to-face discussion in terms of the simultaneous presence of participants and direct interactions.

Through multi-user domain software, each participant in an immersive world is present in a three-dimensional graphical environment through an 'avatar', a graphic representation that emulates real life and interacts in a real situation (Baker, Wentz, & Woods, 2009). Thus, the opportunity offered by virtual environments to interact in real time is not comparable with other formats such as video or radio recording. In this sense, Burdea and Coiffet (2003) highlighted the value of their '3 I's': immersion, interaction and imagination, which enable the bidirectional flow of information between the user and the virtual world. The success of virtual environments has been well documented in different fields such as medicine (Gerald & Antonacci, 2009), industry (Wilson, 2008), entertainment (Sivan, 2008) and education (Bouras & Tsiatsos, 2006; Grunwald & Barak, 2001; Kickmeier-Rust, Bull, & Meissl-Egghart, 2014; Lorenzo, Sicilia, & Sánchez, 2012; Mathers, Goktogen, Rankin, & Anderson, 2012; Sumners, Reiff, & Weber, 2008). In particular, Mamo et al. (2011) reported the success of a virtual environment for soil science activities based on the use of avatars. In turn, authors such as Schmorrow (2009) underlined the potential of virtual environments to change dramatically the way we live, particularly in the areas of education, product development and entertainment.

This chapter reports the experience of creation and usage of an open, virtual, immersive space that overcomes spatial limitations and holds virtual meetings between senior researchers and young scientists. The main purpose was to create a space where young researchers who lack the funding to attend international conferences could present their work, receive feedback from leading experts and thus play an active role in the dissemination of science. Avatars were used to promote interactions and introduce a gaming element. The experience was based on a real, existent conference. It was the European Geosciences Union (EGU) Assembly, which takes place in Vienna (Austria) every year. The first time the conference was also held in the virtual immersive environment, created for that aim, was in 2015. That year was the International Year of Soils, and the initiative was launched in order to cope with the objectives encouraged by the Food and Agriculture Organization of United Nations (FAO) (2014): to increase the information given to all sectors of society to promote the awareness of the fundamental role the soil plays in our lives and to promote, at all levels, policies for and investment in the sustainable management and protection of land resources. Since the duty to make their activities on soil studies became more attractive and the first experience was well received by young researchers, the experience has been repeated. In order to explain the process of design and evaluation of the experiences, this chapter is organized as follows: The next section is devoted to explaining the proposal of virtual conference, including the design of the scientific activities, the virtual platform and tools for evaluating the experience. The third section describes the evaluation of the virtual conferences in 2015 to 2017. Finally, the fourth section extracts conclusions about the whole experience.

Design of the experience

The set of experiences was created by a working group of nine members: Four were Master Students (MS); the rest, teaching staff at the Universities of Cordoba, Malaga and Granada. In addition, 10 senior professors and scientists of the Universities of Valencia (Spain), Madrid (Spain), Elche (Spain), Seville (Spain), Wageningen (Netherlands) and Trier (Germany) and staff from the Institute of Sustainable Agriculture in Cordoba (Spain) collaborated in the scientific discussions during the session. Table 15.1 presents the work stages and activities of the project, grouped into two work packages: A) scientific organization; and B) design and construction of the virtual building similar to the Austrian centre, where the EGU session has regularly been held in recent years. In turn, the last stage was to plan the evaluation of the experience.

Organization of the scientific activities

First, the project of the virtual session was presented to members of the Division of Soil Science Systems at the EGU, who supported it and agreed to include it in the program of the 2015 Annual Assembly to celebrate the International Year of Soils (Table 15.1, A.1). The title of the session was 'SSS1.3. Get immersed in Soil Sciences'. A flyer was prepared on the spot to invite the participants, through media such as Facebook and e-mails.

In order to test the capacity of the server, two months before the conference, a potential group of 15 to 20 young scientists was invited to access the virtual space, configure their avatars and upload all the audio-visual material necessary for the session. A trial run of the contents of the session was then

Table 15.1 Summary of the work stages carried out to prepare the virtual conference.

Work stages	Objectives
A. Scientific Organization	A.1 Dissemination and advertisement of session, as part of EGU
	A.2. Organization of schedule and content of session
	A.3. Participant training
	A.4. Collection/implementation of scientific material for the islands about soils
	A.5. Rehearsal and general trial run of the scientific session
	A.6. Session (see package C, feedback)
B. Immersive World: Design and Construction	B.1 Soil Division centre: rooms, furniture and equipment
	B.2 Basement: rooms, furniture and equipment
	B.3. General trial run
	B.4. Session (see package C, feedback)
	B.5. Video edition of the session

carried out (Table 15.1, A.2). The contents of the manual and the videos were organized into two blocks: i) basic steps for installation, movements of the avatar, appearance and chatting; ii) advanced steps for how to use the full repertoire of gestures, maps, pictures and time in the virtual world. In addition, there was, at least, one individual training session with each researcher taking part (A.3, Table 15.1). All the presentations were exported to the virtual world as interactive panels whose management was controlled by the avatar (Table 15.1, A.4). Finally, the week before the session, there were two additional trials to check the capacity of the server (Table 15.1, A.5 and A.6).

Design of the virtual platform and technical requirements

The main purpose of the design and construction of the platform was to reproduce the characteristics of a forum for face-to-face discussion, as suggested by Rodríguez García and Baños González (2011). The four factors recommended by Dionisio et al. (2013) were also included. Under this perspective, the simulation of the 3D virtual environment was carried out using OpenSim version 0.8.1.1 (http://opensimulator.org/), following the recommendations and scheme of Kappe and Guetl (2009). The Open Simulator project is a server of virtual worlds for creating 3D graphic environments. This is an open source simulator, which through OSGRID (OS = OpenSim + Grid = Mesh), the largest existing network in Open Simulator, enables interaction with different users from a PC. It is written in C# on .NET framework or MONO Project, which has allowed its developers to include new features.

The first step for users is to install FirestormViewer (www.firestormviewer.org/), to access the server and to prepare his/her avatar after receiving a login and a password. Users can select their avatars and begin to interact in the islands of the virtual world equipped for the meeting. The used server, which is dedicated to research and development of new procedures for the improvement of scientific and technological dissemination, presented the following characteristics: 40GB of RAM, 2 CPUs Intel Xeon E5620 2.40GHz 64bit, 5TB hard drive and Ubuntu 10.10. The server was physically installed in the Campus of the University of Córdoba (Spain). The recommended minimum requirements for user equipment are listed in Table 15.2. Further information concerning system requirements may be found at the following webpage: https://secondlife.com/support/system-requirements/.

FirestormViewer (www.firestormviewer.org/) is client software that allows users to access the virtual world. It is based on the LGPL V3 code from Linden Lab and offers a wide range of configuration options. The development of Firestorm is cross-platform, and there are versions for Windows, Linux and Mac OS X operating systems.

Regarding the structure of the immersive world, two islands (Soil Division Center and Basement) were created with different purposes: holding meetings

Table 15.2 Minimum requirements for users of Windows.

Features	Requirements
Internet connection	Optic fiber/ADSL
Operative system	Vista, Windows 7 and Windows 8
Processor	CPU with SSE2, including Intel Pentium 4, Pentium M, Core or Atom, AMD Athlon 64 or later
Memory	1GB
Screen resolution	1024x768 pixels
Graphic card	NVIDIA GeoForce 6600 or later, ATI Radeon 9500 or later Intel 945 chipset

Note: They were compatible with Opensim, which was used because it is quite popular and known; and Firestorm, offering numerous options for reproducing multimedia contents.

and editing avatars, respectively. Some buildings and many of the objects used to build the virtual world were downloaded from the free Zadaroo Internet repository (http://zadaroo.com/), while others were designed on the spot with exported CAD. Finally, to make it possible for users to communicate via voice chat, the platform was linked to an external voice service called Vivox (www.vivox.com/).

Evaluation of the experiences

Impact and feedback metrics

The procedure applied to evaluate the results of the experience was an observational type, with a minimum degree of control and interaction to choose the sample (Alaminos-Chica & Castejón-Costa, 2006). It was based on surveys in which the data were mainly measured on ordinal and categorical scales for statistical treatment. The steps followed to evaluate the impact of the session are summarized in Figure 15.1.

The general objectives of research were defined, hypotheses were made and the operative concepts to evaluate the educative experience discussed. Next, two types of questionnaires were designed: Block A and Block B (Figure 15.1). Questionnaires were drafted and fine-tuned using a pre-test trial; three participants in the session ruled out some questions and improved the contents of the others. The contents of Block A were focused on: 1) Information about the participants' background; 2) The place from which they were going to access the virtual world; 3) Their Information and Communication Technology skills; 4) Personal objectives from the session (questions 1 and 2, Figure 15.1). The participants were also asked to submit a written survey prior to the session (they were handed in anonymously). The objectives and final contents of block B (Figure 15.1) included

Steps - Impact measurements

1. Definition of general objectives– Aspects to consider for a successful and useful virtual meeting

2. Pretest – Characterisation of the participants (Block A); Technical aspects, learning and evaluation and feedback for improvement (Block B)

3. Exploration, discussion and final surveys design:
- **Block A (previous to the session)**
- **Block B (after the session)**

4. Submission to all participants who voluntarily answered the survey after the session (sample)

5. Qualitative and quantitative treatment (statistical analysis)

6. Interpretation of the results

Block B-Contents	Objectives	Format type
Question 1	Characterization of potential failures in relation with the characteristics of the	Closed/ List of categories
Question 2	participants and connection	Open/ Direct
Question 3	Difficulties and potential failures of software	List of categories and open options
Question 4	Minimum resources needed to set up programs/ to acces the immersive world	Closed/ List of categories
Question 5	Description of learning temporal curve	Open/ Direct
Question 6	Evaluate the role of the interaction with other participants for the learning	Closed/Ordinal
Question 7	Evaluate the best resources to learn how to manage the avatar	Closed/ List of categories
Question 8	Determine the strengths of the session	Closed/ List of categories
Question 9	Determine the weaknesses of the session	Closed/ List of categories
Question 10	Rate the overall usefulness of the session	Closed/Ordinal
Question 11	Rate the advantages of the virtual session in relation with the conventional methods	Closed/Ordinal
Question 12	Rate the advantages of the virtual session for the conference	Closed/Ordinal
Question 13	Proposal of improvements	Open

Figure 15.1 Steps to prepare and interpret impact measurements (left) and questions included in Block B (right).

different questions about difficulties in accessing immersive islands (questions 1-3); information about the Internet connection and descriptions of error messages (question 4); evaluation of the organization of spaces, resources and information, style and design, manuals and video-tutorials and training sessions; type of difficulties (configuration, management, chat) the temporal learning curve; evaluation of the interaction with other participants and evaluation of the material for learning how to manage the avatar (question 6); strengths and weaknesses of the session (questions 8 and 9); usefulness of the immersive session in comparison with face-to-face sessions; usefulness of the immersive session for general use in conferences (questions 10-12) and improvements for future sessions (question 13). In the surveys, no questions were guided or restricted, and participants were told that the most important thing was to express their opinions.

The answers to the different questions in Block A were organized into descriptive categories and grouped by different response percentages. This approach was applied to the answers of Block B, 1–3 and 7–9. The numerical evaluation of the tendency and dispersion indices (mean, standard and response percentages) was carried out for questions 4–6 and 10–12. In the case of open questions (4 from Block A and 13 from Block B), a qualitative research procedure was applied, based on the written responses and comparison analyses to look for emerging patterns (Bogdan & Bilken, 1992). The results were organized into descriptive categories and grouped by different response percentages. Finally, any descriptive comments were also analysed as a case study.

Characterization of the participants (Block A)

The total number of speakers in the three editions of the session was 27 (Table 15.3). As can be seen, there were 13 participants and 12 senior scientists involved in the session held in 2015. However, after unfavourable feedback obtained in the first edition about numerous technical failures and the excessive length of the session, the number of participants was reduced. The percentage of PhD students who presented their works was 70%, 75% and 100% for 2015, 2016 and 2017 sessions, respectively.

Table 15.3 Participation data for the period 2015–2017.

Basic information	Year 2015	Year 2016	Year 2017	Total
Number of young scientists (speakers)	13	8	6	27
% PhD students	70	75	100	81
Number of different nationalities	7	4	4	11
Number of medium/seniors scientists involved	12	6*	6*	19

Note: (*)5 senior scientists participated both editions

In order to show how to participate in the virtual conference, a video of the session carried out in 2015 was uploaded in Youtube (www.youtube.com/watch?v=Y7htOZo6VGg). This proved to be extremely useful in the following editions (2016 and 2017). It is also worth noting that researchers of 11 different nationalities contributed to the session (Austrian, Dutch, Chinese, Colombian, English, Finnish, Italian, Mexican, North American, Spanish and Syrian).

Table 15.4 shows an analysis of the basic details of the participants who answered the opinion surveys during the three editions (22 students). The average age of the participants was 32.5, which included both young and senior scientists. As can be observed in Table 15.4, Spanish participants obtained the highest participation rates (65%), mainly as a result of the ease of dissemination and interaction among groups close to the organizers. On the other hand, 67% of people who completed the survey were female, who proved skilful at handling the Office package, social networks and (reasonably) skilful at videogames and the immersive world (Table 15.4, questions 1 and 3). It is significant that 81% attended the session from their offices, and their main motivation could be divided into two categories: i) to present their work in an original way (even 'fearlessly') and ii) to take part in open scientific discussion and/or answer specific questions in their field. It was significant that one Syrian attendant highlighted the benefit of 'crossing scientific borders', as the political situation in his country was difficult and he greatly appreciated being given the opportunity of attending.

Valuation from participants (Block B)

Table 15.5 shows the number of surveys and their analysis indicators (percentage and statistics) for the period as a whole and year by year. For the first three questions (which dealt with problems and technical constraints), it must be stressed that there were far more problems in the year 2015, where the Internet bandwidth and the capacity of the server were not big enough to support between 20 and 30 avatars and a complex infrastructure. This is particularly significant if we consider the answers to question 1 in the years 2016 and 2017, where over 60% of the surveys stated that there were no problems with access to the immersive island. On the other hand, the voice chat was the main source of difficulties (Table 15.5, question 3), independently of the operative system, where it seems that an anti-virus was blocking the sound ports. In 2016 and 2017, the tests carried out prior to the session enabled us to anticipate some problems; however, the variability of the Internet connection can be critical. In fact, the highest marks obtained for the training sessions in question 4 and 9 stress the importance of the technical tests.

Despite the fact that navigation and wayfinding problems in virtual spaces can adversely affect the engagement of the participants (Gregory, Lee, &

Table 15.4 Characterization of the participants for the period 2015–2017.

Questions/Options	Total Years 2015-2016-2017 (n=22; 48% of participants in virtual sessions)
1. Background	
Age	32.5± 8.2
Nationality	65% Spanish; 5% US; 5% English; 5% Mexican; 10% Colombian; 5% Dutch; 5% Finnish
Sex	67% Female; 33% Male
Degree/Studies:	Environmental Science 11%; Geography 22%; Forestry Engineering 27%; Geology 6%; Agronomy Engineering 1%; Civil Engineering 6%; Electronic Engineering 6%; Chemistry 6%
Doctorate	62.0% PhD students
2. Where do you visit the immersive islands from (home, office, cybercafé, etc.)?	81% Office; 5% Lab; 5% Home; 10% EGU
3. Please evaluate your skills in the use of the following IT tools	
Office package	4.4 ±0.7
Social networks	3.9 ±1.1
Videogames/serious games	2.7±1.4
Immersive worlds/Secondlife	2.5±1.6
4. Could you give us a couple of ideas about your objectives in this session?	i) to present work in an original way ii) find open scientific discussion and/or answer specific questions about my field.

Dalgarno, 2016), the positive results obtained in our case in terms of the organization of spaces, resources, information, the manual and video tutorials and their perception on their learning curve (questions 4–5, Table 15.5) suggest that the design, personal support for the participants and the material provided for the session were all of an acceptable standard. The management, in particular, was quick and trouble-free, and it took under half an hour to move, customize and get an avatar speaking (Table 15.5, question 5).

Concerning the quality of the simulation, high marks were awarded to the interaction with the other participants and the organizers, as well as to the sensation of immersion (Table 15.5, question 6). Although this was to be expected, it is important to highlight how the participants started to speak to each other and interact in a more natural way during the training sessions. It was surprising how much the fun atmosphere encouraged participation (see also question 8, Table 15.5), particularly considering the diversity of nationalities,

Table 15.5 Survey about learning aspects and opinions of the impact of the session.

Questions/Options	Year 2015 (n=8; 32%)	Year 2016 (n=6; 43%)	Year 2017 (n=8; 67%)	Total (n=22; 48%)
1. Did you have difficulties in accessing the immersive islands?				
a) Yes, due to poor band width	0.0%	0.0%	11.0%	4.3%
b) Yes, due to the server	50.0%	0.0%	0.0%	17.4%
c) Yes, but I do not know why	50.0%	17.0%	22.0%	30.4%
d) No, everything worked perfectly	0.0%	83.0%	67.0%	47.8%
2. Please complete the following information about your Internet connection if you know:				
a) Band width of your Internet connection for the immersive sessions	ADSL 20-50Mbits	ADSL 20-50Mbits	ADSL 20-50Mbits	ADSL 20-50Mbits
b) Operative System of your computer (M=Mac; Win=Windows)	12.5% M; 87.5% Win	100.0% Win	25% M; 75% Win	12.5% M; 87.5% Win
c) Did you receive error messages? If so, which?	Voice chat	Voice chat	Voice chat	Voice chat
3. Did you have any difficulties? What kind of problems did you have?				
a) Difficulties of access to the immersive islands	22.0%	100%	0.0%	17.0%
b) Difficulties with the configuration	0.0%	0.0%	0.0%	8.3%
c) Difficulties with Voice Chat	78.0%	0.0%	100%	75.0%
d) Difficulties with using an avatar	0.0%	0.0%	0.0%	0.0%
e) Others	0.0%	0.0%	0.0%	0.0%
4. Please rate the importance of the following elements of the immersive islands. (1: not suitable at all; 2: not very suitable; 3: acceptably suitable; 4: suitable; 5: very suitable, cool!)				
a) Organization of spaces	4.0 ±1.4	4.8 ±0.4	4.0 ±0.8	4.2 ±1.0
b) Resources and information	3.9 ±1.0	4.8 ±0.4	4.1 ±0.8	4.2 ±0.9

(Continued)

Table 15.5 (Cont.)

Questions/Options	Year 2015 (n=8; 32%)	Year 2016 (n=6; 43%)	Year 2017 (n=8; 67%)	Total (n=22; 48%)
c) Style and design	4.6 ±0.5	4.8 ±0.4	3.9 ±0.6	4.4 ±0.7
d) Manual and video tutorials	4.3 ±0.7	4.7 ±0.5	4.4 ±0.5	4.4 ±0.6
e) Training sessions (if you used them)	4.3 ±0.6	4.8 ±0.4	5.0 ±0.0	4.8 ±0.5
5. We would like to evaluate your learning curve, so, please, answer the questions.				
a) Minutes taken to learn to walk, run, fly	6.5 ±9.7	3.4 ±3.8	2.2 ±1.8	4.1 ±6.4
b) Minutes taken to learn to sit or take objects	7.6 ±10.3	3.6±3.6	4.3 ±3.3	5.3 ±6.7
c) Minutes taken to learn to customize avatar	12.5±4.6	14.0 ±6.5	8.3 ±7.1	11.4 ±6.2
d) Minutes taken to learn to use the voice chat	8.1 ±5.3	2.2 ±0.8	7.1 ±10.2	6.3 ±7.0
e) Minutes taken to learn to watch a video or view a poster in the immersive island	5.0 ±4.3	2.0 ±0.1	2.0 ±1.5	3.2 ±3.2
6. We would like to know how you rate the inter-action with other partici-pants. Please give a mark from 1 to 5 according to how much you agree (1: Do not agree at all; 5: Totally agree)				
a) Presence of the chairperson is important	3.8 ±1.2	4.8 ±0.4	5.0 ±0.0	4.5 ±0.9
b) Presence of other participants is important	4.3 ±1.2	5.0±0.0	4.8 ±0.5	4.6 ±0.8
c) The sensation of immersion was total	3.6±1.1	4.6 ±0.5	4.4 ±0.9	4.1 ±1.0
7. Which components were the most helpful for man-aging your avatar on the immersive island?				
a) Video tutorials	26.7%	21.4%	11.1%	19.1%
b) Tutorial guide	26.7%	21.4%	33.3%	27.7%
c) The organizers' help	20.0%	35.7%	22.2%	25.5%
d) Other colleagues	13.3%	7.1%	11.1%	10.6%
e) Self-learning	13.3%	14.3%	22.2%	17.0%
f) Others	0.0%	0.0%	0.0%	0.0%

(Continued)

Table 15.5 (Cont.)

Questions/Options	Year 2015 (n=8; 32%)	Year 2016 (n=6; 43%)	Year 2017 (n=8; 67%)	Total (n=22; 48%)
8. What were the main strengths of the session?				
a) On-line participation	42.9%	50.0%	37.5%	42.5%
b) Atmosphere	14.3%	20.0%	12.5%	15.0%
c) Changing the way of participating	7.1%	30.0%	37.5%	25.0%
d) Help and support from presentations	14.3%	0.0%	12.5%	10.0%
e) The duration	14.3%	0.0%	0.0%	5.0%
f) The technical failures (there were few and were resolved quickly)	7.1%	0.0%	0.0%	2.5%
g) Others	42.9%	50.0%	37.5%	42.5%
9. What were the weaknesses of the sessions?				
a) On-line participation	0.0%	0.0%	0.0%	0.0%
b) Atmosphere	0.0%	0.0%	0.0%	0.0%
c) Changing the way of participating	0.0%	0.0%	0.0%	0.0%
d) The help and support given for the presentations	0.0%	0.0%	0.0%	0.0%
e) The duration (too many presentations)	33.3%	0.0%	0.0%	16.7%
f) The duration (too few presentations)	0.0%	0.0%	0.0%	0.0%
g) The technical failures (too many or they were not resolved quickly enough)	66.7%	100.0%	100.0%	83.3%
h) Others	0.0%	0.0%	0.0%	0.0%
10. Please rate the usefulness of the immersive session for the participant (5= very useful; 1= not useful at all)	4.6 ±0.5	5.0 ±0.0	4.7 ±0.5	4.7 ±0.5
11. Please rate the usefulness of the immersive session in comparison with face-to-face sessions (5= immersive sessions are much more useful; 3=same degree of usefulness; 1= face-to-face sessions are much more useful)	3.1 ±0.7	3.8 ±1.0	4.0 ±1.4	3.5 ±0.9

(Continued)

Table 15.5 (Cont.)

Questions/Options	Year 2015 (n=8; 32%)	Year 2016 (n=6; 43%)	Year 2017 (n=8; 67%)	Total (n=22; 48%)
12. Please rate the usefulness of the immersive session for general use in congresses (5= very useful; 1= not useful at all)	4.4 ±0.5	4.3 ±0.6	4.8 ±0.4	4.5 ±0.5
13. If you would like to make a suggestion to improve the session, please let us know.	i) technical measures to solve sound problems, organization and visualization (particularly in the first year); ii) dissemination and iii) innovations in the structure and dynamics of the meeting.			

degrees and ages. The organizers found the role of PhD students who were participating for the first time in an international conference particularly rewarding. Using the English language was a challenge for most of them, and they found it especially motivating to answer questions from senior scientists. As for the resources, the participants particularly appreciated the guide and the help of the organizers when managing the avatar (question 7, Table 15.5). On the other hand, it is easy to understand how the main weaknesses were related to technical problems. The number of talks and participants had to be managed carefully in order to achieve a successful session when working on a very limited budget (funded by the organizers).

Many authors, such as Anderson (1996), Çakir (2002), Kappe and Guetl (2009), have underlined the use of virtual conferences for participation any time/any place. In this case, the evaluation of the usefulness in questions 10, 11 and 12 (Table 15.5) illustrates the helpfulness of these immersive sessions for all types of conferences; they are even considered by some more useful than face-to-face sessions. As regards teams, Warkentin, Sayeed and Hightower (1997) found that face-to-face teams turned out to be more efficient. The need for longer and more intensive contact may justify the differences observed.

Finally, the improvements suggested were grouped in three areas: i) technical measures to solve sound, organization or visualization problems (particularly in the first year); ii) dissemination and iii) innovations in the structure and dynamics of the meeting. All of the above were taken into account, with the exception of the last one, in order to follow the usual structure of the conference. However, structural changes of the session might be crucial in order to optimize its potentiality, particularly in smaller or more specific conferences addressed to young scientists. For instance, the creation of virtual scenarios can support the practical results of the presentations and facilitate their dissemination through educational or informative videos. The creation of work meetings in the virtual countryside or in virtual cafeterias where the speakers present their work in an informal way ('gaming') might improve the contact among researchers and overcome 'stage fright' associated to the first meetings of PhD students. Another interesting point mentioned in the surveys is reducing the carbon footprint, cost and barriers set by age, racial or political differences.

Conclusion

This chapter exposes the potential benefits of organizing virtual conferences and encouraging young scientists by using immersive world experience in today's context of post-economic crisis and outbreak caused by COVID-19. It might prove valuable for PhD students or/and young scientists who feel stage fright derived from the uncertainty of their research or foreign language difficulties. In addition, we presented a new way of increasing the participation of young scientists with a limited budget in international conferences or with travel restrictions. The objectives and stages of work are explained in order to make it transferable to fields other than Soil Sciences. The only aspects that might limit the success of the sessions were technical, and these were essentially related to the Internet connections of the participants and the conference site. To overcome these problems, a training session held before the session would provide valuable opportunities for the participants to start to socialize and pre-empt some technical issues. It is also advisable to plan the available time and be flexible with the objectives of the training in order to anticipate potential errors. On the other hand, it is worth noting that the guide and the organizers' support was indispensable to learning how to manage the avatar and achieving a successful session. Among other strengths, the sensation of immersion was high as a result of the fun atmosphere and the accurate reproduction of virtual scenarios, which looked very like the real conference buildings. According to the participants, it was as useful as or more useful than face-to-face meetings.

Major improvements that could be made on the design include allowing attendants at the real conference to interact in the virtual world with virtual participants, thus increasing the total audience at the conference. Moreover, new formats, such as stories or background sounds, might increase the interaction of the participants and add to the fun element of the session.

Acknowledgments

We are very grateful to Artemi Cerdá and Saskia Keestra for the Soil Science System Division's valuable support in organizing the session. We would also like to thank Vidal Barron, Antonio Jordán, Jose A. Gómez and Manuel Seeger for their valuable contributions to the virtual sessions as senior scientists. We appreciated the contribution of Dr Francisco Montes of the University of Cordoba, director of the

Master program on Representation and Design in Engineering and Architecture, in preparing the virtual space. This project was partially supported by the University of Cordoba (Actividades de Difusión y Divulgación Científica del XXI Programa Propio de Fomento de la Investigación- 2016) and FEDER Funds entitled 'Inmersión en Ciencias del Suelo a través de Avatares - Get immersed in the Soil Sciences: bright ideas shared among avatars'.

References

Alaminos-Chica, A., & Castejón-Costa, J. L. (2006). *Elaboración, análisis e interpretación de encuestas, cuestionarios y escalas de opinión (Preparation, analysis and interpretation of surveys, questionnaires and opinion scales)*. Retrieved from https://rua.ua.es/dspace/bit stream/10045/20331/1/Elaboraci%c3%b3n,%20an%c3%a1lisis%20e%20interpretaci %c3%b3n.pdf

Anderson, T. (1996). The virtual conference: Extending professional education in cyberspace. *International Journal of Educational Telecommunications*, 2(2/3), 121–135.

Baker, S., Wentz, R., & Woods, M. (2009). Using virtual worlds in education: Second life as educational tools. *Teaching and Psychology*, 36, 59–64.

Bogdan, R. C., & Bilken, S. K. (1992). *Qualitative research for education: An introduction to theory and methods*. Boston, MA: Allyn & Bacon.

Bouras, C., & Tsiatsos, T. (2006). Educational virtual environments: Design rationale and architecture. *Multimedia Tools and Applications*, 29(2), 153–173.

Burdea, G., & Coiffet, P. (2003). Virtual reality technology. *Presence: Tele Operators and Virtual Environments*, 12(6), 663–664.

Çakir, A. E. (2002). Virtual communities-a virtual session on virtual conferences. *Behaviour& Information Technology*, 21(5), 365–371.

Dionisio, J. D. N., Burns, W. G. B., & Gilbert, R. (2013). 3D virtual worlds and the metaverse. *ACM Computing Surveys*, 45(3), 1–38.

FAO, Food and Agriculture Organization of the United Nations. (2014). *Global soil partnership*. Retrieved from www.fao.org/globalsoilpartnership/es/

Gerald, S., & Antonacci, D. M. (2009). Virtual world learning spaces: Developing a second life operating room simulation. *EDUCAUSE*. Retrieved from https://er. educause.edu/articles/2009/3/virtual-world-learning-spaces-developing-a-second-life-operating-room-simulation

Gregory, S., Lee, M. J. W., & Dalgarno, B. (Eds.). (2016). *Learning in virtual worlds: Research and applications*. Edmonton, Canada: AU Press, Athabaska University.

Grunwald, S., & Barak, P. (2001). The use of VRML for virtual soil landscape modeling. *Systems Analysis, Modelling, Simulation*, 41, 755–777.

Kappe, F., & Guetl, C. (2009). Enhancements of the realXtend framework to build a virtual conference room for knowledge transfer and learning purposes. In G. Siemens & C. Fulford (Eds.), *Proceedings of ED-MEDIA 2009–World Conference on Educational Multimedia, Hypermedia & Telecommunications* (pp. 4113–4120). Honolulu, HI: Association for the Advancement of Computing in Education (AACE).

Kickmeier-Rust, M. D., Bull, S., & Meissl-Egghart, G. (2014). Collaborative language learning in immersive virtual worlds: Competence-based formative feedback and open learner modeling. *International Journal of Serious Games*, 1(2), 67–74.

Lorenzo, C. M., Sicilia, M. A., & Sánchez, S. (2012). Studying the effectiveness of multi-user immersive environments for collaborative evaluation tasks. *Computers & Education*, *59*, 1361–1376.

Mamo, M., Namuth-Covert, D., Guru, A., Nugent, G., Phillips, L., Sandall, L., McCallister, D. (2011). Avatars go to class: A virtual environment soil science activity. *Journal of Natural Resources and Life Sciences Education*, *40*, 114–121.

Mathers, N., Goktogen, A., Rankin, J., & Anderson, M. (2012). Robotic mission to Mars: Hands-on, minds-on, web-based learning. *Acta Astronautica*, *80*, 124–131.

Moedas, C. (2015). *Open innovation, open science, open to the world*. European Commission Speech. Retrieved from http://europa.eu/rapid/press-release_SPEECH-15-5243_en.htm

Rodríguez García, T. C., & Baños González, M. (2011). E-learning en mundos virtuales 3D. Una experiencia educativa en SecondLife. *Revista ICONO14 Revista científica de Comunicación y Tecnologías Emergentes*, *9*(2), 39–58. doi:10.7195/ri14.v9i2.39

Schmorrow, D. D. (2009). Why virtual? *Theoretical Issues in Ergonomics Science*, *10*(3), 279–282.

Sivan, Y. (2008). 3D3C real virtual worlds defined: The immense potential of merging 3D, community, creation, and commerce. *Journal of Virtual Worlds*, *1*(1), 1–32. Retrieved from http://journals.tdl.org/jvwr/article/viewArticle/278

Sumners, C., Reiff, P., & Weber, W. (2008). Learning in an immersive digital theater. *Advances in Space Research*, *42*, 1848–1854.

Warkentin, M. E., Sayeed, L., & Hightower, R. (1997). Teams: An exploratory study of a web-based conference system. *Decision Sciences*, *28*(4), 975–996.

Wilson, C. (2008). *Avatars, virtual reality technology, and the U.S. Military: Emerging policy issues*. Retrieved from https://fas.org/sgp/crs/natsec/RS22857.pdf

Chapter 16

Educational technologies in the area of ubiquitous historical computing in virtual reality

Giuseppe Abrami, Alexander Mehler,
Christian Spiekermann, Attila Kett, Simon Lööck
and Lukas Schwarz

Introduction

New technologies are being developed at ever-shorter intervals and are being used in more and more areas of application. This regards, for example, *Virtual Reality* (VR) and *Augmented Reality* (AR) devices. However, the use of such technologies has not progressed equally in all sectors in recent years. This concerns especially the field of education and learning (Ott & Freina, 2015). To fill this gap, there are currently far-reaching initiatives in the area of historical education, collected within the framework of the *European Time Machine*[1] project. This project, which encompasses a broad spectrum of scientific disciplines, aims to make the cultural heritage of the European Union virtually accessible. Its novel thematic focus is probably related to the fact that although VR emerged as a topic in the early 1960s, affordable hardware has only been available for a few years (Pelargos et al., 2017). A significant contribution to this development was made by the release of the VR glasses HTC Vive and Oculus Rift. With the help of these devices, new milestones of developing educational technologies and platforms come into sight combining the generation of knowledge with semantic processing, visualization and interaction (Yang, 2018). In addition, the use of technical innovations has reached the end customer segment, so that appropriate hardware equipment can now be financed for educational institutions.

The research on VR is already equipped with a rich terminology, which we partially reconstruct here in order to situate our work. This includes the distinction of immersive VR, semi-immersive VR, non-immersive VR, AR and mixed reality (Martín-Gutiérrez, Mora, Añorbe-Díaz, & González-Marrero, 2017; Pelargos et al., 2017; Riva, 2006):

1. Immersive VR, or even fully immersive VR (Riva, 2006), means completely hiding the physical environment in which a user acts by using appropriate controllers and actuators (e.g. 3D glasses). The 'i' of the attribute *immersive* represents three characteristics of this process: *immersion, interaction* and *imagination* (Bamodu & Ye, 2013). Immersive VR

suggests to its users that they are acting outside the part of reality in which they find themselves: this reality is no longer perceived when a user interacts within a virtual environment through audiovisual and tactile hardware (Sánchez, Lumbreras, & Silva, 1997), which even provides haptic feedback.

2. Semi-immersive VR enables the perception of virtual worlds with multiple projection screens instead of 3D glasses (Martìn-Gutiérrez et al., 2017). CAVE applications are well-known examples of this approach. They take place in a room on whose walls computer-generated visualizations are projected or displayed (Riva, 2006).

3. Non-immersive VR concerns technologies whose users are aware of their external environments. Instead of interactivity, the focus is on viewing: Users look at virtual worlds rather than being located in or interacting with them. Typical hardware is *Samsung Gear VR* and *Google Cardboard* (Pelargos et al., 2017). In addition, conventional 3D visualizations on screen (c.f. Card, Robertson, & Mackinlay, 1991; Ingram, Benford, & Bowers, 1996) or viewed by means of stereoscopic glasses and peripheral controls without haptic feedback (Pick, Weyers, Hentschel, & Kuhlen, 2016; Riva, 2006) also exemplify non-immersive VR.

4. Augmented Reality (AR): Unlike VR, AR does not separate the user from the real environment in which he or she operates. In AR, the environment, which the user sees through a hardware device, is 'complemented' by virtual objects. These objects are visualized (e.g. by transparent holograms). A distinction is made between *image-based* and *location-based* AR. The first variant requires markers for positioning 3D objects; the second one uses GPS coordinates (Özdemir, Sahin, Arcagok, & Demir, 2018). With appropriate hardware, users can interact with virtual objects in AR (e.g., through touch, gestures or voice commands). Typical AR hardware includes tablets and smartphones (Butchart, 2011).

5. Mixed Reality (MR) expands AR by displaying virtual objects not as holograms but as virtual images with more solid structures. Ideally, glasses are used for both AR and MR. In addition, the use of smartphones or tablets is suitable for this purpose, which offers further means of interaction with virtual objects. Well-known examples of MR devices are *Microsoft Hololens*[2] or *Magic Leap One*.[3]

6. Distributed-VR: In addition to the approaches distinguished so far, there are hybrid applications such as *Distributed-VR* or *Network-VR*. The aim of this approach is to have users connect to each other via the Internet in order to interact in VR (Bamodu & Ye, 2013).

Besides the latter classification, we have to distinguish virtual environments and frameworks for generating such environments. To this end, we define virtual environments as computer-based interfaces for generating and interacting with virtual worlds. Using appropriate input and output methods, these interfaces can create spatially independent environments using 3D visualizations. This allows virtual environments to represent or imitate aspects of the real world and imagined worlds, as well as simulate additional properties (Sánchez et al., 1997). Technically speaking, this requires *Head-Mounted Display* s (HMD) that enable the representation of virtual environments depending on body or eye movements of the user (Sutherland, 1968). Although projected images are displayed two-dimensionally, a 3D effect is created by positioning the images relative to the viewer's eyes. HMDs can be used in different configurations, where it depends on the capabilities of the hardware which type (VR or AR) is supported. Based on these preliminaries we can now distinguish *frameworks for generating virtual environments*. The following list includes frameworks that cover the range from fully immersive to non-immersive VR – some of them also support AR and MR:

1. As a virtual online environment, Second Life allows users to interact as virtual avatars with each other or with objects in their environment. At the same time, they can create their own content and exchange it with each other (Potkonjak et al., 2016).
2. As an extensible open-source platform for hosting virtual worlds, OpenSimulator[4] can be used stand-alone or in a network. The last development activity was in June 2018.
3. RealXtrend[5] is based on OpenSimulator and uses visualizations of Second Life. The interaction between users is realized by virtual avatars, for which RealXtrend provides group and object management. The last development activity was in 2014.
4. Open Wonderland[6] is a Java-based open source framework that enables the creation of collaborative virtual 3D environments (Potkonjak et al., 2016). It offers several presentation and interaction facilities like virtual whiteboards, document views and presentations. However, the last development activity was in March 2012.
5. Unreal Engine,[7] which is well known in the gaming community, also allows creating virtual 3D environments. Using suitable hardware, simulations can be generated to ensure full immersion (Zaidi, Moore, & Khanna, 2019). The framework supports various hardware systems (e.g. smartphones, VR glasses) and thus is flexibly usable.
6. The cross-platform game engine Unity 3D[8] also enables the generating of virtual environments (Indraprastha & Shinozaki, 2009). Like Unreal Engine, it can be used on different platforms.

Obviously, these frameworks are not equally versatile, feature-rich, widely used or even being further developed. In any case, VR, as implemented by these frameworks, does not simply mean a visual enrichment of classic 2D media. Rather, immersive VR is a complex, versatile and expandable technology that not only has a supporting effect but also has groundbreaking potential for educational applications. However, the use of VR is not without restrictions and effort. On the one hand, there is the problematic experience of unknown interaction possibilities or the danger of becoming sick through their use (Hettinger & Riccio, 1992). In addition, there is the problem of visualizing complex, overlapping scenarios or designing sufficient interaction possibilities (Krekhov, Cmentowski, Waschk, & Krüger, 2019; Sidenmark, Kiefer, & Gellersen, 2019; Spiekermann, 2017). Users can get lost by not being able to generate adequate situation models with which they can orient themselves in VR. For authoring virtual environments, however, these are not obstacles, but challenges. Following this interpretation, this chapter aims to investigate a novel application scenario in educational sciences with the help of immersive VR and perspective MR. To this end, one has to keep in mind the problems and pitfalls of virtual environments – especially with regard to immersive VR. In order to face these challenges, we provide a requirements analysis and present VAnnotatoR as a framework for generating virtual environments that fulfil most of these requirements.

The chapter is organized as follows: *Virtual environments and historical education* presents a first-requirements analysis for VR systems especially in historical education. *Related tools and projects* discusses related work in the context of these requirements. After presenting and assessing VAnnotatoR in the next Section, *Extension points* explains its future development. The last section concludes with a summary.

Virtual environments and historical education: a requirements analysis

The task of historical education is to convey an understanding of the past by means of the findings of historical science. Despite all didactic and pedagogical challenges, it makes sense to use VR/AR technologies for the transfer of such historical knowledge as explained by Greenwald et al. (2017). In addition, the following aspects and requirements are of particular importance:

1. Realistic visualizations: Textbooks and other documents are limited in the mediation of information about historical contexts by the linearity of the underlying texts and limited 2D visualizations. For historical events to be presented more appropriately, they should be presented more realistically and especially more attractively. This can be done with the help of walkable 3D visualizations.
2. Communicating context-related information: Historical contexts should be conveyed not only through visual reconstructions; they also require a certain amount of information, which has to be prepared and visualized in a suitable form. This should not be realized, as in museums, by text contributions beside exhibits. The animation of historical events,

the integration of such animations or the recourse to historical persons as narrators offer alternatives for expansion.

3. Validity of information: In order to make it more difficult to disseminate false or defamatory information, it is essential that the validity of the information provided in virtual environments be guaranteed and able to be checked at any time. This is certainly the biggest challenge for the use of VR in the field of historical education.

4. Ubiquitous use: VR systems make it possible to inform about historical events by providing an on-site experience independent of one's physical location. For this purpose, it is necessary to geolocalize historical events as much as possible, regardless of the underlying hardware and software solution.

Irrespective of the technological achievements connected with these requirements, it is not possible to play off the dissemination of information in VR against traditional forms of representation in the field of education (Yang, 2018). These traditional methods, which may seem monotonous to younger generations, can renew the fun of learning with new technologies if they actually provide a high-quality learning experience (Yang, 2018).

As in digital laboratories (c.f. Potkonjak et al., 2016), virtual environments provide many possibilities for visualizing and experiencing situations. In any case, the requirements for reducing negative effects in learning are not the same as for laboratory work. In this context, we believe that the following requirements should be met to ensure meaningful and targeted uses of VR:

(A) Flexibility through database support: Virtual environments should allow for simulating different scenarios and environmental conditions. This is not only a matter of creating scenarios, but also of mapping them by means of a suitable database system and making them interactively manipulable. The flexibility addressed here should be based on the underlying data model and its extensibility through context-sensitive modelling.

(B) Collaboration and multi-user mode: In addition to the individual use of virtual environments, their simultaneous and even shared use should be made possible, so that users can collaborate directly in the use of the system. Communicating and collaborating within the same virtual environment in multi-user mode promotes collaborative learning. This scenario allows the creation, monitoring and supervision of complex, interactive scenarios, depending on the assigned task.

(C) Interaction and communication: VR systems should allow for using gestures (e.g. grasping, touching, throwing, pushing) to control interaction with virtual objects. Ideally, they allow for implementing and recognizing gestures so that a dynamic extension of the underlying gesture alphabet is made possible. In this context, gaze and voice control contribute to more flexible systems. Voice control and *Natural Language Processing*

(NLP) should especially be used to enhance communication capabilities in virtual environments.

(D) Decentralization: The underlying technology should enable decentralized, non-proprietary availability of the VR application. It should therefore not require a central server environment: Instead of needing a central server, the application should connect its clients directly with each other.

(E) Open Access: In the context of education and teaching, it is important that VR technologies be freely available via an *Open Access* platform. Ideally, this enables further development by a broad community.

(F) Data protection and security: Data protection and data security are indispensable criteria for any learning application, including giving learners ultimate control over their data, who they share it with and in what form.

(G) Access permissions: Because of the required openness of VR systems, situations can arise in which the use of content and the interaction of users must be further restricted. To ensure this, it is necessary to provide an access rights management system to control the dissemination of content and the availability of its functions.

(H) Portability and platform independence: Due to ever-shorter development phases it is necessary that a VR system remain portable and not be limited to certain hardware platforms. The same application should work, for example, with HDMs, smartphones, tablets, etc. In accordance with Requirement (B), several users should then be able to interact with each other in the same environment independently of their technical devices.

(I) Full 3D: Virtual environments generate added values if their content is presented in 3D. From this point of view, it is less advisable, for example, to present web content 2D or to make file systems available as tree views. In VR systems, the focus is on presenting multimodal content as 3D objects; otherwise, the technology will lag behind the promises of VR.

The fulfilment of these requirements should enable the development of targeted VR applications for different application areas. One of these areas concerns historical education, on which the chapter focuses. It describes educational technology that supports VR[9] in the field of historical computing. For this purpose, the so-called VAnnotatoR (Spiekermann, Abrami, & Mehler, 2018) is described and illustrated as an exemplary application for the use of ubiquitous VR technologies. VAnnotatoR has been developed in the context of practical courses and qualifications at Goethe University Frankfurt. It can be used as an experimental platform for investigating issues of information processing in VR (Kühn, 2018; Spiekermann et al., 2018). One field of application of VAnnotatoR is the project *Stolperwege* Mehler et al. (2017), which aims to model the biographies of victims of the National Socialist regime. In this project, life paths and places of victims are virtually reconstructed and contextualized as stations of these paths, see Figure 16.1 for an illustration: All objects generated from VAnnotatoR's database are

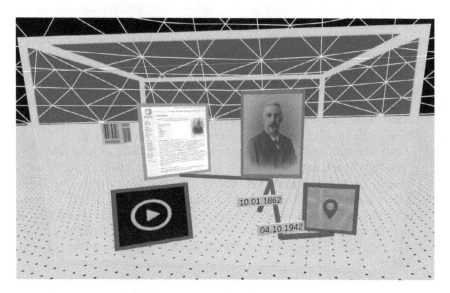

Figure 16.1 VAnnotatoR: Multimodal objects can be visualized, positioned and linked with each other in the virtual environment.

visualized depending on their type. The example shows a compilation of objects compiled for the purpose of documenting the biography of the politician Gustav Hoch. They originate again from the project Stolperwege. The portrait shown originates from the Wikipedia article about Gustav Hoch and is thus linked to its virtual presentation. The portrait represents the person whose days of birth and death are additionally displayed. All of these information objects are located in a green box that illustrates their togetherness (comparable to a non-directional, hierarchical (internally structured) hyperedge). The underlying semantics can also be utilized to create nested groups of objects and to interlink them in the sense of hypergraphs (Abrami, Spiekermann, & Mehler, 2019).

As a platform for the documentation and processing of multimodal information objects, VAnnotatoR can also be used in other project contexts. However, historical education is currently a major field of application for VAnnotatoR and *Stolperwege* is a prototypical example of this. A second application of VAnnotatoR in the context of the *European Time Machine* project is the construction of a virtual model of Frankfurt's historic old town. With a view to these applications, this chapter develops technological and content-related requirements for VR/AR systems for their use in historical education.

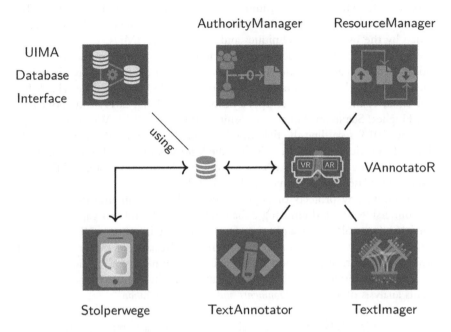

Figure 16.2 VAnnotatoR uses a database for representing and managing multimodal information units. It can use external tools to extend its functionality. By means of
TextImager, texts can be processed using various language-specific NLP tools.
In this way, for example, named entities can be recognized and linked to Wikipedia or similarity relations between text fragments can be computed and visualized in VR. By means of TextAnnotator, VAnnotatoR allows for writing and
annotating texts in VR or correcting the output of its NLP modules. Currently,
extensions of VAnnotatoR are developed, such as resources2city (Kett,
Abrami, Mehler, & Spiekermann, 2018), that can be added as modules.

Related tools and projects

Several projects deal with classifying VR and AR technologies (c.f. Arth
et al., 2015; Bamodu & Ye, 2013; Martín-Gutiérrez et al., 2017; Pick et al.,
2016). Due to the diversity of their underlying tools, we mainly limit our
overview to those with a focus on immersive VR. Two of the main application areas of VR systems are currently medicine and physics. Milán, David
& Stefan (2018), for example, describe a VR system for modelling the nasal
cavity and extending it by volume rendering. To this end, they use 3D
glasses, in which the anatomy of a human head is visualized and contextualized by means of Unity3D. Similar to this project is the work of Marks,
White, and Singh (2017), which focuses on anatomical learning. An example
of non-immersive VR in the field of medicine is the work of de Faria,

Teixeira, de Moura Sousa Júnior, Otoch, and Figueiredo (2016). The authors describe the learning of medical topics as a complex task to be simplified by the use of 3D techniques and stereoscopic HMDs.

Concerning the reconstruction of historical places, there are numerous publications (c.f. Sampaio, Rosario, Gomes, & Santos, 2013), as there are about the use of VR (c.f. Bryan, Campbell, & Mangina, 2018; Greenwald et al., 2017; He, Shen, & Li, 2018; Lee & Spryszynski, 2019; Meng, 2019) and about AR (c.f. Hughes, Stapleton, Hughes, & Smith, 2005; Lee, 2012; Wu, Lee, Chang, & Liang, 2013) regarding the field of education. A system for the acoustic modelling of historical virtual spaces is described, for example, by Postma and Katz (2015). An interesting approach to giving people the impression of flying is Sasaki, Liu, Hasegawa, Hiyama, and Inami (2019).

Currently, few projects or applications for learning in historical contexts use immersive VR and ensuring collaborative use. To fill this gap, we developed VAnnotatoR as an authoring framework for immersive VR to enable the creation of virtual historical environments. Because of the limitations of projects in historical education that provide for immersive VR, the following list gives an overview of selected applications in the context of the requirements analysis of *Virtual environments and historical education*[10]:

1. The project *C1x6* by Kulik et al. (2011) realizes a stereoscopic multi-user display for collaborative work in shared virtual environments. A projection on walls was realized; up to six users can receive different information by means of shutter glasses. C1x6 belongs to the category of semi-immersive VR applications and partly realizes Requirement (B): The application can be used simultaneously but not directly collaboratively. In addition, users cannot all interact with the virtual environment at the same time except via a fixed tracking ball construction. Thus, Requirement (C) is not fulfilled; nor are Requirements (D) (due to a lack of network possibilities) and (E). In our view, Requirement (A) is also not fulfilled due to the lack of a database, while requirements (F), (G) and (H) are not fulfilled due to the experimental set-up of this project.

2. The collaboration of historians and computer scientists led to the reconstruction of *Le Boullongne*, a merchant ship of the French East India Company (Barreau et al., 2015). The aim of this project was to understand the living conditions on board the ship. For this purpose, a simulation of the ocean was created. To virtualize this environment and let the user interact with the ship, Unity3D was employed. However, VR technologies are reduced to the virtualization of CAVE environments based on stereoscopic glasses and control via joysticks. Although Unity3D would allow for fully immersive VR, the project can currently only be classified as semi-immersive or even non-immersive. Since the project does not allow for client networking or collaborative use, it concerns only Requirement (C).

3. The project *Petty* (Doak, Denyer, Gerrard, Mackay, & Allison, 2019) allows for visualizing and manipulating the structure of proteins in virtual environments. It was implemented as a teaching platform based on Unity3D and *Oculus Rift* but can also be used without HMDs on the screen. Petty partially addresses Requirement (C) from the perspective of interaction capacity and by using Unity3D Requirement (H) as well as Requirement (I) from the project context.

4. Peixoto et al. (2019) outline a virtual environment developed in Unity3D for learning a foreign language that uses HTC Vive as an HMD. Formal and informal speech dialogues are virtualized as after-scenario questionnaires. Through Unity3D, this project meets Requirements (H) and (I).

5. In *SplashSim* (Chin et al., 2017), a mobile VR application, users experience the phases of the water cycle from the perspective of a water drop. The employment of immersive VR based on Unity3D in this project provides an educational experience that is hardly possible with traditional methods such as video. By means of Unity3D, this application partly meets Requirement (C) (interaction), without providing sufficient communication possibilities. Since there is no database and no network component for collaborative use, Requirement (H) is the only one that is additionally fulfilled.

6. With *UrbanHistory4D* (Maiwald, Bruschke, Lehmann, & Niebling, 2019) historical cities and buildings are reconstructed and virtualized by means of photogrammetry. AR and VR applications are provided in which users (immersive VR on HMD basis) have to find positions of 3D visualizations with the help of images. UrbanHistory4D uses OpenGL for visualization and OpenCTM for image storage. In addition, CIDOC CRM, a data model for mapping cultural objects, is used, while data is stored in a graph database (Neo4J). The main focus is on the automatic reconstruction of buildings and squares, while the VR and AR applications are still in their initial stages. However, both applications meet requirements (A), (H) and (C), the latter without sufficiently meeting the communication requirement. In any event, the use of a large number of images allows a realistic reconstruction of buildings and squares, but without the mediation of interior views – see Requirement (I).

7. In the *Venice Time Machine*[11] project, a digital reconstruction of historical Venice is created in which a multitude of documents, maps, monographs and manuscripts are digitized (Abbott, 2017). In addition to the virtual reconstruction, the project also aims at the generation and visualization of a social network of the persons mentioned in the digitized texts, which can also be geolocalized. For the reconstruction of buildings and objects, photogrammetry is used. Since we do not have concrete information about the implementation of this project, its assessment in the light of the requirements analysis of *Virtual environments and historical education* has to be omitted here.

These projects do not yet fully meet the requirements for a networked, collaborative and communication-enabling VR application in the field of education. Nevertheless, they are established examples of VR systems in this area of application. Following this overview (see summary Table 16.1), VAnnotatoR is now presented as a platform for VR applications in the field of historical education to meet the requirements analysis of *Virtual environments and historical education*.

VAnnotatoR: a framework for generating virtual environments

This section describes the structure and functionality of VAnnotatoR as a framework for generating virtual environments in the context of ubiquitous historical education. We introduce VAnnotatoR by classifying this system in the light of the requirements analysis from *Virtual environments and historical education*.

VAnnotatoR, which is implemented in Unity3D, offers a variety of functions for various application areas. It can be used with the HMDs HTC Vive and Oculus Rift. Although any hardware platform supported by Unity3D can be deployed by VAnnotatoR, no other HMDs have been tested to date. Using controllers with haptic feedback, VAnnotatoR belongs to the class of immersive VR systems. In addition to the controllers of the HMDs, VAnnotatoR can be operated by means of Leap Motion[12] and data gloves[13] (Kühn, 2018). With the help of these input devices, much more complex gestures can be performed than with conventional control devices. These VR devices help to fulfil requirement (C), whereby interaction possibilities (controller or glove-based) are ensured as is verbal communication via the HMDs.

Table 16.1 Overview of the projects and their fulfilment of the requirements defined in Section Virtual environments and historical education.

Project/Requirement	A	B	C	D	E	F	G	H	I	Technology
CIx6	−	±	−	−	−	−	−	−	−	semi-immersive VR
Le Boullongne	−	−	+	−	−	−	−	−	−	semi-immersive VR
Petty	−	−	±	−	−	−	−	+	−	immersive VR
Peixoto et al.	−	−	−	−	−	−	−	+	+	immersive VR
SplashSim	−	−	±	−	−	−	−	+	−	immersive VR
UrbanHistory4D	+	−	+	−	−	−	−	+	±	immersive VR/AR
VAnnotatoR	+	+	+	+	+	+	+	+	+	immersive VR/AR

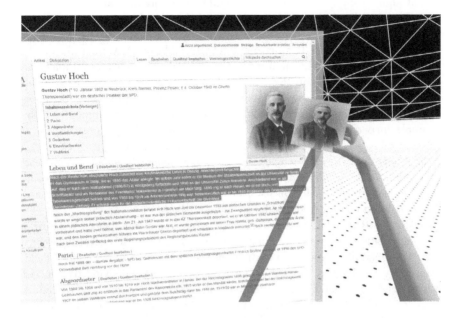

Figure 16.3 Processing of an external resource (URL) within a virtual browser.

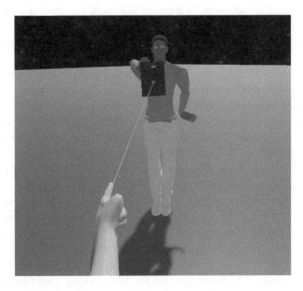

Figure 16.4 To fulfil Requirement (B), a network component for the simultaneous communication and collaboration among users is needed.

Through its implementation in Unity3D, VAnnotatoR can run on different platforms. Due to the homogeneity of this development environment, fundamental changes to VAnnotatoR can be easily ported. In this sense, VAnnotatoR also fulfils Requirement (H). In addition, VAnnotatoR can be used as a single or a distributed multi-user system. This allows multiple users to work simultaneously in the same virtual environment at the same or different physical locations by (cooperating in) manipulating the same or different virtual objects; Figure 16.4 show corresponding examples: In this example *users can see representations of each other and exchange virtual objects. In this example of VAnnotatoR, user A has created a text in a virtual book that he offers to user B in the same virtual space. User B performs a pointing gesture, which allows the selection or use of distant objects. Alternatively, the user can move through the room and grab the book from the hand of his interlocutor.* In this way, requirements (B) and (D) are addressed.

VAnnotatoR can be expanded by connecting it to a number of systems for semi-automatic processing of natural language. Figure 16.2 schematically depicts how VAnnotatoR is connected to the underlying database and to a range of additional services. Due to its database integration and the underlying data model, a high degree of flexibility in the sense of Requirement (A) can be achieved. As a result, all objects and environments used in VAnnotatoR are stored in and generated from this database. A flexible data model allows the annotation and use of multimodal information units (Abrami, Mehler, & Spiekermann, 2019), including situation modelling and the modelling of courses of events (Mehler, Abrami, Spiekermann, & Jostock, 2018).

Texts, images, 3D objects, 'walkable' 3D buildings, video and audio content can be stored, visualized and used in VAnnotatoR – see Figure 16.1 for an example. In addition, URLs can be processed via a virtual browser, which gives access to the content of the respective website by 'cutting out' text or images using drag and drop and making them processable, annotatable and networkable as virtual objects – see Figure 16.3 for an example. VAnnotatoR's database utilizes the *UIMA-Database Interface* (Abrami & Mehler, 2018), a dynamic interface for UIMA document databases. This database was originally created as the result of NLP analyses of biographical documents, stored as UIMA documents, within the *Stolperwege* project. However, VAnnotatoR is not limited to this database, but can utilize various database paradigms, especially the one of graph databases.

Using ResourceManager and AuthorityManager (Gleim, Mehler, & Ernst, 2012), content from different provenances can be managed and access to this content restricted by assigning appropriate user and group access rights: information objects can then be stored directly in the database or alternatively as object references in ResourceManager. By means of ResourceManager and AuthorityManager, which are part of the *eHumanities Desktop* (Gleim et al., 2012), and their planned release on GitHub as open access applications, VAnnotatoR addresses the requirements (E), (F) and (G).

It is generally important to ensure the longevity, portability and extensibility of the software solution platform used (requirements E and H). With Unity3D, these requirements can be met: Unity3D has a very active developer community; its use in the gaming market is widespread and the flexibility and portability is guaranteed. VAnnotatoR allows the visualization of multimodal objects and the execution of various virtual operations on these objects (Mehler et al., 2018). Among other things, so-called portals, virtual boxes and multimodal surfaces can be freely created by the user to process information objects and to network them:

1. *Portals* are used as link anchors (e.g. to generate previews of linked (3D) objects). See Figures 16.5 and 16.6. If, for example, a person's birthplace is to be viewed in the context of her or his virtualized home, this can be done with the help of a portal that the user can activate like a virtual analogue to a hyperlink in order to 'browse' to this virtualized birthplace: When entering the portal, the user arrives at the displayed target object, that is, her or his position is virtually moved to the position of this object. In any event, the preview in the portal depends on the data type of the referenced object – in this way, for example, 3D buildings are distinguished from documents.

2. Using *surfaces*, users can generate storage, presentation and interaction planes – see Figure 16.6 for an example. Surfaces can be generated manually on any plane of a 3D object (by freehand drawing). Alternatively, they are semi-automatically computed on user-defined planes as shown in Figure 16.6. Surfaces can then be linked together, filled with content (texts, images, videos, etc.) or linked to action elements (buttons, sliders, etc.). In this way, VAnnotatoR enables its users to use the virtual environment as a storage and writing medium and to enrich it continuously with information – comparable to a 3D wiki since the surfaces can be shared among different users.

3. Thirdly, *virtual boxes* can be created as containers in which any (copy of) virtual objects of the virtual environment can be stored; see Figure 16.6 for an example. A container can also be used as a portal by allowing users to enter the space defined by the box. In this way, boxes can be recursively nested within each other, creating hierarchies of interactive spaces for the storage, presentation and interaction with virtual media. Since these nested boxes can be shared among the users of VAnnotatoR (in terms of authorship and readership), a real 3D alternative to hypertexts (such as wikis) in conventional 2D hypermedia is created.

Geolocalization is essential for VR applications in historical education (Greenwald et al., 2017). For this purpose, VAnnotatoR can be supplemented by geocoordinates. All virtual objects are located in the so-called *real-world space* at their corresponding coordinates. The real-world space is a special virtual room that uses OpenStreetMap to provide a plane on which users can

Figure 16.5 A portal represents a hyperlink to an object within the virtual environment and displays a preview of it in a circle, which can be positioned anywhere in the virtual space.

navigate. Objects (texts, images, videos and 3D representations of people, buildings, events, etc.) are then located in this space at the position corresponding to their geocoordinates, provided the coordinates are available in VAnnotatoR. In combination with AR and MR components, which are available in VAnnotatoR, users can switch back and forth between the objects aligned in this way in reality and the virtual world (Mehler et al., 2018).

This functionality helps meet Requirement (I). Furthermore, a realistic visualization of situations, a context-related representation of information as well as ubiquitous computing are realized (see *Virtual environments and historical education*). The validity of the data stored, managed and displayed by VAnnotatoR must be monitored by experts in the respective discipline. In this context, the validity of the virtualizations of the buildings included in VAnnotatoR is partly ensured by reference to corresponding archive material. Regardless of the technical implementation, this is a very sensitive problem; its handling requires caution and transparent documentation.

Figure 16.6 VAnnotatoR enables the creation of virtual surfaces at any position in the virtual space.

VAnnotatoR is not limited to the field of historical education. VAnnotatoR has already been tested for modelling virtual cities (Kett et al., 2018). The flexibility of VAnnotatoR's data model, its modular architecture and its functional scope allow us to speak of it – to the best of our knowledge – as the first framework that implements immersive VR for various application areas according to the requirements analysis of *Virtual environments and historical education.*

Extension points

VAnnotatoR is developed regularly and continuously. The next development steps will focus on the following main areas:

1. Improving the AR/MR component: The AR component of VAnnotatoR is based on Google Tango. Since this project was officially completed, the AR component of VAnnotatoR is to be converted to ARCore.[14] ARCore enables better processing of real environment

information and a higher performance rate. In addition, we will experiment with mixed-reality glasses.

2. Implementation of a more dynamic and context-related communication solution: Since only audio communication with all users of a virtual room is currently possible, selective and group-related voice transmission and reception will be further developed. This avoids flooding the audio channel and allows 'private' conversations.

3. Publication on GitHub: In order to facilitate the use of VAnnotatoR and to share it with a broad community, it will be published on GitHub. The authors believe that this will provide a versatile extension and the generation of further ideas for the realization of a meaningful and 3D-driven immersive VR.

In addition to the specific evaluations that were performed based on respective use cases (c.f. Kühn, 2018; Spiekermann, 2017), an overall evaluation of VAnnotatoR will be performed. This evaluation could be embedded in a concrete application of historical education in order to demonstrate its benefit in the field of education.

Conclusion

In this chapter, we focused on the potential of immersive VR. In addition to the comparison of frameworks, selected tools and applications for general and specific use in historical education were presented. Furthermore, a requirements analysis for a meaningful use of immersive VR in education was specified. In accordance with this analysis, existing projects and applications were assessed. VAnnotatoR was presented and described as a framework for the generation of immersive virtual environments in general and for historical education in particular. Since VAnnotatoR fulfils all listed requirements for a meaningful immersive VR, its application in the field of education is reasonable. After being published on GitHub as an open access application, a free and decentralized use of VAnnotatoR will be guaranteed.

Applying VR and perspective MR in education is becoming increasingly realistic. Research in this field is still in its infancy but is also on the rise thanks to the ever-faster development of hardware and the low-cost use in the private and public sectors. However, portability, openness and extensibility are indispensable criteria for the development of appropriate educational technologies. For this purpose, we have developed VAnnotatoR and continue to develop it.

Acknowledgement

The work on this chapter was partly funded by the *Förderfonds Lehre* of Goethe-University of Frankfurt.

Notes

1 https://www.timemachine.eu/
2 https://www.microsoft.com/en-us/hololens
3 https://www.magicleap.com/
4 http://opensimulator.org
5 https://realxtend.org
6 http://openwonderland.org/
7 https://www.unrealengine.com
8 https://unity3d.com/de/unity
9 The chapter therefore deals less with pedagogical or didactic aspects that have already been discussed elsewhere (c.f. He et al., 2018; Vehrer & Pongracz 2019).
10 See Potkonjak et al. (2016) for the projects and the development of a more general scope regarding the use of virtual laboratories.
11 https://vtm.epfl.ch/
12 https://www.leapmotion.com/
13 https://hi5vrglove.com/
14 https://developers.google.com/ar/

References

Abbott, A. (2017, June). The 'time machine' reconstructing ancient Venice's social networks. *Nature, 546*, 341–344. doi:10.1038/546341a

Abrami, G., & Mehler, A. (2018). A UIMA database interface for managing NLP-related text annotations. In *Proceedings of the 11th Edition of the Language Resources and Evaluation Conference, May 7–12*. Miyazaki, Japan.

Abrami, G., Mehler, A., & Spiekermann, C. (2019, July). Graph-based format for modeling multimodal an-notations in Virtual Reality by means of VAnnotatoR. In C. S. M. Antona (Ed.), *Proceedings of the 21st International Conference on Human-Computer Interaction, HCII 2019* (pp. 251–358). Cham: Springer.

Abrami, G., Spiekermann, C., & Mehler, A. (2019). VAnnotatoR: Ein Werkzeug zur Annotation multimodaler Netzwerke in dreidimensionalen virtuellen Umgebungen. In P. Sahle (Ed.), *Proceedings of the 6th Digital Humanities Conference in the German-Speaking Countries, DHD 2019* (pp. 354–355). Frankfurt, Germany.

Arth, C., Grasset, R., Gruber, L., Langlotz, T., Mulloni, A., & Wagner, D. (2015). The history of mobile augmented reality. *CoRR, abs/1505.01319*. Retrieved from http://arxiv.org/abs/1505.01319

Bamodu, O., & Ye, X. (2013, April). Virtual reality and virtual reality system components. *Advanced Materials Research, 765–767*, doi:10.2991/icsem.2013.192

Barreau, J.-B., Nouviale, F., Gaugne, R., Bernard, Y., Llinares, S., & Gouranton, V. (2015, June). An immersive virtual sailing on the 18th-century ship Le Boullongne. *Presence Teleoperators & Virtual Environments, 24*. doi:10.1162/PRES a 00231

Bryan, S. J., Campbell, A., & Mangina, E. (2018, August). Scenic spheres – An AR/VR educational game. In *2018 IEEE Games, Entertainment, Media Conference (GEM)* (pp. 1–9). doi:10.1109/GEM.2018.8516456

Butchart, B. (2011). *Augmented reality for smartphones*. Bath: University of Bath.

Card, S., Robertson, G. G., & Mackinlay, J. (1991, 01). The information visualizer, an information workspace. In *Proceedings of CHI'91* (pp. 181–186). doi:10.1145/108844.108874

Chin, N., Gupte, A., Nguyen, J., Sukhin, S., Wang, G., & Mirizio, J. (2017, November). Using virtual reality for an immersive experience in the water cycle. In *2017 IEEE MIT Undergraduate Research Technology Conference (URTC)* (pp. 1–4). doi:10.1109/URTC.2017.8284185

de Faria, J. W. V., Teixeira, M. J., de Moura Sousa Júnior, L., Otoch, J. P., & Figueiredo, E. G. (2016). Virtual and stereoscopic anatomy: When virtual reality meets medical education. *Journal of Neurosurgery JNS*, *125*(5), 1105–1111. Retrieved from https://thejns.org/view/journals/j-neurosurg/125/5/article-p1105.xml

Doak, D. G., Denyer, G. S., Gerrard, J. A., Mackay, J. P., & Allison, J. R. (2019). Peppy: A virtual reality environment for exploring the principles of polypeptide structure. *BioR, xiv.* doi:10.1101/723155

Gleim, R., Mehler, A., & Ernst, A. (2012). SOA implementation of the eHumanities desktop. In *Proceedings of the Workshop on Service-Oriented Architectures (SOAS) for the Humanities: Solutions and Impacts, Digital Humanities 2012*, Hamburg, Germany.

Greenwald, S. W., Kulik, A., Kunert, A., Beck, S., Fröhlich, B., Cobb, S., … Maes, P. (2017). Technology and applications for collaborative learning in virtual reality. In B. K. Smith, M. Borge, E. Mercier, & K. Y. Lim (Eds.), *Making a Difference: Prioritizing Equity and Access in CSCL, 12th International Conference on Computer Supported Collaborative Learning (CSCL) 2017* (Vol. 2). Philadelphia, PA: International Society of the Learning Sciences.

He, L., Shen, Q., & Li, R. (2018). Analysis and reflection on the relationship between the vision of embodied cognitive and VR educational games. In *International Conference on Management, Economics, Education, Arts and Humanities (MEEAH 2018)* (Vol. 291, pp. 48–53). Shenzhen, China.

Hettinger, L. J., & Riccio, G. E. (1992). Visually induced motion sickness in virtual environments. *Presence: Teleoperators and Virtual Environments*, *1*(3), 306–310. Retrieved from doi:10.1162/pres.1992.1.3.306

Hughes, C. E., Stapleton, C. B., Hughes, D. E., & Smith, E. M. (2005, November). Mixed reality in education, entertainment, and training. *IEEE Computer Graphics and Applications*, *25*(6), 24–30. doi:10.1109/MCG.2005.139

Indraprastha, A., & Shinozaki, M. (2009, January). The investigation on using unity3D game engine in urban design study. *ITB Journal of Information and Communication Technology*, *3*, 1–18. doi:10.5614/itbj.ict.2009.3.1.1

Ingram, R., Benford, S., & Bowers, J. (1996). Building virtual cities: Applying urban planning principles to the design of virtual environments. In *Proceedings of the ACM Symposium on Virtual Reality Software and Technology (VRST96)* (pp. 83–91). ACM Press.

Kett, A., Abrami, G., Mehler, A., & Spiekermann, C. (2018). Resources2City explorer: A system for generating interactive Walkable virtual cities out of file systems. In P. Baudisch & A. Schmidt (Eds.), *Proceedings of the 31st ACM User Interface Software and Technology Symposium* (pp. 123–125). Berlin, Germany.

Krekhov, A., Cmentowski, S., Waschk, A., & Krüger, J. H. (2019). Deadeye visualization revisited: Investigation of preattentiveness and applicability in virtual environments. *CoRR, abs/1907.04702.* Retrieved from http://arxiv.org/abs/1907.04702

Kühn, V. R. (2018). *A gesture-based interface to VR* [Bachelor] (Bachelor thesis). Goethe University of Frankfurt. Retrieved from http://publikationen.ub.uni-frankfurt.de/frontdoor/index/index/docId/50915

Kulik, A., Kunert, A., Beck, S., Reichel, R., Blach, R., Zink, A., & Froehlich, B. (2011). C1x6: A Stereoscopic six-user display for co-located collaboration in shared virtual environments. In *Proceedings of the 2011 SIGGRAPH Asia Conference* (pp. 188:1–188:12). New York, NY: ACM. Retrieved from doi:http://doi.acm.org/10.1145/2024156.2024222.

Lee, K. (2012, March 01). Augmented reality in education and training. *TechTrends, 56*(2), 13–21. Retrieved from doi:10.1007/s11528-012-0559-3.

Lee, M., & Spryszynski, A. (2019, January 1). Personalizing VR educational tools for English language learners. In C. Trattner, D. Parra, & N. Riche (Eds.), *Joint Proceedings of the {ACM} {IUI} 2019 Workshops co-located with the 24th {ACM} Conference on Intelligent User Interfaces (ACM IUI), 2327* (Vol. 2327). Los Angeles, USA.

Maiwald, F., Bruschke, J., Lehmann, C., & Niebling, F. (2019, July). A 4D information system for the exploration of multitemporal images and maps using photogrammetry, web technologies and VR/AR. *Virtual Archaeology Review, 10*(21), 1–13. doi:10.4995/var.2019.11867

Marks, S., White, D., & Singh, M. (2017). Getting up your nose: A virtual reality education tool for nasal cavity anatomy. In *SIGGRAPH Asia 2017 Symposium on Education* (pp. 1: 1–1:7). New York, NY: ACM. Retrieved from doi:10.1145/3134368.3139218.

Martín-Gutiérrez, J., Mora, C. E., Añorbe-Díaz, B., & González-Marrero, A. (2017). Virtual technologies trends in education. *Eurasia Journal of Mathematics, Science and Technology Education, 13*(2), 469–486. Retrieved from doi:10.12973/eurasia.2017.00626a.

Mehler, A., Abrami, G., Bruendel, S., Felder, L., Ostertag, T., & Spiekermann, C. (2017). Stolperwege: An app for a digital public history of the Holocaust. In *Proceedings of the 28th ACM Conference on Hypertext and Social Media* (pp. 319–320). New York, NY: ACM. Retrieved from doi:10.1145/3078714.3078748.

Mehler, A., Abrami, G., Spiekermann, C., & Jostock, M. (2018). VAnnotatoR: A framework for generating multimodal hypertexts. In *Proceedings of the 29th ACM Conference on Hypertext and Social Media*. New York, NY: ACM.

Meng, X. (2019). Formal analysis and application of the new mode of 'VR+ education'. *ITM Web Conferences, 26*, 01014. Retrieved from doi:10.1051/itmconf/20192601014.

Milán, M., David, W., & Stefan, M. (2018). Extending a virtual reality nasal cavity education tool with volume rendering. In Sasha Nikolic, Mark J. W. Lee *2018 IEEE International Conference on Teaching, Assessment, and Learning for Engineering (TALE)* (pp. 811–814). Wollongong, NSW, Australia.

Özdemir, M., Sahin, C., Arcagok, S., & Demir, M. (2018, April). The effect of augmented reality applications in the learning process: A meta-analysis study. *Eurasian Journal of Educational Research (EJER), 74*, 165–186. doi:10.14689/ejer.2018.74.9

Ott, M., & Freina, L. (2015). A literature review on immersive virtual reality in education: State of the art and perspectives. In *Proceedings of eLearning and Software for Education (eLSE)* (Issue 1, pp. 23–24, 133–141). Bucharest, Romania.

Peixoto, B., Pinto, D., Krassmann, A., Melo, M., Cabral, L., & Bessa, M. (2019). Using virtual reality tools for teaching foreign languages. In A. Rocha, H. Adeli, L. P. Reis, & S. Costanzo (Eds.), *New knowledge in information systems and technologies* (pp. 581–588). Cham: Springer International Publishing.

Pelargos, P. E., Nagasawa, D. T., Lagman, C., Tenn, S., Demos, J. V., Lee, S. J., Yang, I. (2017). Utilizing virtual and augmented reality for educational and clinical enhancements in neurosurgery. *Journal of Clinical Neuro-Science, 35*, 1–4. Retrieved from doi:10.1016/j.jocn.2016.09.002.

Pick, S., Weyers, B., Hentschel, B., & Kuhlen, T. W. (2016, April). Design and evaluation of data annotation workflows for CAVE-like virtual environments. *IEEE Transactions on Visualization and Computer Graphics, 22*(4), 1452–1461. doi:10.1109/TVCG.2016.2518086

Postma, B. N. J., & Katz, B. F. G. (2015, November 01). Creation and calibration method of acoustical models for historic virtual reality auralizations. *Virtual Reality, 19*(3), 161–180. Retrieved from doi:10.1007/s10055-015-0275-3.

Potkonjak, V., Gardner, M., Callaghan, V., Mattila, P., Guetl, C., Petrovi´c, V. M., & Jovanovi´c, K. (2016, April). Virtual laboratories for education in science, technology, and engineering. *Computer & Education, 95*(C), 309–327. Retrieved from doi:10.1016/j.compedu.2016.02.002.

Riva, G. (2006). Virtual reality. In M. Akay (Ed.), *Wiley encyclopedia of biomedical engineering* (Vol. 4, pp. 1–17). London: American Cancer Society. doi:10.1002/9780471740360. ebs1266

Sampaio, A. Z., Rosario, D., Gomes, A., & Santos, J. (2013). Virtual reality applied on civil engineering education: Construction activity supported on interactive models. *International Journal of Engineering Education, 29*(6), 1331–1347.

Sánchez, J., Lumbreras, M., & Silva, J. (1997). Virtual reality and learning: Trends and issues. In *Proceedings of the 14th International Conference on Technology and Education.* (pp. 10–13). Oslo, Norway.

Sasaki, T., Liu, K.-H., Hasegawa, T., Hiyama, A., & Inami, M. (2019). Virtual super-leaping: Immersive extreme jumping in VR. In *Proceedings of the 10th Augmented Human International Conference 2019* (pp. 18:1–18:8). New York, NY: ACM. Retrieved from doi:10.1145/3311823.3311861.

Sidenmark, L., Kiefer, N., & Gellersen, H. (2019). Subtitles in interactive virtual reality: Using gaze to address depth conflicts. In *Workshop on Emerging Novel Input Devices and Interaction Techniques* (pp. 1–6) Osaka, Japan.

Spiekermann, C. (2017). *Ein Text-Editor für die Texttechnologie in der dritten Dimension* (Bachelor thesis). Goethe University of Frankfurt.

Spiekermann, C., Abrami, G., & Mehler, A. (2018). VAnnotatoR: A gesture-driven annotation framework for linguistic and multimodal annotation. In *Proceedings of the Annotation, Recognition and Evaluation of Actions (AREA 2018) Workshop* (pp. 1–6) Miyazaki, Japan.

Sutherland, I. E. (1968). A head-mounted three dimensional display. In *Proceedings of the December 9–11, 1968, Fall Joint Computer Conference, Part I* (pp. 757–764). New York, NY: ACM. Retrieved from doi:10.1145/1476589.1476686.

Vehrer, A., & Pongracz, A. (2019, February). Generation management trends in VR education. In S. Gyula (Ed.), *Coginfocom 2018 Proceedings* (pp. 399–403). Piscataway, NJ: IEEE Computational Intelligence Society.

Wu, H.-K., Lee, S. W.-Y., Chang, H.-Y., & Liang, J.-C. (2013). Current status, opportunities and challenges of augmented reality in education. *Computers & Education, 62,* 41–49.

Yang, K. (2018). Dual dimensions of VR education development: Vision and technology direction. In *3rd International Conference on Education, e-Learning and Management Technology (EEMT 2018)* (Vol. 220, pp. 469–483). Atlantic Press. doi:https://doi.org/10.2991/iceemt-18.2018.93

Zaidi, S. F. M., Moore, C., & Khanna, H. (2019). Towards integration of user-centered designed tutorials for better virtual reality immersion. In *Proceedings of the 2nd International Conference on Image and Graphics Processing* (pp. 140–144). New York, NY: ACM. Retrieved from doi:10.1145/3313950.3313977.

Virtual and augmented reality applications for environmental science education and training

Yusuf Sermet and Ibrahim Demir

Introduction

Cyberinfrastructure systems and applications are broadly used for information retrieval and management in the environmental domain (Essawy et al., 2018; Li, Lam, Qiang, Zou, & Cai, 2015; Muste et al., 2012; Rathje et al., 2017). Integration of new technologies, including web-based platforms with real-time knowledge-generation capabilities, into environmental problem-solving paved the way for realistic simulations of environmental conditions for in-depth analysis (Demir, Yildirim, Sermet, & Sit, 2018; Jones et al., 2018). Evaluation of natural events for inspection and planning purposes require the combined analysis and optimization of various datasets (e.g. digital elevation model, weather conditions, forecasting models, infrastructure information, financial data, vulnerable population) (Demir, & Szczepanek, 2017, Krajewski et al., 2017; Sit, Sermet, & Demir, 2019). Complemented by real-world physics and environmental dynamics, these parameters can effectively be presented in a virtual environment (Boulos, Lu, Guerrero, Jennett, & Steed, 2017).

With the increased prevalence of smartphones and popularity of artificial intelligence, substantial research and development have been made in pursuit of more cost-effective and high-performance sensor technologies (Deng, Yu, Yuan, Wan, & Yang, 2013; Li, 2016) and graphical processing units, which led to the production of affordable virtual and augmented reality (AR) devices (Anthes, García-Hernández, Wiedemann, & Kranzlmüller, 2016). These developments allowed researchers in many fields (e.g. astronomy, psychology, medicine) to create controlled virtual environments that allow users to interact with digitally generated stimuli (Cipresso et al., 2018; Freina & Ott, 2015; Joda, Gallucci, Wismeijer, & Zitzmann, 2019). In the field of environmental sciences and disaster management, public, scientists, decision-makers and professionals can benefit from virtual reality (VR) and AR applications to simulate various environmental scenarios for a realistic and safe workspace that allows repetition and precise measurements (Hsu et al., 2013; Nunes, Lucas, Simões-Marques, & Correia, 2018).

In this chapter, we provide a variety of use cases (i.e. applications) that utilize VR and AR in disaster management and environmental data retrieval, analysis and visualization. Design goals of these applications broadly include increasing public awareness regarding natural disasters with engaging graphics and interaction, communicating environmental information efficiently and effectively to educate K-12 and college-level students, providing a decision support system for environmental planning and disaster management, training first responders and maintenance staff, and advancing conventional real-time environmental data retrieval and processing.

The remainder of this chapter is organized as follows. We provide a literature review to summarize the previous work on implementing AR/VR in natural disaster sciences, and describe the use cases focusing on the recreation of a realistic flood scenario with purposes of increasing awareness, providing decision support and educating stakeholders. Afterwards, we focus on AR/VR applications in real-time environmental data acquisition, its processing and visualization. Finally, conclusions are provided along with the future directions.

Background

Various studies have shown that VR and AR can be used to advance conventional disaster management and response approaches (Alharthi et al., 2018; Jung, Cho, & Jee, 2016; Schwarz, Binetti, Broll, & Mitschele-Thiel, 2016; Sharma et al., 2019; Vichitvejpaisal, Yamee, & Marsertsri, 2016). One of the most prominent ways of applying AR/VR in environmental science is on smartphones due to their prevalence. Using smartphones, many studies showed the potential and benefits of using AR to access and display disaster data in its geospatial context (Itamiya, Tohara, & Nasuda, 2019). Tsai and Yau (2013) presented a mobile application that calculated the best route for evacuation from disaster areas and informed the user by outlining the route on the camera feed of the smartphone with AR. The Whistland system (Luchetti, Mancini, Sturari, Frontoni, & Zingaretti, 2017) is an example of retrieving crowdsourced disaster-related information from a real-time Twitter feed for display as an AR overlay to the smartphone camera to visualize data and information on their originating sources, and it also provides detailed analysis on a web-based analytics application. Mirauda, Erra, Agatiello and Cerverizzo (2018) developed a mobile application to provide hydrological sensor measurements and model results in an intuitive and context-informed way using AR overlays to augment points of interest (e.g. hydrometric stations). Veas, Grasset, Ferencik, Grünewald and Schmalstieg (2013) introduced a mobile AR application for on-site enhanced environmental monitoring and demonstrated it with two case studies yielding positive results from the participants. Fedorov, Frajberg and Fraternali (2016) presented a unique approach for utilizing computer vision techniques to identify mountain silhouettes and compare the extracted information to available digital elevation model (DEM) data in order to annotate the mountain and provide useful information (e.g. peak name, distance) to users as AR overlays.

In addition to data retrieval and presentation, AR/VR solutions are developed for visualizing data resources and analysing information in-situ or in virtual environments (Reyes & Chen, 2017). Ready, Dwyer and Haga (2018) presented a virtual reality application for HTC Vive that recreates a 3D model for Japan, consisting of terrain and buildings, allowing a user to interact with various data resources to access hydrological time-series data in an easily interpretable way for disaster management. Haynes, Hehl-Lange and Lange (2018) developed a mobile AR application for visualizing potential floods on site and integrating real-time sensor readings (e.g. water level, soil moisture and humidity) with the vision of allowing stakeholders to use the application for flood risk management. In their after-experiment survey, the results show that users who were involved in flood management and experienced with smartphone usage while having less experience in 3D modelling found the AR application's visualizations easy to understand. Macchione, Costabile, Costanzo and De Santis (2019) proposed a virtual environment to recreate an urban environment (e.g. buildings, streams, roads, levees, textures) to simulate hydraulic dynamics during different flood scenarios using an open-source 3D graphics creation application (i.e. Blender).

Several recent studies presented how AR/VR can be used for immersive disaster simulations for education, emergency management, decision-making and evacuation drills (Bernhardt et al., 2019; Mitsuhara, Shishibori, Kawai, & Iguchi, 2016; Ooi, Tanimoto, & Sano, 2019; Pratama, Fardhosseini, & Lin, 2018; Smith & Ericson, 2009). Kawai, Mitsuhara and Shishibori (2015) proposed an AR-based tsunami evacuation drill system in which the users are required to escape from a disaster scenario in a limited period of time. The disaster simulations are processed server-side and transferred over the Internet to the client device for display in smart glasses (i.e. Moverio). Iguchi, Mitsuhara and Shishibori (2016) developed a gamified disaster-evacuation training framework with a specific emphasis on supporting teachers educating students on disaster response. The system allows users to immerse themselves in various scenarios using smartphones and interact with virtual students via voice commands. Federal Emergency Management Agency (FEMA) offered IMMERSED, an HTC Vive-based VR experience to educate community leaders and the public on flood mitigation strategies by letting users experience several scenarios (e.g. exploring damage in a flooded neighbourhood, leading a stranded person to a safe zone from a flooded school). The application walks the user through the same scenarios while describing different types of actions for hazard mitigation planning (FEMA, 2018). Wang, Hou, Miller, Brown and Jiang (2019) described a VR-based flood risk management system that aims to simulate floods for Sponge cities by integrating hydrodynamic models and topographic data into a 3D environment developed for Oculus Rift and presented a case study for Fengxi, China.

AR/VR applications for disaster preparedness and management

AR and VR applications present an opportunity to develop fully immersive experiences to recreate real-time and historical disaster scenarios in a controlled experimental environment that allows repetition. Two case studies (i.e. Flood Action VR and HoloFlood) are presented in this section to demonstrate the workflow of creating both VR and AR solutions for disaster education, preparedness and management. Various data resources (e.g. hydrological, geographical, meteorological) have been utilized to power both applications, retrieved from organizations including the United States Geological Survey, National Oceanic and Atmospheric Administration, The Weather Channel, Iowa Flood Center and ArcGIS City Engine.

When simulating any natural event, one of the pillars of success is the accurate representation of the environment and underlying dynamics. In the case of flooding, high-resolution terrain along with elevation metadata is vital for water inundation and flow calculations. For the case studies, DEM data is used to recreate the world surface and enhanced by satellite images mapped on 3D terrain objects. Critical infrastructures (e.g. buildings, bridges, dams, roads) and objects with secondary importance (e.g. trees, traffic lights, park benches) are retrieved from ArcGIS. For natural events, disaster (e.g. flood extent, depth, return period, watershed characteristics) and weather-related (e.g. precipitation duration and intensity, wind speed and direction, humidity, temperature, visibility) data are retrieved from historical sources, model forecasts and real-time sensor readings. These data resources are available for use in specific application scenarios depending on context and device capabilities.

Although different use cases may require the use of specific resources and integration of different capabilities, the basis (i.e. the core) of the mixed reality (XR)-based disaster management applications is the procedural generation of realistic environmental scenes. This includes high-resolution terrain models (i.e. DEM), satellite imagery, roads, buildings and infrastructure models, textures and their appropriate placement on the scene, which requires the clamping of structures to the terrain. While they are not directly linked to the disaster simulation, objects that enhance the realization experience (e.g. trees, electric poles, park benches, traffic lights and signs) can be included as long as the performance of the device is capable of rendering the scenes.

The main development environments for the framework are Unity3D and ESRI City Engine. Unity3D is a cross-platform game-engine capable of producing AR and VR experiences, and ESRI City Engine is a 3D modelling software focused on generating virtual urban environments. The main reasons for choosing these platforms are their advanced physics capabilities, rich 3D resources and export functionalities that allow flexible development and easy integration. The core 3D components of the immersive disaster management and education framework, as described in the previous paragraph, are modelled and constructed (e.g. clamping of buildings onto 3D terrain object) using City Engine and exported in FBX file format to be used for scene generation in the game engine. Disaster simulations, water physics, object animations and interaction methods are then developed using the game engine, which has the capability of creating immersive experiences that can be ported into various AR/VR headsets and presentation channels (i.e. smartphones, web-based platforms) with little modifications to the original application. Figure 17.1 describes system architecture for creating an immersive disaster management and education framework (e.g. Flood Action VR, HoloFlood) using real-time and historical environmental datasets.

Case study on VR

Flood Action VR is a virtual reality framework that utilizes real-time and historical weather, disaster and geographic data to construct a 3D gaming environment to increase public awareness for extreme events (Figure 17.2). It also provides an immersive and interactive environment for training and education on disaster preparedness and response (Sermet & Demir, 2018b). It integrates a voice-enabled intelligent assistant (i.e. The Flood Expert, Sermet & Demir, 2018a) capable of comprehending and responding to complex environmental queries in natural language due to its integration with an information-centric flood ontology (Sermet & Demir, 2019). The main focus of the game is to let users achieve several tasks (e.g. escaping from the flood zone, rescuing those in need and transporting medicine and emergency supplies) within a limited time during an extreme disaster scenario while simulating intense weather conditions. The scenarios can be based upon real events and forecasts as well as custom setups. In-game navigation is done flying a rescue drone. Interactions with the system can be made in different forms including voice-based natural language commands and default input

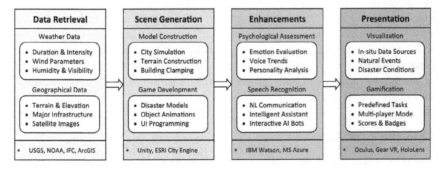

Figure 17.1 System-level architecture for an immersive disaster management and education framework.

Figure 17.2 Screenshots from Flood Action VR game for Samsung Gear VR.

methods (e.g. gesture, controller, touchpad) of the client device. When users interact with the system or other players use their voice, the system is able to analyse voice trends, thus determining emotional and psychological states.

In addition to the base 3D model of a location, Flood Action VR integrates several enhancements for complete immersion using real-time or historical weather conditions in various aspects of the scene. Weather conditions (e.g. precipitation type and intensity, cloudiness, visibility) are set up using retrieved weather data. Utilizing the wind speed and direction, a directional wind animation is created, allowing interaction with other 3D objects in the scene. High-quality tree models are animated by the effect of the wind and placed roadside and in parks. To avoid the high computational cost of animating tree and leaf models with the wind, a conditional rendering mechanism is implemented to change the quality of the tree and cancel the wind-affected animation as the user gets away from the tree. Most importantly, realistic water objects are created using the retrieved flood scenarios and animated in accordance with the environmental conditions (e.g. wind, sun, floating objects). Properties of the water objects include environment reflection, refraction of colour and distortion and the shape and speed of the waves, which can be adjusted according to the computational capabilities of the client device.

Case study for AR

HoloFlood (Demir et al., 2018) is an AR framework for simulating historical, current or forecasted flood scenarios as holograms, structured from the 3D model of selected locations. It also provides property-specific estimations for structural and content damage as well as the vulnerable population. Scientists, decision-makers, emergency responders and stakeholders can use HoloFlood to examine the ways a city would be affected by different types of floods and benefit from HoloFlood as a decision support tool during disaster planning and response situations. It allows collaborative inspection of the holographic simulation by multiple stakeholders to pave the way for next-generation decision support systems. The application is mainly designed for use with see-through displays (e.g. Microsoft (MS) HoloLens) (Figure 17.3) and smartphones with augmented reality capabilities.

Main uses of the system are as follows: The routes for emergency responders and evacuation of affected citizens can be analysed by considering a variety of possibilities in terms of speed and safety. Safe and accessible areas and locations can be determined to transport and deliver emergency supplies such as medication and food. By using the estimations for flood damage and vulnerable populations at a property during a flood with a certain extent, evacuation priorities and the most efficient allocation of resources can be determined to minimize the loss of lives and economic damage. Floodplain managers can utilize the system for damage estimation based on the HAZUS (a standardized methodology for estimating potential damage from natural disasters including floods) dataset as well as the data collected from tax assessors, where available (Yildirim & Demir, 2019).

AR/VR applications for environmental visualization and data analysis

Massive amounts of environmental data are being generated at a rapidly increasing pace due to developments and investments in sensor technologies

Figure 17.3 A snapshot of HoloFlood placed on a conference room table.

(Ebert-Uphoff et al., 2017) and crowdsourcing (Sit et al., 2019), which are fuelled by the increased awareness of sustainability (Bibri, 2018) and climate change (Weber et al., 2018) as well as the efforts for disaster preparedness and mitigation. Making good use of these large-scale datasets require intelligent and efficient approaches for access, analysis and communication to stakeholders (Demir & Beck, 2009; Krajewski et al., 2017). These approaches include the presentation of structured data via web-based platforms in forms of 2D visualizations and interactive tools (Demir, Jiang, Walker, Parker, & Beck, 2009) and intuitive and gamified decision-support frameworks to allow stakeholders to make informed decisions (Carson et al., 2018). AR and VR can be utilized to develop next-generation data retrieval, on-site analysis and in-depth visualizations in the environmental field as highlighted by the case studies described in the remainder of this section.

Environmental data retrieval and sensing

AR can help develop modern data sensing approaches. It provides an opportunity for the user to perform complex measurements and data collection with intuitive methods. Sermet, Sit, Villanueva and Demir (2019) presented several geometry-based approaches to measure water stages using prevalent sensors found in smartphones. All approaches presented in the study require a user to take a picture of a point of interest (i.e. an intersection of a water body with land) in order to assess the real-world elevation of the surface of the water body (Figure 17.4a). The study outlines how AR beacons and known structures can be used as reference points to calibrate sensor readings, perform more accurate surveys, guide users to survey locations that are in more need of data points and present previous measurements for that location and relevant information as AR overlays.

In addition to data sensing, AR-based cyber tools can serve as practical intermediaries to communicate raw data and information to users in the appropriate spatiotemporal context. As an example, a smartphone-based AR application is developed (Demir et al., 2018) to allow the enhancement of a real-time camera feed by creating interactive AR layers (i.e. overlays) for nearby sensors (e.g. water level sensor, rain gauge, soil moisture gauge) to access data resources (Figure 17.4b). The application filters the sensors based on proximity determined by the user and resizes the representative icons to create a perception of distance.

Another use case for enhanced data communication is the inspection and measurement of power line sag using AR-enabled smartphone applications (Sermet, Demir, & Kucuksari, 2018). An Android application was developed to effectively and safely inspect overhead power line sag in terms of the line's sag tolerance and distance to nearby obstacles (e.g. trees) and ground using image processing. For known locations, information boxes are generated with various useful information including the last maintenance

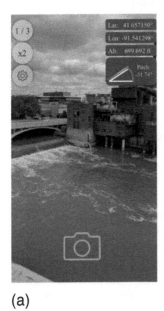

(a)   (b)

Figure 17.4 (a) Smartphone-based stream stage measurement (b) AR layers for visualizing
nearby sensors on a smartphone.

date, previous sag measurements with neighbouring poles and action messages to reflect whether the pole or line needs maintenance. These boxes
are overlaid to the camera stream and placed on top of the electric poles on
sight using AR (Figure 17.5).

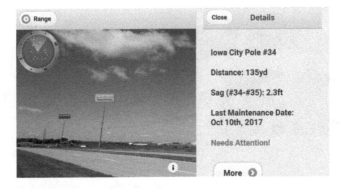

Figure 17.5 A screenshot from the Android application to show AR overlays for power
line inspection.

Hydrological simulations and disaster education

A major motivation for the use of AR/VR in disaster sciences is the education of the public, students in K-12 or college level students concerning hydrological processes and natural disasters. XR technologies can bring the fun factor to the education applications with gamification and the interactive nature of these platforms. XR can allow students to experiment with environmental phenomena to see outcomes that are impractical or impossible to reproduce in real life. An example of such initiatives is the web-based hydrological simulation system (Demir, 2014) developed at the University of Iowa. The system can simulate hydrological concepts (e.g. watershed, precipitation, river network, flood inundation and mitigation) that are controlled by the instructor and students to create different flood scenarios and implement flood mitigation strategies while providing realistic visualizations to assess the potential structural and environmental damage. The system is accessible from a web browser as a 3D interactive environment, on smartphones as an AR application using a marker (Figure 17.6a) and on VR devices (e.g. Oculus Rift) as an immersive VR application.

In addition to education, augmenting real-life locations that are of interest to stakeholders is an effective tool in increasing awareness. The literature suggests that a notable percentage of people are undermining the effects of disasters, which contributes to the lack of preparatory activities, leading to increased damages and casualties (Burningham, Fielding, & Thrush, 2008). A realistic flood visualizer has been developed (Demir et al., 2018) using 360-degree panoramic imagery by integrating a layer of advanced water simulation (Figure 17.6b). The flood visualizer allows users to choose any place on a 2D map that has 360-degree imagery available and generates interactive VR that can be viewed on a web platform, VR headsets and smartphones. The main advantage of the tool is to provide a unique and immersive experience of how floods affect communities, giving users a feeling of empathy. Thus, it paves the way for individuals to take roles in disaster preparedness efforts by increasing their interest.

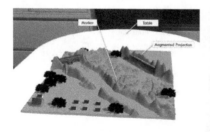 

Figure 17.6 a) A snapshot of an educational hydrological simulation environment
b) A screenshot of panoramic imagery augmented with realistic flood visualization.

Concluding remarks and future directions

The use of AR and VR technologies shows great potential for applications in environmental and disaster studies in the contexts of decision-making, education and awareness. Conventional data-sensing approaches can be complemented with modern data-collection methods using AR to reduce the cost of sensor deployment and maintenance in terms of invested time and resources and increase data coverage complementing conventional sensor technologies. Furthermore, AR-based data-collection approaches can enable citizen science applications for crowdsourcing geospatial data, thus decreasing the cost of computational resources supported by an agency or an organization. These developments can be facilitated by several factors including advancements in mobile sensor technologies in terms of accuracy, size and cost. Another factor is the newly available 5G cellular network that will result in increasing mobile streaming capabilities for faster transfers of complex and high-resolution 3D models, denser sensor coverage and data points with a more comprehensive and detailed reporting.

Immersive simulation environments can support advanced analysis and scenario evaluation applications in decision support systems. The presented applications serve as prototypes and a demonstration of the potential of AR and VR applications in environmental science education and training. They also highlight various opportunities for advancement and directions for future research. Collaborative activities in immersive simulations are vital for allowing stakeholders from different physical locations to work on a common goal. AR and VR applications can support the new science of socio-hydrology, which treats people as an important part of the water cycle through water consumption, pollution of freshwater resources, policies and technology (Sivapalan, Savenije, & Blöschl, 2012). For 3D representation of real-world features, structural and terrain-related data need to be shared in a consensual format for easy integration to immersive systems to support the vision of global and generalized simulation platforms. Physics-based scientific dynamics and animations need to be incorporated into these applications to examine the chain-reactions caused by extreme events and human intervention. Benefiting the recent developments in deep learning and artificial intelligence in general, detailed simulations of people and their behaviours during various environmental scenarios can be developed and integrated into immersive frameworks.

References

Alharthi, S. A., LaLone, N., Khalaf, A. S., Torres, R., Nacke, L., Dolgov, I., & Toups, Z. O. (2018, January). Practical insights into the design of future disaster response training simulations. In *Proceedings of the 15th International ISCRAM Conference*. Retrieved from http://par.nsf.gov/biblio/10061145.

Anthes, C., García-Hernández, R. J., Wiedemann, M., & Kranzlmüller, D. (2016, March). State of the art of virtual reality technology. In *2016 IEEE Aerospace Conference* (pp. 1–19). IEEE.

Bernhardt, J., Snelllings, J., Smiros, A., Bermejo, I., Rienzo, A., & Swan, C. (2019). Communicating hurricane risk with virtual reality: A pilot project. *Bulletin of the American Meteorological Society, 100*(10), 1897–1902.

Bibri, S. E. (2018). The IoT for smart sustainable cities of the future: An analytical framework for sensor-based big data applications for environmental sustainability. *Sustainable Cities and Society, 38*, 230–253.

Boulos, M. N. K., Lu, Z., Guerrero, P., Jennett, C., & Steed, A. (2017). From urban planning and emergency training to Pokémon Go: Applications of virtual reality GIS (VRGIS) and augmented reality GIS (ARGIS) in personal, public and environmental health. *International Journal of Health Geographics, 16*(7). https://ij-healthgeographics.biomedcentral.com/articles/10.1186/s12942-017-0081-0.

Burningham, K., Fielding, J., & Thrush, D. (2008). 'It'll never happen to me': Understanding public awareness of local flood risk. *Disasters, 32*(2), 216–238.

Carson, A., Windsor, M., Hill, H., Haigh, T., Wall, N., Smith, J., Muste, M. (2018). Serious gaming for participatory planning of multi-hazard mitigation. *International Journal of River Basin Management, 16*(3), 379–391.

Cipresso, P., Giglioli, I. A. C., Raya, M. A., & Riva, G. (2018). The past, present, and future of virtual and augmented reality research: A network and cluster analysis of the literature. *Frontiers in psychology, 9*, 2086.

Demir, I. (2014). Interactive web-based hydrological simulation systems as an education platform using augmented and immersive reality. In *The Annual Conference of American Society for Engineering Education*. North Midwest Section Conference. 3. https://ir.uiowa.edu/aseenmw2014/fluids_classroom_innovations/1B/3/

Demir, I., & Beck, M. B. (2009, April). GWIS: A prototype information system for Georgia watersheds. In *Proceedings Georgia Water Resources Conference: Regional Water Management Opportunities*, Paper 6.6.4.

Demir, I., Jiang, F., Walker, R. V., Parker, A. K., & Beck, M. B. (2009, October). Information systems and social legitimacy scientific visualization of water quality. In *2009 IEEE International Conference on Systems*, Man and Cybernetics (pp. 1067–1072). IEEE.

Demir, I., & Szczepanek, R. (2017). Optimization of river network representation data models for web-based systems. *Earth and Space Science, 4*(6), 336–347.

Demir, I., Yildirim, E., Sermet, Y., & Sit, M. A. (2018). FLOODSS: Iowa flood information system as a generalized flood cyberinfrastructure. *International Journal of River Basin Management, 16*(3), 393–400.

Deng, Z., Yu, Y., Yuan, X., Wan, N., & Yang, L. (2013). Situation and development tendency of indoor positioning. *China Communications, 10*(3), 42–55.

Ebert-Uphoff, I., Thompson, D. R., Demir, I., Karpatne, A., Guereque, M., Kumar, V., Smyth, P. (2017, September). A vision for the development of benchmarks to bridge geoscience and data science. In *7th International Workshop on Climate Informatics*. https://par.nsf.gov/biblio/10057023.

Essawy, B. T., Goodall, J. L., Zell, W., Voce, D., Morsy, M. M., Sadler, J., Malik, T. (2018). Integrating scientific cyberinfrastructures to improve reproducibility in computational hydrology: Example for HydroShare and GeoTrust. *Environmental Modelling & Software, 105*, 217–229.

Fedorov, R., Frajberg, D., & Fraternali, P. (2016, June). A framework for outdoor mobile augmented reality and its application to mountain peak detection. In

International Conference on Augmented Reality, Virtual Reality and Computer Graphics (pp. 281–301). Cham: Springer.

FEMA. (2018). *IMMERSED: A VR experience about flood & resilience*. [online]. Retrieved from www.fema.gov/immersed. [Accessed 14 August 2019].

Freina, L., & Ott, M. (2015, April). A literature review on immersive virtual reality in education: State of the art and perspectives. In *The International Scientific Conference eLearning and Software for Education* (Vol. 1, p. 133). "Carol I" National Defence University.

Haynes, P., Hehl-Lange, S., & Lange, E. (2018). Mobile augmented reality for flood visualisation. *Environmental Modelling & Software, 109*, 380–389.

Hsu, E. B., Li, Y., Bayram, J. D., Levinson, D., Yang, S., & Monahan, C. (2013). State of virtual reality based disaster preparedness and response training. *PLoS Currents, 5*. https://www.ncbi.nlm.nih.gov/pmc/articles/PMC3644293/

Iguchi, K., Mitsuhara, H., & Shishibori, M. (2016, December). Evacuation instruction training system using augmented reality and a smartphone-based head mounted display. In *2016 3rd International Conference on Information and Communication Technologies for Disaster Management (ICT-DM)* (pp. 1–6). IEEE.

Itamiya, T., Tohara, H., & Nasuda, Y. (2019, March). Augmented reality floods and smoke smartphone app disaster scope utilizing real-time occlusion. In *2019 IEEE Conference on Virtual Reality and 3D User Interfaces (VR)* (pp. 1397–1398). IEEE.

Joda, T., Gallucci, G. O., Wismeijer, D., & Zitzmann, N. U. (2019). Augmented and virtual reality in dental medicine: A systematic review. *Computers in Biology and Medicine, 108*, 93–100.

Jones, C. S., Davis, C. A., Drake, C. W., Schilling, K. E., Debionne, S. H., Gilles, D. W., Weber, L. J. (2018). Iowa statewide stream nitrate load calculated using in situ sensor network. *JAWRA Journal of the American Water Resources Association, 54*(2), 471–486.

Jung, S. U., Cho, H., & Jee, H. K. (2016, November). An AR-based safety training assistant in disaster for children. In *SIGGRAPH ASIA 2016 Posters* (p. 49). ACM.

Kawai, J., Mitsuhara, H., & Shishibori, M. (2015). Tsunami evacuation drill system using smart glasses. *Procedia Computer Science, 72*, 329–336.

Krajewski, W. F., Ceynar, D., Demir, I., Goska, R., Kruger, A., Langel, C., Small, S. J. (2017). Real-time flood forecasting and information system for the state of Iowa. *Bulletin of the American Meteorological Society, 98*(3), 539–554.

Li, K., Lam, N. S., Qiang, Y., Zou, L., & Cai, H. (2015). A cyberinfrastructure for community resilience assessment and visualization. *Cartography and Geographic Information Science, 42*(sup1), 34–39.

Li, Y. (2016). *Integration of MEMS sensors, WiFi, and magnetic features for indoor pedestrian navigation with consumer portable devices* (Doctoral dissertation). University of Calgary.

Luchetti, G., Mancini, A., Sturari, M., Frontoni, E., & Zingaretti, P. (2017). Whistland: An augmented reality crowd-mapping system for civil protection and emergency management. *ISPRS International Journal of Geo-Information, 6*(2), 41.

Macchione, F., Costabile, P., Costanzo, C., & De Santis, R. (2019). Moving to 3-D flood hazard maps for enhancing risk communication. *Environmental Modelling & Software, 111*, 510–522.

Mirauda, D., Erra, U., Agatiello, R., & Cerverizzo, M. (2018). Mobile augmented reality for flood events management. *Water Studies, 47*, 418–424.

Mitsuhara, H., Shishibori, M., Kawai, J., & Iguchi, K. (2016, July). Game-based evacuation drills using simple augmented reality. In *2016 IEEE 16th International Conference on Advanced Learning Technologies (ICALT)* (pp. 133–137). IEEE.

Muste, M. V., Bennett, D. A., Secchi, S., Schnoor, J. L., Kusiak, A., Arnold, N. J., Rapolu, U. (2012). End-to-end cyberinfrastructure for decision-making support in watershed management. *Journal of Water Resources Planning and Management, 139*(5), 565–573.

Nunes, I. L., Lucas, R., Simões-Marques, M., & Correia, N. (2018, August). An augmented reality application to support deployed emergency teams. In *Congress of the International Ergonomics Association* (195–204). Cham: Springer.

Ooi, S., Tanimoto, T., & Sano, M. (2019, March). Virtual reality fire disaster training system for improving disaster awareness. In *Proceedings of the 2019 8th International Conference on Educational and Information Technology* (pp. 301–307). ACM.

Pratama, L. A., Fardhosseini, M. S., & Lin, K. Y. (2018). *An overview of generating vr models for disaster zone reconstruction using drone footage* (pp. 336–344). Auckland, New Zealand: The University of Auckland.

Rathje, E. M., Dawson, C., Padgett, J. E., Pinelli, J. P., Stanzione, D., Adair, A., Esteva, M. (2017). DesignSafe: New cyberinfrastructure for natural hazards engineering. *Natural Hazards Review, 18*(3), 06017001.

Ready, M., Dwyer, T., & Haga, J. H. (2018). Immersive visualisation of big data for river disaster management. In *Workshop on Immersive Analytics: Exploring Future Visualization and Interaction Technologies for Data Analytics, Phoenix, AZ.*

Reyes, M. E. P., & Chen, S. C. (2017, April). A 3D virtual environment for storm surge flooding animation. In *2017 IEEE Third International Conference on Multimedia Big Data (BigMM)* (pp. 244–245). IEEE.

Schwarz, A., Binetti, J. C., Broll, W., & Mitschele-Thiel, A. (2016). New technologies and applications in international crisis communication and disaster management. *The Handbook of International Crisis Communication Research, 43*, 465.

Sermet, M. Y., Demir, I., & Kucuksari, S. (2018, September). Overhead power line sag monitoring through augmented reality. In *2018 North American Power Symposium (NAPS)* (pp. 1–5). IEEE.

Sermet, Y., & Demir, I. (2018a). An intelligent system on knowledge generation and communication about flooding. *Environmental Modelling & Software, 108*, 51–60.

Sermet, Y., & Demir, I. (2018b). Flood action VR: A virtual reality framework for disaster awareness and emergency response training. In *ACM SIGGRAPH 2019 Posters (SIGGRAPH '19), Association for Computing Machinery, New York, NY, USA, Article 27, 1–2. doi: 10.1145/3306214.3338550*

Sermet, Y., & Demir, I. (2019). Towards an information centric flood ontology for information management and communication. *Earth Science Informatics, 12*(4), 541–551.

Sermet, Y., Villanueva, P., Sit, M. A., & Demir, I. (2020). Crowdsourced approaches for stage measurements at ungauged locations using smartphones. *Hydrological Sciences Journal, 65*:5, 813–822.

Sharma, S., Devreaux, P., Sree, S., Scribner, D., Grynovicki, J., & Grazaitis, P. (2019). Artificial intelligence agents for crowd simulation in an immersive environment for emergency response. *Electronic Imaging, 2019*(2), 176–181.

Sit, M., Sermet, Y., & Demir, I. (2019). Optimized watershed delineation library for server-side and client-side web applications. *Open Geospatial Data, Software and Standards, 4*(1), 8.

Sit, M. A., Koylu, C., & Demir, I. (2019). Identifying disaster-related tweets and their semantic, spatial and temporal context using deep learning, natural language processing and spatial analysis: A case study of Hurricane Irma. *International Journal of Digital Earth, 12*(11), 1205–1229.

Sivapalan, M., Savenije, H. H., & Blöschl, G. (2012). Socio-hydrology: A new science of people and water. *Hydrological Processes, 26*(8), 1270–1276.

Smith, S., & Ericson, E. (2009). Using immersive game-based virtual reality to teach fire-safety skills to children. *Virtual Reality, 13*(2), 87–99.

Tsai, M. K., & Yau, N. J. (2013). Improving information access for emergency response in disasters. *Natural Hazards, 66*(2), 343–354.

Veas, E., Grasset, R., Ferencik, I., Grünewald, T., & Schmalstieg, D. (2013). Mobile augmented reality for environmental monitoring. *Personal and Ubiquitous Computing, 17*(7), 1515–1531.

Vichitvejpaisal, P., Yamee, N., & Marsertsri, P. (2016, July). Firefighting simulation on virtual reality platform. In *2016 13th International Joint Conference on Computer Science and Software Engineering (JCSSE)* (pp. 1–5). IEEE.

Wang, C., Hou, J., Miller, D., Brown, I., & Jiang, Y. (2019). Flood risk management in sponge cities: The role of integrated simulation and 3D visualization. *International Journal of Disaster Risk Reduction, 39*, 101139.

Weber, L. J., Muste, M., Bradley, A. A., Amado, A. A., Demir, I., Drake, C. W., Thomas, N. W. (2018). The Iowa Watersheds Project: Iowa's prototype for engaging communities and professionals in watershed hazard mitigation. *International Journal of River Basin Management, 16*(3), 315–328.

Yildirim, E., & Demir, I. (2019). An integrated web framework for HAZUS-MH flood loss estimation analysis. *Natural Hazards, 99*(1), 275–286.

Chapter 18

ViMeLa

An interactive educational environment for the mechatronics lab in virtual reality

*Toomas Tikk, Rain Eric Haamer, Dorota Kamińska,
Anna Firych-Nowacka, Slawomir Wiak, Najmeh Rezaei,
Marcin Lefik, Grzegorz Zwoliński, Tomasz Sapiński,
Goga Cvetkovski, Lidija Petkovska, Paolo Di Barba,
Maria Evelina Mognaschi, Mihail Digalovski, Maja
Celeska and Gholamreza Anbarjafari*

Introduction

Traditional education and teaching methods, although with significantly improved teaching techniques, cannot sufficiently keep the interest of the students that grew up with Internet, mobiles and tablets (Heradio, de la Torre, & Dormido, 2016). Especially sensitive to these issues are students in engineering, in particular, in mechatronics (Abulrub, Attridge, & Williams, 2011). Modern information technology is rapidly being adopted in Mechatronics Engineering education as a tool for enriching the practical experience of the students. The practical training is a vital part of Mechatronics Engineering education (Piovesan, Passerino, & Pereira, 2012). However, the high cost needed to implement laboratory experiments (for educational purposes) led to development of virtual facilities in which physical systems can be virtually controlled via Virtual Reality (VR) simulations (Brown & Green, 2016). Multimedia and VR technologies offer great potential for presenting theory and laboratory experiments in an enhancing and interesting but economical way (Anbarjafari, Haamer, Lüsi, Tikk, & Valgma, 2019; Kamińska et al., 2019).

Mechatronics is synergy and interaction of mechanical, electrical and computer systems (Wikander, Torngren, & Hanson, 2001), as seen in Figure 18.1. Hence, it is an interactive combination of mechanical engineering, electronic control and computer technology, with the aim of achieving an ideal balance between mechanical structure and its overall control and performance.

Currently, mechatronics classes are divided into two parts: theoretical lectures and laboratory courses with experiments following the 'learning by doing' model. Expensive equipment and limited time for training do not provide sufficient educational platforms (Petrović, Nikolić, Jovanović, &

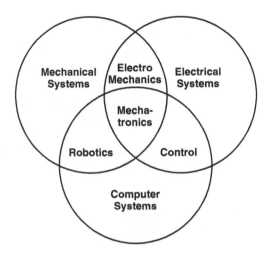

Figure 18.1 Structure and key elements of mechatronics.

Potkonjak, 2016; Popescu, Stoian, Petrisor, & Popescu, 2015). In some cases, students simulate scenarios on the computer and only later learn how mechatronic systems and devices operate in reality. For some students this approach appears too abstract and does not fully reflect the physical phenomena of particular processes.

The described drawbacks of mechatronics study are greatly improved when classroom teaching is supported by VR technology and VR tools. Virtual laboratories are a large part of these solutions. The students are able to visualize abstract concepts, to observe events at micro or macro scales, to visit various environments and interact with events and devices that usually due to place, time or safety factors are unavailable. VR laboratory simulations provide an interactive experience. Users can move freely around the environment, interact with objects, carry out tests and make decisions and mistakes until they have mastered the subject. As a result, students and graduates are better able to master and apply their knowledge in practice.

Use-cases of ViMeLa

The ViMeLa project proposes a solution for this problem by giving future students the opportunity to learn mechatronics concepts in an engaging and cost-effective environment. The project is based on a blended-learning method combining theoretical classes and VR as an experimentation tool that is more effective than purely face-to-face classes. The project consists of three unique scenarios:

1. Construction, operating principles and performance of electric motors
2. Industrial automation solution for controlling the process of sorting packages in a high storage warehouse
3. Construction and tuning of an automatic waste sorting line

The innovation of the proposed concept lies in developing an original and novel mechatronic learning system, which is based on VR technology in a factory, as seen in Figure 18.2, where the working spaces for the three scenarios are placed. In these scenarios, students will be able to observe, enter and move around, with a possibility to make dynamical changes in each scenario.

The project is primarily meant for three target groups:

- students of mechatronics
- universities and other academic institutions
- businesses seeking trained personnel

Scenario 1: Construction, operating principles and performance of electric motors

Assembling of electrical motors: In this part of Scenario 1, in a created VR environment, students will become familiar with properties of different types of electric motors, as well as their construction. The 3D motor models that are designed are based on authentic devices, according to their technical documentation.

The different 3D parts for various electric motors are placed on a shelf. The user will have the task of assembling a certain type of electric motor based on a selection defined for the exercise. This means that in order to realize the task the student will have to select from the shelf the appropriate 3D motor parts (stator, rotor with shaft, permanent magnets, housing, brushes, rotor bars etc.).

Figure 18.2 Factory hall created in ViMeLa project using VR.

After the assembling process is finished, using the VR tools, the completed motor will be automatically assessed, giving the students appropriate feedback. If the electric motor is not correctly put together, the user will have two more chances to properly assemble the object. For the time being 3D parts are made for the following electrical machines: permanent magnet synchronous motor (PMSM), three phase induction motor, switched reluctance motor, DC commutator motor, permanent magnet DC commutator motor and permanent magnet generator. The components of a switched reluctance motor created in VR environment and a partly assembled motor are presented in Figure 18.3 (a) and (b).

Investigation of operating principles of PMSM: In the second part of Scenario 1 the user will be able to observe the working principles and to perform various investigations of a pre-defined model of PMSM.

First, the student will have to place the tested motor on the testing bench and make appropriate connections with a power supply, control and adequate instrumentation. When the connections are realized, the user will receive information on whether the wiring is properly done. Here the user will also have two more attempts to realize the correct connections. After the connections are properly done, the user can proceed to the investigation of operating principles of the studied PMSM at different working conditions, by changing voltage, frequency and load. The measured values of voltages, frequency, input currents, input power, speed and torque are presented on a display.

The VR testing environment will enable the user to perform an even more hazardous investigation, such as an overload of the motor, for which the user will get a certain signalization of the problematic working condition.

Scenario 2: Industrial automation solution for controlling the process of sorting packages in a high storage warehouse

The goal is to familiarize the end users with the functional principles of industrial automation and the details of the most important components necessary to control the process of sorting packages in a high storage warehouse. Through

(a) components of the motor parts in VR look

(b) Partly assembled motor

Figure 18.3 Switched reluctance motor in VR environment. (a) Components of the motor parts in VR look. (b) Partly assembled motor.

the course of this scenario, the students will learn about pneumatic actuator construction and rules for selecting proper pneumatic actuators for a particular task and will be able to master the fundamentals of PLC programming.

The VR environment in this exercise is a representation of the final part in the process of production and distribution of electric motors. The high storage warehouse, where the motors are stacked, consists of racks, a lift platform, a roller-belt conveyor, a pneumatic cylinder for transferring the packages on the racks, a device with electric drive for stacking pallets on and retrieving pallets from shelves, a PLC controller with power supply board and several different sensors, actuators and pneumatics components.

Through the use of VR, students have the opportunity to interact with each element of the controlling line, learn about the construction of pneumatic actuators, operate the sorting line, select proper sensors and assemble the sorting line from partial elements, while 'being present' in a simulation of an actual working environment. Every actuator used in this exercise can be disassembled providing the possibility for the students to get acquainted with its construction. Each part has an attached description (containing the name, purpose, type of material, etc.) and can be viewed from any side or angle.

Moreover, it is possible to run a simple simulation of particular actuators working in a pneumatic system with solenoid valves and damping valves. During this simulation, the students have the possibility to adjust the force and speed of the piston and model the operation of the actuator with an incorrect connection of the pneumatic system.

As mentioned before, all elements of the exercise are created in VR as interactive models, including the PLC controllers. The user will be able to program the controller in VR using a ladder diagram (containing basic elements such as logic functions, slope detection, time blocks, counters, etc.). The sorting line will be launched according to the user's programming. The students will be able to individually assess the correctness of the created programming and experience full-scale effects of potential errors or misconfiguration. Additionally, this scenario includes states of emergency that may lead to equipment damage.

After learning the basics (e.g. principle of operation, construction, types of components), students start to arrange the whole process by

- selecting appropriate components for particular process;
- programming the PLC controller (i.e. to ensure appropriate package sorting according to colour, size, etc.) and avoid collisions or unintentional stopping of the sorting line.

It is assumed that the students should experience positive and negative outcomes while programming the controlling line. Negative outcomes include wrongly programed PLC controllers or component selection. In such a case, packages can fall, stack, push each other etc. In addition, to emphasise learning to react to states of emergency, the VR environment provides controls similar to those in the real world (i.e. buttons and switches used for emergency shutdown or for manual mode, e.g. reversing the belt conveyor or the lift platform).

Scenario 3: A waste sorting line with belt

This scenario is composed of two sub-scenarios: Scenario A, domestic waste sorting line and Scenario B, industrial waste sorting line. The user can choose, at the beginning of the VR tutorial session, to sort domestic waste or industrial waste. Figure 18.4 illustrates the overview of scenario 3.

Scenario A aims to build and use a waste sorting line able to segregate materials like plastic, glass and organic waste. In Scenario B the user can sort other kinds of materials (e.g. the ferromagnetic and the conductive materials).

The system is composed of sensors, actuators and a single belt whose velocity is set *a priori*. The waste is assumed to exit from an automatized dispenser and falls on the belt. At the beginning of the tutorial session, the user has to design the sorting line, by choosing the sensors and actuators available in the library, and set their positions along the belt. The user has to set the position of the containers for various materials.

There is one magnetic actuator and two kinds of sensors (inductive and capacitive). The user can set their properties (e.g. frequency and magnitude of current or voltage). In order to make the Scenario work, the characterization of the sensors and actuators in terms of input–output transfer function is modelled with Finite Element Models.

Figure 18.4 An overview of the waste sorting scenario for the ViMeLa project.

Field models of sensors and actuators

The developed scenario has two types of sensors: an inductive sensor for ferro-magnetic and conductive objects and a capacitive sensor that senses dielectric permittivity. The former must be implemented with a frequency between 50Hz to 100kHz. When a conductive objective is in front of the sensor, the impedance of the coil becomes lower. In turn, when a ferromagnetic object-ive is in front of the sensor, the impedance of the coil becomes higher. The sensor in VR mimics these sensing lines using three basic 3D shapes. The resulting sensor field is not completely realistic, but in terms of the scenario it performs enough like real-life to be used as a realistic approximation.

The capacitive sensor is able to sense objects with different dielectric per-mittivity. The capacitive sensor consists of two electrode plates: one grounded and the other fed by AC voltage. The piece of waste to be detected and sorted should pass through these plates. When a dielectric objective is in the middle of the plates, the capacitance of the sensor becomes higher.

As with the inductive sensor, the capacitive sensor uses three detection fields in order to mimic realistic detections. The fields are spaced out based on size and model detection areas for 20%, 50% and 100% actual capaci-tance. The capacitive sensor has three changeable parameters:

- the applied voltage of the electrode (V)
- the frequency of the source (f)
- the number of electrode plates (m) m=1,2,3.

This sensor can be described using a linear transfer function shown in (1). In it, the three aforementioned variables are defined by the user while the rest are defined by the scenario. This allows the sensing current (eqn. 1) to be derived based on the capacitance of the detected material.

$$I = \frac{V}{\left|\frac{1}{j\omega C}\right|} = V2\pi fC [\text{A}]. \tag{1}$$

The current that capacitive sensor is capable of detecting should be in the following range (eqn 2):

$$50[\mu A] \le I \le 10[mA]. \tag{2}$$

By considering that the capacitance in our project is changing in the range $[1.64\text{x}10^{-12}, 9.31\text{x}10^{-12}]$ [F] and the voltage is changing from 100 mV to 20V, the current will be in the range of 10.33 mA to 23.4 mA. By consid-ering the feasible range of current based on (2), for output current in the range of 10.33 mA to mA, the current is not in the detectable range, so no output signal is generated. In the range of 10 mA to 23.4 mA, the sensor will experience overcurrent and can be damaged in real life. To mimic this the virtual sensor first trips an alarm and over time will cease to function. This means only a current in the range of will be detected and sent forward to the actuators. To accommodate for the wide ranges and magnitudal differences in the adjustable ranges, the scales in the scenario are logarithmic.

Scenario 3 is based on a tangible task of sorting waste into different containers. The scenario is set up as a mini factory with a waste conveyor belt, electric actuators, capacitive and inductive sensors as well as a waste generator. The main task for the student is to set the parameters for the sensors (current, frequency, voltage) determining the sensor field, delays between detections and the travel time of the detection signal to a specific actuator. This exercise provides a basic understanding of capacitive and inductive sensor parameters along with an applied overview of how a simple sorting line functions. During the VR tutorial session, a user may choose to practice on Scenario A or Scenario B, but during tasks these will be predefined by the instructor.

Development

The most relevant concern during discussions for the scenario were centralized around the differences between real and virtual worlds. These issues were primarily centred around hardware limitations and general optimization questions: Do we have realistic detection fields, proper theoretical current calculation models, photorealistic visuals and component-accurate models?

For any given exercise, a far more important task was a realistic detection algorithm. It is possible to develop a VR world without a realistic setting and physical parameters. For instance, if there is glass bottle, then the object could just have a tag that indicates it as such. Passing this in front of a sensor would then yield a binary detection that would travel to an actuator, which pushes the object. This would heavily optimize the application side but would not be realistic enough for the given environment. The detection should instead be dependent on capacity, inductivity, distance, sensor frequency, voltage, orientation and so on. Thus, the largest portion of the workload was devoted to developing a close to real life approximation of different material parameters and sensor functionalities.

As in the real world, students need to configure sensors and parameters with the utmost care in the virtual one. The main difference in the two is that in the virtual one, overloading sensors or causing edge case scenarios will not result in a costly mistake and can instead be used for learning.

Platform

The project was developed in the Unity3D game engine. This choice provided several advantages in the visual aspects as Unity already contains an optimized rendering engine. Despite the advantages, the models still had to be developed externally. The hardware that we used is the HTC Vive headset with two standard controllers. This limited our means of interaction with the scenario, removing the sense of weight and touch. The student would thus lose the ability to tell components apart solely based on how they felt in their hand and would instead have to rely on the visual appearance of the object alone.

In an ideal case, the factory would look as close to realistic as possible with correct models, textures, lights and ambiance, but are all of these required to perform and learn a task? Modern students have grown up with high quality games with stunning visuals, and this can create expectations for any virtual world, even those meant for learning. In the scope of the exercise it has low importance, which means it is not wise to spend too much energy on visuals, but the application still has an obligation to leave a good first impression. From the point of view of completing an exercise, it is essential to create an intuitive enough system for a student to instantly understand it and enter intended values for a given setup or to tune the parameters of a conveyor system. In the end a balance was found between the realistic nature of the scenario and its intuitive user interaction system.

Scene components

The system is composed of sensors, actuators, sorting bins, a conveyor belt, a waste dispenser and the waste itself. Each of the components has its own custom models and behavioural logic. The waste is comprised of domestic and industrial components. Each kind of waste contains appropriate capacitive and inductive information the sensors can detect.

The waste will be placed on the belt by the automatic dispenser and will be removed from the scene if it enters one of the sorting bins. The scenario starts with the user being given a task of designing the general structure of the sorting line. This consists of sensor and actuator placement as well as the setting up of their interconnections. These components will be available on a virtual shelf and can be created at will if any of them is lost in the scenario.

The actuators in the scenario serve the purpose of moving trash items from the belt into the trash bins. The actuators have configurable push distances and speeds, but these will not play a huge roll in the scenario setup. The main functionality stems from the signal delay between the sensor and actuator.

The belt speed will determine the time it takes different objects to pass by the sensors and actuators; this is important as, without trial and error, the belt speed will determine the delays the students will have to design. In

Figure 18.5 Actuators on the conveyor line. (a) Capacitive sensor with adjustable parameters (b) Framework of the Evaluation tool Results of the evaluation.

order to further solidify this fact, the speed of the belt as well as the trash dispensing speed will vary between exercises. During training, however, both the dispensing and belt speeds will be adjustable by the user.

Due to their complexity, the actuators and sensors come with their own parametrized logic. The task for the user is to adjust the parameters for each of these components to complete the provided sorting task. The user will have to adjust not only the sensor to actuator signal timings, but also the exact voltage and frequency levels for each sensor. Incorrect parameter initialization can cause unintended actuator activations, detections to not occur or damage to the virtual sensors, which will incur a fail state. Figure 18.5 illustrates the actuator and sensor adjustment views.

The waste containers serve the purpose of waste removal from the scene as well as a grading mechanism based on the number of correctly sorted objects. Their locations will be adjustable by the user but can also be predefined in order to increase the complexity of a given scenario.

Conclusions

In today's digital world, finding new ways to teach students is more difficult than ever. When technologies such as mobile phones, tablets and game consoles are highly advanced, finding educational engagement with modern technology in the classroom can be even harder. Hence, VR has become an important and useful tool in engineering education. The use of VR in teaching mechatronics provides a unique opportunity to create a truly exciting and engaging learning experience for students. The chapter presents main features of the ViMeLa project, which intends to introduce an innovative concept of teaching mechatronics using VR and to bring industry into the classroom. In a virtual factory, students will learn the basics of mechatronics, experiencing three scenarios in the frame of the project.

Acknowledgements

This publication has been co-funded by the Erasmus+ Programme of European Union (Strategic Partnership, ViMeLa, 2017-1-PL01-KA203-038675) and reflects only the views of the authors; the National Agency and European Commission cannot be held responsible for any use that may be made of the information contained therein. Virtual Mechatronic Laboratory http://vimela.p.lodz.pl/

References

Abulrub, A. H. G., Attridge, A. N., & Williams, M. A. (2011, April). Virtual reality in engineering education: The future of creative learning. In *2011 IEEE Global Engineering Education Conference (EDUCON)* (pp. 751–757). IEEE.

Anbarjafari, G., Haamer, R. E., Lüsi, I., Tikk, T., & Valgma, L. (2019). 3D face reconstruction with region based best fit blending using mobile phone for virtual reality based social media. *Bulletin of the Polish Academy of Sciences: Technical Sciences.* 67(1), pp. 125–132.

Brown, A., & Green, T. (2016). Virtual reality: Low-cost tools and resources for the classroom. *TechTrends*, 60(5), 517–519.

Heradio, R., de la Torre, L., & Dormido, S. (2016). Virtual and remote labs in control education: A survey. *Annual Reviews in Control, 42*, 1–10.

Kamińska, D., Sapiński, T., Wiak, S., Tikk, T., Haamer, R. E., Avots, E., Anbarjafari, G. (2019). Virtual reality and its applications in education: Survey. *Information, 10*(318), 1–20.

Petrović, V. M., Nikolić, B., Jovanović, K., & Potkonjak, V. (2016, June). Development of virtual laboratory for mechatronic systems. In *International Conference on Robotics in Alpe-Adria Danube Region* (pp. 622–630). Cham: Springer.

Piovesan, S. D., Passerino, L. M., & Pereira, A. S. (2012). Virtual reality as a tool in the education. *International Association for Development of the Information Society.*295–298.

Popescu, D., Stoian, V., Petrisor, A., & Popescu, R. (2015). Virtual engineering for mechatronics laboratory. In *2015 Proceedings of 6th International Conference "Computational Mechanics and Virtual Engineering" (COMEC)* (pp. 316–322). 15–16 October 2015, Braşov, Romania.

Wikander, J., Torngren, M., & Hanson, M. (2001). The science and education of mechatronics engineering. *IEEE Robotics & Automation Magazine, 8*(2), 20–26.

Lessons learnt from virtual reality in education

Linda Daniela

Virtual reality (VR), mixed reality (MR) and augmented reality (AR) are opportunities created by digital solutions and have been known about for quite some time, but the potential of these technological solutions in education has not yet been fully explored. If we believe that education is the gateway to higher achievement, new innovations and a better society, then we need to realize that education must seek and offer solutions to each new area that can make a significant contribution to education and society as a whole. This book has brought together researchers who have given their insight into VR capabilities to improve the acquisition of specific knowledge, to measure knowledge progress and to make processes that would otherwise be more expensive, more dangerous, more time-consuming and less effective.

I am grateful to the authors who contributed to the book by preparing their chapters on the results of their research, using their knowledge of the use of VR in the education process and providing insights into their research processes. The information in this book should be useful for students who are studying to become teachers, and it should also be useful for teachers, tutors and academics working with students as well as for VR developers who want the experiences that they developed to be useful in educational processes. All in all, under the unifying element of innovative pedagogical solutions, the book has brought together very diverse ideas on how to use virtual solutions in education in each of its three subsections: 1) VR in Humanities and Social Sciences; 2) Concepts of VR and 3) VR in Sciences and Medical Education.

Lana Frančeska Dreimane opened the first subsection with a chapter on her development of a learning experience assessment tool consisting of 3 macrocriterions, 21 criterions. The evaluation tool provided in this chapter could fit into different learning contexts to ensure that the learning content is effective. It will also help VR experience developers understand what educational goals the product can achieve, as it allows the alignment between the instructional, pedagogical and VR learning environments to be outlined to ensure and strengthen the efficiency of the VR learning design and instructional strategies.

In the following chapter, Yipaer Aierken and I continued the topic of evaluating VR experiences, and we proposed a tool that can be used to evaluate the experiences of virtual museums from an educational perspective. In our chapter, we introduced the reader to rubric design principles and the process of the evaluation of virtual museums; we believe that this tool could be useful for teachers who would like to utilize relevant virtual museum experiences and for developers of VR experiences who would like these experiences to be used in an educational context. Often, VR experiences are offered because they can provide access to information that would not otherwise be available, but it is also important to be aware of educational needs. This tool will therefore be useful for teachers when selecting the most appropriate experiences based on specific educational needs.

The potential of VR in entrepreneurship education was analysed by Marko Orel; he concludes that VR enables individuals to step into immersive environments, engage in social interactions with other peers, visualize actions that are relevant to a particular learning outcome and reflect on their actions. However, he notes that it also has a number of limitations that need to be considered in the future development of these solutions: i) VR is still underdeveloped, and environments have functionality issues; ii) its usage is a costly solution for enhanced learning in group and teacher-led classes; and iii) a lack of understanding on what to expect regarding the VR experience within the education processes makes the training of both learning staff and students a necessary pre-teaching process. These findings point to further research directions that can be developed in both the field of educational sciences and ICT.

Joshua A. Fisher, for his part, came up with ideas for using MR in dramaturgical pedagogy and developed classifications of MR interactions paired with participatory performance methods. He believes that MR's capacity for interactive, spatial and visual representations of abstract and concrete ideas allows for new avenues of critical reflection. Fisher also describes different ways of mixing technological solutions with dramaturgical pedagogy, which on the one hand makes processes more interactive and, on the other, teaches students to use the various digital solutions available, in this case MR solutions.

From a higher education perspective, the immersive world was analysed by Elvira Fernández-Ahumada and her colleagues; they developed study materials by developing six working packages using a 3D virtual environment. As a result of the study, it was concluded that the use of immersive materials in teaching improves learning outcomes, promotes creativity and improves interdisciplinary collaboration, demonstrating that, today, different disciplines are interconnected and that the development of a variety of innovative study/teaching materials must take a pedagogical perspective into account in order for the learning process to be successful.

Tomas Blazauskas and Daina Gudoniene discussed the use of VR experiences to enrich the learning process, focusing on the mental-physical combination in VR. They examined the various VR experiences available in Lithuania and conducted a qualitative evaluation from an educational perspective, focusing on whether the experiences available support mental processes and whether active human involvement is possible. As a result, they concluded that experiences requiring not only mental but also physical activity are more conducive to learning content.

In his chapter, Oli Howson analysed the potential of VR in the school environment and provided insights into the challenges that reduce the likelihood of VR being used in schools, despite its potentially positive impact on the learning process. He analysed the various resources available and sites where learning resources can be developed, looking at specific case studies, and concluded that VR has great potential to transform learning. This chapter is valuable because, in addition to analysing various VR possibilities and specific areas in which VR is used in the school environment, the author has identified issues including not only the cost in developing VR experiences and the availability of technology, but also the teacher time needed to organize learning using VR experiences. It is also necessary to be aware of such a perspective, because often, behind the various innovations and the needs of students, practical things are forgotten, such as the teacher time required for installing different technologies and wiring, not to mention the time needed for designing new teaching materials.

In the next section, Neus Lorenzo Galés and Ray Gallon argue that pedagogy is capable of blending the Industry 4.0 ecosystem with SDGs requiring new literacies, especially transliteracy, as learning clearly needs to take place in a transmedia context. They believe that, for a technology transformed learning environment, we need: i) significant transformations related to the treatment of information input, processes and output and to know what the role of the teacher is in these processes; ii) meaningful transformations of teaching and learning processes when using VR/AR devices and iii) important transformations connected to the expression, dissemination and sharing of information, leading to the creation of new values. The authors analysed specific cases and concluded that the use of VR in the learning process can be valuable from the point of view of teaching and that it can also be useful for learners who are at risk of social exclusion.

The section continues with ideas on trustworthiness in a VR environment, summarized by Davide Salanitri, Glyn Lawson and Brian Waterfield. The authors conducted an experimental study testing the factors that affect trust. They concluded that the successful implementation of VR systems requires those systems to be trustworthy. This applies in every field in which VR systems are implemented, but special attention should be given to systems built for educational purposes. The study had conflicting results. While technology acceptance and usability were found to be related to trust, its presence was not, demonstrating the need for further research into technology acceptance and usability in order to make learning more effective and create innovative technological solutions for not only for entertainment purposes, but also allowing teachers to choose VR solutions to transform the learning process.

Michael Spitzer, Manfred Rosenberger and Martin Ebner offered ideas to improve the mechanical engineering preparation process. In their chapter, a HoloLens app and a CAD/Simulation workflow were introduced to visualize CAD models, sensors and the simulation data of a test run on an air condition system test bed; they described the use of HoloLens in different learning scenarios. Using qualitative research methods, they tested how technology-enhanced prototypes contributed to the acquisition of knowledge relevant to operating in an environment that could be dangerous if certain knowledge and competences are not acquired. The authors recommend being mindful of the pedagogically sound organization of the learning process, both in defining goals and providing support to students in the learning process.

Relatively similar ideas are summarized in the next chapter, where Gregory Quinn and Fabian Schneider analyse how to use VR solutions to improve STEM learning processes. They give insight into the general concept of novel methods to facilitate both free and scripted learning, enhanced by haptic interaction and augmented via digital simulations. Initial trials were carried out in VR on an HTC Vive and in MR with Microsoft's HoloLens. At the end of the chapter, the authors offer a complete spectrum of potential mediums for a new age of digital-analogue hybrid learning.

Jin Rong Yang, Fabian Hadipriono Tan and Adrian Hadipriono Tan describe fuzzy angular models and 3D models on a construction method assessment on the Great Wall of China in Jinshanling as a case study and analyse how VR or AR can enable further knowledge acquisition for students in courses on the history and heritage of civil engineering.

The first chapter in the final subsection is devoted to ideas about how VR can be used for teaching clinical skills in medical education, and Charles Hand, Raphael Olaiya and Mohammed Elmasry describe various ideas on how to change the traditional education process in the training of medical staff. The authors also pointed to some drawbacks that have already been described in the literature: i) VR is used for simple manipulation but does not ensure that VR's potential is used for more complex concepts and ii) the graphics used are often of poor quality and therefore cannot replace a human-led learning process.

Next, Hai Chien Pham and his colleagues describe the VR pedagogical model for safety education and offer a virtual photoreality-based learning framework. The authors have developed 20 accident case studies that students had to analyse. Their preliminary findings revealed that a VP-based pedagogy approach can significantly support learners in acquiring safety knowledge and professional skills, thus improving construction safety education.

A different perspective on the use of VR was chosen by Encarnación V. Taguas and her colleagues. They propose the use of VR to organize professional conferences where PhD students can exchange ideas; this would, at the same time, reduce the cost of attending conferences and the consumption of other resources when going to conferences. To some extent, it can be seen as contributing to the development of a sustainable society. As the authors point out, the positive aspects include reduced anxiety that may arise from speaking to strange audiences, because the researcher's avatar performs at these virtual conferences.

Giuseppe Abrami and his colleagues focus on aspects of historical education and VAnnotatoR, which is a versatile framework for the creation and use of virtual environments that serves to model historical processes in historical education. In their chapter, the building blocks of VAnnotatoR and its applications in historical education are described. The authors believe that there are a number of important aspects when learning history in a virtual environment, such as i) flexibility through database support; ii) collaboration and multi-user modes; iii) interaction and communication; iv) decentralization; v) open access; vi) data protection and security; vii) access permissions; viii) portability and platform independence and ix) full 3D.

Next, Yusuf Sermet and Ibrahim Demir analysed virtual and augmented reality solutions that can be used for disaster education, preparedness and management. They chose two specific cases to create in VR, and the main development environments for the framework were Unity3D and ESRI City Engine. Unity3D is a cross-platform game engine capable of producing augmented and VR experiences, and ESRI City Engine is 3D modelling software focused on generating virtual urban environments. They also propose system-level architecture for an immersive disaster management and education framework.

In the final chapter of the book, Toomas Tikk and his colleagues explore the possibilities of learning mechatronics in VR and propose their ViMeLa project, offering future students the opportunity to learn mechatronics concepts in an engaging and cost-effective environment. The project is based on a blended-learning method combining theoretical classes and VR, and it was developed in the Unity3D game engine as an experimentation tool that is more effective than face-to-face classes. The project consists of three unique scenarios: i) the construction, operating principles and performance of electric motors; ii) industrial automation solutions for controlling the process of sorting packages in a high storage warehouse and iii) the construction and tuning of an automatic waste sorting line.

All in all, the chapters in the book provide insight into different ideas on how VR solutions can be used in education and i) offer solutions for analysing VR experiences from an educational perspective; ii) analyse the concrete results achieved through VR solutions and iii) offer specific scenarios for developing and improving VR experiences.

The chapters in this book provide many interesting ideas on how to combine educational needs with technological capabilities, but there is a need to continue both the research and analysis of the proposed solutions in order to help teachers, tutors and academics see the applicability of these products in teaching. There is also a need to develop further innovative ideas to make these products and solutions more accessible and usable. Despite the great amount of work and information we have collected in this volume, we cannot assume that the work has now been completed and that all the answers can be found in these chapters. Many more projects, studies, articles and books will need to follow in order to strengthen our knowledge and competences in the use and development of VR.

Index